CASES AND APPLICATIONS

Organization Theory

SECOND EDITION

CASES AND APPLICATIONS

Organization
Theory

SECOND EDITION

Richard L. Daft
TEXAS A&M

Kristen D. Skivington
MICHIGAN STATE UNIVERSITY

Mark P. Sharfman
PENNSYLVANIA STATE UNIVERSITY

West Publishing Company
ST. PAUL   NEW YORK   LOS ANGELES   SAN FRANCISCO

Art: Rolin Graphics
Cover Design: Peter Thiel

COPYRIGHT © 1984 By WEST PUBLISHING COMPANY
COPYRIGHT © 1987 By WEST PUBLISHING COMPANY
50 W. Kellogg Boulevard
P.O. Box 64526
St. Paul, MN 55164–1003

Printed in the United States of America

Library of Congress Cataloging in
  Publication Data
ISBN: 0–314–28488–5
1st Reprint—1987

Contents

II Design and Structure 64

Bureaucracy

Technology

Structure

III Internal Organizational Processes 153

Goals and Effectiveness

Control and Information

IV   Organizational Dynamics 245

Change

Organizational Culture

Power and Politics

V View From the Top 313

Preface

The purpose of this book is to provide a set of organization theory cases and exercises that are theoretically relevant and meaningful in application. As an academic discipline, organization theory concepts pertain to everyday management problem solving and decision making. The challenge facing organization theory instructors is to teach theoretical concepts and also to show how these concepts can be used in practical application. From our own teaching experience, challenging case problems can make the difference between a good organization theory course and a great one. The goal of this book is to provide supplementary case material that is both interesting and practical and that will help students become more competent and more informed about organizations. The second edition helps translate organization theory concepts into relevant applications by including cases which have the following features.

1. The second edition contains more than 40 percent new material, and several of the carryover cases have been updated. Because the field of organization theory changes rapidly, it is essential that the materials be fresh. With the development of new organizational forms and even new industries, the cases and exercises were selected to reflect this evolution.

2. There is more emphasis on "problem-oriented" cases in this edition. This means that several of the cases are longer, and the student has the opportunity to see theoretical issues revealed in less than ideal ways. Students then have the opportunity to diagnose problems, suggest alternatives, and recommend solutions. The student gets to grapple with the issues in much the same way as a manager in industry. The problem-oriented cases are excellent vehicles for group projects that let students apply what they have learned.

3. The cases cover the breadth of organization theory topics, especially topics that have emerged in recent years. Several cases pertain to traditional topics such as environment, bureaucracy, technology, and structure. New cases have been included to reflect emerging issues in organizations, such as management information systems and corporate culture.

Cases also address high technology industries such as aerospace, bioengineering, computers, and telecommunications. Cases have been included to reflect the rise in the service sector, and cases also cover broader issues such as corporate social responsibility, government/business relationships, and retrenchment.

4. Cases were selected because of their high interest level for students. The cases represent real people in real organizations. They are not fictional and are not written from secondary material. A major criterion for selection was that they be well written and enjoyable to read. Most of the cases have been classroom tested on students.

5. Several improvements have been made in the experiential exercises. Feedback from users of the first edition indicated difficulty in using some of the exercises. A great deal of effort has been put into the design of the student exercises to ensure that they are meaningful and that the instructions are clear. Some of the new exercises could actually do double duty. They are interesting as classroom activities and can also be modified and used for diagnosis or training in organizations.

6. The Instructor's Manual has been changed to provide more information to instructors. For some cases, material included in the Instructor's Manual provides a recent update on the status of the company. Discussion questions for each case have been added to the Manual for instructors who like to use questions to focus student preparation for class discussion. The topic matrix has been included in the Instructor's Manual but not in the casebook itself. A complexity scale has been added to indicate the complexity of each case. These changes, in addition to the substantive discussion of each case and exercise, makes the Manual more helpful for instructors.

ACKNOWLEDGMENTS

This book, like most books, reflects the ideas and hard work of a number of people. First and foremost, we would like to thank the case authors. They studied organizations, wrote the cases, and gave us permission to use their work. We would also like to thank the publishers who granted us permission to use their previously published materials.

We also extend appreciation to administrators and colleagues at Texas A&M and Penn State University who were helpful and supportive during development of the second edition. Michael Hitt, Management Department Head, and Bill Mobley, Dean of the College of Business at Texas A&M, and Charles Snow, Management Department Head, and Eugene Kelly, Dean of the College of Business Administration at Penn State, have created excellent climates for research of all sorts, and have provided many of the resources for this project. Several colleagues at Texas A&M and Penn State have provided assistance and intellectual stimulation along the way. We especially thank Jim Dean, Barbara Gray, Don Hellriegel, and Jim Skivington. Special recognition must go to the individuals who gave us painstaking reviews of the first edition. Their assistance made the creation of the new edition far easier. Many thanks to Robert Allison of Wayne State, John Clarry of Penn State, Larry French from University of Texas–Arlington, William Ickinger of Tulane, Carol Sales of Brock University, and Jim Swenson of Moorehead State.

For assistance with typing, permissions, and hundreds of other details we are especially grateful to Laura Frye, Shirley Rider, Diane Snyder, and Phyllis Washburn.

We also thank the editors at West. Esther Craig and Dick Fenton were, as usual, extraordinary. Jean Cook in production and Beth Kennedy in marketing also were extremely helpful. Without the collective tolerance, encouragement and assistance from the staff at West this edition would not have been completed.

Our final note of appreciation goes to the professors and students who used the first edition. We have created this new volume for you. It is our hope that this edition has furthered the original goal of making the concepts and discoveries of organization theory available to students and practition-

ers through the teaching process. The comments, support, and interest in the first edition showed us there was a demand for a supplementary casebook, and in some ways this book was meeting that demand.

R.L.D.

M.S.

K.D.S.

A General Diagnostic Model for Organizational Behavior: Applying a Congruence Perspective

Most of the job of management is the struggle to make organizations function effectively. The work of society gets done through organizations, and the function of management is to get those organizations to perform that work.

The task of getting organizations to function effectively is a difficult one, however. Understanding one individual's behavior is a challenging problem in and of itself. A group, made up of different individuals and multiple relationships among those individuals is even more complex. Imagine, then, the mind boggling complexity inherent in a large organization made up of thousands of individuals, hundreds of groups, and relationships among individuals and groups too numerous to count.

In the face of this overwhelming complexity, organizational behavior must be managed. Ultimately the work of organizations gets done through the behavior of people, individually or collectively, on their own or in collaboration with technology. Thus, central to the management task is the management of organizational behavior. To do this, there must be the capacity to *understand* the patterns of behavior at individual, group and organizational levels, to *predict* what behavioral responses will be elicited by different managerial actions, and finally to use understanding and prediction to achieve *control*.

How can one achieve understanding, prediction, and control of organizational behavior? Given its inherent complexity and enigmatic nature, one needs tools to help unravel the mysteries, paradoxes, and apparent contradictions that present themselves in the everyday life of organizations. One kind of tool is the conceptual framework or model. A model is a theory which indicates which factors (in an organization, for example) are most critical or important. It also indicates how these factors are related, or which factors or combination of factors cause other factors to change. In a sense, then, a model is a roadmap that can be used to make sense of the terrain of organizational behavior.

Source: Written by David A. Nadler and Michael L. Tushman. Published by permission of the authors, who retain all rights. A version of this paper was originally published in J. R. Hackman, E. E. Lawler, and L. W. Porter (eds.), *Perspectives on Behavior in Organizations* (New York: McGraw-Hill, 1977).

The models we use are critical because they guide our analysis and action. In any organizational situation, problem solving involves the collection of information about the problem, the interpretation of that information to determine specific problem types and causes, and the development of action plans. The models that individuals hold influence what data they collect and what data they ignore; models guide how people attempt to analyze or interpret the data they have; finally models aid people in choosing action plans.

Indeed, anyone who has been exposed to an organization already has some sort of implicit model. People develop these roadmaps over time, building on their own experiences. These implicit models (they usually are not explicitly written down or stated) guide behavior (Argyris & Schon, 1974). These models also vary in quality, validity, and sophistication depending on the nature and extent of the experiences of the model builder, his or her perceptiveness, his/her ability to conceptualize and generalize from experiences, etc.

We are not solely dependent, however, on the implicit and experience based models that individuals develop. The last four decades have witnessed intense work including research and theory development related to organization behavior (see, for example, Dunnette, 1976). It is therefore possible to think about scientifically developed explicit models for the analysis of organizational behavior and for use in organizational problem solving.

This paper will present one particular research and theory based model. It is a general model of organizations. Rather than describing a specific phenomenon or aspect of organizational life (such as a model of motivation or a model of organizational design) it attempts to provide a framework for thinking about the organization as a total system. The major thrust of the model is that for organizations to be effective, their subparts or components must be consistently structured and managed—they must approach a state of congruence.

The paper will be organized into several sections. In the first section we will discuss the basic view of organizations which underlies the model—systems theory. In the second section we will present and discuss the model itself. In the third section, we will present an approach to using the model for organizational problem analysis. Finally, we will discuss some of the implications of this model for thinking about organizations.

A BASIC VIEW OF ORGANIZATIONS

There are many different ways of thinking about organizations. Typically when a manager is asked to "draw a picture of an organization" he/she responds with some version of a pyramidal organizational chart. The model this rendition reflects is one which views the most critical factors as the stable formal relationships among the jobs and formal work units that make up the organization. While this clearly is one way to think about organizations, it is a very limited view. It excludes factors such as leader behavior, the impact of the environment, informal relations, power distribution, etc. Such a model can only capture a small part of what goes on in an organization. It is narrow and static in perspective.

Over the past twenty years there has been a growing consensus that a viable alternative to the static classical models of organizations is to think about organizations as social systems. This approach stems from the observation that social phenomena display many of the characteristics of natural or mechanical systems (Von Bertalanffy, 1968, Buckley, 1967). In particular it is argued that organizations can be better understood if they are considered as dynamic and open social systems (Katz & Kahn, 1966; 1978).

What is a system? In the simplest of

terms, a system is a set of interrelated elements. These elements are related; thus change in one element may lead to changes in other elements. An *open system* is one that interacts with its environment. Thus it is more than just a set of interrelated elements. Rather, these elements make up a mechanism that takes input from the environment, subjects it to some form of transformation process, and produces output (Exhibit 1). At the most general level, it should be easy to visualize organizations as systems. Let's consider a manufacturing plant, for example. It is made up of different related components (different departments, jobs, technologies, etc). It receives input from the environment, including labor, raw material, production orders, etc., and subjects those inputs to a transformation process to produce products.

Organizations as systems display a number of basic systems characteristics. Katz and Kahn (1966; 1978) discuss these in detail, but a few of the most critical characteristics will be mentioned here. First, organizations display degrees of internal *interdependence* (Thompson, 1967). Changes in one component or subpart of an organization frequently has repercussions for other parts—the pieces are interconnected. Returning to our manufacturing plant example, if changes are made in one element (for example, the skill levels of the people hired to do jobs), other elements will be affected (the productiveness of equipment used, the speed or quality of production activities, the nature of supervision needed, etc.). Second, organizations have the capacity for *feedback* (see Exhibit 1). Feedback is information about the output of a system that can be used to control the system (Weiner,

1950). Organizations can correct errors and indeed change themselves because of this characteristic (Bauer, 1966). If, in our plant example, the plant management receives information about the declining quality of its product, it can use this information to identify factors in the system itself that contribute to this problem. It is important to note that, unlike mechanized systems, feedback information does not always lead to correction. Organizations have the potential to use feedback and be self-correcting systems, but they do not always realize this potential.

A third characteristic of organizations as systems is *equilibrium*. Organizations develop energy to move towards states of balance. When an event occurs that puts the system out of balance, it reacts and moves towards a balanced state. If one work group in our plant example were suddenly to increase its performance dramatically, it would throw the system out of balance. This group would be making increasing demands on the groups that supply it with information or materials to give it what it needs. Similarly, groups that work with the output of the high performing group would feel the pressure of work in process inventory piling up in front of them. Depending on the pay system used, other groups might feel inequity as this one group begins to earn more. We would predict that some actions would be taken to put the system back into balance. Either the rest of the plant would be changed to increase production and thus be back in balance with the single group, or (more likely) actions would be taken to get this group to modify its behavior to be consistent with the levels of performance of the rest of the system (by removing workers, limiting supplies, etc.). The point is that somehow the system would develop energy to move back towards a state of equilibrium or balance.

Fourth, open systems display *equifinality*. In other words, different system configura-

EXHIBIT 1 . THE BASIC SYSTEMS MODEL

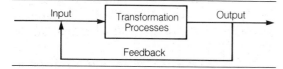

tions can lead to the same end or lead to the same type of input-output conversion. This means there is not a universal or "one best way" to organize. Finally, open systems need to display *adaptation*. For a system to survive it must maintain a favorable balance of input or output transactions with the environment or it will run down. If our plant produces a product for which there are decreasing applications, it must adapt to the environmental changes and develop new products or ultimately the plant will simply have to close its doors. Any system therefore must adapt by changing as environmental conditions change. The consequences of not adapting to the environment can be seen in the demise of many once prosperous organizations (such as the eastern railroads) which did not alter in response to environmental changes.

Thus systems theory provides a different way of thinking about the organization, in more complex and dynamic terms. While systems theory is a valuable basic perspective on organizations, it is limited as a problem solving tool. The reason is that as a model systems theory is too abstract to be used for day to day organizational behavior problem analysis. Because of the level of abstraction of systems theory, we need to develop a more specific and pragmatic model based on the concepts of the open systems paradigm.

A CONGRUENCE MODEL OF ORGANIZATIONAL BEHAVIOR

Given the level of abstraction of open systems theory, our job is to develop a model which reflects the basic systems concepts and characteristics, but which will also be more specific and thus more usable as an analytic tool. In this section, we will describe a model which attempts to specify in more detail what are the critical inputs, what are the major outputs, and what are the transformation processes that characterize organizational functioning.

The model puts its greatest emphasis on the transformation process and in particular reflects the critical system property of interdependence. It views organizations as made up of components or parts which interact with each other. These components exist in states of relative balance, consistency, or "fit" with each other. The different parts of an organization can fit well together and thus function effectively, or fit poorly, thus leading to problems, dysfunctions, or performance below potential. Given the central nature of these "fits" among components in the model, we will talk about it as a *congruence model of organizational behavior*, since effectiveness is a function of the congruence among the various components.

The concept of congruence is not a new one. Homans (1952) in his pioneering work on social processes in organizations emphasized the interaction and consistency among key elements of organizational behavior. Leavitt (1965) for example identified four major components of organization as being people, tasks, technology and structure. The model we will present here builds on these views and also draws from fit models developed and used by Seiler (1967), Lawrence and Lorsch (1969) and Lorsch & Sheldon (1972).

It is important to remember that we are concerned about modeling the *behavioral* system of the organization—the system of elements that ultimately produce patterns of behavior and thus performance of the organization. In its simplest form we need to deal with the questions of what inputs does the system have to work with, what outputs does it need to and actually produce, and what are the major components of the transformation process, and how do these components interact with each other.

Inputs

Inputs are those factors that are, at any one point in time, the "givens" that face the organization. They are the material that the organization has to work with. There are several different types of inputs, each of which presents a different set of "givens" to the organization. (See Exhibit 2 for an overview of inputs.)

The first input is the *environment*, or all of those factors outside of the boundaries of the organization being examined. Every organization exists within the context of a larger environment which includes individuals, groups, other organizations and even larger social forces, all of which have a potentially powerful impact on how the organization performs (Pfeffer & Salancik, 1978). Specifically, the environment includes markets (clients or customers), suppliers, governmental and regulatory bodies, labor unions, competitors, financial institutions, special interest groups, etc. The environment is critical to organizational functioning (Aldrich & Pfeffer, 1976). In particular, for purposes of organizational analysis, the environment has three critical features. First, the environment makes demands on the organization. For example, it may require the provision of certain products or services, at certain levels of quality or quantity. Market pressures are particularly important here. Second, the environment may place constraints on organizational action. It may limit the types of kinds of activities in which an organization can engage. These constraints could range from limitations imposed by scarce capital, all the way to governmental regulatory prohibitions. Third, the environment provides opportunities which the organization can explore. In total, then, the analysis of an organization needs to consider what factors are present in the environment of the organization, and how those factors individually or in relation to each other create demands, constraints, or opportunities.

EXHIBIT 2 KEY ORGANIZATIONAL INPUTS

Input	Environment	Resources	History	Strategy
DEFINITION	All factors, including institutions, groups, individuals, events, etc. outside of the boundaries of the organization being analyzed, but having a potential impact on that organization.	Various assets that organization has access to, including human resources, technology, capital, information, etc. as well as less tangible resources (recognition in the market, etc.).	The patterns of past behavior, activity, and effectiveness of the organization which may have an effect on current organizational functioning.	The stream of decisions made about how organizational resources will be configured against the demands, constraints and opportunities, within the context of history.
CRITICAL FEATURES OF THE INPUT FOR ANALYSIS	▪ What demands does the environment make on the organization? ▪ Environment puts constraints on organizational action.	▪ What is the relative quality of the different resources that the organization has access to? ▪ To what extent are resources fixed, as opposed to flexible in their configuration?	▪ What have been the major stages or phases of development of the organization? ▪ What is the current impact of historical factors such as strategic decisions acts of key leaders crises core values & norms?	▪ How has the organization defined its core mission, including: ▪ What markets it serves ▪ What products/ services it provides to these markets ▪ On what basis does it compete ▪ What supporting strategies has the organization employed to achieve the core mission ▪ What specific objectives have been set for organizational output?

The second input is the *resources* of the organization. Any organization faces its environment with a range of different assets to which it has access and which it can employ. These include human beings, technology, capital, information, etc. Resources can also include certain less tangible assets such as the perception of the organization in the marketplace, or a positive organizational climate. A set of resources can be shaped, deployed, or configured in different ways by an organization. For analysis purposes, there are two features that are of primary interest. One aspect of resources concerns the relative quality of those resources, or what value they have in light of the nature of the environment. The second factor concerns the extent to which resources can be reconfigured, or how fixed or flexible different resources are.

The third input is the *history* of the organization. There is growing evidence that the contemporary functioning of many organizations is greatly influenced by events in the past (see Levinson, 1972; 1976). In particular, it is important to understand what have been the major stages or phases of development of the organization over time (Galbraith & Nathanson, 1978) as well as understanding what is the current impact of events that occurred in the past such as key strategic decisions that were made, the acts or behavior of key leaders in the past, the nature of past crises and the organizational responses to them, and the evolution of core values and norms of the organization.

The final input is somewhat different from the others in that it in some ways reflects some of the factors in the environment, resources, and history of the organization. The fourth input is *strategy*. We will use this term in its most global and broad context (Hofer & Schendel, 1978) to describe the whole set of decisions that are made about how the organization will configure its resources against the demands, constraints and opportunities of the environ-

ment within the context of its history. Strategy refers to the issue of matching the organization's resources to its environment, or making the fundamental decision of "what business are we in?" For analysis purposes, several aspects of strategy are important to identify (Katz, 1970). First is what is the core mission of the organization, or what has the organization defined as its basic purpose or function within the larger system or environment? The core mission includes decisions about what markets the organization will serve, what products or services it will provide to those markets, or what basis it will use to compete in those markets. Second, strategy includes the specific supporting strategies (or tactics) that the organization will employ or is employing to achieve its core mission. Third is the specific performance or output objectives that have been established.

Strategy is perhaps the most important single input for the organization (see discussion in Nadler, Hackman & Lawler, 1979). On one hand, strategic decisions implicitly determine what is the nature of the work that the organization should be doing, or the tasks that it should perform. On the other hand, strategic decisions, and particularly decisions about objectives, serve as the basis for determining what the outputs of the system should be. Based on strategy, one can determine what is the desired or intended output of the system.

In summary, there are three basic inputs: environment, resources, and history, and a fourth input, strategy, which reflects how the organization chooses to respond to or deal with those other inputs. Strategy is critical because it determines the work that the organization should be performing and it defines the nature of desired organizational outputs.

Outputs

Outputs describe what the organization produces, how it performs, or globally, how effective it is. There has been a lot of discussion about what makes for an effective organization (see Steers, 1978; Goodman & Pennings, 1978; Van de Ven & Ferry, 1980). For our purposes, however, it is possible to identify a number of key indicators of organizational output. First, we need to think about system output at different levels (see Exhibit 3). Obviously we can think about the output that the system itself produces, but we also need to think about the various other types of output that contribute to organizational performance, such as the functioning of groups or units within the organization as well as the functioning of individual organization members.

At the organizational level, three factors are important to keep in mind in evaluating organizational performance. The first factor is goal attainment, or how well the organization meets its objectives (usually determined by strategy). A second factor is resource utilization or how well the organization makes use of resources that it has available to it. The question here is not just whether the organization meets its goals but whether it realizes all of the potential performance that is there and whether it achieves its goals by continuing to build resources or by "burning them up" in the process. A final factor is adaptability, or whether the organization continues to position itself in a favorable position vis-a-vis its environment—whether it is capable of changing and adapting to environmental changes.

Obviously, these organizational level outputs are contributed to by the functioning of groups or units (departments, divisions, or other subunits within the organization). Organizational output also is influenced by individual behavior, and certain individual level outputs (affective reactions such as satisfaction, stress, or experienced quality of working life) may be desired outputs in and of themselves.

The Organization as a Transformation Process

So far, we have defined the nature of inputs and outputs for the organizational system. This approach leads us towards thinking about the transformation process. The question that any manager faces, given an environment, a set of resources, and history, is "How do I take a strategy and implement it to produce effective organizational, group/unit, and individual performance?"

In our framework, the means for implementing strategies, or the transformation mechanism in the system is *the organization*. We therefore think about the organization and its major component parts as the fundamental means for transforming energy and information from inputs into outputs (see Exhibit 4). The question then is what are the key components of the organization, and what is the critical dynamic which describes how those components interact with each other to perform the transformation function?

Organizational Components

There are many different ways of thinking about what makes up an organization. At this point in the development of a science of organizations, we probably do not know what is the one right or best way to describe the different components of an organization. The question then is to find approaches for describing organizations that are useful, help to simplify complex phenomena, and help to identify patterns in what may at first blush seem to be random sets of activity. The particular approach

EXHIBIT 3 KEY ORGANIZATIONAL OUTPUTS

ORGANIZATIONAL FUNCTIONING
- Goal Attainment
- Resource Utilization
- Adaptability

GROUP/UNIT FUNCTIONING

INDIVIDUAL FUNCTIONING
- Behavior
- Affective Reactions

EXHIBIT 4   THE ORGANIZATION AS A TRANSFORMATION PROCESS

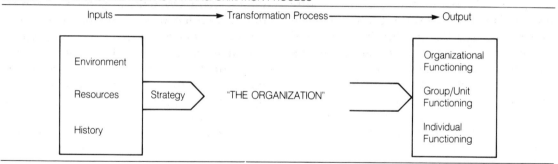

here views organizations as composed of four major components: (1) the task, (2) the individuals, (3) the formal organizational arrangements, and (4) the informal organization. We will discuss each one of these individually. (See Exhibit 5 for overviews of these components.)

The first component is the *task* of the organization. The task is defined as the basic or inherent work to be done by the organization and its subunits. The task (or tasks) is the activity the organization is engaged in, particularly in light of its strategy. The emphasis is on the specific work activities or functions that need to be done, and their inherent characteristics (as opposed to characteristics of the work created by how the work is organized or structured in this particular organization at this particular time). Analysis of the task would include a description of the basic work flows and functions, with attention to the characteristics of those work flows such as the knowledge or skill demands made by the work,

EXHIBIT 5   KEY ORGANIZATIONAL COMPONENTS

Component	Task	Individual	Formal Organizational Arrangements	Informal Organization
DEFINITION	The basic and inherent work to be done by the organization and its parts.	The characteristics of individuals in the organization.	The various structures, processes, methods, etc. that are formally created to get individuals to perform tasks.	The emerging arrangements including structures, processes, relationships, etc.
CRITICAL FEATURES OF EACH COMPONENT	▪ The types of skill and knowledge demands the work poses. ▪ The types of rewards the work inherently can provide. ▪ The degree of uncertainty associated with the work, including factors such as interdependence, routineness, etc. ▪ The constraints on performance demands inherent in the work (given a strategy).	▪ Knowledge and skills individuals have. ▪ Individual needs and preferences. ▪ Perceptions and expectancies. ▪ Background factors.	▪ Organization design, including grouping of functions, structure of subunits, and coordination and control mechanisms. ▪ Job design. ▪ Work environment. ▪ Human resource management systems.	▪ Leader behavior. ▪ Intragroup relations. ▪ Intergroup relations. ▪ Informal working arrangements. ▪ Communication and influence patterns.

the kinds of rewards the work inherently provides to those who do it, the degree of uncertainty associated with the work, and the specific constraints inherent in the work (such as critical time demands, cost constraints, etc.) The task is the starting point for the analysis, since the assumption is that a primary (although not the only) reason for the organization's existence is to perform the task consistent with strategy. As we will see, the assessment of the adequacy of other components will be dependent to a large degree on an understanding of the nature of the tasks to be performed.

A second component of organizations concerns the *individuals* who perform organizational tasks. The issue here is identifying the nature and characteristics of the individuals that the organization currently has as members. The most critical aspects to consider include the nature of individual knowledge and skills, the different needs or preferences that individuals have, the perceptions or expectancies that they develop, and other background factors (such as demographics) that may be potential influences on individual behavior.

The third component is the *formal organizational arrangements*. These include the range of structures, processes, methods, procedures, etc., that are explicitly and formally developed to get individuals to perform tasks consistent with organizational strategy. Organizational arrangements is a very broad term which includes a number of different specific factors. One factor of organizational arrangements is organization design, how jobs are grouped together into units, the internal structure of those units, and the various coordination and control mechanisms used to link those units together (see Galbraith, 1977; Nadler, Hackman & Lawler, 1979). A second factor in organizational arrangements is how jobs are designed (Hackman & Oldham, 1980) within the context of organizational designs. A third factor is the work environment, which includes a number of factors which characterize the immediate environment in which work is done, such as the physical working environment, the work resources made available to performers, etc. A final factor includes the various formal systems for attracting, placing, developing, and evaluating human resources in the organization.

Together, these factors combine to create the set of organizational arrangements. It is important to remember that these are the formal arrangements, formal in that they are explicitly designed and specified, usually in writing.

The final component is the *informal organization*. In any organization, while there is a set of formal organizational arrangements, over time another set of arrangements tends to develop or emerge. These arrangements are usually implicit and not written down anywhere, but they influence a good deal of behavior. For lack of a better term, these arrangements are frequently referred to as the informal organization and they include the different structures, processes, arrangements, etc., that emerge over time. These arrangements sometimes arise to complement the formal organizational arrangements by providing structures to aid work where none exist. In other situations they may arise in reaction to the formal structure, to protect individuals from it. It may therefore either aid or hinder organizational performance.

A number of aspects of the informal organization have a particularly critical effect on behavior, and thus need to be considered. The behavior of leaders (as opposed to the formal creation of leader positions) is an important feature of the informal organization, as are the patterns of relationships that develop both within and between groups. In addition, there are different types of informal working arrangements (including rules, procedures, methods, etc.) that develop. Finally, there are the various communication and influence patterns that combine to create the informal organization design (Tushman, 1977).

Organizations can therefore be thought of as a set of components, the task, the individuals, the organizational arrangements, and the informal organization. In any system, however, the critical question is not what the components are, but rather the nature of their interaction. The question in this model is, then, what is the dynamic of the relationship among the components? To deal with this issue, we need to return to the concept of congruence or fit.

The Concept of Congruence

Between each pair of inputs, there exists in any organization a relative degree of congruence, consistency, or "fit." Specifically, the congruence between two components is defined as follows:

the degree to which the needs, demands, goals, objectives and/or structures of one component are consistent with the needs, demands, goals, objectives and/or structures of another component.

Congruence, therefore, is a measure of the goodness of fit between pairs of components. For example, consider two components, the task and the individual. At the simplest level, the task can be thought of as inherently presenting some demands to individuals who would perform it (i.e., skill/knowledge demands). At the same time, the set of individuals available to do the tasks have certain characteristics (i.e., levels of skill and knowledge). Obviously, when the individual's knowledge and skill match the knowledge and skill demanded by the task, performance will be more effective.

Obviously, even the individual-task congruence relationship encompasses more factors than just knowledge and skill. Similarly, each congruence relationship in the model has its own specific characteristics. At the same time, in each relationship, there also is research and theory which can guide the assessment of fit. An overview of

the critical elements of each congruence relationship is provided in Exhibit 6.

The Congruence Hypothesis

Just as each pair of components has a degree of high or low congruence, so does the aggregate model, or whole organization, display a relatively high or low level of system congruence. The basic hypothesis of the model builds on this total state of congruence and is as follows:

other things being equal, the greater the total degree of congruence or fit between the various components, the more effective will be the organization, effectiveness being defined as the degree to which actual organization outputs at

EXHIBIT 6   DEFINITIONS OF FITS

Fit	The Issues
Individual-organization	To what extent individual needs are met by the organizational arrangements. To what extent individuals hold clear or distorted perceptions of organizational structures, the convergence of individual and organizational goals.
Individual-task	To what extent the needs of individuals are met by the tasks. To what extent individuals have skills and abilities to meet task demands.
Individual-informal organization	To what extent individual needs are met by the informal organization. To what extent does the informal organization make use of individual resources, consistent with informal goals.
Task-organization	Whether the organizational arrangements are adequate to meet the demands of the task, whether organizational arrangements tend to motivate behavior consistent with task demands.
Task-informal organization	Whether the informal organization structure facilitates task performance, whether it hinders or promotes meeting the demands of the task.
Organization-informal organization	Whether the goals, rewards, and structures of the informal organization are consistent with those of the formal organization.

individual, group, and organizational levels are similar to expected outputs, as specified by strategy.

The basic dynamic of congruence thus views the organization as being more effective when its pieces fit together. If we also consider questions of strategy, the argument expands to include the fit between the organization and its larger environment. An organization will be most effective when its strategy is consistent with the larger environment (in light of organizational resources and history) and when the organizational components are congruent with the tasks to be done to implement that strategy.

One important implication of the congruence hypotheses is that organizational problem analysis (or diagnosis) involves description of the system, identification of problems, and analysis of fits to determine the causes of problems. The model also implies that different configurations of the key components can be used to gain outputs (consistent with the systems characteristic of equifinality). Therefore the question is not finding the "one best way" of managing, but of determining effective combinations of components that will lead to congruent fits among them.

The process of diagnosing fits and identifying combinations of components to produce congruence is not necessarily intuitive. A number of situations which lead to congruence have been defined in the research literature. Thus, in many cases fit is something that can be defined, measured, and even quantified. There is, therefore, an empirical and theoretical basis for making assessment of fit. In most cases, the theory provides considerable guidance about what leads to congruent relationships (although in some areas the research is more definitive and helpful than others). The implication is that the manager who is attempting to diagnose behavior needs to become familiar with critical aspects of relevant organizational behavior models or theories so that he or she can evaluate the nature of fits in a particular system.

The congruence model is thus a general organizing framework. The organizational analyst will need other, more specific "sub models" to define high and low congruence. Examples of such submodels that might be used in the context of this general diagnostic model would be (1) Job Characteristics model (Hackman & Oldham, 1980) to assess and explain the fit between individuals and tasks as well as the fit between individuals and organizational arrangements (job design); (2) Expectancy Theory models of motivation (Vroom, 1964; Lawler, 1973) to explain the fit between individuals and the other three components; (3) the Information Processing model of organizational design (Galbraith, 1973; Tushman & Nadler, 1978) to explain the task-formal organization and task-informal organization fits; or (4) an Organizational Climate model (Litwin & Stringer, 1968) to explain the fit between the informal organization and the other components. These models and theories are listed as illustrations of how more specific models can be used in the context of the general model. Obviously, those mentioned above are just a sampling of possible tools that could be used.

In summary, then, we have described a general model for the analysis of organizations (see Exhibit 7). The organization is seen as a system which takes inputs and transforms them into outputs. At the core of the model, the transformation process is the organization, seen as composed of four basic components. The critical dynamic is the fit or congruence among the components. We now turn our attention to the pragmatic question of how to use this model for analyzing organizational problems.

A PROCESS FOR ORGANIZATIONAL PROBLEM ANALYSIS

The conditions that face organizations are

EXHIBIT 7   A CONGRUENCE MODEL FOR ORGANIZATIONAL ANALYSIS

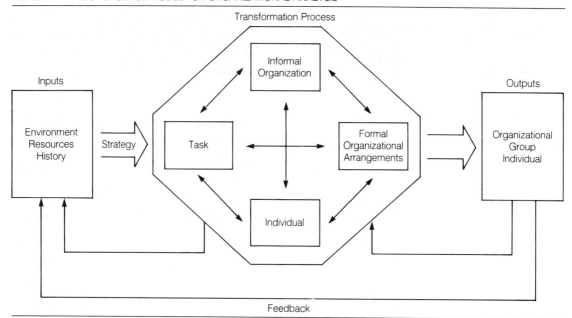

frequently changing, and as a consequence, managers are required to continually engage in problem identification and problem solving activities (Schein, 1970). To do this managers must be involved in gathering data on the performance of their organizations, comparing these data to desired performance levels, identifying the causes of problems, developing and choosing action plans, and finally implementing and evaluating these action plans. These phases can be viewed as a generic problem solving process. For long term organizational viability, some sort of problem solving process needs to continually be in operation (Schein, 1970; Weick, 1969).

Experience with using the congruence model for organizations to do problem analysis in actual organizational settings has led to the development of an approach to using the model, based on the generic problem solving processes described above (see Exhibit 8). In this section, we will walk through this process, describing the different steps in the process and discussing

how the model can be used at each stage. There are eight specific steps in the problem analysis process, and each one will be described separately.

1. *Identify symptoms:* In any situation there is initial information that presents itself as indications that problems may exist. We can think of this information as symptomatic data. These data tell us that a problem might exist, but they do not usually indicate what the problem is or what the causes are. Symptomatic data are important to note, however, since the symptoms or problems that present themselves may be important indicators of where to look for more complete data.

2. *Specify inputs:* Having noted the symptoms, the starting point for analysis is to identify the system and the environment in which it functions. This means collecting data about the nature of environment, the type of resources the organization has, and the critical aspects of its

EXHIBIT 8 BASIC PROBLEM ANALYSIS STEPS
USING THE CONGRUENCE MODEL

Step	Explanation
1. Identify symptoms	List data indicating possible existence of problems.
2. Specify inputs	Identify the system. Determine nature of environment, resources, and history. Identify critical aspects of strategy.
3. Identify outputs	Identify data that defines the nature of outputs at various levels (individual, group/unit, organization)—should include Desired outputs (from strategy) Actual outputs being obtained.
4. Identify problems	Identify areas where there are significant and meaningful differences between desired and actual outputs. To the extent possible, identify penalties, i.e., specific costs (actual and opportunity costs) associated with each problem.
5. Describe components of the organization	Describe basic nature of each of the four components with emphasis on their critical features.
6. Assessment of congruence (fits)	Do analysis to determine relative congruence among components (draw on submodels as needed).
7. Generate hypotheses to identify causes	Analyze to associate fit with specific problems.
8. Identify action steps	Indicate what possible actions might deal with causes of problems.

history. Input analysis also involves identifying what the strategy of the organization is, including its core mission, supporting strategies, and objectives.

3. *Identify outputs:* The third step is an analysis of the outputs of the organization at the individual, group, and organizational level. Output analysis actually involves two elements. The first is to define what is the desired, or planned output. This usually can be obtained from an analysis of strategy which should explicitly or implicitly define what the organization is attempting to achieve in terms of output or performance indicators. The second is to collect data that would indicate what type of output the organization is actually achieving.

4. *Identify problems:* Symptoms indicate the possibility of problems. For our purposes, we will define problems as the differences between expected output and actual output. A problem exists when a significant and meaningful difference is observed between output (at any level) that is desired or planned and the output that is actually being obtained. Thus problems would be discrepancies (actual vs. expected) of organizational performance, group functioning, and individual behavior or affective reactions. These data thus tell us that problems exist, but they do not specify what the causes are.

Where data are available, it is frequently useful to also identify what are the costs associated with the problems, or the *penalties* that the organization incurs by not fixing the problem. Penalties might be actual costs (increased expenses, etc.) or opportunity costs, such as revenue that could be realized if the problem were not there.

5. *Describe organizational components:* The next step begins analysis to determine the causes of problems. Data are collected about the nature of each of the four major organizational components, including information about the component and its critical features in this organization.

6. *Assess congruence (fits):* Using the data collected in step 5 as well as applicable submodels or theories, an assessment is made of the positive or negative fit between each of the pairs of components.

7. *Generate hypotheses about problem causes:* Having described the components and assessed congruence, the next step is to link together the congruence analysis with the problem identification (step 4). Given the analysis, which poor fits seem to be associated with or account for the output problems that have been identified. The patterns of congruence and incongruence which appear to cause the patterns of problems are determined.

8. *Identify action steps:* The final step in problem analysis is to identify possible action steps. These steps might range from specific changes to deal with relatively obvious problem causes on one hand, to additional data collection to test the hypotheses developed concerning relatively more complex problems and causes.

In addition to these eight steps identified, some further steps need to be kept in mind. Having identified possible actions, problem solving involves making predictions about the consequence of those actions, choosing particular action steps, implementing those action steps, and evaluating the impact of those actions. In each case, it is, of course, important to have a general diagnostic framework to monitor what the effects of actions are.

The congruence model and this problem analysis process outline are tools for structuring and dealing with the complex reality of organizations. Given the indeterminate nature of social systems, there is no one best way of handling a particular situation. The model and the process do, however, facilitate one in collecting data, analyzing the meaning of that data, and making decisions about possible action. If these tools have merit, then it is up to the manager to use them along with his or her intuitive sense (based on experience) to make the appropriate set of diagnostic, evaluative, and action decisions over time.

FUTURE DIRECTIONS

The model that we have presented here reflects a particular way of thinking about organizations. If that perspective has merit, then it may make sense to think about the possible extensions of that model as a tool to think about more complex problems or to structure more complex situations. A number of directions for further thought, research, and theory development are as follows:

1. *Organizational change:* The issue of organizational change has received a good deal of attention from managers and academics alike. The question is how to implement organizational changes effectively. Much talk has centered on the lack of a general model of organizational change. In one sense, however, it is hard to think about a general model of organizational change in the absence of a general model of organizations. The congruence perspective outlined here may provide some guidance and direction towards the development of a more integrated perspective on the processes of organizational change. Initial work in that area (Nadler, 1981) is encouraging in terms of the applicability of the congruence model to the change issue.

2. *Organizational development over time:* There has been a growing realization that organizations grow and develop over time, that they face different types of crises, evolve through different stages, and develop along some predictable lines (see for example Greiner, 1972; Galbraith and Nathanson, 1978). A model of organizations such as the one presented here might be a tool for developing a typology of growth patterns by indicating what are the different configurations of task, individual, organizational arrangements and informal organizations that might be most appropriate for organizations in different environments and at different stages of development.

3. *Organizational pathology:* Organizational problem solving ultimately requires some sense of what types of problems may be encountered and kinds of patterns of causes one might expect. It is reasonable to assume that most problems that organizations encounter are not wholly unique, but rather predictable problems that one might expect. The view, often heard, that "our problems are unique" reflects in part the fact that there is no framework of organizational pathology. The question is, are there certain basic "illnesses" which organizations suffer? Can a framework of organizational pathology, similar to the physician's framework of medical pathology be developed? The lack of a pathology framework in turn reflects that lack of a basic functional model of organizations. Again, development of a congruence perspective might be able to provide a common language to use for the identification of general pathological patterns of organizational functioning.

4. *Organizational solution types:* Closely linked to the problem of pathology is the problem of treatment, intervention, or solutions to organizational problems. Again, there is a lack of a general framework to consider the nature of organizational interventions. In this case, too, the congruence model could have value as a means for conceptualizing and ultimately describing the different intervention options available in response to problems (see one attempt at this in Nadler & Tichy, 1980).

SUMMARY

This paper has presented a general approach for thinking about organizational functioning and a process for using a model to analyze organizational problems. This particular model is one way of thinking about organizations. It clearly is not the only model, nor can we claim that it definitively is the best model. It is one tool, however, that appears to be useful for structuring the complexity of organizational life, and helping managers in creating, maintaining, and developing effective organizations.

REFERENCES

Aldrich, H. E., & Pfeffer, J. Environments of organizations. *Annual Review of Sociology*, 1976, 2, 79–105.

Argyris, C., & Schon, D. A. *Theory in practice.* San Francisco: Jossey-Bass, 1974.

Bauer, R. A. Detection and anticipation of impact: The nature of the task. In R. A. Bauer (Ed.), *Social indicators*, pp. 1–67. Boston: M.I.T. Press, 1966.

Buckley, W. *Sociology and modern systems theory.* Englewood Cliffs, N.J.: Prentice-Hall, 1967.

Dunnette, M. D. *Handbook of industrial and organizational psychology.* Chicago: Rand-McNally, 1976.

Galbraith, J. R. *Designing complex organizations.* Reading, Mass.: Addison-Wesley, 1973.

——, *Organization design.* Reading, Mass.: Addison-Wesley, 1977.

——, & Nathanson, D. A. *Strategy implementation: The role of structure and process.* St. Paul, Minn.: West, 1978.

Goodman, P. S., & Pennings, J. M. *New perspectives on organizational effectiveness.* San Francisco: Jossey-Bass, 1977.

Greiner, L. E. Evolution and revolution as organizations grow. *Harvard Business Review*, 1972.

Hackman, J. R., & Oldham, G. A. *Work redesign.* Reading, Mass.: Addison-Wesley, 1979.

Hofer, C. W., & Schendel, D. *Strategy formulation: Analytical concepts.* St. Paul, Minn.: West, 1978.

Homans, G. C. *The human group.* New York: Harcourt Brace Jovanovich, 1950.

Katz, D., & Kahn, R. L. *The social psychology of organizations*, New York: Wiley, 1966, 2d ed., 1978.

Katz, R. L. *Cases and concepts in corporate strategy.* Englewood Cliffs, N.J.: Prentice-Hall, 1970.

Lawler, E. E. *Motivation in work organizations.* Belmont, Calif.: Wadsworth, 1973.

Lawrence, P. R., & Lorsch, J. W. *Developing organizations: Diagnosis and action.* Reading, Mass.: Addison-Wesley, 1969.

Leavitt, H. J. Applied organization change in industry. In J. G. March (Ed.), *Handbook of organizations*, pp. 1144–1170. Chicago: Rand-McNally, 1965.

Levinson, H. *Organizational diagnosis.* Cambridge, Mass.: Harvard, 1972.

——, *Psychological man.* Cambridge, Mass.: Levinson Institute, 1976.

Litwin, G. H., & Stringer, R. A. *Motivation and organizational climate.* Boston: Harvard University Graduate School of Business Administration, 1968.

Lorsch, J. W., & Sheldon, A. The individual in the organization: A systems view. In J. W. Lorsch and P. R. Lawrence (Eds.), *Managing group and intergroup relations.* Homewood, Ill.: Irwin-Dorsey, 1972.

Nadler, D. A. An integrative theory of organizational change. *Journal of Applied Behavioral Science*, 1981 (in press).

——, & Tichy, N. M. The limitations of traditional intervention technology in health care organizations. In N. Margulies & J. A. Adams, *Organization development in health care organizations*. Reading, Mass.: Addison-Wesley, 1980.

——, Hackman, J. R., & Lawler, E. E. *Managing organizational behavior*. Boston: Little, Brown, 1979.

Salancik, G. R., & Pfeffer, J. *The external control of organizations*. New York: Wiley, 1978.

Schein, E. H. *Organizational psychology*. Englewood Cliffs, N.J.: Prentice-Hall, 1970.

Seiler, J. A. *Systems analysis in organizational behavior*. Homewood, Ill.: Irwin-Dorsey, 1967.

Steers, R. M. *Organizational effectiveness: A behavioral view*. Pacific Palisades, Calif.: Goodyear, 1977.

Thompson, J. D. *Organizations in action*. New York: McGraw-Hill, 1967.

Tushman, M. L. A political approach to organizations: A review and rationale. *Academy of Management Review*, 1977, 2, 206–216.

Van de Ven, A., & Ferry, D. *Organizational assessment*. New York: Wiley Interscience, 1980.

Von Bertalanffy, L. *General systems theory: Foundations, development applications* (Rev. ed.). New York: Braziller, 1968.

Vroom, V. H. *Work and motivation*. New York: Wiley, 1964.

Weick, K. E. *The social psychology of organizing*. Reading, Mass.: Addison-Wesley, 1969.

Wiener, N. *The human use of human beings: Cybernetics and society*. Boston: Houghton Mifflin, 1950.

CASES AND APPLICATIONS

Organization Theory

SECOND EDITION

I

Open Systems

Environment

Organizations as Systems

1

They Sang the Low Down, Loss of Market Share Blues

Ten years ago it was a solid, profitable small business, locally and privately owned, in its third generation of family management. Its single consumer product, which enjoyed steady and effortless sales, was number one in its market, its share an enviable 29%.

Five years ago that good fortune had been turned to bad by competition from a national giant. The firm was still profitable, but it had fallen to number two on a market share that had dwindled to 14%.

Three years ago the situation had grown still worse, thanks to persistent competition and a catastrophic product quality problem. Market share was down to 6%. The company had to make a comeback—or go out of business.

Today, market share is up to 10%, and it's expected to hit 13% for 1980.

The company is Dixie Brewing Co. of New Orleans. The product is Dixie Beer. The fight to bring it back is a lesson in imaginative marketing—a demonstration that one industry's routine procedures may be revolutionary strategies in another. The

managers of Dixie Brewing have looked beyond their industry, beyond the company's successful past, for new and creative ideas.

The Dixie Brewing Co. was founded in 1907 by Valentine Merz, who took on 10 competing local breweries in the New Orleans market. By 1970, only three local breweries were still doing business, and Dixie was the best-selling beer in New Orleans. Sure, there were dozens of domestic and foreign imports sold there. But Dixie had a price advantage, and in those days the price of a beer was more important than brand. Dixie, though, had a brand advantage as well: It had the image of *the* local beer in the Jefferson and Orleans parishes (metropolitan New Orleans), which accounted for 75% of sales.

The company appeared to have few problems. The presidency had passed to the founder's grandson, Cyril Mainergra. Ownership was closely held within the Mainergra family, a compatible group. Dixie Beer practically sold itself. A Dixie salesman would simply walk into a tavern and buy everyone a Dixie. At a supermarket the

Written by John R. Halbrooks. Reprinted with the permission of *INC.* Magazine, September, 1980. Copyright © 1980 by INC. Publishing Company, 38 Commercial Wharf, Boston, MA 02110.

salesman simply asked the manager how much beer he needed that week.

But in 1970 all that began to change. Philip Morris acquired the Miller Brewing Co., nationally number seven (although barely a factor in New Orleans), and threw all its marketing expertise toward making Miller High Life number one in the nation. No longer would Miller compete on price; they began to sell image. By 1975 Miller was number four among all brewers and number one in New Orleans, its share of the market 17%.

While Miller was aggressively marketing its beer nationwide, Dixie continued to do business as usual, selling its beer as casually as though it were just a distributor. By 1975, Dixie's share of its market had dropped from 29% to 17.5%. Dixie, however, was still *the* local beer. Sales slipped only slightly during the Miller onslaught. The market was growing, and Dixie still produced 220,000 barrels annually.

Then in July, 1975, Dixie laid a new floor in its brewhouse. Some phenol, an acidic compound in the flooring, leaked into open cooling vats in the cellars below, contaminating make-up water. That contaminated water was pumped upstairs and brewed into beer. Although the bad beer did not prove toxic, its terrible medicinal taste made it impossible to drink.

That medicinal-tasting beer, unfortunately, went out to taverns and stores around New Orleans over the Fourth of July, traditionally the biggest week of the year for beer sales, bigger even than Mardi Gras. And to compound the error, Dixie was slow to trace the source of contamination. For three weeks, bad beer was replaced with more bad beer.

The results were catastrophic. Over a six-week period, Dixie's sales fell by 55%. The image of the local beer was shattered, and Dixie settled into a slow, steady sales decline.

As soon as the contamination problem had been solved, president Cyril Mainergra set to work resuscitating Dixie. In December 1975 Mainergra hired Dan Hooten, an aggressive young district field sales manager at Lever Bros., as sales manager. A month later, Mainergra hired Robert Oertling as Dixie's brewmaster. He told Hooten and Oertling that they had his blessing to do whatever needed to be done to save Dixie Brewing Co.

Together, Hooten and Oertling began a much-needed plant modernization that consumed $500,000 in 1976 alone. At the same time, they instituted a cost-cutting program that eliminated truck routes and streamlined the bottling and garage operations.

Hooten's efforts to stop the erosion in sales were hampered by Dixie's poor image. "I remember calling on one tavern," Hooten says. "The manager threw me out, said he'd never serve Dixie, that we were a schlock operation. Well, I'm like anyone else. You tell me often enough that I'm not going to make it and I get stubborn. Dammit, we are going to make it."

By the fall of 1977, though, it was clear that stubbornness alone wouldn't save Dixie. Market share was down to 6%, and traditional sales methods had done nothing to slow the decline. Hooten was desperate to get Dixie back into the hands of New Orleans beer drinkers. If conventional methods didn't work, they would try unconventional methods.

Hooten's first inspiration was a sample giveaway—unheard of in the beer industry, but common in supermarket merchandising. One weekend, he handed out 60,000 six-packs of Dixie in residential neighborhoods around the city. The flood of free beer did what it was meant to do—it prevented Dixie's sales from sinking further.

The giveaway's success showed Hooten that what was routine procedure in one industry might be revolutionary in another. He decided that to survive Dixie would have to acquire an eye for the unorthodox, an ability to look beyond its own industry and its past successes for new creative ideas.

Hooten didn't know what those ideas-would be. Surprised by the success of the giveaway, he hadn't planned any followup. Now he began to search for another marketing coup that would feed the momentum of Dixie's turnaround.

At this point, in December 1977, Cyril Mainergra died of a heart attack. The Mainergra family asked Dan Hooten to become president of the company.

Half a year later, Hooten found the marketing technique he was looking for. Like the beer sampling, the idea came from grocery marketing. Hooten decided to try using coupons—on a grand scale.

In June 1978, Hooten took out a full-page ad in New Orleans's morning newspaper, the *Times-Picayune*. The ad described the brewery's quality control improvements and invited everyone to try some Dixie beer for free. At the bottom of the ad was a "Dixie Bill" that could be mailed to the brewery for a coupon worth $1.80 toward the purchase of a six-pack of Dixie Beer.

It was hard to believe anything so prosaic as coupons could generate such excitement. "I don't think anything like this had ever been tried before in the beer industry," says Hooten. The reaction was explosive. An AP photo of Hooten holding a six-pack of Dixie and a copy of the ad was picked up by newspapers all over the country. Papers in Canada, England, and Australia also ran the photo.

With the morning circulation of over 200,000, the *Times-Picayune* had printed nearly half a million dollars' worth of Dixie Bills. "If they'd all been redeemed," Robert Oertling admits, "it would have bankrupted us." Hooten budgeted for 10 times the average coupon redemption, or about 125,000 returns, and held his breath. When the totals were tabulated, 94,000 bills had been redeemed.

"After our beer sampling," says Hooten, "we'd failed to follow up with effective ad-vertising. This time we were ready." Television testimonials by delighted new Dixie fans began to work their magic. In 1978, Dixie's sales increased by 9% over 1977 to 127,000 barrels.

With Dixie's sales climbing at last, Hooten began to do something that had never been done before at the Dixie Brewing Co. He began to *sell* beer. Dixie had always operated on the assumption that beer sold itself. In fact, nearly all breweries worked on that assumption. In the 1950s and 1960s, beer companies were primarily production-oriented; beer was differentiated less by brand than by price. But in the 1970s, Miller's marketing onslaught changed the rules of the game. Miller rocked the industry by leaping from seventh to second position among all brewers in only seven years.

Hooten's response to the marketing challenge was not to mimic Miller, but to examine the very basis of sales in the beer industry. What he found was that beer was sold with a single sales force and a single sales pitch.

"I had found it very difficult," Hooten says, "to sell to a tavern manager, who looks at profit by the unit, and then switch to a supermarket, where the manager is concerned about volume and profit per linear foot."

Hooten's unorthodox solution to this dichotomy was to split his sales force. It was his twist on a practice common in the grocery industry, where sales is divided into product groups. Hooten had only one product, but he had two quite dissimilar sales outlets.

So Hooten hired a sales manager, Ron Sprinkle, like himself a Lever Bros. veteran. In early 1979, Hooten and Sprinkle set about breaking Dixie's sales force into an on-premise group (restaurants and taverns) and an off-premise group (groceries and convenience stores).

In on-premise sales, Dixie continues to emphasize the rebuilding of Dixie's representation in taverns and restaurants around New Orleans. Tom Murry, Dixie's on-premise sales manager, has pushed aggressive service and a more professional sales approach (stressing profitability and return on investment) that attempts to give the manager "a reason to buy." These efforts have won Dixie 40 new accounts in the first quarter of 1980.

But clearly, it is off-premise sales that offer Dixie its greatest immediate potential for growth. Off-premise sales account for two-thirds of Dixie's total barrelage. "We began to do more and more that was not all that new in the grocery industry," says Ron Sprinkle, "but was new in the beer industry. The beer companies lag about 10 to 15 years behind other consumer product companies."

Dixie sales supervisors had worked in relative autonomy before Ron Sprinkle conducted a sales analysis of 90 stores and drew up coverage plans for sales calls. Sales supervisors began to call on better accounts more frequently. And Sprinkle had supervisors begin to lavish attention on the headquarters of food store chains, which in the past had received mailings but had rarely been called on. Sprinkle saw that although stores often operated as individual profit centers, it was headquarters that set policy. By selling headquarters, Dixie could make gains in a dozen stores at once.

The manager of the off-premise sales division, Tom Voelkel, compiled data on market brand and package ranking from state tax figures to provide his sales supervisors with support in their sales presentations. But, as Ron Sprinkle says, "It's not so much the figures as the way you use them that's important."

Voelkel massages data and statistics so well he seems to find a way to use any figure to his advantage. When he enters a grocery, Voelkel knows immediately what sales tack he will take. If he is pushing Dixie's bread-and-butter 12-ounce one-way (nonreturnable) package, he may suggest increasing Dixie's shelf space at the expense of Miller. When the store manager refuses, saying that Miller is his best-selling beer, Voelkel is ready with a market breakdown that shows Dixie's 12-ounce package outsells Miller's 16-ounce package. "Why not give us some of that 16-ounce space?" he will ask.

Perhaps the most unusual tactic Dixie has employed involves its private-label beer. Dixie had been producing its beer under special labels for certain grocery chains, but it had never exploited the natural marketing advantage a private label gave it—the foot in the door for Dixie sales supervisors.

Sprinkle and Voelkel conducted a study of private-label beer sales at Schwegmann Giant Super Markets, whose 10 stores do about 30% of the grocery business in the city. They then made a slide presentation before Schwegmann's buying committee.

In every store that was surveyed, Schwegmann's Beer was positioned down among the economy brands. Miller and Anheuser-Busch, the market leaders, held prime space—at eye level as the consumer turned the corner.

Dixie's presentation to Schwegmann's was an appeal to logic and reason. Why position Schwegmann's Beer down among the economy brands? Taking Schwegmann's Beer—and Dixie, of course—and putting them next to the premium brands dramatizes the price differential. An attractive price and good shelf position is bound to increase sales of Schwegmann's Beer, which will draw customers to Schwegmann's stores. And the higher the sales of both Schwegmann's and Dixie, the greater Dixie's barrelage and the lower its costs.

So, Dixie suggested, why not let us work with your managers to set your stores? Unfolding diagrams to show Schwegmann's exactly how Dixie would display and stock beer at each outlet, Dixie won store-setting privileges for all Schwegmann stores.

Dixie is confident that in the 60 stores it

helps set today—a figure Hooten is sure Dixie can double—its beer is well positioned, all its packages are available, and it won't get caught out of stock.

Hooten also broke with tradition by budgeting generous amounts for advertising Dixie. Convincing beer drinkers that "local is better" is critical to Dixie's success, he and Sprinkle believe. They spend $2 a barrel on advertising (a figure even national brewers did not exceed until recently) to let local beer drinkers know that Dixie is fresher and that the brewery represents a tradition in New Orleans that should not die out. "Dixie is as much a part of New Orleans," Sprinkle says, "as red beans and rice, as the French Quarter itself."

So far Hooten's search for unorthodox solutions to Dixie's problems has paid off. By the end of 1979, Dixie had passed a faltering Schlitz for third position on New Orleans beer charts with about 10% of the market. By year-end, Hooten wants a 13% market share and a shot at Anheuser-Busch. Miller's astonishing 47% market share looks unassailable in the near future.

The hopes for the boost that will push Dixie up over the top and back into profits ride on another unlikely hero, the "long neck," the 12-ounce returnable bottle that has suffered at the hands of the convenient throw-aways. The long neck offers almost double the profit margin of the non-returnable because it can simply be refilled and sent back out.

Miller and Anheuser-Busch, which ship from Fort Worth and Houston respectively, downplay the long neck because of high freight costs. Many merchants also look down on the long neck because they don't like to bother with returnable bottles.

Yet, despite recalcitrant merchants and the lack of enthusiasm by the national breweries, the long neck made an imperceptible advance in 1979 after a decade of falling sales. And Dixie's long neck was up 9% in the first quarter of 1980 over the same period a year before.

In a marketing test last year, Dixie introduced the long neck in several stores. The results showed that the long neck did not cannibalize Dixie's other packages, but ate into competitors' sales. Dixie's total sales volume in those stores increased by between 24% and 60%.

Hooten has high hopes for the long neck. It is symbolic, as is Dixie, of everything the major brewers are not. And it represents Dixie's new marketing strategy: to look to the past or the future, in your own backyard or outside the industry, for new ideas. Dan Hooten has made the unorthodox orthodox at the Dixie Brewing Co.

2

Pine Mountain State University

BACKGROUND

Pine Mountain is a university of 22,000 students located in the southeastern United States. It offers a full range of programs at both the undergraduate and graduate levels, including the doctorate in 17 areas. The college was founded in 1873 as a small private liberal arts college. It became a state teachers college in 1927 and a full-fledged state university in 1946. During the last 30 years enrollment has increased by 10,000 students from 12,000 to 22,000.

The school is one of two major universities in the state. It is located in a town of about 50,000 residents situated in a rural area. The closest large city (population 250,000) is about 90 miles away.

There are five other state-supported colleges in the state. Only one of these is a major university; the others are teacher colleges. The other major state university is located in a major metropolitan area with a population of about one million. Its enrollment is about 17,000 students, most of whom are enrolled in the night program.

This other university offers doctorates only in business and in education. Its enrollment has increased greatly in the past 15 years from 3,000 to its present level.

The state in which both universities are located has been severely affected by a national recession. Unemployment in the state has averaged 10.5% over the past 18 months. Inflation has averaged about 8% for each of the last two years. The state legislative allocation for higher education has not increased during the past two years. During the 1960s, the allocation increased an average of 10% each year.

THE SITUATION

Pine Mountain State recently completed a reorganization in order to better deal with what its top administration believed to be the contingencies in the environment. As they saw it, the university was faced with several key problems listed below:

1. how to cope with increasing enrollments in the face of a decline in real

From B. J. Hodge and William P. Anthony, *Organizational Theory: An Environmental Approach.*
Copyright © 1979 by Allyn & Bacon, Inc. Reprinted with permission.

dollar allocations (adjusted for inflation) from the legislature,

2. how to cope with increasing calls for accountability and financial responsibility continually being made by various legislators and the state board of trustees,
3. how to manage the internal operations of the university to better cope with the increase in enrollments, faculty, and staff that occurred during the late 1960s and early 1970s,
4. what posture it should take in relation to its sister university in the urban area, and
5. how to develop other sources of funds from alumni, foundations, corporations, and the federal government to supplement legislative appropriations.

After extensive study, the top administrative staff of Pine Mountain State developed a comprehensive reorganization plan that established several new units of the university and consolidated others. The role of most of the units was redefined. The intent of the reorganization was to keep the university in better tune with its environment so that it could more easily assess environmental opportunities and constraints in order to react more quickly with an appropriate response. Exhibits 2–1 and 2–2 show both the old and the new formal organizational structures of the university.

The new structure has been in operation for about 18 months. The top administrators believe the structure is enabling the university to better respond to its environment. However, they realize continuing adjustments need to be made, so an organizational development committee was established to monitor and receive inputs on the implementation of the new structure. The committee is to evaluate the inputs and to pass them on to the top administrators. The committee was formed at the time of reorganization but has only met three times since reorganization.

THE ISSUES

Since the reorganization, the following criticisms have been raised by the faculty, students, legislature, board of trustees, alumni, and federal government.

Legislature

The university seems top heavy with administrators. At a time of financial austerity it does not seem appropriate to create so many new, highly-paid positions.

Trustees

Pine Mountain State spends for administration twice the amount spent by the other major state university and four times the amount spent by a teachers college. Even worse is the fact that the budgeting and accounting system is less accurate now than it was before.

Students

The registration process is worse than ever. The lines are longer and it is more difficult to get the classes desired. Classes are overcrowded; professors are never around for counseling and advising. Parking is terrible—there is never a place to park now. The top administration is isolated and is not responsive to the needs of the students. The president is unwilling to meet with students to discuss their problems.

Faculty

The president is impossible to contact. There are too many levels of administration; everything is too centralized. An individual college cannot do its own fundraising, alumni relations, purchasing, or publicity without first going through the appropriate university office. There is no money for new faculty positions or for raises since the administration has taken all new positions and money. The internal allocation of resources is unfair. Arts and Sciences receives too many resources compared to its enrollment, while the professional colleges that have experienced tremendous student growth do not get enough.

Alumni

The university seems to be more coordinated now than in the past. Instead of being contacted by four or five different people for financial contributions, only one contact is made by the development office. The alumni affairs office seems to have good current addresses on all alumni.

Federal government

The accounting and management of feder-

ally sponsored research seems to be better coordinated. The university now has one main office concerned with this effort.

Since the reorganization, financial gifts from alumni have increased from $40,000 annually to about $500,000 annually. Gifts from corporations and foundations have increased from $15,000 to $100,000 annually. Federal government grants have decreased from $12,000,000 annually to $9,500,000 annually. Legislative appropriations have remained constant at $48,000,000 annually. Tuition for a 14-hour load has increased from $210 per quarter to $260 per quarter.

EXHIBIT 2-1   PINE MOUNTAIN STATE UNIVERSITY'S OLD ORGANIZATION CHART

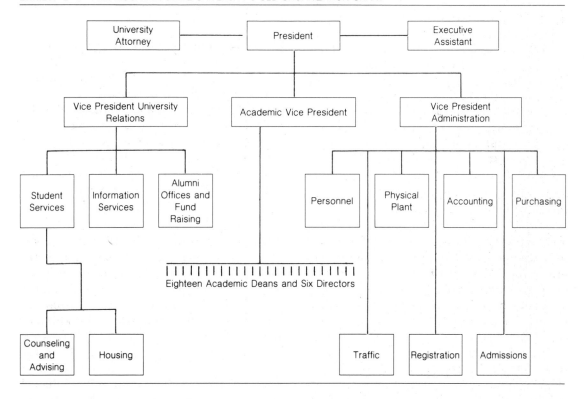

EXHIBIT 2-2 PINE MOUNTAIN STATE UNIVERSITY'S NEW ORGANIZATION CHART

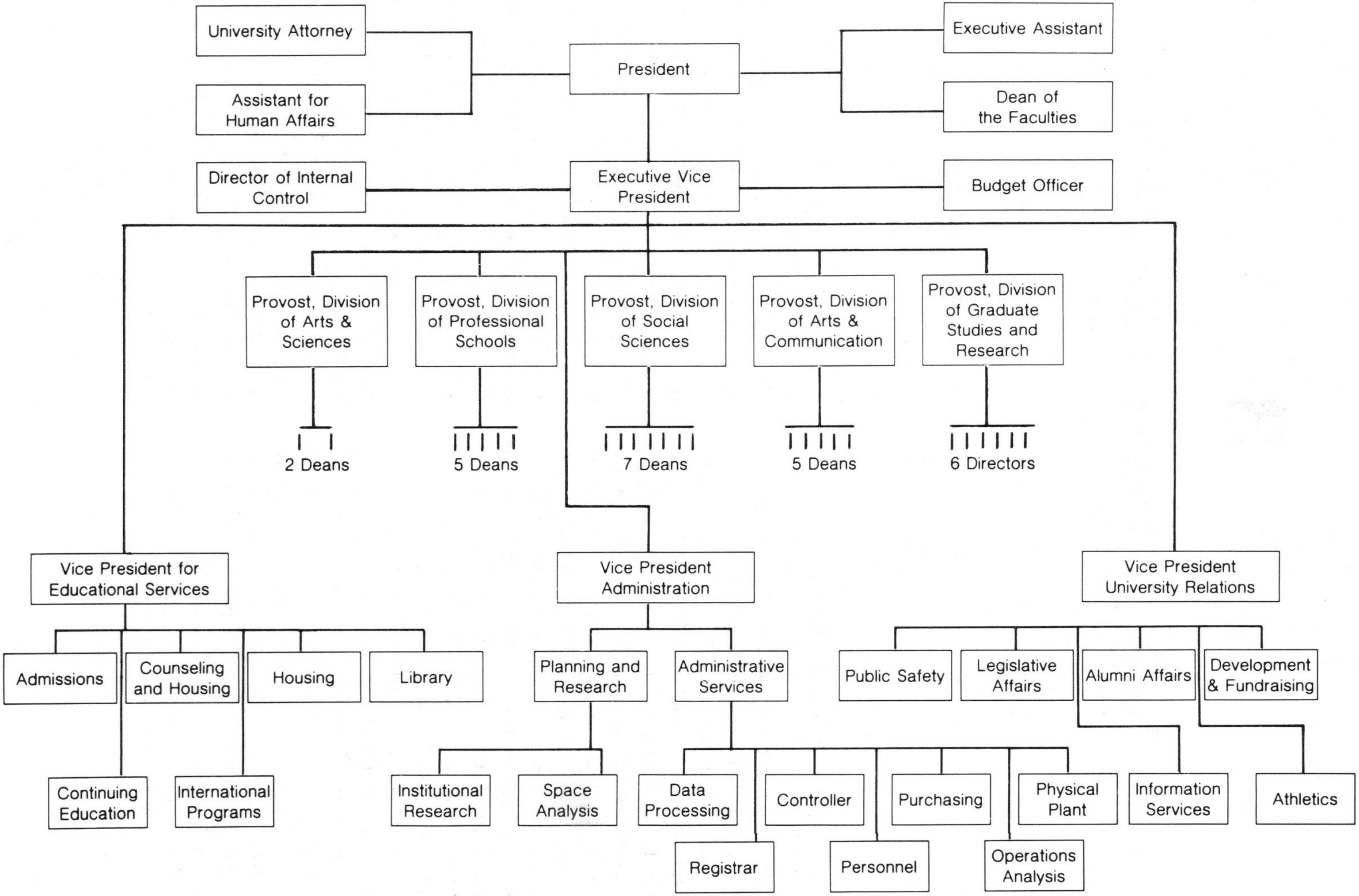

3

First National City Bank

The First National City Bank was founded in 1955 by William Jacks, who owned a controlling interest in the bank. His family had been in banking for many years, and he saw this as an opportunity to apply his banking and management experience to his own bank. The bank was located in a rapidly growing urban area in Arizona. During the initial years, First National City Bank concentrated on two goals: attracting and retaining depositors through personal service, and establishing a reputation as a safe and solid financial institution. The goals were successful, and the bank grew to $475 million in assets by 1974.

During the late 1970s, the bank's growth slowed, and Bill Jacks and the bank experienced some reversals. Two new branch locations were closed because they could not show a profit. One of the branches was located in a nearby city that had a large population of ethnic and minority people. The other branch had been located near a major university where most of the residents were college students. In both cases, the First National City branches seemed unable to attract depositors and borrowers from their local areas. The Bank did not have a positive reputation with those population segments, and did not seem to have the flexibility or types of service desired by potential customers.

By 1978, Bill Jacks began to replace some middle managers, hoping to bring in new energy and fresh ideas. Bill Jacks still believed that a bank succeeded because of its safety as a financial institution, and because it established personal relationships with middle class customers. He passed this philosophy and other management ideas on to the new managers. He stressed a traditional management structure, including centralized decision making and standardized procedures. All branch banks were encouraged to offer the same services, and many decisions were passed up the

Written by Richard L. Daft. From: *Organizations: A Micro/Macro Approach* by Richard L. Daft and Richard Steers. Copyright © 1986 by Scott, Foresman and Company. Reprinted by permission.

hierarchy to the top. Vertical communication and "following the rules" were deemed a safe and responsible management approach for a community bank.

As the new managers gained experience in the bank, they began to propose changes. One branch manager suggested that each of the branch locations establish an advisory board. The purpose of the advisory board would be to select people from the surrounding community to serve on a committee that would serve as a liaison between the community and First National City Bank and make recommendations to management. The advisory boards would be composed of the bank manager, Bill Jacks, and important people from the local area, such as business people, women, minority group members, or college students. The manager who proposed the idea argued that advisory board members could counsel prospective customers about bank services and in general provide good information to the bank manager and promote good will for the bank.

Another new manager proposed that the bank engage in more advertising and public relations. She argued that bank employees should become more involved in community groups, such as the Chamber of Commerce and United Way. She also argued that the bank should make a contribution to the State Association of Bankers to support lobbyists working at the state capitol to increase the interest rate ceilings, and to support lobbyists working in Washington to influence bank regulation.

As Bill Jacks considered these and other proposals, deregulation of banks became a hot topic in Washington. Deregulation had been successful in other industries, and President Carter signed into law the Depository Institutions Deregulation Act of 1980. President Reagan encouraged continued deregulation through the Depository Institutions Act of 1982. These changes dramatically affected the industry climate of banks. New powers were given to thrift institutions—credit unions, savings and loan associations—to compete directly with banks in business and consumer lending, retirement annuities, and other services. Deregulation also gave banks the freedom to become financial supermarkets and provide services such as the sale of stocks and bonds, to offer high interest rates, and to charge for services. The new regulations seemed to favor large banks because interstate banking and bank holding companies were possible.

Bill Jacks and the other managers were very uncertain about the impact of deregulation on First National City Bank. A bank consultant was hired to assess the impact of deregulation on First National City's strategy. The consultant said that as deregulation was implemented over the next three years, the bank will need, "a strong commitment to the development and delivery of new products. Moreover, customer loyalty will fade and price competition combined with technological advances and internal efficiencies will be essential for maintaining and increasing a customer base."

A university professor conducted a survey of successful community banks to learn how they were coping with deregulation. The survey found that successful banks were making changes in four areas: (1) asset-liability management, (2) cost control, (3) marketing, (4) pricing and non-interest income. Better asset-liability management in many banks was accomplished through a new asset-liability committee that helped the bank make a transition to variable-rate loans, make loans according to profit margin, and explore new investment opportunities. Cost control was accomplished through technology and data processing, such as automated tellers and the automatic transfer of funds. New marketing techniques included market segmentation and the packaging of new products for each segment. Money market accounts, discount brokerage services, increased advertising, retirement accounts, and other marketing ideas were being adopted. Important new income was also being derived from non-interest sources for successful community banks. Seventy-five percent of the banks increased fees for returned checks, overdrafts and checking account services. Fees were also increased for routine balance inquiries and saving accounts.

In January of 1983, Bill Jacks felt overwhelmed, and wondered whether he was up to managing the bank. The bank had grown little over five years, and was losing market share to other, often recently established banks. Two of the newer managers quit out of frustration over not having impact on bank policy. The impact of bank deregulation was difficult to anticipate, and he was not sure how the bank should respond. Two of the brightest young managers in the bank had been to see him about a change in management structure and approach. They encouraged the creation of several internal committees to study the problems and to coordinate the needs of each department and branch. They also suggested the bank begin planning for the addition of new departments that would be responsible for new electronic technology, new services, and stronger advertising. "The banking industry is becoming more complex and it's changing rapidly," one manager argued, "and if we don't adapt to it we will be left behind." Bill Jacks also thought back to earlier proposals, such as for advisory boards, on which he had not acted. Could the bank afford to invest in advertising, lobbying, new technology, and new departments? Would customers pay fees for services that had been provided free? Should the bank provide non-banking services? Could all of these activities be coordinated when things change so quickly? If he was unable to resolve these problems, Bill Jacks thought the best thing might be to retire and perhaps sell his interest in the bank to someone else.

4

Let Them Make Mudpies

Jack Wells shifted uneasily in his chair. He was not happy about this. Not one bit. "They say a bureaucrat knows he's going to have a bad day when he shows up for work and finds a camera crew from '60 Minutes' in his office," he said, forcing a smile. "Maybe I should get somebody else in here." He picked up his telephone and dialed for help.

Wells is the chief financial officer in the Seattle regional office of the Small Business Administration. He is a short, rotund, good-natured sort of fellow, with thinning, gray hair and a slightly crimson face, which at the moment was clouded with worry. No camera crew from "60 Minutes" had been waiting for him when he arrived for work that morning, but he seemed to feel he was in for a bad day nonetheless. "I don't think I can talk about a specific case without some kind of letter from the company," he said.

The company in question was Imré Corp., a young biotechnology concern that had applied in September 1982 for a so-called SBA guaranty loan of $250,000 (mean-ing that the SBA would guarantee up to 90% of the amount lent by the participating bank). The money was to be used for equipment needed to start production of a promising new anti-cancer device.

Good intentions aside, Imré appeared to be a solid candidate for the loan. For one thing, its request had already passed through the credit department of Rainier National Bank, Seattle's second largest commercial bank, which has an excellent record of reviewing SBA loan applicants. Imré had emerged with flying colors. Indeed, the bank was so enthusiastic that it had decided to submit the application under a special program reserved for eligible loans of unusually high quality.

The SBA, however, had not shared Rainier's enthusiasm. Seven times, the application had been sent in for review; seven times, it had been turned down. By the time the process had run its course, five crucial months had passed, and Imré was fighting for its survival. Faced with mounting debts, a shattered credit rating, and dwindling operating capital, Imré's owner-operators had no choice but to turn to venture capitalists, even at the risk of giving up control of their company.

The perplexing part of all this was that, during the entire period, the company had always appeared to be on the verge of getting the loan. Granted, the SBA had raised various questions along the way, but Imré had systematically answered each one:

Would the U.S. Food and Drug Administration allow the sale and use of the biological material in the device? Imré obtained a letter of approval from the FDA.

Was there enough demand for the product? Imré gave the SBA letters from three well-known researchers at major medical institutions, stating their intention to acquire, among them, more than half of the first year's production. The company also provided the names, addresses, and telephone numbers of nine other researchers who were ready to place orders whenever Imré was ready to accept them.

Could they manufacture the device as cheaply as they claimed? Imré brought in an independent expert—a faculty member in the University of Washington's microbiology department—who affirmed, in writing, that the company's cost estimates were accurate.

Was the collateral sufficient to protect the government against default? Imré pointed out that the SBA would have a lien on its laboratory equipment, which was worth $335,000 new and which could be resold for 50% to 70% of its current catalog price. Beyond that, the three principal officers offered personal guarantees totaling $250,000.

And so it went. For every objection, Imré was able to give a logical, documented response. Moreover, the SBA seemed to be receptive. As the weeks went by, Imré's officers and representatives had numerous meetings and discussions with SBA officials, including Jack Wells. Each time, the officials would listen, ask questions, hear the evidence, and encourage Imré to resubmit its formal application. But then back would come another letter of rejection.

When it was all over, Imré's people seemed more baffled than bitter. Why had they been led on? And what was the SBA's *real* reason for turning down the loan?

Some suggested that the agency was out of its depth. In the final analysis, they averred, its officers were unwilling to take a chance on a technology, a product, and a market that they did not understand. "They have a problem with high-technology loans, and they know it," said Jere Glover, a Washington lawyer and former SBA official, whom Imré had retained to help present its case. "If this [application] had been for a car wash or a restaurant, it would have sailed right through."

But Jack Wells, for his part, was not about to concede that point. Although he could not discuss the specifics of the Imré case, he was happy to address the broader issues. "In today's world, we talk a lot about high technology," he said. "In the old days, it was called 'new inventions.' It's all the same thing. As loan officers, we really don't care if a product is the most wonderful thing in the world or not. It could be a new fishing rod. It could be a manufacturing process. Why, . . ."

His face brightened. He leaned forward. "Why, you could be down on the Duwamish River making *mudpies*. If you can make 'em cheaply enough, and if you can show us there's a demand, the chances are we'll loan you the money for a *dredge*." He beamed as if he had scored a telling point.

As it happened, he had.

Mudpies have never held much appeal for Dr. Frank Jones. Cats are his weakness. His laboratory at Memorial Sloan-Kettering Cancer Center in New York City is piled high with slide cases bearing the names of his patients: "Fluffy," "Romeo," "Felix," "Trucker," "Magoo," and the like. Elsewhere, the shelves and counters are cluttered with the usual paraphernalia of research laboratories—chemicals, petri dishes, flasks—but here and there you can find a personal touch. Taped to a shelf near Jones's work space, for example, is a saying from a fortune cookie. It reads, "Man can cure disease but not fate."

Indeed, you can almost sense fate lurking about this laboratory, peering over the shoulders of the scientists. Here, after all, is where man intrudes on the domain of God—often at his own peril. As if to press the point, the freezers have stickers that say "BIOHAZARD" and labels that say "Contains feline leukemia virus."

Feline leukemia virus is the real object of Jones's fascination. It is the pathogen responsible for various types of cancer in cats. Not all cats with the virus develop cancer, but those that do generally die within four months. In recent years, scientists have been studying feline leukemia virus partly for love of cats, even more for love of man, hoping to learn something about human cancer along the way.

Frank Jones has been active in that quest, first at the University of Washington in Seattle, then at Sloan-Kettering. In his spare time, he has served as the guiding spirit behind Imré, as well as chairman of the board and chief executive officer. To a large extent, in fact, it is his company. Although others run it and share in its ownership, Jones is the one who provided the vision and assembled the team.

"Generally speaking, scientists are not good businesspeople," he says, sitting in a coffee shop on Second Avenue in Manhattan. "I'm a scientist." Nobody seeing him would think to argue. Without his white lab coat, Jones looks as though he has on someone else's clothes.

"I read through a few prospectuses [of biotechnology companies], and I looked at their structure," Jones goes on. "I even drew up some organizational maps. And I began to see what they're missing. Businesspeople. A salesperson. A financial person. Somebody to handle production . . .

"And another thing. There is usually no product. They all have the product on the come, but it's not up there. So I thought it was important to have a product on line."

In fact, Imré does have a product on line—a device that is used for filtering blood plasma. It is called a Prosorba column and looks more or less like a clear plastic car filter filled with sand. The latter is no illusion. Prosorba is sand (technically, silica), coated with protein A, a well-known natural substance.

A Prosorba treatment is roughly comparable to kidney dialysis. The patient is hooked up to a machine that withdraws blood and separates it into plasma and cells. After passing through the column, the plasma is recombined with the cells, and the blood flows back to the patient. By all accounts, the procedure is relatively painless and simple.

In 1978 and 1979, Jones and his assistant, Lois Yoshida, conducted a series of experiments at the University of Washington on five cats that had cancer caused by feline leukemia virus. They set up a system for filtering each cat's blood plasma, using a glass column containing a certain kind of dead bacteria that have a natural coating of protein A (the same active ingredient as in Prosorba). Scientists had determined that this protein can latch on to circulating immune complexes, pulling them out of the plasma as it flows by.

Jones did not invent the technique of removing immune complexes by means of a protein A column, but he was one of the first to use it in a clinical setting, and the results were startling. All five cats responded to the treatment within two weeks. Three showed significant, long-term improvement—including two with no further signs of virus or cancer.

And Jones was not alone. Other researchers were using protein A to treat cancer in dogs and even in humans. In case after case, they reported a significant reduction in the size of tumors.

Mulling over the results of his cat experiments, Jones realized that there was going to be a market for these devices—one that could eventually grow to staggering proportions. "Whether we would make [the device], or someone else would make it, I didn't know," he says. "But I was convinced it would be made."

Lynn Berry, for one, believed that Imré would make it. She is a loan officer at the Ballard office of the Rainier National Bank, where the company's vice-president, John J. King, opened up a corporate checking account in June 1982. He told her a little bit about Frank Jones and the protein A column. "I thought it was great," she says.

And, in the summer of 1982, few doubted that Imré (at that time known as Immune Response Systems Inc.) would soon be in production. The company had just completed a private placement of $210,000. King had located an ideal building in northwest Seattle. Meanwhile, Richard Hargreaves, Imré's chief technician, was hard at work in a laboratory affiliated with The Fred Hutchinson Cancer Research Center.

Behind all this was a plan. In essence, it called for production to begin modestly in September and then build. To generate immediate cash flow, Imré would sell pure protein A to selected researchers at a discount from the market price. The emphasis, however, was on developing the market for Prosorba columns as quickly as possible. If all went well, the company expected to be strong enough by January to negotiate a favorable deal with venture capitalists, thereby obtaining the funds to launch full-scale production in 1983. Already, the esteemed venture capital firm of Allen & Co. had expressed strong interest in Imré. Charles Allen himself had invested $40,000 in Imré in the names of members of his family.

Of course, even the best plan cannot be implemented without the right people, but, on that score as well, Imré seemed to be in rather good shape. In addition to King and Hargreaves, Jones had brought in Peter A. Rueckert, a 36-year-old Austrian with an MBA from the University of California at Berkeley, who was serving as Imré's president. He was the marketing specialist and was eminently qualified for the job. Before joining Imré, he had been the marketing manager and had run the West German subsidiary of Cordis Dow Inc., a leading manufacturer of dialysis equipment. Before that, he had spent four years with subsidiaries of Gambro AB, a Swedish-based medical supply company. Of all the members of the team, Rueckert had the best understanding of the market and the competition. He also had personal contacts with potential customers all over Europe. And he believed that Imré's prospects were excellent.

Most of the others shared his optimism. There was, however, one thing that stood in the way: money. The initial $210,000, from the private placement, was barely enough to cover the costs of establishing a formal presence in Seattle—office, desks, letterhead, copier, and the like. It did not come close to paying for the laboratory equipment needed to start production of the columns. For that, Imré would require an additional $250,000 or so. The burden of raising these funds fell squarely on the shoulders of Imré's vice-president in charge of finance, Arthur Karuna-Karan.

Karan was the newest member of Imré's crew. "Serendipity" is how Jones describes the way Imré found him. The company had been looking for help with its private placement, when Jones's wife, Carol, came across Karan's "job wanted" ad in *Science* magazine. The contact was made, and given his excellent credentials, Jones hired him on a consulting basis. In about two weeks, he had lined up $95,000 in investments. Soon after, he signed on as Imré's chief financial officer.

His primary responsibility at Imré was to raise funds for the laboratory equipment. Banker friends in New York suggested he try the SBA. That sounded like a good idea, so in July 1982 he dropped by the New York office, where he received a very friendly reception. He got more encouragement in Denver, where he discussed the idea with a loan officer at a bank. When he finally arrived in Seattle in August, one of the first things he did was to set up a meeting with Lynn Berry.

Karan went to the meeting with John King, and Berry showed up with Hal Greider, a Rainier loan officer for more than 25 years. They listened intently as Karan and King explained the ins and outs of Prosorba. The more they heard, the more they liked. "My father died of cancer of the esophagus, and my aunt lost a breast to cancer," says Berry. "Here was a benign treatment. Anybody who's had experience with cancer would have to be enthusiastic."

The bankers asked for additional financial information and gave Karan and King the standard SBA application form. "After looking everything over, we felt that the loan should be made," says Berry. "We sent it dow. to the credit administration [of Rainier], and they agreed to make the loan, subject to SBA approval."

Moreover, the bank decided to submit the application under the so-called Certified Lenders Program, which guarantees a quick response from the SBA, based on a bank's strong record of reviewing SBA applications. Rainier was one of only two certified lenders in Seattle, and it had rarely been turned down on a loan submitted under the program. "I was really very optimistic, because of the project itself and also because of the bank's history with the SBA," says Berry. After arranging for the formal submission of the application, she left on two weeks' vacation.

Something happened while Berry was away. The bank is reluctant to discuss the matter, but the application was not sent in. Instead, it wound up on the desk of a junior bank officer named Phil Milne, who looked it over and decided to reject it. Milne's secretary may even have called the SBA. In any case, Milne showed up at Imré and announced that the company was not an appropriate candidate for an SBA loan. "Then he says, 'Let me know if I can help you out in the future,' " says King.

When Berry returned, she was furious. She quickly got the decision reversed and submitted the application, but there was a lingering suspicion that some damage may have been done. The first hint of trouble came in September, when Berry and Karan went down to the district SBA office to discuss the loan. The person they met with was Arthur S. Blanco, chief of the district's financing division.

Art Blanco is a bulldog of a man, who describes himself as "hard-nosed." He was certainly not enthralled with Imré. Berry considered his reaction "unenthusiastic." Karan thought it was "hostile."

"He looked over the application and said, 'I don't see anyone here with management experience,' " says Karan. "Lynn pointed out that I have a Harvard MBA. He said, 'That doesn't mean he can manage a company.' So Lynn mentioned that I had managed a lab in Malaysia. He said, 'That's more relevant.' "

Karan was beginning to get a little nervous. In September, he had replaced Rueckert as president of Imré and so he had primary responsibility for keeping the ball rolling. And the ball *was* rolling, despite the delay in getting the loan. Imré had gone ahead and ordered enough lab equipment to start making protein A on a modest scale, using Lynn Berry as a reference. Meanwhile, Jones continued to fill out his crew. The latest recruit was Dr. Joseph Balint, a leading protein A researcher. He would run Imré's lab.

So a lot was riding on the SBA's decision, more with each passing week. Karan remained optimistic. "I still believed that, under the Certified Lender Program, the bank more or less had the power to authorize the loan, and the SBA was just checking the details." To cover his bets, however, he began to look for outside help, and his search soon led him to a Washington lawyer by the name of Jere Glover.

A former deputy chief counsel for advocacy with the Small Business Administration, Glover has a well-deserved reputation as a man who can do business with the SBA. He is often asked to represent companies seeking to do just that. When Karan called, Glover agreed only to look at Imré's file. "I prescreen these things," he says. "If it's a shitty case—and a lot of them are—I won't take it."

The material arrived a few days later. Glover studied it himself, then ran it by an associate. He had his brother, a doctor, read through the scientific papers. "It looked doable," he says. "There was enough documentation to show that this wasn't a flier. I concluded that a reasonable SBA loan officer would look at the application and approve it." He decided to take on the case.

Karan had told him about the difficulties with Blanco, so Glover began by calling Robert Caldwell, deputy administrator of the Seattle region, whom he happened to know. "[Caldwell] said, 'No question, we have a real problem with innovation loans, but we're trying to deal with it,' " says Glover. "He told me, 'You know how hard it is to do a new horizon. We're used to doing restaurants and car washes.' He said he'd check on the case. I told him to let me know if there was a problem."

In the meantime, there was the FDA to deal with. To Karan, Blanco's request seemed a little like asking a restaurant owner for written FDA approval to sell hamburgers. Nevertheless, he did what he could to abide by it. After numerous telephone calls, however, it became apparent that the questions required answers from various divisions of the agency. Moreover, Karan found it hard to persuade anyone long-distance of the urgency of the situation. Finally, he decided that he had to go to Washington himself.

In the middle of November, Karan showed up at the office of Alzena G. Darr of the FDA's Division of Compliance Operations. She seemed willing to help and began by calling Blanco. As she spoke with him, a frown came over her face. "When she got off, she said, 'This had better be letter perfect. That man is not your friend,' " says Karan. For the next three hours, he sat in her office while she gathered the necessary information and drafted the letter. She then called Blanco back and read it to him. He said it would do.

Karan returned to Seattle, confident that Imré's troubles were over. "I really thought that was it," he says. On November 30, the bank formally resubmitted the application, with all the additional information. On December 1, it was formally denied.

Imré's people were shocked. Only later did some of them feel anger. "Why did they put us through all that?" Karan asks today. "Why did they make us go to all the trouble and expense of getting that FDA letter when they were going to turn us down on the basics? Small businesses don't *have* time and money to waste."

Indeed, the rejection letter—signed by Blanco—did not even mention protein A. Rather it gave three reasons for denying the loan guaranty:

- The SBA did not believe Imré would be profitable enough to repay the loan. The projected markets were considered "quite speculative," and Blanco did not accept the earnings projections. He suggested that Imré seek financing through a small business investment company.
- Imré had the ability "to raise additional equity funds from stockholders and/or the public sale of stock." Therefore it was ineligible for SBA assistance, "because of policy reasons."
- The collateral was not sufficient to protect the government's interests.

Now it is fair to say that these were not

the strongest grounds on which to base the decision. To begin with, the SBA is not *allowed* to use "insufficient collateral" as a primary reason for denying an application. If it were, very few restaurants or shopping center stores would ever get SBA financing. In Imré's case, moreover, the collateral was enough to cover the government's exposure, and then some.

As for raising the funds by other means, various Imré representatives had aleady tried. Not surprisingly, they had found that the company would have to give up a significant amount of equity, and perhaps even control of its destiny, to take any of the courses mentioned by Blanco. He might as well have suggested that they seek acquisition by Johnson & Johnson, or that they move their operation to Japan—both of which would have achieved the same purpose. The truth was that he could not reject the loan on these grounds either.

So that left the question of Imré's ability to repay. The application had, in fact, included detailed information about manufacturing costs, general operating expenses, and anticipated revenues, all reasonably well documented. Glover, for one, thought the case had been very convincing, but Blanco was clearly not convinced. Glover called him to find out why. "He told me the financials were wrong. They didn't accord with the industry averages," says Glover. "I asked him, 'What industry?' He told me they looked at the average return on sales in the chemicals industry and the pharmaceuticals industry. In other words, they were looking at the ratios for long-established companies across their entire product line and comparing those to Imré. It was ridiculous." Karan later said it was like estimating the market value of a diamond by looking at the price of coal.

Karan became convinced that the SBA simply needed more information. He wrote a very humble letter, criticizing the inadequacies of Imré's original presentation and explaining with painstaking clarity the his-

tory of protein A and Jones's research; the reasons for Imré's high efficiency and low costs; the nature of the market; the company's strategy; and on and on. To this, he added supporting documents. He showed the letter to Glover and submitted it to Lynn Berry at Rainier, who included it with her formal request for reconsideration of Imré's loan guaranty application. On December 13, the application was again denied.

Nevertheless, on January 5, another rejection letter went out—this one signed by Robert Caldwell himself, on behalf of the regional administrator. "To me, that one was the biggest surprise," says Karan.

That same day, Glover telephoned Caldwell who said, "Why don't you come on out here." Within hours, Glover was on a flight to Seattle.

At that point, Glover hardly knew what to think. "I could not see any factual basis for being turned down, so I had to assume we were dealing with a personality clash, or some other unspoken factor," he says. To be blunt, he could not rule out the possibility that racism was playing a role. Karan has dark skin. So he arranged for a kind of mass meeting with the SBA. Aside from Glover himself, Lynn Berry would be there, as well as King, Rueckert, Balint, and Karan. "I wanted [the SBA officials] to see who was involved," says Glover. "I mean, here we had a couple MBAs, a couple of PhDs, an entrepreneur with other small businesses, a marketing specialist. It really was a model company."

The meeting on Friday, January 7, lasted about an hour and a half. Jack Wells represented the regional office. From the district office came deputy director Don Smith. Glover presented the case for Imré. Some technical questions about the columns had arisen. The company could not sell them in assembled form without something known as an investigational device exemption (IDE) from the FDA. Glover explained that the FDA had already granted such exemptions to several investigators and would routinely grant one to Imré as well. While the paperwork was being completed, the columns would simply be shipped unassembled. Thereupon, Glover proceeded to demonstrate how easily the columns could be put together by the investigators themselves.

Smith asked about demand for the product. Glover presented letters from Dr. William I. Bensinger of The Fred Hutchinson Cancer Research Center and Dr. Richard A. Willson of the Harborview Medical Center, both in Seattle. The letters showed that, together, they planned to acquire more than a third of the first year's production. (Later, another large order came in from Dr. Donald J. Higby of Roswell Park Memorial Institute in Buffalo.)

But what about all the other people who had supposedly expressed interest in the columns? Rueckert said that he could not take specific orders without knowing when the columns could be delivered. Smith understood that, but couldn't Imré come up with something more? Rueckert said he would put together a list of the strongest prospects, and the SBA could then verify their interest directly. (After the meeting, he drew up a list of 12 likely customers, their addresses and phone numbers.)

But was there really a market for these columns? Smith asked. With that, Glover went to town. "I said, *'Is there a market?* Look at laetrile. Look at the thousands and thousands of dollars people spend on a treatment with *no* scientific support.' I said, 'I'll tell you what. I'll run an ad in the Seattle newspaper saying, "Possible cancer cure. If interested in purchasing, please contact the head of the SBA." Let's just see what happens.' Smith said, 'No need. You've convinced me.' "

Not a single member of the Imré contingent left the meeting with the slightest doubt that they had, indeed, convinced Smith and the others. "I remember that Jack Wells gave a little speech about

mudpies," King recalls. "He said, 'Why, if you show us you can make mudpies and can sell mudpies, we'll give you the money to help you do it.' "

Smith and Wells told them to put in a whole new application. Glover saw this as a face-saving way to overturn the original decision. "They said, 'Resubmit. We'll put it through real quick.' And Smith told me, 'Don't complicate it with a lot of scientific bullshit. Make it simple, like selling mudpies. . . . He was very encouraging. I mean, like, 'You've certainly answered all my questions.' "

That afternoon, Glover and Karan dropped by to see Bob Caldwell, who had already heard about the meeting from Jack Wells. Caldwell was beaming. "He said, 'I hear you did a great job,' " Glover recalls. " 'That's really good. This is the kind of loan we should be making.' "

"[Caldwell] seemed very pleased," Karan agrees.

Glover himself was sky high. "We all have good days and bad days," he says. "Well, that was one of my best. . . . When I walked out of that meeting, I'd have given 10-to-1 odds that the loan would go through without a problem. After talking to Caldwell, I'd have given 100-to-1 odds."

On January 10, Rainier National Bank formally submitted a new application for an SBA loan guaranty to cover a $250,000 loan to Imré Corp. On January 19, it was formally rejected. The rejection letter was signed "Arthur S. Blanco."

And that was pretty much the end of it.

To be sure, they went through the motions a couple more times. As the weeks passed, more orders for columns came in, some of them unsolicited. Twice, Lynn Berry called up Don Smith with news. Twice, he encouraged her to ask for reconsideration. Twice, she was turned down. By the end, the process had taken on overtones of a sadomasochistic ritual.

The people at Imré, meanwhile, had turned elsewhere. Since December, Jones had been working in New York to line up a venture capital deal. Allen & Co. was still very interested, but, with the collapse of the SBA gambit, Imré found itself in a weak bargaining position. The business plan was all but dead. The company was in no position to produce much of anything. Worse yet, time was running out. Imré's operating capital was nearly gone, and it had no credit to speak of. What is more, its various suppliers were anxious to be paid.

For the next two months, Imré's people clawed and scrambled and somehow survived. They had some help—mainly from Lynn Berry of Rainier and from Jerry Brown, district credit manager of their major supplier, VWR Scientific Inc. In addition, they managed to obtain enough short-term financing to start producing columns on a small scale.

As it turned out, those two months were all they needed. In March, they worked out a deal with Allen & Co. for nearly $1.5 million in venture capital. They immediately began to consider taking the company public, hoping to raise the additional capital needed to make up for lost time.

Although Imré appeared to be out of the woods, the SBA episode had taken its toll. Karan estimated that Imré lost about $300,000 in total revenues because of the delay in production, not to mention about $30,000 in expenses connected with the application. In addition, the drain on management time was enormous, amounting to more than 40 man-days for Karan alone. Moreover, at least one key person decided not to join the company because of the uncertainty surrounding the loan, and Karan's own position within Imré was seriously weakened, since he bore primary responsibility—and hence blame—for the effort. In May, he resigned as president.

Most important, however, the episode cost Imré's people a significant portion of ownership, and it may have cost the company its competitive edge. Six months is a long time in the life of a new technology. In

September, Imré had almost no competition, but since then, a couple of giants seem to be getting ready to join the fray.

Of course, Imré still enjoys the advantage that comes with being small. "We're out there in Seattle," says Jones, who moved there himself early in May. "We don't go home at five o'clock. We can move a lot faster than a big company." And if one good thing did come out of the SBA affair, it is a sense of determination and togetherness that is almost tangible around the office and laboratory.

Lynn Berry, for one, still believes that Imré will make it. "I don't doubt it. I have no doubts whatsoever," she says. "They've been struggling since last June, and they're still around. They're not going to throw up their hands and walk away. And I think that the SBA is going to feel some regret" when Imré becomes a very successful company.

But, even today, Berry doesn't fully understand why the SBA rejected the application. Nor does anybody else around Imré. "It came down to the fact that they simply didn't believe the numbers," says King, who replaced Karan as president. "That's about all you can say for sure."

"I'd like to think it was an isolated case, but I'm afraid that's not the situation," says Glover in his office a few blocks from the SBA's national headquarters. "In this environment of 'quality' loans, I think any innovative company has got an uphill road. Maybe you'll be lucky if you put together a factual presentation and run into [a loan officer] with a desire to make good, innovative loans. But the average Joe is probably in trouble. As far as Seattle is concerned, God help the sucker."

He doesn't hide his anger, but one can also detect a note of regret. "I was truly shocked by what happened," he says. "I mean, I worked for the SBA. I know the SBA. I wasn't selling them a turkey. . . . This one really offends me." He pauses, then snorts derisively. "Mudpies!"

5

Death of a Computer

Almost immediately, people at Texas Instruments were calling it Black Friday. Early in the afternoon of October 28, 1983, the rumors began to fly, and at the company's Lubbock-based consumer products group, the rest of the day was chaotic. Middle managers called employees in, a few at a time, to tell them that yes, it was true and there was nothing that could be done, and then everyone in Lubbock was on the phone to friends at all the other TI facilities, and by four o'clock, when the official corporate announcement was released to the press, there wasn't a soul at the company who hadn't heard the bad news. Texas Instruments, the company that had put more computers into American homes than anyone else, was pulling out of the home computer business.

Who could have imagined that it would end this way? Only a year earlier the consumer products group had been the toast of Texas Instruments, and the TI home computer, the 99/4A, its biggest success. Back then, TI people talked about the 99/4A with awe. It was destined to dominate the home computer business, they said. It was going to reach $1 billion in sales. It was going to be the biggest winner in the history of the company. Back then, TI assembly lines in Lubbock were cranking out five thousand computers a day, and that still didn't keep up with the demand.

THE TI CULTURE

The microprocessor is one of the great inventions of the age, as seminal a step in the development of the modern computer as the invention of the silicon chip was in the late fifties. The silicon chip made it possible to put complicated electronic circuitry on a tiny piece of silicon; the microprocessor made it possible to compress an entire computer onto a chip not much larger than a postage stamp. Today there are any number of microprocessors inside a personal computer (different chips control the graphics and the memory and so on), but the central microprocessor, called the CPU, is the computer's brain, the thing that reads the bits of information sent to it.

Written by Joseph Nocera. Reprinted with permission from the April issue of *Texas Monthly*, copyright © 1984, by *Texas Monthly*.

Although selling consumer items like pocket calculators and computers is what gives Texas Instruments visibility, the company's biggest profits have always been made in less glamorous ways, chief among them the manufacture of silicon chips, which it sells in huge lots, at low prices, to other companies. Getting the volume up and the price down has always been the linchpin of TI's sales strategy. And so it was with microprocessors. Although TI did not invent the microprocessor—the credit for that goes to a Silicon Valley company named Intel—the company quickly asserted its superiority in the marketplace with its first chip, introduced in 1974, a four-bit chip called the TMS 1000. (The term "four bits" means that the circuitry can handle four bits of information at once. It is a measure of complexity and also of speed; an eight-bit chip can work twice as fast as a four-bit chip.) The TMS 1000 soon became the most ubiquitous chip in the business, used in video games, calculators, microwave ovens, and hundreds of other electronic products; to date, more than 100 million TMS 1000's have been sold.

TI's second-generation microprocessor was the 9900, but though it was a quantum leap technologically, it was a flop in the marketplace. It failed in part because it was too far ahead of the field; while Intel and everyone else were just beginning to make eight-bit microprocessors, TI leapfrogged them and made the sixteen-bit 9900. The idea was that the 9900 would make the eight-bit competition instantly obsolete and this new TI microprocessor, like the TMS 1000 before it, would become the industry standard. Instead, the industry flocked to the eight-bit microprocessors and left the 9900 dying on the vine. But to back down and build eight-bit microprocessors like everyone else was an abhorrent idea for TI, a company where managerial decisions are shaped by an internal framework that is a culture all its own.

TI is run by engineers for engineers.

Both Mark Shepherd and J. Fred Bucy began their TI careers as engineers, and almost all of its top managers have engineering backgrounds. Thus, they understand the needs of engineers—the need for autonomy, for instance. Despite the company's size, the TI chain of command is quite short, and Bucy and Shepherd try not to get in the way of managers who are doing well. The company never skimps on its research and development budget, no matter what its cash-flow needs might be. R & D, which is what engineers live for, is at the heart of Texas Instruments' technological success.

But engineers have other, psychic needs, and these too have become a part of the TI culture. One is the desire to accomplish things oneself, from scratch, rather than using existing products. At TI this frame of mind has led to an obsessive dislike of—and even contempt for—other companies' products. A former TI employee remembers once suggesting in a meeting that a computer design might be improved with a common eight-bit microprocessor called the Z–80. Fred Bucy flung a book listing the different TI chips in the direction of the man and said huffily, "Show me where it's listed here." End of discussion.

Given that corporate culture, there wasn't much doubt that TI would stand by its own microprocessor, the 9900, rather than conform to a marketplace that wanted eight bits instead of sixteen. Conforming would be an admission of defeat. The preferred solution was to find an internal use for the 9900 that would make it profitable. One possibility was to build·a consumer product, a computer, that would be driven by the 9900 microprocessor. It was a classic Texas Instruments solution—TI divisions have always been able to post profits by selling components to other TI divisions—but it also meant that TI would be building a computer to fit its microprocessor rather than the other way around. Though no one could know it at the time, the TI culture had just led the company into its first big home computer mistake.

The TI machine was going to be the first computer designed for Everyman. Did Everyman need—or even want—a computer in his home? That was impossible to say, since no such product existed and since most Americans had no feel for how a computer might be useful. That's what made the venture so risky. In the late seventies computers still seemed exotic. Yet TI was unperturbed by the prospect of trying to create a market from scratch. After all, hadn't the company created the market for the pocket calculator? Hadn't it made digital watches popular? Hadn't it taken a dozen other inventions and turned them into commercial successes? The feeling at TI was that it had a knack for consumer electronics and that its knack would come to the fore again, with the home computer. TI would put out a computer that was just powerful enough to entice the average person to take the plunge—no word processing, but plenty of educational programs for the kids—yet inexpensive enough that the plunge wouldn't break the bank. On the basis of price alone, TI thought, the machine would sell. Convincing people that they needed it could come later.

It wasn't long before events began to conspire against the consumer division's carefully laid plans. First, the man who had devised the strategy quit in frustration over the problems he faced in Lubbock—particularly the inability to hire the outside engineers he thought he needed. Then his chief supporter back in the Dallas headquarters took an overseas assignment.

To make matters even more complicated, there was another management shuffle in 1978, and the man put in charge of developing the home computer was an engineer whose previous job had been to design the expensive business computer. He didn't see the home computer in quite the same way that his predecessor had, and by the time he finished tinkering with the design, it was no longer a $400 machine but an $1150 machine. Then, although TI had announced that the computer would be ready by the middle of 1979, the engineers didn't shake all the bugs out of the system until the first few months of 1980, thus missing an opportunity to cash in on the 1979 Christmas season. And finally, when the new 99/4 hit the computer stores, it turned out that the average American had no idea what to do with a home computer and wasn't interested in paying $1150 for one. To the great dismay of everyone at Texas Instruments, the 99/4, four years and $10 million or so in the making, was a bomb.

The keyboard is what computer people most remember about the TI 99/4 home computer. The keyboard somehow became the symbol for everything that was wrong with the machine. It was not modeled after a typewriter, as most personal computer keyboards were. Instead, it looked like an elongated calculator keyboard, with stubby little keys that popped through the plastic casing. TI had chosen a calculator keyboard because most of the engineers who developed the 99/4 had cut their teeth on calculators; that was the technology they knew best and could produce most inexpensively. But a short time before the 99/4 came out, another company had put a calculator keyboard on a personal computer. The keyboard was widely criticized, and out of that experience grew a belief that calculator keyboards wouldn't cut it. Texas Instruments, so intent on putting out its own product, scarcely noticed.

The lesson of the calculator keyboard was not that it was an engineering mistake—at bottom, it really didn't matter what kind of keyboard you used—but that it was a *marketing* mistake. And the same applied to other facets of the machine. Using the 9900 microprocessor, for instance, was good for the Texas Instruments division that made the chip, but it caused far more problems than it was worth. Because

TI's chip division had to make a profit despite the low demand, the cost to the consumer division was very high—about $20 a unit compared to about $4 for most of the popular eight-bit microprocessors. Because it had been designed for industrial uses, it did not adapt well to a consumer system; the advantage of having a sixteen-bit microprocessor was negated by the circuitous way programs had to be written for it. And because nobody else in the industry was using it, independent software companies, the third-party vendors, as they're called, had no incentive to write programs for it. The independents liked to write programs that could be easily adapted to different computers. They couldn't do that with the 99/4.

WHAT'S THIS THING FOR, ANYWAY?

By the fall of 1980, with Texas Instruments selling fewer than a thousand computers a month, the people in the consumer products group had come to the not unexpected conclusion that it was time to go back to the drawing board. Peter Bonfield, then the head of the home computer division, felt that the most critical flaws in the 99/4 were its price and its 9900 microprocessor, so he asked his engineers to design a computer that used a different microprocessor and that cut the cost in half.

The new design had been slapped together by a small group of engineers. The engineers' new design kept the 9900 microprocessor (there wasn't any getting around that) and the main circuitry of the machine but changed the way the computer looked. Now the computer had a typewriter keyboard. The keyboard had also been separated from the screen—unbundling the system, it's called—so that the screen became optional. (The keyboard could be attached to a television set.) They also drew up proposals for cutting down the number of chips needed to run the

computer, which had the effect of dramatically cutting costs.

By the summer of 1981, after months of working up prototypes, getting the kinks out of the system, and passing the various radiation tests mandated by the Federal Communications Commission, the 99/4A was ready. The basic cost of the computer to the retailer was $340—and the price to the consumer, without peripherals, was going to be $550. Don Bynum had done his job. But would it sell?

Why do you need a home computer? It is hard to imagine a more basic question, but no one in the home computer business has come up with a compelling answer. It is hard to sell a product when you can't tell people why they need it.

For years now, we've been hearing that the day will come when the computer will revolutionize the way we live. There's a feeling among computer people that they are not only on the frontier of the American economy but also on the frontier of American life itself. Scratch a computer engineer, and you'll most likely find a visionary, someone who foresees the day when computers will do everything but prepare dinner.

The man whose job it was to answer that question at TI was William J. Turner, and he was that rarest of birds at Texas Instruments, an outsider. He had been hired away from Digital Equipment Corporation, an important maker of minicomputers, in May 1980 and had been named marketing manager for TI's consumer products group. Although he had a degree in mathematics, he had gotten his job precisely because he wasn't an engineer. Turner had spent his career marketing computers. At 36, he was the same age as his counterpart in engineering, Don Bynum, but he was shorter and thinner, almost completely bald, with sharp features and a sharp New England accent.

He brought to the home computer division something it hadn't had before: a sales mentality. Bill Turner was gung ho about whatever product he was selling, upbeat and enthusiastic no matter what the actual state of affairs. He was great with numbers and projections. In meetings he always had a chart that proved beyond all doubt that the home computer was about to turn the corner.

He came to his job with two crucial theories. First, he believed that you couldn't sell a home computer in a computer store. Computer stores were meant for people who already knew something about computers or who were serious enough about them to spend several thousand dollars on one. Those people were not likely to wind up buying a home computer. Turner wanted to get the 99/4A placed in the kind of retail stores that already carried the company's pocket calculator, stores like Penney's and Sears and Montgomery Ward. From the day he walked in the door, Turner spent much of his time building up this retail network, and he was good at it. Every month he would report new successes. Toys Я Us had signed up; K Mart had signed up; even 7-Eleven was on the verge of signing up before the roof fell in at TI. The engineers hated the thought of their machine's being sold in stores like 7-Eleven, and they complained about it, but it was mostly their pride that was hurt. Turner was right.

Turner's second theory was that the price of the 99/4A had to be a lot lower. If the price was low enough, it wouldn't matter that the home computer was more toy than tool. People would buy it on a lark. Bill Turner wanted to sell price, and that became the cornerstone of his marketing strategy. It didn't hurt his standing in the company that he was advocating the one strategy that TI's management had always felt most comfortable with.

So in the months after the 99/4A was introduced, Turner began bringing the list price of the 99/4A down, from $550 to $450 to $375. He did this partly by making what

seemed to be outrageous volume projections and then hustling up new retail outlets to absorb that volume. He also pushed Bynum's engineers to find ways to lower the cost of the machine, by simplifying the design, eliminating chips, and so on. That way the profit margin on each computer remained steady—40 per cent—while the price went down. With each new round of cost cutting, the engineers became increasingly unhappy with Turner, for they felt he was pushing them to do too much too fast. But no one could argue with the results. TI had once produced fewer than eight thousand 99/4's a month; it was now producing that many 99/4A's in a good week. That wasn't enough for the consumer products group, with its large overhead and R & D budget, to turn a profit, but it was more than enough to make people believe Turner when he pulled out his latest chart and said the 99/4A was about to take off.

By then, however, Texas Instruments was not the only company in the home computer business. Atari, the video game maker, had had a computer out for some time that was under $1000—the Atari 400. Several toy companies, particularly Mattel and Coleco, were trying to get out of video game consoles (which wouldn't have a chance if home computers really hit) and into home computers. Timex had a home computer in development, which it hoped would establish an entirely new market, the under-$100 computer. And then there was Commodore. Nine months after TI put the 99/4A on the retail shelves of America, the Commodore Corporation, of King of Prussia, Pennsylvania, introduced its first home computer. It was called the Vic 20, and it came on the market at $299.

LAUNCHING THE GREAT PRICE WAR

Talk to anyone who ever worked on the 99/4A and you'll get the same story. The Vic 20 couldn't compare with the 99/4A. It was true. While the 99/4A didn't measure up to the more expensive small business computers, it looked spectacular next to the Vic 20. The Vic 20 had a measly 4K of memory, while the 99/4A had 16K. The Vic 20 used an old-style eight-bit microprocessor, while the 99/4A had the sixteen-bit 9900. The Vic 20 had only about forty chips in its entire system; the 99/4A had sixty. There was no question that the TI computer was a far more powerful, far more sophisticated system, "a Cadillac competing against Chevys," as Don Bynum used to say.

The 99/4A's advantages, however, didn't necessarily translate into sales. The computer business didn't work that way anymore and hadn't for some time—and nobody understood that better than Jack Tramiel, the president of Commodore. Although he has recently resigned from his position, Tramiel remains a near-mythic figure in the computer business. He has a reputation as a tough, driven entrepreneur who through shrewd dealing and brilliant marketing single-handedly built Commodore into a major force in the computer business. When Tramiel set out to conquer the home computer market he knew as well as anyone that the Vic 20 was no match for the TI 99/4A on the basis of performance. He also knew that the 99/4A was no match for the Vic 20 on the basis of price. Once before, Commodore had put out a product in a market where its chief competitor was TI: a line of digital watches. TI started a price war and drove Commodore out of the market. Tramiel was not about to let that happen again. No matter how low the 99/4A went in price, Tramiel's machine could go lower. It simply cost less to build.

In retrospect Bill Turner's great mistake, as big a mistake as the original decision to use the 9900 microprocessor, was creating a marketing strategy that lived and died on price alone. He had other options. He could have promoted the 99/4A's superiority to the Vic 20 and justified a higher price on that basis. He could have tried harder to answer the question of why consumers needed to buy his home computer. But it is not just in retrospect that this is obvious; it should have been clear at the time. As soon as the Vic 20 came on the market, some Texas Instruments engineers took it apart and analyzed its insides. They poked fun at what they found, but it was apparent that it was cheaper to make. The Vic 20's cost advantage was no deep, dark secret.

In meetings Turner would rage about the Vic 20, talk about "destroying Commodore," but out there on the retail shelves, it was Commodore that was winning.

And why not? Most customers didn't know the difference between eight bits and sixteen bits. Neither did most of the people working in the stores. And Texas Instruments was doing nothing to explain the difference. All the customer knew was that two computers were sitting side by side on a shelf and one cost $300 and the other less than $250. The choice seemed obvious. Even though the 99/4A was doing better than it ever had before, it was still being outsold by the Vic 20 on the order of two to one. To Turner, the situation was intolerable.

On September 1, 1982, at a time when the 99/4A was selling for about $300 and the Vic 20 for $250, Texas Instruments announced a rebate for the computer that effectively lowered the price to $199. This time there was no cost cutting by the engineers to match the price cut. The profit margin on the 99/4A was halved, but Turner wasn't worried about that. That same day Commodore dropped the price of its machine $40 to match TI's. The price war was on.

FROM $20 MILLION TO $200 MILLION OVERNIGHT

For the next four months Turner's price strategy worked like a charm. The fall and winter of 1982 were Turner's time of triumph, for in those months the 99/4A became the machine Texas Instruments had always wanted it to be, a computer the average American would buy. Almost as soon as the price cut was announced, home computer sales rocketed, and to the people at the consumer products group—indeed, to people throughout the company—the turn of events was astonishing. Turner was suddenly a corporate superstar at TI, the marketing genius, the outsider who had shown the engineers how to sell a computer. The retail network now constituted some 12,000 stores; the 99/4A was outselling the Vic 20 three to one; and a $20 million business had become, overnight, a $200 million business. Who could argue with that? Bucy and Shepherd were happy to leave Turner alone. That was the way TI always treated its winners.

With things going so well for the 99/4A, Turner and the consumer products group made their next big mistake. They got greedy. Timex had a dinky little computer on the market that cost about $100; it wasn't much, but it was selling, and Turner decided to go after it. He had Bynum pull together some engineers, and they undertook a crash program to develop a competitive product to be called the 99/2. Several other computers were competing in the $500 to $1000 price range, and Texas Instruments had long been developing a computer for that market: the 99/8, known by the code name "Armadillo." (Commodore was developing a computer for the same market, which became the enormously successful Commodore 64.) Partly it was good marketing strategy to come in behind the original computer with a more advanced computer like the 99/8; that's the way markets evolved. But who cared if Timex was selling some $100 computer that couldn't do much? Was that really the direction in which the market was going? It seemed that Turner and Texas Instruments simply wanted it all.

TI's extraordinary fall and winter had brought forth from Bill Turner some extraordinarily optimistic forecasts for the future. According to his projections, 1983 would be the year of the home computer. Nearly seven million would be sold that year, he predicted, more than triple the two million sold in 1982. And of that seven million, he estimated—promised, actually—that three million would be sold by Texas Instruments (whereas about 500,000 had been sold in 1982). Most analysts thought those figures were way too high; they were predicting sales in the area of four million. But Turner was undeterred. The home computer revolution had begun, he said, and TI was about to take over the market. The analysts, on the other hand, said that with the price so low and the machines so limited, most people thought of the home computer as a toy, which meant that sales would always peak in the months before Christmas. To them, that timing had as much to do with TI's success in late 1982 as the price war did. Turner, in contrast, was predicting that every month from now on was going to be about twice as good as December 1982—the best month ever for the 99/4A. With Bucy and Shepherd in tow, he was going full steam ahead.

PULLING THE PLUG

. . . the fall came very, very quickly. In January Commodore cut the price of the Vic 20 to $125; a few weeks later TI was forced to follow suit. The inevitable had happened: the 99/4A was no longer making a profit; it was merely breaking even. But there were plenty of orders from retailers, much of it on backlog since Christmas, so Turner kept pushing the computers out.

On April 4 Commodore cut the price of the Vic 20 to $99, thus putting Turner in an untenable position. It cost more than $99 to manufacture the 99/4A. He stalled for time, announcing that TI would offer a new rebate on the home computer by June. But it wasn't good enough. Now the Vic 20 was back where it had been before the price war began—sitting next to the 99/4A on retail shelves, at a much cheaper price. At the same time, with the Vic 20 so inexpensive, the market for the Timex product dried up completely. That was the thing about the computer business; there was no telling what the market would be like by the time your product was ready. Texas Instruments quietly canceled the 99/2, the machine that was supposed to compete with Timex, before it ever came out. Now people in the consumer products group were beginning to see the handwriting on the wall.

In late April the numbers caught up with Turner. Because the consumer products group was adhering to Turner's forecast, the TI assembly lines kept pushing out computers as fast as they could. But now computers began coming back to TI. Just because a retailer had a machine on the shelves didn't mean he had actually bought it. He had the right to return it—that was the way the market had evolved. Retailers had so many TI machines that they couldn't take any more, and since the machine wasn't selling, many of them began to send some back to make room for other products. "Sales" that had been posted by Turner were revised and lowered. It wasn't going to be December all year round. Turner's optimistic projections were crashing down around him.

There was really nothing that could be done quickly. The mistakes were too big, and they had been allowed to go on too long. By the second quarter of 1983, anyone who followed American business knew the Texas Instruments home computer was in danger. It was then that Shepherd and Bucy announced that the company had lost $119 million that quarter because of the home computer.

Pulling the plug on the home computer three months later was an act of mercy—it put the home computer division out of its misery. Could the situation have been turned around eventually? Possibly. But it would have taken new products and new strategies and new approaches in the marketplace. And most of all, it would have taken time, which Texas Instruments didn't think it could afford. The stock was dropping because analysts had become so soured on the 99/4A. The losses were continuing to mount; in the third quarter TI took a $300 million bath. When Bucy and Shepherd looked into the tunnel, they could see no light. All they could see was computers and software and peripherals everywhere, and nobody who wanted to buy them. In the end, Texas Instruments was just too big and bulky, with too much overhead and too much cultural baggage to respond to a volatile market. The home computer market belonged to the nimble— to the companies that could adapt quickly, the companies that understood that marketing was everything. In that sense, perhaps TI was doomed from the start.

6

Rondell Data Corporation

"God damn it, he's done it again!"

Frank Forbus threw the stack of prints and specifications down on his desk in disgust. The Model 802 wide-band modulator, released for production the previous Thursday, had just come back to Frank's Engineering Services Department with a caustic note that began, "This one can't be produced, either ..." It was the fourth time Production had kicked the design back.

Frank Forbus, director of engineering for Rondell Data Corp., was normally a quiet man. But the Model 802 was stretching his patience; it was beginning to look just like other new products that had hit delays and problems in the transition from design to production during the eight months Frank had worked for Rondell. These problems were nothing new at the sprawling old Rondell factory; Frank's predecessor in the engineering job had run afoul of them too, and had finally been fired for protesting too vehemently about the other departments. But the Model 802 should have been different. Frank had met two months before (July 3, 1978) with the firm's president, Bill Hunt,

and with factory superintendent Dave Schwab to smooth the way for the new modulator design. He thought back to the meeting ...

"Now we all know there's a tight deadline on the 802," Bill Hunt said, "and Frank's done well to ask us to talk about its introduction. I'm counting on both of you to find any snags in the system, and to work together to get that first production run out by October second. Can you do it?"

"We can do it in Production if we get a clean design two weeks from now, as scheduled," answered Dave Schwab, the grizzled factory superintendent. "Frank and I have already talked about that, of course. I'm setting aside time in the card room and the machine shop, and we'll be ready. If the design goes over schedule, though, I'll have to fill in with other runs, and it will cost us a bundle to break in for the 802. How does it look in Engineering, Frank?"

"I've just reviewed the design for the second time," Frank replied. "If Ron Porter can keep the salesmen out of our hair, and avoid any more last minute changes, we've got a shot. I've pulled the draftsmen off three other overdue jobs to get this one out. But, Dave, that means we can't spring engineers loose to confer with your production people on manufacturing problems."

"Well, Frank, most of those problems are caused by the engineers, and we need them to resolve the difficulties. We've all agreed that production bugs come from both of us bowing to sales pressure, and putting equipment into production before the designs are really ready. That's just what we're trying to avoid on the 802. But I can't have 500 people sitting on their hands waiting for an answer from your people. We'll have to have *some* engineering support."

Bill Hunt broke in, "So long as you two can talk calmly about the problem I'm confident you can resolve it. What a relief it is, Frank, to hear the way you're approaching this. With Kilmann (the previous director of engineering) this conversation would have been a shouting match. Right, Dave?" Dave nodded and smiled.

"Now there's one other thing you should both be aware of," Hunt continued. "Doc Reeves and I talked last night about a new filtering technique, one that might improve the signal-to-noise ratio of the 802 by a factor of two. There's a chance Doc can come up with it before the 802 reaches production, and if it's possible, I'd like to use the new filters. That would give us a real jump on the competition."

Four days after that meeting, Frank found that two of his key people on the 802 design had been called to Production for emergency consultation on a bug found in final assembly: two halves of a new data transmission interface wouldn't fit together because recent changes in the front end required a different chassis design for the back end.

Another week later, Doc Reeves walked into Frank's office, proud as a new parent, with the new filter design. "This won't affect the other modules of the 802 much," Doc had said. "Look, it takes three new

cards, a few connectors, some changes in the wiring harness, and some new shielding, and that's all."

Frank had tried to resist the last-minute design changes, but Bill Hunt had stood firm. With a lot of overtime by the engineers and draftsmen, Engineering Services should still be able to finish the prints in time.

Two engineers and three draftsmen went onto 12-hour days to get the 802 ready, but the prints were still five days late reaching Dave Schwab. Two days later, the prints came back to Frank, heavily annotated in red. Schwab had worked all day Saturday to review the job, and had found more than a dozen discrepancies in the prints—most of them caused by the new filter design and insufficient checking time before release. Correction of those design faults had brought on a new generation of discrepancies; Schwab's cover note on the second return of the prints indicated he'd had to release the machine capacity he'd been holding for the 802. On the third iteration, Schwab committed his photo and plating capacity to another rush job. The 802 would be at least one month late getting into production. Ron Porter, Vice President for Sales, was furious. His customer needed 100 units *NOW*, he said. Rondell was the customer's only late supplier.

"Here we go again," thought Frank Forbus.

COMPANY HISTORY

Rondell Data Corp. traced its lineage through several generations of electronics technology. Its original founder, Bob Rondell, had set the firm up in 1920 as "Rondell Equipment Co." to manufacture several electrical testing devices he had invented as an engineering faculty member at a large university. The firm branched into radio broadcasting equipment in 1947, and into data transmission equipment in the early 1960s. A well-established corps of direct sales people, mostly engineers, called on industrial, scientific and government accounts, but concentrated heavily on original equipment manufacturers. In this market, Rondell had a long-standing reputation as a source of high-quality, innovative designs. The firm's salespeople fed a continual stream of challenging problems into the Engineering Department, where the creative genius of Ed "Doc" Reeves and several dozen other engineers "converted problems to solutions" (as the sales brochure bragged). Product design formed the spearhead of Rondell's growth.

By 1978, Rondell offered a wide range of products in its two major lines. Broadcast equipment sales had benefitted from the growth of UHF TV and FM radio; it now accounted for 35% of company sales. Data transmission had blossomed, and in this field an increasing number of orders called for unique specifications, ranging from specialized display panels to entirely untried designs.

The company had grown from 100 employees in 1947 to over 800 in 1978. (Exhibit 6–1 shows the current organization chart of key employees.) Bill Hunt, who had been a student of the company's founder, had presided over most of that growth, and took great pride in preserving the "family spirit" of the old organization. Informal relationships between Rondell's veteran employees formed the backbone of the firm's day-to-day operations; all the managers relied on personal contact, and Hunt often insisted that the absence of bureaucratic red tape was a key factor in recruiting outstanding engineering talent. The personal management approach extended throughout the factory. All exempt employees were paid on a straight salary plus a share of the profits. Rondell boasted an extremely loyal group of senior employees, and very low turnover in nearly all areas of the company.

The highest turnover job in the firm was Frank Forbus's. Frank had joined Rondell in January of 1978, replacing Jim Kilmann,

who had been director of engineering for only 10 months. Kilmann, in turn, had replaced Tom MacLeod, a talented engineer who had made a promising start, but had taken to drink after a year in the job. MacLeod's predecessor had been a genial old timer who retired at 70 after 30 years in charge of engineering. (Doc Reeves had refused the directorship in each of the recent changes, saying, "Hell, that's no promotion for a bench man like me. I'm no administrator.")

For several years, the firm had experienced a steadily increasing number of disputes between research, engineering, sales, and production people—disputes generally centered on the problem of new product introduction. Quarrels between departments became more numerous under MacLeod, Kilmann, and Forbus. Some managers associated those disputes with the company's recent decline in profitability—a decline that, in spite of higher sales and gross revenues, was beginning to bother people in 1977. President Bill Hunt commented:

Better cooperation, I'm sure, could increase our output by 5–10% . I'd hoped Kilmann could solve the problems, but pretty obviously he was too young, too arrogant. People like him—that conflict type of personality—bother me. I don't like strife, and with him it seemed I spent all my time smoothing out arguments. Kilmann tried to tell everyone else how to run their departments, without having his own house in order. That approach just wouldn't work, here at Rondell. Frank Forbus, now, seems much more in tune with our style of organization. I'm really hopeful now.

Still, we have just as many problems now as we did last year. Maybe even more. I hope Frank can get a handle on Engineering Services soon . . .

THE ENGINEERING DEPARTMENT: RESEARCH

According to the organization chart (see Exhibit 6–1), Frank Forbus was in charge of

EXHIBIT 6-1 RONDELL DATA CORPORATION 1978 ORGANIZATION CHART

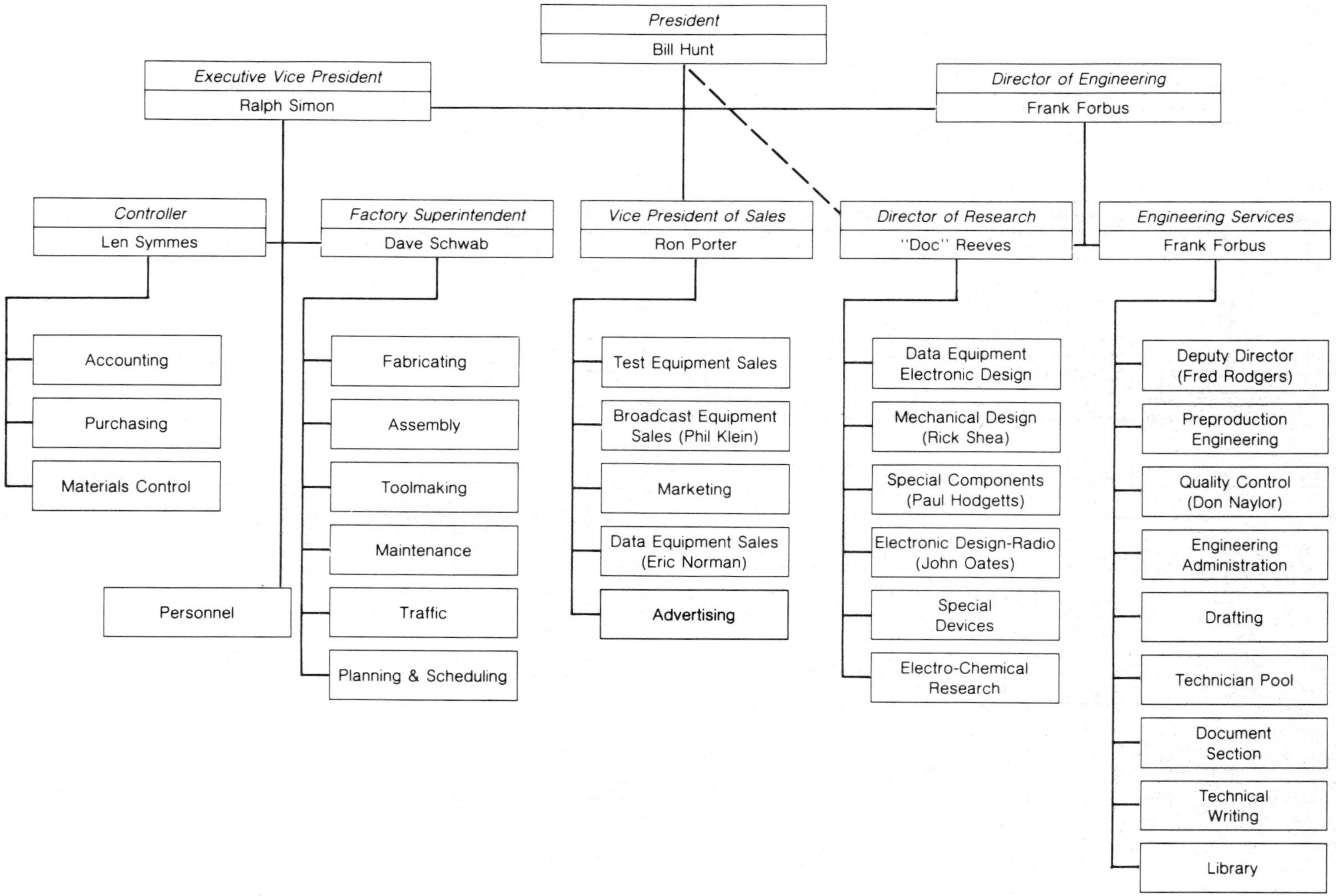

```
                              President
                              Bill Hunt
                                  |
              Executive Vice President
                   Ralph Simon
                        |
  ┌─────────────────────┼─────────────────────┬─────────────────────┐
  |                     |                      |                     |
Controller      Factory Superintendent   Vice President of Sales  Director of Research   Director of Engineering
Len Symmes          Dave Schwab               Ron Porter           "Doc" Reeves              Frank Forbus
  |                     |                      |                      |                        |
Accounting          Fabricating        Test Equipment Sales   Data Equipment          Engineering Services
Purchasing          Assembly           Broadcast Equipment    Electronic Design         Frank Forbus
Materials Control   Toolmaking         Sales (Phil Klein)     Mechanical Design             |
                    Maintenance        Marketing              (Rick Shea)             Deputy Director
Personnel           Traffic            Data Equipment Sales   Special Components      (Fred Rodgers)
                    Planning &         (Eric Norman)          (Paul Hodgetts)        Preproduction Engineering
                    Scheduling         Advertising            Electronic Design-Radio Quality Control (Don Naylor)
                                                              (John Oates)           Engineering Administration
                                                              Special Devices        Drafting
                                                              Electro-Chemical       Technician Pool
                                                              Research               Document Section
                                                                                     Technical Writing
                                                                                     Library
```

both research (really the product development function) and engineering services (which provided engineering support). To Forbus, however, the relationship with research was not so clear-cut:

Doc Reeves is one of the world's unique people, and none of us would have it any other way. He's a creative genius. Sure, the chart says he works for me, but we all know Doc does his own thing. He's not the least bit interested in management routines, and I can't count on him to take any responsibility in scheduling projects, or checking budgets, or what-have-you. But as long as Doc is director of research, you can bet this company will keep on leading the field. He has more ideas per hour than most people have per year, and be keeps the whole engineering staff fired up. Everybody loves Doc—and you can count me in on that, too. In a way, he works for me, sure. But that's not what's important.

"Doc" Reeves—unhurried, contemplative, casual, and candid—tipped his stool back against the wall of his research cubicle and talked about what *was* important:

Development engineering. That's where the company's future rests. Either we have it there, or we don't have it.

There's no kidding ourselves that we're anything but a bunch of Rube Goldbergs here. But that's where the biggest kicks come from—from solving development problems, and dreaming up new ways of doing things. That's why I so look forward to the special contracts we get involved in. We accept them not for the revenue they represent, but because they subsidize the basic development work which goes into all our basic products.

This is a fantastic place to work. I have a great crew and they can really deliver when the chips are down. Why, Bill Hunt and I (he gestured toward the neighboring cubicle, where the president's name hung over the door) are likely to find as many people here at work at ten p.m. as at three in the afternoon. The important thing here is the relationships between people; they're based on mutual respect, not on policies and procedures. Administrative red tape is a pain. It takes away from development time.

Problems? Sure, there are problems now and then. There are power interests in production, where they sometimes resist change. But I'm not a fighting man, you know. I suppose if I were, I might go in there and push my weight around a little. But I'm an engineer, and can do more for Rondell sitting right here, or working with my own people. That's what brings results.

Other members of the Research Department echoed Doc's views and added some additional sources of satisfaction with their work. They were proud of the personal contacts they built up with customers' technical staffs—contacts that increasingly involved travel to the customers' factories to serve as expert advisors in preparation of overall system design specifications. The engineers were also delighted with the department's encouragement of their personal development, continuing education, and independence on the job.

But there were problems, too. Rick Shea, of the mechanical design section, noted,

In the old days I really enjoyed the work—and the people I worked with. But now there's a lot of irritation. I don't like someone breathing down my neck. You can be hurried into jeopardizing the design.

John Oates, head of the radio electronic design section, was another designer with definite views:

Production engineering is almost nonexistent in this company. Very little is done by the preproduction section in engineering services. Frank Forbus has been trying to get preproduction into the picture, but he won't succeed because you can't start from such an ambiguous position. There have been three directors of engineering in three years. Frank can't hold his own against the others in the company. Kilmann was too aggressive. Perhaps no amount of tact would have succeeded.

Paul Hodgetts was head of special components in the R & D department. Like the rest of the department he valued bench work. But he complained of engineering services.

*The services don't do things we want them to do.
Instead, they tell us what they're going to do. I
should probably go to Frank, but I don't get any
decisions there. I know I should go through
Frank, but this holds things up, so I often go
direct.*

THE ENGINEERING DEPARTMENT:
ENGINEERING SERVICES

The Engineering Services Department provided ancillary services to R & D, and
served as liaison between engineering and
the other Rondell departments. Among its
main functions were drafting; management
of the central technicians' pool; scheduling
and expediting engineering products; documentation and publication of parts lists
and engineering orders; preproduction engineering (consisting of the final integration
of individual design components into
mechanically compatible packages); and
quality control (which included inspection
of incoming parts and materials, and final
inspection of subassemblies and finished
equipment). Top management's description
of the department included the line, "ESD
is responsible for maintaining cooperation
with other departments, providing services
to the development engineers, and freeing
more valuable people in R & D from essential activities which are diversions from
and beneath their main competence."

Many of Frank Forbus's 75 employees
were located in other departments. Quality
control people were scattered through the
manufacturing and receiving areas, and
technicians worked primarily in the research area or the prototype fabrication
room. The remaining ESD personnel were
assigned to leftover nooks and crannies
near production or engineering sections.

Frank Forbus described his position:

*My biggest problem is getting acceptance from
the people I work with. I've moved slowly rather
than risk antagonism. I saw what happened to
Kilmann, and I want to avoid that. But although
his precipitate action had won over a few of the*
*younger R & D people, he certainly didn't have
the department's backing. Of course it was the
resentment of other departments which
eventually caused his discharge. People have been
slow accepting me here. There's nothing really
overt, but I get a negative reaction to my ideas.*

*My role in the company has never been well
defined, really. It's complicated by Doc's unique
position, of course, and also by the fact that ESD
sort of grew by itself over the years, as the
design engineers concentrated more and more on
the creative parts of product development. I wish
I could be more involved in the technical side.
That's been my training, and it's a lot of fun. But
in our setup, the technical side is the least
necessary for me to be involved in.*

*Schwab (production head) is hard to get along
with. Before I came and after Kilmann left, there
were six months intervening when no one was
really doing any scheduling. No work loads were
figured, and unrealistic promises were made
about releases. This puts us in an awkward
position. We've been scheduling way beyond our
capacity to manufacture or engineer.*

*Certain people within R & D, for instance John
Oates, head of the radio electronic design
section, understand scheduling well and meet
project deadlines, but this is not generally true of
the rest of the R & D department, especially the
mechanical engineers who won't commit
themselves. Most of the complaints come from
sales and production department heads because
items—like the 802—are going to production
before they are fully developed, under pressure
from sales to get out the unit, and this snags the
whole process. Somehow, engineering services
should be able to intervene and resolve these
complaints, but I haven't made much headway so
far.*

*I should be able to go to Hunt for help, but he's
too busy most of the time, and his major interest
is the design side of engineering, where he got
his own start. Sometimes he talks as though he's
the engineering director as well as president. I
have to put my foot down; there are problems
here that the front office just doesn't understand.*

Sales people were often observed taking
their problems directly to designers, while
production frequently threw designs back

at R & D, claiming they could not be produced and demanding the prompt attention of particular design engineers. The latter were frequently observed in conference with production supervisors on the assembly floor. Frank went on:

The designers seem to feel they're losing something when one of us tries to help. They feel it's a reflection on them to have someone take over what they've been doing. They seem to want to carry a project right through to the final stages, particularly the mechanical people. Consequently, engineering services people are used below their capacity to contribute and our department is denied functions it should be performing. There's not as much use made of engineering services as there should be.

Frank Forbus's technician supervisor added his comments:

Production picks out the engineer who'll be the "bum of the month." They pick on every little detail instead of using their heads and making the minor changes that have to be made. The fifteen-to-twenty-year people shouldn't have to prove their ability any more, but they spend four hours defending themselves and four hours getting the job done. I have no one to go to when I need help. Frank Forbus is afraid. I'm trying to help him but he can't help me at this time. I'm responsible for fifty people and I've got to support them.

Fred Rodgers, who Frank had brought with him to the company as an assistant, gave another view of the situation:

I try to get our people in preproduction to take responsibility but they're not used to it and people in other departments don't usually see them as best qualified to solve the problem. There's a real barrier for a newcomer here. Gaining people's confidence is hard. More and more, I'm wondering whether there really is a job for me here.

(Rodgers left Rondell a month later.) Another of Forbus's subordinates gave his view:

If Doc gets a new product idea you can't argue. But he's too optimistic. He judges that others can do what he does—but there's only one Doc Reeves. We've had 900 production change orders this year—they changed 2,500 drawings. If I were in Frank's shoes I'd put my foot down on all this new development. I'd look at the reworking we're doing and get production set up the way I wanted it. Kilmann was fired when he was doing a good job. He was getting some system in the company's operations. Of course, it hurt some people. There is no denying that Doc is the most important person in the company. What gets overlooked is that Hunt is a close second, not just politically but in terms of what he contributes technically and in customer relations.

This subordinate explained that he sometimes went out into the production department but that Schwab, the production head, resented this. Personnel in production said that Kilmann had failed to show respect for oldtimers and was always meddling in other departments' business. This was why he had been fired, they contended.

Don Taylor was in charge of quality control. He commented:

I am now much more concerned with administration and less with work. It is one of the evils you get into. There is tremendous detail in this job. I listen to everyone's opinion. Everybody is important. There shouldn't be distinctions—distinctions between people. I'm not sure whether Frank has to be a fireball like Kilmann. I think the real question is whether Frank is getting the job done. I know my job is essential. I want to supply service to the more talented people and give them information so they can do their jobs better.

THE SALES DEPARTMENT

Ron Porter was angry. His job was supposed to be selling, he said, but instead it had turned into settling disputes inside the plant and making excuses to waiting customers. He jabbed a finger toward his desk:

You see that telephone? I'm actually afraid nowadays to hear it ring. Three times out of five, it will be a customer who's hurting because we've failed to deliver on schedule. The other two calls will be from production or ESD, telling me some schedule has slipped again.

The Model 802 is typical. Absolutely typical. We padded the delivery date by six weeks, to allow for contingencies. Within two months the slack had evaporated. Now it looks like we'll be lucky to ship it before Christmas. (It was now November 28.) We're ruining our reputation in the market. Why, just last week one of our best customers—people we've worked with for 15 years—tried to hang a penalty clause on their latest order.

We shouldn't have to be after the engineers all the time. They should be able to see what problems they create without our telling them.

Phil Klein, head of broadcast sales under Porter, noted that many sales decisions were made by top management. Sales was understaffed, he thought, and had never really been able to get on top of the job.

We have grown further and further away from engineering. The director of engineering does not pass on the information that we give him. We need better relationships there. It is very difficult for us to talk to customers about development problems without technical help. We need each other. The whole of engineering is now too isolated from the outside world. The morale of ESD is very low. They're in a bad spot—they're not well organized.

People don't take much to outsiders here. Much of this is because the expectation is built up by top management that jobs will be filled from the bottom. So it's really tough when an outsider like Frank comes in.

Eric Norman, order and pricing coordinator for data equipment, talked about his own relationships with the production department:

Actually, I get along with them fairly well. Oh, things could be better, of course, if they were more cooperative generally. They always seem to say, "It's my bat and my ball, and we're playing by my rules." People are afraid to make production mad; there's a lot of power in there. But you've got to understand that production has its own set of problems. And nobody in Rondell

is working any harder than Dave Schwab to try to straighten things out.

THE PRODUCTION DEPARTMENT

Dave Schwab had joined Rondell just after the Korean War, in which he had seen combat duty (at the Yalu River) and intelligence duty at Pyong Yang. Both experiences had been useful in his first year of civilian employment at Rondell's: the wartime factory superintendent and several middle managers had been, apparently, indulging in highly questionable side deals with Rondell's suppliers. Dave Schwab had gathered evidence, revealed the situation to Bill Hunt, and had stood by the president in the ensuing unsavory situation. Seven months after joining the company, Dave was named Factory Superintendent.

His first move had been to replace the fallen managers with a new team from outside. This group did not share the traditional Rondell emphasis on informality and friendly personal relationships, and had worked long and hard to install systematic manufacturing methods and procedures. Before the reorganization, production had controlled purchasing, stock control, and final quality control (where final assembly of products in cabinets was accomplished). Because of the wartime events, management decided on a check-and-balance system of organization and removed these three departments from production jurisdiction. The new production managers felt they had been unjustly penalized by this organization, particularly since they had uncovered the behavior that was detrimental to the company in the first place.

By 1978, the production department had grown to 500 employees, of whom 60% worked in the assembly area—an unusually pleasant environment that had been commended by *Factory* magazine for its colorful decoration, cleanliness, and low noise level. An additional 30% of the work force, mostly skilled machinists, staffed the finishing and fabrication department. About 60 others performed scheduling, supervisory, and maintenance duties. Production workers were nonunion, hourly-paid, and participated in both the liberal profit-sharing program and the stock purchase plan. Morale in production was traditionally high, and turnover was extremely low. Dave Schwab commented:

To be efficient, production has to be a self-contained department. We have to control what comes into the department and what goes out. That's why purchasing, inventory control, and quality ought to run out of this office. We'd eliminate a lot of problems with better control there. Why, even Don Naylor in QC, would rather work for me than for ESD; he's said so himself. We understand his problems better.

The other departments should be self-contained, too. That's why I always avoid the underlings, and go straight to the department heads with any questions. I always go down the line.

I have to protect my people from outside disturbances. Look what would happen if I let unfinished, half-baked designs in here—there'd be chaos. The bugs have to be found before the drawings go into the shop, and it seems I'm the one who has to find them. Look at the 802, for example. (Dave had spent most of Thanksgiving Day [it was now November 28] red-pencilling the latest set of prints.) ESD should have found every one of those discrepancies. They just don't check drawings properly. They change most of the things I flag, but then they fail to trace through the impact of those changes on the rest of the design. I shouldn't have to do that.

And those engineers are tolerance crazy. They want everything to a millionth of an inch. I'm the only one in the company who's had any experience with actually machining things to a millionth of an inch. We make sure that the things that engineers say on their drawings actually have to be that way and whether they're obtainable from the kind of raw material we buy.

That shouldn't be production's responsibility, but I have to do it. Accepting bad prints wouldn't let

us ship the order any quicker. We'd only make a lot of junk that had to be reworked. And that would take even longer.

This way, I get to be known as the bad guy, but I guess that's just part of the job. (He paused with a wry smile). Of course, what really gets them is that I don't even have a degree.

Dave had fewer bones to pick with the sales department because, he said, they trusted him.

When we give Ron Porter a shipping date, he knows the equipment will be shipped then.

You've got to recognize, though, that all of our new product problems stem from sales making absurd commitments on equipment that hasn't been fully developed. That always means trouble. Unfortunately, Hunt always backs sales up, even when they're wrong. He always favors them over us.

Ralph Simon, age 65, executive vice president of the company, had direct responsibility for Rondell's production department. He said:

There shouldn't really be a dividing of departments among top management in the company. The president should be czar over all. The production people ask me to do something for them, and I really can't do it. It creates bad feelings between engineering and production, this special attention that they [R & D] get from Bill. But then Hunt likes to dabble in design. Schwab feels that production is treated like a poor relation.

THE EXECUTIVE COMMITTEE

At the executive committee meeting of December 6, it was duly recorded that Dave Schwab had accepted the prints and specifications for the Model 802 modulator, and had set Friday, December 29, as the shipping date for the first 10 pieces. Bill Hunt, in the chairperson's role, shook his head and changed the subject quickly when Frank tried to open the agenda to a discussion of interdepartmental coordination.

The executive committee itself was a brainchild of Rondell's controller, Len Symmes, who was well aware of the disputes that plagued the company. Symmes had convinced Bill Hunt and Ralph Simon to meet every two weeks with their department heads, and the meetings were formalized with Hunt, Simon, Ron Porter, Dave Schwab, Frank Forbus, Doc Reeves, Symmes, and the personnel director attending. Symmes explained his intent and the results:

Doing things collectively and informally just doesn't work as well as it used to. Things have been gradually getting worse for at least who years now. We had to start thinking in terms of formal organization relationships. I did the first organization chart, and the executive committee was my idea too—but neither idea is contributing much help, I'm afraid. It takes top management to make an organization click. The rest of us can't act much differently until the top people see the need for us to change.

I had hoped the committee especially would help get the department managers into a constructive planning process. It hasn't worked out that way because Mr. Hunt really doesn't see the need for it. He uses the meetings as a place to pass on routine information.

MERRY CHRISTMAS

"Frank, I didn't know whether to tell you now, or after the holiday." It was Friday, December 22, and Frank Forbus was standing awkwardly in front of Bill Hunt's desk.

"But, I figured you'd work right through Christmas Day if we didn't have this talk, and that just wouldn't have been fair to you. I can't understand why we have such poor luck in the engineering director's job lately. And I don't think it's entirely your fault. But . . ."

Frank only heard half of Hunt's words, and said nothing in response. He'd be paid through February 28 . . . He should use the time for searching . . . Hunt would help all he could . . . Jim Kilmann was supposed to be doing well at his own new job, and might need more help . . .

Frank cleaned out his desk, and numbly started home. The electronic carillon near his house was playing a Christmas carol. Frank thought again of Hunt's rationale: conflict still plagued Rondell—and Frank had not made it go away. Maybe somebody else could do it.

"And what did Santa Claus bring you, Frankie?" he asked himself.

"The sack. Only the empty sack."

7

Artisan Industries

Artisan Industries was a nine-million-dollar-a-year, family-run manufacturer of wooden decorative products.

They were approaching their first fall sales season since last year's successful turnaround under the direction of the new 29-year-old President, Bill Meister. Last fall had begun with a year-to-date loss of $125,000 and, through Meister's actions, had ended with a $390,000 profit. This had been the first profit in several years and capped a challenging eight months for the new president.

Meister had hired his first man while his father was still president, bringing in 27-year-old Bob Atwood from the local office of a "Big Eight" firm to begin modernizing the accounting system. On June 10th, 1977, Bob was in Bill's office for further and, he hoped, final discussion of plans for this fall season. Artisan's sales were quite seasonal and on June 10th there were about two more months during which production would exceed sales. Atwood, concerned with the company's limited capital, proposed a production plan to hold the inventory build-up to $1,600,000, or about twice

the level shown on the last full computer listing.

The president, based on his feel for conditions after the successful 1976 season and viewing sales in the first weeks of 1977, believed total sales for this year would really beat Bob's estimate of the same as last year's and reach $9,000,000. But he would like to have stronger support for his opinions; a lot rested on this estimate. If sales were much beyond their plans he could expect to lose most of them and create difficulties with his customers. New customers might even be lost to the competition. Bill was also concerned with developing contingency plans for dealing effectively with the potential oversold condition. Besides getting more production from the plants at the last minute, there might be good ideas that involved the customers and salespeople. For example, if all orders couldn't be filled, should some be fully shipped and others dropped, or should all be shipped 75–95% complete? Overall in 1976 orders had been shipped 75% complete and during the peak months this had fallen to 50%. Partial shipments might be a way to keep eve-

Reprinted by permission of Frank C. Barnes, Associate Professor, University of North Carolina at Charlotte.

ryone happy. If orders are canceled should they be the ones from the small "mom and pop" stores or the large department stores? The small stores are more dependable customers, but on the other hand large department stores systematically evaluate suppliers on their order completion history. Also the department store buyers must commit funds when they place an order, thus their resources are idle until the order is filled. There are potential benefits from good communications, for if you inform the buyer of any delay quickly he can cancel that order and order something he can get. Such sensitivity to the customer's needs could win the company many friends and aid Meister in building a desirable reputation. On the other hand, poor communication could cause the opposite. Meister wondered if there was some way to usefully involve the salespeople, many of whom had left a sales representative organization six months earlier to work solely for Artisan.

After about mid-August total annual sales were limited to what had been built up in inventory beforehand and production through mid-November. Thus holding back now put a lid on total sales for the season.

If, on the other hand, the sales plan was not reached there could also be serious consequences. Last year after the fall sales period the inventory loan had been paid off for the first time since the 1960s. This had made a very favorable impression on the lending institutions and brought a reduction in the high interest rates (from 12% to 10¼%). They considered Bill a "super-star," with his youth, professional appearance, and modern ideas, and their fears for the Artisan loan were diminishing. Trouble at this time might erase all this and suggest last year was just a fluke.

If sales didn't materialize, inventories could be held down by cutting back on production. But Bill believed the plants operate inefficiently during any cutbacks and such moves very likely saved nothing. He

held a similar opinion of temporary second shifts. In many past years over-production early in the year had resulted in big layoffs in December and January and in the financial drain of carrying over large inventories. Meister was highly interested in building an effective work environment for people at Artisan, where attitudes were historically poor. The employees—workers and supervisors—had little exposure to "professional" managers and had much to learn. The long process had been begun, but a layoff now could undermine all his efforts and, he felt, lose him what little confidence and support he had been able to encourage.

The strategy for this fall was of critical importance to Bill and his hopes for Artisan and his future.

ARTISAN'S HISTORY

Artisan Industries is the product of a classical entrepreneur—W.A. (Buddy) Meister. After a variety of attempts at self-employment, such as running a dry-cleaning shop, a food shop, and an appliance store, he began to have some success making wooden toys. One try in 1950 with his father and brothers failed, leaving Buddy with an old tin building and some worn-out equipment.

During the next few years Buddy put his efforts into making a collection of 10 to 15 toys, sold via direct mail, house-to-house, on television, and on the roadside, all without a sales representative. One day a visiting gummed-tape salesman offered to take on the line and a pattern of using outside sales reps was established.

The first attempt at a trade show was a last-minute entry into the regional gift show 40 miles away. Out of sympathy for Buddy, Artisan was allowed to pay the $25-a-week rent after the show. Buddy brought home $3,000 in sales but lacked the money to produce them until a friend offered a loan. The orders were produced in a dirt-floor barn. In the following months, Buddy and his wife drove off to other markets, showing the goods in their motel room.

In 1953 sales reached $15,000, then climbed to $30,000 in 1954, $60,000 in 1955, and $120,000 in 1956. Then in April the plant, or barn, burned down destroying everything. With hardly a delay Buddy jumped into rebuilding and sales continued to double. In 1958, success allowed Artisan to move into a 30,000-square-foot building and continue using its two old buildings for finishing and shipping. Then in March of 1960 these two burned down. Again Buddy fought back and sales doubled into 1961. The rate of growth slowed to 50% in 1962.

The third and most disastrous fire occurred in February of 1963. The entire main plant was burned to the ground with the exception of the new office, which stood under one foot of water and was damaged by smoke and water. The company was in the middle of manufacturing its show orders and the only thing saved was the inventory in the paint shop. All the jigs were burned and before work could begin new jigs and patterns had to be made. "Only the plant in Spencer, built only a year before, saved us. The entire operation, with the exception of the office, was moved to Spencer, and working three shifts, we were able to keep most of the 200 employees. Many employees worked night and day for approximately six months to help us get on our feet again." Before Christmas of 1963 the company was back in full operation in the main plant.

Sales reached $4 million in 1967 and $8 million in 1972. During that six-year span Buddy's five children reached ages to begin full-time jobs in the company. The youngest, Bill, was last to join. Typical of the youngest, he had it best, having all the "toys" his father could provide. He attended Vanderbilt, where he majored in Business Administration and the "good life." But his good time was at last interrupted by graduation and retirement to Artisan.

Bill wanted no major role in the company but over the next three years found himself getting more involved. Buddy had developed no modern management systems; accounting was ineffective, sales was in the control of outside reps, manufacturing was outdated and unprofessional. The lack of order fit Buddy's style—close personal control and manipulation. As the company problems increased, family conflict intensified. Bill's older brother lost the support of his father and the support of the other side and left. Bill moved up to the role of spokesman for a change.

In early 1975, though sales were booming, the financial situation at Artisan was "tight." A second shift was in operation, though production was generally inefficient. By October sales had slackened and in November, to hold inventories down, layoffs began. Accounts receivable were worsening and the worried bankers were forcing the company to pay off some of its $2,500,000 loan. The inventory was reduced some and accounts payable were allowed to increase. In December the plant was closed for three weeks and $100,000 in cash was raised through a warehouse sale. But in the end, 1975 closed with a loss of over a million dollars.

As 1976 began the sales picture looked bad. Even with the large inventory there was difficulty shipping because it contained the wrong things. Since it tied up capital, production of salable items was limited. There were more layoffs and shutdowns in January. Some old suppliers cut off the company's credit. In February, under the threat of the local bank calling the loan, Bill and Bob negotiated a new loan with a New York firm. This was composed of an inventory loan with a ceiling of $500,000, an accounts receivable loan of up to $1 million, and a long-term loan on the warehouse and real estate of approximately $350,000. "The package was finalized and the funds transferred about one week prior to payment deadline with the Bank. Had we not completed the deal with the other group, there was no way we could have made the $25,000 payment," according to Bill.

As the troubles deepened in the spring, Buddy had few solutions and, worse, blocked Bill's actions. The atmosphere in the company became grim. As Bill put it: "It became a fight between who was going to make decisions about what. Through the spring the conflict between us continued at a heightened pace. The effect was that most people became very nervous because no one understood who was really in control. With the company in the financial condition it was then, the last thing it needed was a power struggle over who should be in charge. So in April I went to Buddy and explained the situation that the company needed one person who was clearly in authority and in control, that one person would be better than two, and that I felt that he should leave or I should leave. He suggested that since he had gotten there first, I should leave." Bill went to the mountains for good.

But two weeks later, under pressure from the lenders, Buddy stepped aside and Bill became the chief executive.

In May 1976 when Bill Meister became president, Artisan was in critical condition. Sales had fallen off dramatically, there had been little profit for three years, the number of employees had fallen from 600 to 370, modern management systems existed in no area of the company, and there were few qualified managers. "When I took over, sales were running 50% off and we could not get a line of credit through our suppliers, we were on a cash basis only, inventory was still relatively high, accounts receivable were running over 120 days, manufacturing was without anyone in charge, and the company was sustaining a loss of approximately $10,000 a week. The general situation looked pretty hopeless."

BILL MEISTER'S FIRST YEAR AS PRESIDENT

When Bill became president in May changes began. Although Bill controlled many of the changes, others were the result of actions by his managers or outside forces. By mid-summer of 1976 he had reestablished contact with a business professor he particularly respected at his alma mater and was in regular contact with a management professor at a local school. The small number of trained managers, their lack of experience, and the absence of cooperation among them was a serious handicap to his rebuilding effort. He hoped interaction with the professors would make up for the lack of inside managers to interact with.

Exhibit 7–1 shows the organization chart in June 1977. Buddy moved up to Chairman, but remained around the office. Bill's sister Edith and Uncle Sam helped in the sales area. Another sister, Sally, worked for Bob Atwood in accounting. A new man, Will Shire, was over production, mainly Plant One. Two long-term men, Charles Scott and Jack Lander, headed the plants. Two other long-term employees were in management: Cal Robb over the computer and Richard Bare over purchasing. A young man, Richard Barnes, had been hired recently for plant engineering. Paul Morgan had been with Artisan about two years in design.

Marketing

The company was one of four making up the wooden decorative products industry. Sales were seasonal, peaking with the Christmas period. Artisan's customers were some 13,000 retail shops that were serviced by outside sales representatives. Regional market shows were an important part of the marketing activity. The product line consisted of over 1,400 items and included almost anything for the customer. The largest item was a tea-cart and the smallest a clothes-pin type desk paper clip. New

EXHIBIT 7-1 ORGANIZATION CHART—ARTISAN INDUSTRIES—JUNE 1977

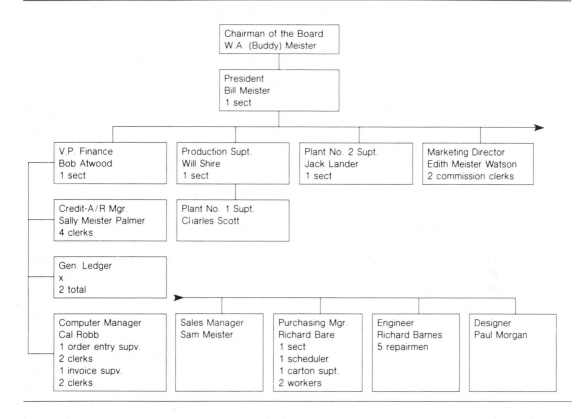

products were continually coming up; about 100 a year were added to the line. Practically no items were ever dropped. The top 100 products averaged 5,000 units a year. The first 25 items had double the sales units of the next group. Two hundred and fifty sold over 1,000 units. The average wholesale price was $3.75. The top item sold 31,000 units last year for about $75,000 in sales. The 200th had sales over $10,000.

Marketing was the function where Bill wanted to spend most of his time. His father had left this mainly with outsiders, but Bill was determined to put the company in charge of its own marketing. He attended all shows and found out firsthand what was going on. He felt the outside sales reps had let Artisan slide into making anything they could sell easily, regardless of costs and profits.

Bill hired a local young man with good design talent, but little experience, to set up a design department. They soon came up with a new "theme" line of items that became the talk of the industry, and Bill planned to try others. He engaged a New York advertising agency for a professional program of advertising in the trade journals and publicity in the newspapers. He produced an artistic catalog with color photographs rather than the dull listing used before.

There had been no price increases in quite a while, and with the recent inflation Atwood estimated the current sales prices would not yield a profit. In mid-October an immediate price increase appeared imperative if 1976 was to end with a profit. But there was great concern about the advisability of such action in the middle of the major sales season. Also, waiting on new price lists to institute the increase in an ordinary manner would not accomplish a 1976 profit; orders already acknowledged or in-house, but not yet acknowledged, exceeded what could be shipped. In fact, as Bill, his sister Edith from sales, Bob Atwood, the computer manager, Cal Robb, and the university professor met to decide what to do, a 30-page order from one store chain for $221,000 at the old prices sat in front of them. Bob and Cal took the position that no further orders should be acknowledged until the customer had been written that prices were increased and asked to mail a reconfirmation if they still wanted the goods. Edith felt the price increase was very risky and would be very difficult to implement at this time, if even possible. But she had difficulty explaining her views and Bob, with Cal, out-talked her. Bill listened to their arguments as little was accomplished. Only when the consultant added his weight to Edith's views and pointed out the manipulation and lack of good problem-solving did any practical ideas develop.

A 16% price increase was instituted immediately. The orders awaiting acknowledgment were examined that afternoon and on a priority basis the salespeople were called and informed of the necessity of the increase and asked to contact their customers for immediate approval. When possible, and with moderation, orders at the new prices were given priority over those at the old prices. Within a few days the new prices were contributing to profits.

Bill's most aggressive move was to cancel, in November 1976, the company's long agreement with E. Fudd Associates, a sales representative firm. Accounting for 60% of their sales, Fudd, with 50 salespeople, had handled Artisan's business in about 20 states for many years, and had even lent the company money during the previous December. But Fudd was an old-style "character" much like Buddy—and Bill had

been unable to systematically discuss market strategies or improvement ideas with him. Bill felt the 15% commission Fudd was setting could be better used as 10% directly to the salespeople and 5% in a company-controlled advertising budget.

Bill had planned to deal with E. Fudd Associates after the first of the year. It would take careful action to break with Fudd and assist any reps wishing to go independent on Artisan's line. But an accidental leak forced Bill's hand in the middle of the critical sales season. Bill did not back off but broke with Fudd immediately. Fudd countered with suits against Artisan, threats of displacing Artisan's goods with others, claims of tossing Artisan out of major regional market shows, and even withholding back, unpaid commissions on salespeople going with Artisan. Fudd spread rumors of Artisan's impending bankruptcy and sued any sales reps leaving him. Though there were bad moments, Bill held firm and in a few weeks it was over. Bill had gotten all the sales personnel he wanted, was lined up for his own space in the critical shows, and the rumors were going against Fudd.

Accounting

With the hiring of Bob Atwood in the fall of 1975, improvement in the accounting systems began, though slowly. By the spring of 1977 the outside service bureau had been replaced by a small in-house computer to handle order-entry and invoicing, including an inventory listing.

The small computer system was delivered in January of 1977. Prior to that $85,000 to $100,000 a year had been spent for assistance from the service bureau. This assistance had been primarily invoicing. After orders were manually checked for accuracy and credit, they went to the service bureau where a warehouse picking ticket was prepared. Then after shipment a form went back to initiate the invoice. Besides invoicing, they produced a monthly statement of bookings and shippings that summarized activity by item, customer, and state. The bureau was not involved with accounts receivable; aging was a manual process that took 30 days and was possibly only accurate to within $25,000. In 1975 checks had been posted, taking about three hours per day, and then forwarded directly to the lender. This had added three to four days of work for Atwood.

The computer had caused a small management crisis for Bill. Cal Robb and Bob Atwood, neither of whom had any special knowledge or experience with computers, had selected the system they wanted with no help beyond that of computer salespeople. With only verbal agreements and several contract notebooks from the supplier, they pressured Bill for his approval. When he failed to act they saw him as foot-dragging and lacking respect for their opinions. With the counsel of the university consultant, Bill took the unpopular step of sending them back to prepare a proper proposal and timetable. In work with the vendor, several serious omissions were found and corrected, and all agreed the further documentation had been worthwhile. Bill approved the project.

The new system consisted of a 48K "small" computer with a 450-line-per-minute printer—two disc drives with two million bytes each, and seven CRTs. Monthly rental amounted to about $4,000. The software was developed in-house by Robb using basic systems supplied by the vendor at no charge. Robb was the only staff for the computer. He was 36, with a business administration degree with some concentration in accounting from a good state university. Prior to Atwood's hiring he had been controller.

By May, inventory accounting was on the computer. The inventory listings computing EOQs were available but inaccurate. Atwood believed a couple of months of debugging was necessary before computer inventory control would be possible. The data needed for the EOQ model were all old and inaccurate; lead times, prepared by a consultant years ago, were considered by all to be way off. They and the standards hadn't been studied in five to six years. For now Atwood felt these listings would be of some help in operating the existing production scheduling system. (EOQ stands for the Economic Order Quantity inventory model.)

By June, invoicing was fully on the computer and the lender had stopped requiring the direct mailing of checks. About 3,000 invoices were prepared each month. The A/R systems, including statements and weekly aging of delinquent accounts, were operational, and about 2,500 statements were being prepared monthly. The controller felt both systems were running well and providing for good control. The computer supplier felt they had been lucky to get the system operational as quickly as they did. (A/R means accounts receivable, A/P means accounts payable.)

Cal expects inventory control will be on the computer by February. In another month he will add A/P payroll and general ledger. Production control must wait on others' work and input.

Monthly preparation of financial statements had begun in January. Production costing for the statements had been based on historical indices, but Bob reported little resulting error. The statements were out, in typed form, 30 days after the close of the period.

Production

There were two plants, roughly identical and five miles apart, each with about 60,000 square feet. Kiln dry lumber, mainly high-quality Ponderosa Pine, was inventoried in truck trailers and covered sheds at the rear of the plant. The lumber width, totally random, depended on the tree, and the length was from 8–16 feet, in multiples of two. The thickness started at the lumber mill at 4, 5, or 6 "quarter" ("quarter" meaning ¼ inch, therefore 4 quarters is 1"). By the time it reached the plant it was about ⅛" less.

The rough mill foreman reviewed the batch of production orders he was given about every week and decided on the "panels" the plant would need. A panel is a sheet of wood milled to a desired thickness and with length and width at the desired dimension or some multiple. Clear panels, ones with no knots, can be made from lower grade lumber by cutting out the defects and then gluing these smaller pieces into standard panels. Artisan did no such gluing but cut high-quality, clear lumber directly to the desired length and width. The necessary panels would be made up in the rough mill from lumber or from purchased glued panels. Artisan spent about as much on purchased panels as it did on raw lumber, paying about twice as much for a square foot of panel as for a square foot of lumber. Surfacers brought the wood to the desired thickness, the finished dimension plus some excess for later sanding. Rip saws cut the lumber to needed width and cut-off saws took care of the length. About 30 people worked in this area, which had about 12% of the labor cost.

The plant superintendent worked with the machine room foreman to decide on the sequence in which orders would be processed. Scheduled due-dates for each department were placed on the orders in production control but they followed up on the actual flow of orders only if a crisis developed. In the machine room 22 workers (17% of the labor cost) shaped panels to the final form. The tools included shapers, molders, routers, and borers. Patterns and jigs lowered the skill requirements, still the highest in the plant. This part of the plant was noisiest and dustiest.

In the third department, sanding, the parts were sanded by women working mainly at individual stations. There were 24 people here. The sanded components were moved to a nearby temporary storage area on the carts, which originated at machining. It was estimated there were 6–8 wooden parts in an average item. In addition there were purchased parts such as turnings and glass or metal parts. Sanding added about 19% of the direct labor to the products.

The assembly foreman kept an eye on the arrival of all parts for an order. Assembly began when all parts were available. Eighteen people assembled the items using glue, screws, nail guns, or hammer and nails. Jigs assisted the work where possible and usually only one person worked on an order. Fourteen percent of direct labor derived from this step. Little skill was needed and dust and noise weren't a problem.

The assembled items were moved promptly to the separate finishing area. Here they were dipped by hand into stains and sprayed with several clear coats. After oven-drying they proceeded to packing. Most were packed individually into cartons made in the company's small plant. Finishing and packing employed about 50 people and accounted for 34% of direct labor costs. The new 60,000 square foot finished goods warehouse was two miles away.

The labor rates ranged from $2.65 to $5.60 per hour. The average was probably $3.00, with about a dozen people making over $4.00. Factory overhead was about 60% of direct labor. Labor costs as a percent of the wholesale selling price ran about 20%; direct material, 35%. Variable costs totaled about 75%, with about another $1,800,000 in total company fixed costs. There was a three percentage point difference between the plants in labor costs. The capacity of the plant with 150 people working was estimated to be less than $110,000 a week. Indirect labor amounted to about 12% of plant overhead.

Most jobs did not require high skill levels. The average jobs in the rough mill and machine room, where the skilled jobs were, required no more than five weeks to master because the person would usually already have advanced skills. Elsewhere a week was adequate. Everyone but the supervisors and workers considered the work pace quite slow.

Production Scheduling

The production control department began the scheduling process. Exhibit 7–2 outlines the production scheduling system. About every week, sometimes longer, the clerk prepared a batch of production orders for each plant. Several factors determined when a batch of orders was prepared: whether the plants said they needed more work, how sales were doing, what the situation was in the warehouse, etc. The clerk examined the "Weekly Inventory Listing" for items that appeared low and the file of "Progress Control Charts" to see if the items were already on a production order. He converted the information to an available supply in weeks and selected any with less than eight weeks. If the total of orders gotten this way did not add up to an aggregate amount he had in mind, such as $60,000 to $100,000, he went back through the lists for more things to run.

"Production Sheets," or shop orders, were prepared for each item. These contained a drawing and a list of materials and process steps. The data were already pre-

EXHIBIT 7–2 PRODUCTION SCHEDULING SYSTEM

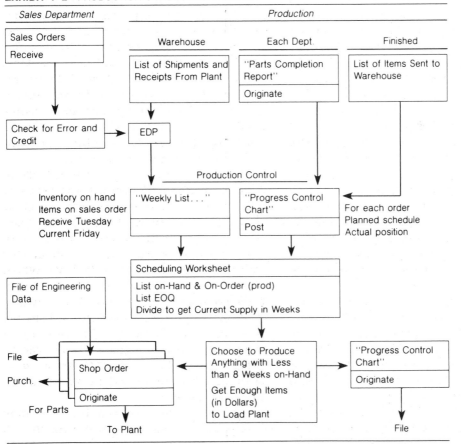

pared and came from consultant studies several years old. The order contained a date the part was due through each department based on standard lead times, for example, one week in the rough mill, three days in machining, etc. The actual work in the plant at the time did not alter leadtimes. At the same time a "Progress Control Chart" was prepared for each order. These remained in production control to trace the flow of orders.

The batch of orders was then handed to the plant superintendent who decided exactly how the items would be run. Daily each department gave production control a "Parts Completion Report," listing production from that department—order number, part number, and number produced. The production control clerk posted this information to the "Progress Control Charts." This reporting cycle used to be every two hours. The clerk reported these charts were not actually used to control production progress; they aided in locating an order if a question arose, but one still had to go out on the floor to be sure.

A brief look at the inventory listing for December showed the first 20 items were 23% of the inventory value. The 10th group of 20 items was 2% of inventory; the cumulative value to this point was 82%. The fortieth item had $1,800 in inventory and the two-hundredth $625.

Turning through the notebook for Plant One "Process Control Charts" on one day showed almost 300 open orders, perhaps 30–50% past the due date. Several items had two or even three different production orders two weeks or so apart. The order size appeared to average 200 at most. One in 10 was for more than 250 pieces. Only a couple were for 500 or more; the maximum was 1,000 pieces. The typical items appeared to contain about six parts and each took three to five processing steps.

The engineer was trying to estimate standards for new items as they were priced. A quick look at eight of them showed a total of 1,800 minutes of set-up time for the eight and a total of 6,400 minutes per 100 units of runtime. The set-up times ranged from 100 to 250 minutes for the products, but several of the parts required no set-up in some departments and where there was set-up it amounted to 25% to 50% of the run time for 100. Many parts required less than 30 minutes of processing in a department. The lot size on these ranged from 100 to 200 units; seven were priced around $4.00 and one at $25.00.

Production Problems

Bill feels production efficiency is a major problem. In talks with machinery salespeople and other visitors to the plant over recent years, Bill has come to feel the machinery is generally appropriate. But based on guesses about his competitors he feels his labor costs must be reduced. Earlier attempts to work with the plant superintendents and the various supervisors to systematically improve output met with no success. The supervisors had been unable to identify the needs for change in the plant or to develop the programs for bringing about improvement. To help the supervisors begin to improve their operations, a weekly production meeting was begun in June 1976. At the meeting the supervisors were to examine the total dollar output and total labor cost for each plant for the past week, compare it to the labor percent goal, 16%, set by Bill, and think about what could be done to improve operations for the coming week. Data on department performance was not available. During the first several meetings, the visiting consultant had to provide direction and ideas; the plant superintendent and his supervisors volunteered no ideas about what specifically limited last week's output. Bill reported some discussion of problems began three or four months later. It was Bill's opinion that this kind of thinking and planning was not required under his father's management. The supervisors in general felt nothing was wrong in the plant and really seemed puzzled at the thought of doing anything except continuing what they had always done.

In March of 1977, after a good deal of thought and search Bill hired two young men for the production system. One man, Will Shire, aged 28, was hired to be general superintendent over everyone in production, and the other, Richard Barnes, aged 27, was to be manufacturing engineer. It appeared the plant simply needed good management rather than any single big change that could be brought from the outside. Both of these men were young, college trained, and experienced in a wood industry.

Significant resistance from the old superintendent and most of the supervisors seemed probable. Consequently, the new men were briefed on this problem. As expected, things did not advance smoothly. Even as the new men gained familiarity with the operation no significant changes were observed. The expected complaints and rumors were heavy, and Bill ignored them as best he could. However after three months on the job the complaints still persisted and, more importantly, the new superintendent did not appear to have command of the situation. He had not developed his appraisal of what needed to be done and had no comprehensive plan for improvement. Bill recently received very good evidence that Will had some major difficulties in supervising people. One of the supervisors who did not appear to be a part of the rumor campaign and was conscientiously concerned about the company gave Bill examples of the new man's mistakes. Bill felt he may have made a mistake in hiring Will.

Richard's responsibilities have also been narrowed to more technical tasks. He is supervising the five-person repair crew, engineering some of the new products, examining the procedures for producing samples of new products, and beginning to examine a major redesign of the rough-mill area.

Major Competitor's Production

The major competitor is Sand Crafters, Inc. A managerial person familiar with both operations provided these comments. Demand for Sand Crafters' products exceeded their capacity and this, in the person's opinion, was the main reason Artisan existed. Their sales were somewhat less than Artisan's, they had no debt, and their equipment was described as new. They were located in a small community where the workers were relatively skilled for this kind of business. The work force was primarily white male. The manager characterized the Artisan worker as about $2/3$ as good as Sand Crafters. The workers in the third company in the industry were rated as $1/2$. The quality of manufacture of Sand Crafters was considered first, Artisan second, and the third company a close third. Sand Crafters' weakness was in poor engineering of the products and an outdated approach to marketing. Sand Crafters schedules long runs in manufacturing with the objective of having three months' stock of top priority items. They do not use the EOQ Model because they are limited in their work-in-process space.

In describing the Artisan manufacturing system, the person noted that two-thirds of the equipment is idle at any time, and that neither capacity nor optimum production mix have yet been determined. The largest run size he claimed to have seen had been 250. Setup costs he estimated to average $30. He commented that this was the least directed operation he had ever seen, with the slowest pace and the lowest level of knowledge of this type of work. He felt its employees knew only the simple way of doing the job. Only one man in the company, for example, was able to count the board feet of lumber and there was no lumber rule in the plant. He stated that this was a skill that the smallest cabinet shop would have and that it was essential for any kind of usage control.

The Workforce

Bill was greatly interested in the newest concept of management, frequently pointing to the latest book or sending a copy of an article to his managers or anyone with whom he was interacting. The behavioral writings made a lot of sense to him and he was very perceptive of behavioral processes in meetings or situations. The participative management systems and cooperative team environments were ones Bill wanted for Artisan. However he recognized his managers and the work force were not ready for this yet. His managers manipulated more than cooperated, and the workers were neither skilled nor very productive. When he discussed the workers' desires with the supervisors he was told they wanted a retirement program and higher pay, nothing else. Bill felt this was really what the supervisors themselves wanted.

As a basis for beginning change in this area, an outside consultant conducted an employee attitude survey in May 1977. All employees in the company were assisted in small groups in completing the written questionnaire. The questionnaire was designed: (1) to find out what they wanted, for example, more pay, retirement plans, more or less direction, etc.; (2) to gain insight into the probable impact of participative man-

agement moves; (3) to establish benchmarks of employee satisfaction so that changes over time could be monitored; (4) to develop an objective profile of the workers; and (5) to look for significant differences in attitudes between the various stratifications possible.

The survey included questions developed specifically for this situation as well as a highly regarded attitude instrument, the Job Descriptive Index (JDI). Although the wording is considered simple, many of the workers did not understand such words as "stimulating," "ambitious," or "fascinating," and it became necessary to read the entire questionnaire to them.

The study showed minorities accounted for 80% of the 300 employees; white females were the largest group at 40%. The workforce was 58% female, 57% white, and 39% over 45 years old. As many people have been with the company under two years as over 10 years—24%. The pay was only a little above the legal minimum, but many workers felt fortunate to have their jobs. There did not appear to be a "morale" crisis; the five JDI measures located the company in about the middle of the norms. The supervisory group was highest in "morale" while management was lowest.

Exhibit 7–3 summarizes the Job Descriptive Index scores. The numbers in parentheses show the norms.

Employees were also questioned about a number of aspects of their work climate

EXHIBIT 7–3 SUMMARY OF JDI SCORES BY LEVEL (PERCENTILE)

Group	Number	Overall	Attitude Towards:				
			Coworker	Work	Supervision	Promotion	Pay
(Maximum score)		25	54	54	54	27	27
Total Company	318	17.4	41.2	32.3	40.4	11.1	7.1
Management	7	15.9	38.0	39.4	48.0	18.7	15.9
(%)			(35)	(60)	(70)	(80)	(55)
Office	18	16.6	45.8	36.6	47.4	6.9	7.7
(%)			(60)	(50)	(65)	(50)	(25)
Supervision	13	19.7	46.8	39.2	46.1	16.1	12.2
Plant No. 1 Hourly	141	17.1	40.4	31.6	38.4	11.7	6.6
Plant No. 2 Hourly	101	18.1	39.8	31.3	42.6	11.0	5.9

that could be improved. Exhibit 7–4 shows these questions.

Their expressed view of the organizational climate was relatively good. They claimed to enjoy their work, looked for ways to improve it, and felt expected to do a good job. They especially felt their co-workers were good to work with and felt part of a team. They appeared to like their supervision.

Their views did not suggest need for a different manner of supervision. And they did not respond positively to the suggestions of being more in charge of themselves, did not feel strongly about having more of a say in how things are done, and didn't feel there were too many rules.

The survey revealed no critical problems, differences between groups were not extreme, and the resulting view of the worker was moderate. However the workers were relatively unsophisticated and there was concern they might not have expressed themselves on the instrument.

EXHIBIT 7–4 RESULTS OF ATTITUDE SURVEY: MAY, 1977

What is your opinion on the following statements? Do you agree or.disagree?	Average Employee Response
I enjoy taking the test.	3.97
My pay is fair for this kind of job.	2.26
My coworkers are good to work with.	4.14
My complaints or concerns are heard by management.	3.22
Things are getting better here.	3.45
The supervisors do a poor job.	2.35
I am fortunate to have this job.	3.95
Working conditions are bad here.	2.55
I benefit when the company succeeds.	3.11
I have all the chance I wish to improve myself.	3.19
The company is well run.	3.29
Communications are poor.	2.91
I don't get enough direction from my supervisor.	2.56
I enjoy my work.	4.13
I look for ways to improve the work I do.	4.21
I need more of a chance to manage myself.	3.11
I don't expect to be with the company long.	2.35
Morale is good here.	3.55
We all do only what it takes to get by.	2.19
I am concerned about layoffs and losing my job.	3.51
I like the way my supervisor treats me.	4.02
We need a suggestion system.	3.75
I want more opportunity for advancement.	3.86
My supervisor knows me and what I want.	3.56
We are not expected to do a very good job here.	2.01
There are too many rules.	2.58
I feel like part of a team at work.	3.82
The company and my supervisor seek my ideas.	3.06
I can influence dept. goals, methods and activities	3.01
There is too much "family" here.	2.77
This company is good for the community.	4.22

5 = Strongly agree
1 = Strongly disagree

THE MEETING WITH BOB ON JUNE 10th

The last months of 1976 had been very good in spite of fears caused by the price increase and the changes in the sales organization, and had resulted in a $390,000 profit. Bob Atwood reported that the original plan for 1977 had been for no major changes—a regrouping, doing as in late 1976, just better. However there was no formal written plan. As actual sales in January and February ran well ahead of the prior year, production was allowed to stay higher than the plan. Bill believed Bob's estimate of sales at $6.5 million was very low. A quite conservative estimate, he felt, was $9.0 million. This level became accepted as the premise for production planning in the first part of the year. But March and April were disappointing and May was only fair. Bill still felt the $9 million was reasonable, as the normal retail sales patterns had been upset by inflation and the fuel crisis. But he recognized the risks and was concerned. He hoped the gift shows in July would settle what 1977 would hold.

On June 10, 1977, Bob Atwood had returned to Bill's office to press for some decision on the inventory level. He wanted Bill to pull back on plans for 1977. As sales had been slower coming in and inventories had increased more than expected, Bob had become increasingly worried. The level on the last full inventory listing prepared about six weeks before stood at $800,000 in wooden goods. The current level was nearer $1,100,000. From a financial perspective Bob was willing to accept a level as high as $1,600,000. But this called for limiting production now. His report dated May 13th presented several alternative production levels for the fall, comparing particularly $600,000 and $720,000 per month. The advantages and disadvantages of $600,000 vs. $720,000 production levels are as follows:

Advantages and Disadvantages

Advantages of $600,000 Production Level:

1. Reduces scope of operation to afford high degree of control.
2. Maintains positive cash flow position for remainder of year.
3. Maintains more liquid corporate position.

Disadvantages of $600,000 Production Level:

1. More customer dissatisfaction from possible low service level.
2. Probable lost sales if orders increase.

Advantages of $720,000 Production Level:

1. High service level to accounts.
2. Low probability of decrease in service if orders increase.

Disadvantages of $720,000 Production Level:

1. Risk of inventory buildup.
2. Risk of being in a "lay off" situation if orders do not increase.

He advocated a $60,000 per month level.

Bob recommended they immediately cut production and make Richard Bare, the purchasing agent, production control manager with the responsibility for guiding the controlled inventory buildup. Since the desired total inventory level of $1,600,000 was twice the level shown on the last computer listing that included recommended run sizes (EOQs), he felt they could use this part of the computer system as a guide in selectively increasing the inventory. They could double either the Re-Order Points (ROPs) or the lead times in the computer, return the report, and use the new EOQs to double the inventory in a balanced form. Bob felt there had been unnecessary delay in making a decision and was impatient for Bill to put this to rest without further delay.

8

Organizational Diagnosis Questionnaire

INSTRUCTIONS FOR USE OF THE ODQ

Goals

I. To assistant participants in understanding the process of organizational diagnosis.
II. To show participants how the various formal and informal aspects of an organization work together.
III. To provide participants with a method for understanding the functioning of the internal environment of an organization.

Group Size

May be administered individually or in small groups of six to eight. May be used with students as a training tool or as part of an organizational analysis.

Time Required

Approximately two hours.

Materials

I. A copy of the Organizational Diagnosis Questionnaire (ODQ) and score sheet for each participant.
II. A newsprint flip chart or chalk board for the instructor.

Physical Setting

A room large enough so that individuals/ groups can work undisturbed. Movable chairs should be provided.

Process

STEP 1. *Introduction (10 min.)*

The instructor announces the goals of the activity distributing copies of the ODQ, its score sheet and the associated handout. The participants are instructed to read the handout.

STEP 2. *Overview (15 min.)*

The instructor presents an overview of the Weisbord Six Box Organizational model, provides examples and elicits questions.

Source: The ODQ and its introduction were prepared By Robert C. Preziosi. Reprinted from: J. William Pfeiffer & John E. Jones, (Eds.), The 1980 Annual Handbook for Group Facilitators, San Diego, CA: University Associates, Inc., 1980. Used with permission.

STEP 3. *Complete the ODQ (30 min.)*

Participants are told to think of an organization with which they have some knowledge. This can be a firm where they have worked, a club to which they belonged etc. They are told to think of that organization as they respond to the items on the ODQ.

STEP 4. *Score the ODQ (10 min.)*

After completing the ODQ, the instructor explains the scoring system and participants score their own questionnaire.

STEP 5. *Small Group Discussion (15 min.)*

Participants are then asked to form small groups and discuss why the organizations they analyzed came out the way they did.

STEP 6. *Change Strategies (10 Min.) (Optional)*

Participants are asked to think of activities they might instigate in their organizations to change some of the negative issues that surfaced in their analysis.

STEP 7. *Large Group Discussion (20 min.) (Optional)*

Instructor brings the entire group together and solicits volunteers to discuss the specifics of their particular organization.

INTRODUCTION TO THE QUESTIONNAIRE

Both internal and external organization development (OD) consultants at some point in the consulting process must address the question of diagnosis. Recently the need for two levels of diagnosis, preliminary and intensive, was addressed (Lippitt & Lippitt, 1978). The purpose of the Organizational Diagnosis Questionnaire (ODQ) is to provide survey-feedback data for intensive diagnostic efforts. Use of the questionnaire either by itself or in conjunction with other information-collecting techniques (such as direct observation or interviewing) will provide the data needed for identifying strengths and weaknesses in the functioning of an organization and/or its subparts. The questionnaire produces data relative to informal activity.

A meaningful diagnostic effort must be based on a theory or model of organizational functioning. This makes action research possible as it facilitates problem identification, which is essential to organization development. One of the more significant models in existence is Weisbord's (1976) Six-Box Organizational Model (Exhibit 8–1). Weisbord's model establishes a systematic approach for analyzing relationships among variables that influence how an organization is managed. It provides for assessment in six areas of formal and informal activity: purposes, structure, relationships, rewards, leadership, and helpful mechanisms. The outer circle in Exhibit 8–1 determines an organizational boundary for diagnosis. This boundary clarifies the functioning of the internal environment, which is to be analyzed to the exclusion of the external environment.

The Instrument

The Organizational Diagnosis Questionnaire (ODQ) is based on Weisbord's practitioner-oriented theory. The ODQ generates data in each of Weisbord's suggested six areas as well as in a seventh, attitude toward change. This item was added as a helpful mechanism for the person involved in organizational diagnosis. In attempting any planned-change effort in an organization it is wise to know how changeable an organization is. Such knowledge helps the change agent understand how to direct his efforts.

Thirty-five items compose the ODQ, five in each of the seven variables. Respondents are asked to indicate their current views of their organization on a scale of 1 to 7, with a score of 4 representing a neutral point.

EXHIBIT 8-1   THE SIX-BOX ORGANIZATIONAL MODEL[1]

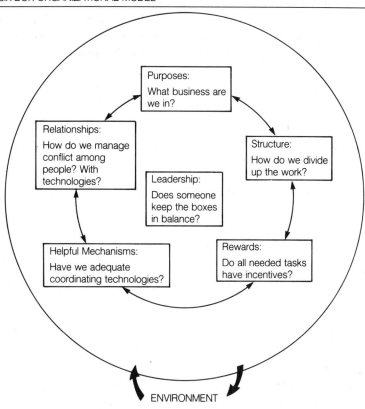

[1] Reproduced from M. R. Weisbord, Organizational diagnosis: Six places to look for trouble with or without a theory, *Group & Organization Studies*, 1976, *I* (4), 430-447, by permission of the publisher and the author.

Uses of the ODQ

The ODQ can be administered to a work unit, an entire organization, or a random sample of each. It might also be used to analyze staff or line functioning as well as to assess the thinking of different levels of management or supervision. It should be administered by the consultant or process facilitator in order to insure that an adequate explanation of the questionnaire and its use will be given. The consultant could also train others to administer the questionnaire.

Administration and Scoring   The administrator of the questionnaire must emphasize to the respondents that they be open and honest. If they are not, data that yield an inaccurate assessment of the organization on any or all of the seven variables may be produced. All ODQ statements are positive and can easily be discerned as such, which may influence the manner in which the respondents react to the questionnaire.

Scoring the questionnaire may be done in more than one way. Aggregate data will be most useful; an individual's set of responses is not significant. A self-scoring sheet is provided for each individual. Individual scoring sheets could then be tabulated by the consultant, an assistant, or, for large-scale studies, a computer.

Processing the Data   Once aggregate data have been collected, they must be processed. The first task is to prepare a bar or line graph (or any similar technique) to present the data so that they can be readily understood. The consultant/facilitator should present the data first to the organization's president or the work unit's supervisor (whichever is applicable) to establish understanding, commitment, and support.

Next, a meeting with the work group is essential. During this meeting the consultant/facilitator must weave a delicate balance between task and maintenance issues in order to be productive. During this meeting a number of things take place: information is presented (feedback); information is objectively discussed; group problem solving is encouraged; brainstorming for solutions is facilitated; alternative solutions are evaluated against criteria; a solution is chosen; an action plan is developed; and a plan for future evaluation is determined. This process is presented in detail in Hausser, Pecorella, and Wissler (1977).

The ODQ produces information about the informal system. As Weisbord suggested, the formal system must be considered also. A consultant/facilitator may review an organization's charter, operations manual, personnel policies, etc. Gaps between the two systems lead to a diagnosis of what is not happening that should be happening, or vice versa.

In sum, the ODQ is useful for diagnostic efforts insofar as it provides data about people's perceptions of their organization. It is an instrument that may be used separate from or in addition to other information-collecting techniques.

REFERENCES

Hausser, D. L., Pecorella, P. A., & Wissler, A. L. *Survey-guided development: A manual for consultants.* San Diego, CA: University Associates, 1977.

Lippitt, G., & Lippitt, R. *The consulting process in action.* San Diego, CA: University Associates, 1978.

Weisbord, M. R. Organizational diagnosis: Six places to look for trouble with or without a theory. *Group & Organization Studies*, 1976, 1(4), 430–447.

ORGANIZATIONAL DIAGNOSIS QUESTIONNAIRE

From time to time organizations consider it important to analyze themselves. It is necessary to find out from the people who work in the organization what they think if the analysis is going to be of value. This questionnaire will help the organization that you work for analyze itself.

Directions: Do not put your name anywhere on this questionnaire. Please answer all thirty-five questions. *Be open and honest.* For each of the thirty-five statements circle only *one (1)* number to indicate your thinking.

    1—Agree Strongly
    2—Agree
    3—Agree Slightly
    4—Neutral
    5—Disagree Slightly
    6—Disagree
    7—Disagree Strongly

1. The goals of this organization are clearly stated.

   1   2   3   4   5   6   7

2. The division of labor of this organization is flexible.

   1   2   3   4   5   6   7

3. My immediate supervisor is supportive of my efforts.

   1   2   3   4   5   6   7

4. My relationship with my supervisor is a harmonious one.

   1   2   3   4   5   6   7

5. My job offers me the opportunity to grow as a person.

   1   2   3   4   5   6   7

6. My immediate supervisor has ideas that are helpful to me and my work group.

   1   2   3   4   5   6   7

7. This organization is not resistant to change.

   1   2   3   4   5   6   7

8. I am personally in agreement with the stated goals of my work unit.

   1   2   3   4   5   6   7

9. The division of labor of this organization is conducive to reaching its goals.

   1   2   3   4   5   6   7

10. The leadership norms of this organization help its progress.

   1   2   3   4   5   6   7

11. I can always talk with someone at work if I have a work-related problem.

   1   2   3   4   5   6   7

12. The pay scale and benefits of this organization treat each employee equitably.

   1   2   3   4   5   6   7

13. I have the information that I need to do a good job.

   1   2   3   4   5   6   7

14. This organization is not introducing enough new policies and procedures.

   1   2   3   4   5   6   7

15. I understand the purpose of this organization.

   1   2   3   4   5   6   7

16. The manner in which work tasks are divided is a logical one.

   1   2   3   4   5   6   7

17. This organization's leadership efforts result in the organization's fulfillment of its purposes.

   1   2   3   4   5   6   7

18. My relationships with members of my work group are friendly as well as professional.

   1   2   3   4   5   6   7

19. The opportunity for promotion exists in this organization.

   1   2   3   4   5   6   7

20. This organization has adequate mechanisms for binding itself together.

   1   2   3   4   5   6   7

21. This organization favors change.

   1   2   3   4   5   6   7

22. The priorities of this organization are understood by its employees.

   1   2   3   4   5   6   7

23. The structure of my work unit is well

designed.

1   2   3   4   5   6   7

24. It is clear to me whenever my boss is attempting to guide my work efforts.

1   2   3   4   5   6   7

25. I have established the relationships that I need to do my job properly.

1   2   3   4   5   6   7

26. The salary that I receive is commensurate with the job that I perform.

1   2   3   4   5   6   7

27. Other work units are helpful to my work unit whenever assistance is requested.

1   2   3   4   5   6   7

28. Occasionally I like to change things about my job.

1   2   3   4   5   6   7

29. I desire less input in deciding my work-unit goals.

1   2   3   4   5   6   7

30. The division of labor of this organization helps its efforts to reach its goals.

1   2   3   4   5   6   7

31. I understand my boss's efforts to influence me and the other members of the work unit.

1   2   3   4   5   6   7

32. There is no evidence of unresolved conflict in this organization.

1   2   3   4   5   6   7

33. All tasks to be accomplished are associated with incentives.

1   2   3   4   5   6   7

34. This organization's planning and control efforts are helpful to its growth and development.

1   2   3   4   5   6   7

35. This organization has the ability to change.

1   2   3   4   5   6   7

ODQ SCORING SHEET

Instructions: Transfer the numbers you circled on the questionnaire to the blanks below, add each column, and divide each sum by five. This will give you comparable scores for each of the seven areas.

Relationships

4 _____

11 _____

18 _____

25 _____

32 _____

Total _____

Average _____

Purposes

1 _____

8 _____

15 _____

22 _____

29 _____

Total _____

Average _____

Rewards

5 _____

12 _____

19 _____

26 _____

33 _____

Total _____

Average _____

Structure

2 _____

9 _____

16 _____

23 _____

30 _____

Total _____

Average _____

Helpful Mechanisms

6 _____

13 _____

20 _____

27 _____

34 _____

Total _____

Average _____

Leadership

3 _____

10 _____

17 _____

24 _____

31 _____

Total _____

Average _____

Attitude Toward Change

7 _____

14 _____

21 _____

28 _____

35 _____

Total _____

Average _____

ODQ PROFILE AND INTERPRETATION SHEET

Instructions: Transfer your average scores from the ODQ Scoring Sheet to the appro- priate boxes in the figure below. Then study the background information and in- terpretation suggestions that follow.

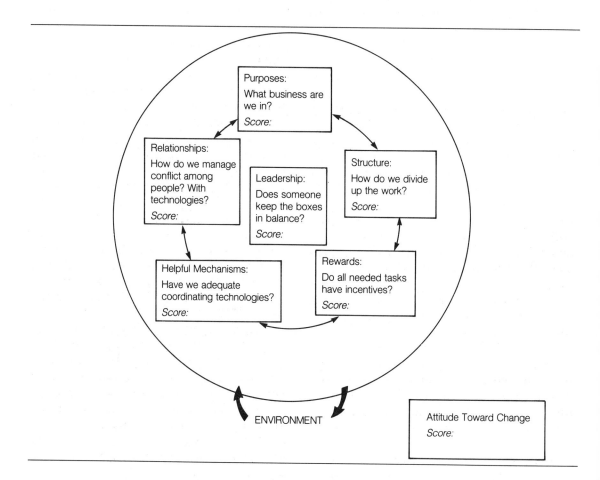

Background

The ODQ is a survey-feedback instrument designed to collect data on organizational functioning. It measures the perceptions of persons in an organization or work unit to determine areas of activity that would benefit from an organization development effort. It can be used as the sole data-collection technique or in conjunction with other techniques (interview, observation, etc.).

Weisbord's Six-Box Organizational Model (1976) is the basis for the questionnaire, which measures seven variables: purposes, structure, relationships, rewards, leadership, helpful mechanisms, and attitude toward change. The first six areas are from Weisbord's model, while the last one was added to provide the consultant/facilitator with input on readiness for change.

The instrument and the model reflect a systematic approach for analyzing relationships among variables that influence how an organization is managed. The ODQ measures the informal aspects of the system. It may be necessary for the consultant/ facilitator also to gather information on the formal aspects and to examine the gaps between the two.

Using the ODQ is the first step in determining appropriate interventions for organizational change efforts. Its use as a diagnostic tool can be the first step in improving an organization's or work unit's capability to serve its clientele.

Interpretation and Diagnosis

A crucial consideration is the diagnosis based upon data interpretation. The simplest diagnosis would be to assess the amount of variance for each of the seven variables in relation to a score of 4, which is the neutral point. Scores above 4 would indicate a problem with organizational functioning. The closer the score is to 7 the more severe the problem would be. Scores below 4 indicate the lack of a problem, with a score of 1 indicating optimum functioning.

Another diagnostic approach follows the same guidelines of assessment in relation to the neutral point (score) of 4. The score of each of the thirty-five items on the questionnaire can be reviewed to produce more exacting information on problematic areas. Thus diagnosis would be more precise. For example, let us suppose that the average score on item number 8 is 6.4. This would indicate not only a problem in organizational purpose, but also a more specific problem in that there is a gap between organizational and individual goals. This more precise diagnostic effort is likely to lead to a more appropriate intervention in the organization than the generalized diagnostic approach described in the preceding paragraph.

Appropriate diagnosis must address the relationships between the boxes to determine the interconnectedness of problems. For example, if there is a problem with relationships, could it be that the reward system does not reward relationship behavior? This might be the case if the average score on item 33 was well above 4 (5.5 or higher) and all the items on relationships (4, 11, 18, 25, 32) averaged above 5.5.

II

Design and Structure

9

Outdoor Outfitters, Ltd.

The early 1970s witnessed an explosion of interest in outdoor activities such as camping, backpacking, canoeing, and hiking. This trend substantially increased sales of recreation vehicles, including four-wheel drives, campers, and trail bikes. But Outdoor Outfitters, Ltd., a small chain of mountain equipment suppliers, was determined to carry only ecologically safe and sound items—those that are noiseless, nondestructive, and self-propelled. They furthered this image by sponsoring free outdoor country and bluegrass music concerts and other events. A recent catalog of Outdoor Outfitters, Ltd. carried this message:

WE HAVE COMPLETED OUR REMODELING!!!

Over the past few months, Outdoor Outfitters, Ltd. has been expanding (thanks to your patronage). During that time the store was a mess and service was a little ... confusing, at best. But that's over with now.

We have enlarged and remodeled our showroom. The walls and display fixtures are done with some beautiful locally milled poplar boards and

our stone work with local rip rap. We're ready for business now, so stop in and take a look at our new store.

Our People *Outdoor Outfitters, Ltd. is staffed by individuals who have been involved in outdoor activities for years. We actively use the equipment we sell and can give competent advice on its selection and usage. Educating the public is one of our main concerns and with this in mind, we sponsor educational seminars and trips throughout the year.*

Our Products *The companies ... whose products we carry manufacture some of the finest outdoor recreation equipment in the world. From the Appalachians to the Himalayas, the products we handle have been tested and refined by generations of outdoorsmen.*

The term "leisure goods" is appropriate to recreation equipment since they are used in one's spare time. Hence, sales depend on the excess time available to the potential purchaser. While the work week has remained constant at 40 hours since World War II, the average work year has been reduced by longer vacations and additional paid holidays. Now up to one-third

Reprinted by permission of Paul Miesing, Assistant Professor, School of Business, State University of New York at Albany.

of the average American's time can be considered "free" or unoccupied. Much of this time is spent with the family, and leisure is now considered a necessity by many.

Recreation expenditures also depend on the money available to the potential buyer. Sales of these items generally keep pace with disposable income. Of these expenditures, approximately $12 billion a year is spent on sporting goods, with camping, skiing, and fishing equipment purchases equalling nearly $.5 billion each. Although growth for this industry is expected to surpass the economy as a whole, it should not match the rate experienced in the '60s and early '70s due to the dampening effects of inflation. (See Exhibit 9–1).

Typically, buyers of leisure-oriented goods search for and demand information, are emotionally involved with their purchase, and have the option of postponing it. And since these goods satisfy needs for self-fulfillment and self-expression, there is little brand loyalty. Instead, purchasers are tremendously influenced by friends, experts, and magazine editorials. Furthermore, since first-time purchasers also tend to fall in the 19–24-year-old age group and are extremely fearful of making a wrong choice, these individuals are avid comparison shoppers, take longer to decide, and are price conscious. In short, the "right" equipment is usually one that is economically painless yet chic. On balance, the net result has been larger sales of quality and durable items, with the weakest sellers being the inexpensive ends of the lines.

In addition to time, money, and psychological fulfillment, demand for recreation equipment is also influenced by available "support" facilities, such as the mountains and streams of the nearby environment. Jefferson City, a middle-sized university town and headquarters for Outdoor Outfitters, Ltd., is well-suited for this since it is situated close to many national parks and national forests.

The area also draws thousands of visitors each year as a major tourist and recreational center. This attraction is reflected in the town's annual general merchandise sales (including variety and general stores) of around $50 million, with an identical amount attributed to department store sales. In addition, the median age—heavily influenced by the student population—is 28 for men and 30 for women, with approximately one-fourth of the workforce considered professionals and one-half considered white-collar.

Outdoor Outfitters, Ltd. was started in 1972 as the outgrowth of an M.B.A. thesis at the State University in Jefferson City. Having experienced several setbacks during

EXHIBIT 9–1 OUTDOOR OUTFITTERS, LTD.
Financial Statistics for Selected Firms For 1977

	5-yr. Avge. ROE	1-yr. Avge. ROE	5-yr. Avge. ROC	1-yr. Avge. ROC	Net Profit Margin	5-yr. Avge. Sales
AMF, Inc	13.3%	12.9%	8.9%	9.7%	3.3%	8.8%
Brunswick	12.3%	10.9	9.5	8.6	4.0	11.1
Fuqua	5.3	10.5	4.9	7.3	2.7	10.2
Recreation Industry Median	12.7	13.3	9.5	10.1	3.8	10.9
All Leisure Industry Median	15.1	17.5	11.1	12.7	5.4	11.2

ROE=return on equity

ROC=return on capital

1973, it was sold by the founder in 1974. The company then began to reach a very good average annual growth rate as several additional stores were gradually opened along the foothills of the nearby mountain range, with Jefferson City serving as the center for these distant operations. However, sales at the Jefferson City store began to level off during the renovation in 1976 and 1977. Although some momentum was lost at this branch, it did not prevent the company as a whole from maintaining its above-average growth rate.

The location of the Jefferson City store was well-suited. The only local store carrying specialized recreation goods (except for several discount and general department stores), it was set in off the main thoroughfare through town—accessible, yet isolated. The store itself was somewhat disorganized, but this appearance only emphasized the casual atmosphere of the place.

With knowledgeable sales help, there was originally little need for direction by the managers. But the increase in size also brought about an increase in complexity, and so the acquirers decided to organize the operations by geographic area (see Exhibit 9–2) and to centrally manage the branches so as to achieve scale economies and greater purchasing power. The local managers retained the authority to stock,

promote, and staff their branches within the budgetary guidelines. In addition, all the managers would attend monthly meetings that—among other things—determined the inventory to be purchased.

One aspect of this reorganization included a formal inventory control system, whereby items would be ordered monthly based on the prior year's sales. Actual stock levels were then recorded from sales tickets for the past week. Management planned to check this running tabulation periodically for accuracy of item, code number, color, and size, and to readjust any discrepancies. Examination of four random sales days revealed that, whereas the other branch stores averaged 4.5 recording errors per day, the Jefferson City store averaged 9 recording errors per day over the same period. (See Exhibit 9–3 for relative productivity estimates.)

Management also attempted to coordinate the stores with inter-company store transfers of merchandise. The company's purchaser relies heavily on reports from the manufacturers' representatives on which items are selling well, so he would determine each store's requirements and make allocations as he saw fit. Imbalances between local supply and demand required special shipping arrangements between branches, causing both delays and unnecessary expenses. Although the other stores averaged 7.5 such transfer requests per week, the Jefferson City branch made 11.5 inter-store transfer requests per week.

Special order requests also boosted costs. Generally under $50 each, every special order requires 15 minutes of processing time, both going out and coming in. In addition, costs add up for shipping and handling, telephone, administration, errors—and occasionally the cost of a customer failing to pick up a special order. As a result, management is considering instituting a service charge for special orders, or perhaps offering a discount to customers willing to switch preference toward items in stock.

EXHIBIT 9–2 OUTDOOR OUTFITTERS, LTD.
Organization Chart

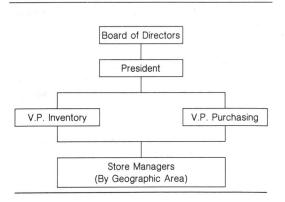

EXHIBIT 9–3   OUTDOOR OUTFITTERS, LTD.
Relative Productivity of Jefferson City
Store

	Jefferson City Store	Average For Other Branches
Number Part-Time Employees	9	7
Number Full-Time Employees	2	2
Annual Employee-Hours	7,000	6,000
Sales per Employee-Hour	$32	$24

But so far, the sales help is reluctant to either request deposits for special orders or to recommend substitutions.

The Jefferson City store sales projections for 1978 have been lowered by 10% and profits by 20% based on early figures (at a time when other local businesses expect increased sales of 10%). The store's president wrote a recent memo, excerpted here:

Our current sales staff at the Jefferson City store consists of young, part-time individuals. As such, they continue to demonstrate an independence not welcome considering our recent setbacks. They are arrogant and impolite to customers. Their work pace is slow, and they avoid responsibility, claiming an unfamiliarity with our established procedures. They are obviously unaware of the costs involved for their practices.

They continue to recommend items to our customers that they enjoy rather than attempt to sell what's on hand. This only leads to expensive imbalances in our inventory, interstore transfers, and special orders. In addition, they are sloppy and careless in their recording of items sold, further throwing off our inventory control. I really don't think they take this business seriously. Finally, they have demonstrated resistance to our improved system of operations and sabotage every new procedure we attempt to introduce. In short, they apparently do not have our interests at stake but only their own. With this in mind, I suggest we immediately replace the Jefferson City sales staff with more experienced full-time professional salesmen.

All these problems are now coming to a head. Management is contemplating further expansion by diversifying into such items as sportswear, cross-country skies, and even snowmobiles. In order to better implement this planned growth, management feels it needs to tighten the reins on the operations so that the various stores will be better coordinated. This need was particularly evident when the Jefferson City store introduced sports-shirts. Resentment from the sales help resulted in low sales, even though they might have earned a high commission on them.

10

How Sears Became a High-Cost Operator

In 1973, when Sears, Roebuck & Co. moved its headquarters, it seemed fitting that it was placed in the world's tallest building. Sears had always been associated with superlatives—biggest, best, and sharpest. The envy of its competitors, the huge retailer was second to none in its ability to ferret out innovative products and to get suppliers to provide them at the lowest cost. Its mail-order catalog was the largest of its kind, and its 860 stores, many of which were located in the first suburban shopping centers, represented the epitome of convenience. Its staff was huge—more than 400,000 employees—and where other retailers made do with just two buyers for a single line of merchandise, Sears could seek out sources with as many as 10.

But no one is envying the giant today. It has become the highest-cost mass merchandiser in the business, with general and administrative expenses siphoning off 29% of its sales dollars, compared with 23% for J. C. Penney Co. and 19% for K-Mart Corp. One competitor estimates that Sears would need to "weed out at least $100 million a year" to be competitive with low-cost retailers such as K-Mart. He guesses that, with Sears's "cumbersome" cost structure, Sears needs a 50% markup to make a profit on items that competitors need mark up only 35%.

Indeed, Sears's merchandising profit margin plunged to 2.2% in 1979 from 3.1% in 1976 and is expected to fall even further when 1980 figures are tallied. Its merchandising profits have slipped precipitously to $367 million in 1979 from $439 million in 1976 on stagnant annual sales of about $17 billion in the same period. In the first nine months of 1980, earnings plunged an additional 80% from the same period in 1979 on sales of $12 billion. Further, its credit-card operations lost $8.1 million in the first nine months of 1980. Wall Street has graded this performance by pushing the stock near its 20-year low.

TRIAL AND ERROR

Indeed, the only bright spots in an otherwise dismal scene are Sears's insurance

Reprinted from the February 16, 1981, issue of *Business Week* by special permission, copyright © 1981 by McGraw-Hill, Inc.

and real estate operations, areas that have little to do with the company's traditional retailing business. As if to underline the despair over its core business, last year Chairman Edward R. Telling reorganized Sears into a semiholding company, in effect divorcing himself from the actual management of the troubled retailing operation. The rationale was that the move would allow Telling, a merchandising executive, to concentrate on new growth opportunities. Says Telling, "Businesses with the greatest growth potential and most promise will undoubtedly be those that have first call on assets."

Still, Sears's retailing operations account for 68% of overall revenues, and Telling cannot cut them off at the pockets without creating a fatal wound. The new managers of the operations have invested in some significant changes, such as centralizing purchasing stations, early-retirement incentives, and store modernization. And Telling is demonstrating a willingness to enter new retail growth areas: on Jan. 22, Sears announced the opening of five freestanding business machine stores that are to be the front-runners of a network of stores geared to capitalize on the growing interest in electronic equipment from both business managers and home users.

Whether the stores are successful or not, they represent a newly focused approach to revitalizing Sears's merchandising operations and a distinct change from the series of erratic and seemingly unrelated moves that Sears's managers have made in seeking financial recovery. Indeed, Sears's apparent trial-and-error approach to managing its way out of trouble has given aid and comfort to its competitors. As K-Mart and Dayton Hudson's Target Stores chain solidified their reputations as savvy discounters, and specialty shops such as Herman's and Toys Я Us wooed customers with in-depth inventories of single lines, Sears lost customers. A sample of its scattershot approach includes the following:

1. An attempt to lure more affluent people into its solid blue-collar customer base by stocking expensive, high-fashion merchandise. Ignoring its own image as the provider of merchandise for America's heartland, Sears also missed one of its great opportunities: capitalizing on the back-to-nature trend characterized by the *Whole Earth Catalog*. The company neglected to use its mail-order catalog to compete with sellers of health foods and simple tools. Meanwhile, the affluent showed little interest in clothing or jewelry sporting the Sears label, and its traditional customers were turned off by the new and higher prices.

2. Sears then decided to woo the specialty stores' customers by stocking products in depth. Customers still saw no reason to buy sporting equipment at Sears rather than at Herman's, for one, and grew even more confused about why to buy at Sears at all. Sears wound up with expensive inventory nightmares and no increased sales. "We tried to be too many things to too many people and got our merchandise stretched too thin," recalls a former Sears buyer.

3. K-Mart's customers became the next target. In 1977, as Telling became chairman, Sears embarked on an only-too-successful price war, shooting sales up 16%. But when the euphoria died down, management discovered that the price cuts had destroyed profits. Earnings for the merchandise group in 1977 fell more than 10%.

4. Suppliers became another target of Sears's floundering tactics. Expecting that Sears's buying muscle would keep suppliers in line, Telling ordered a get-tough policy with the company's suppliers, informing them that Sears would no longer inventory products that were slow sellers in the stores. Instead, suppliers found new customers and expanded their lines of branded merchandise. For example, in 1972 Sears accounted for

61% of Whirlpool Corp.'s sales. In 1979, sales of refrigerators, washers, and other appliances Sears bought from Whirlpool to sell under the Kenmore name accounted for only 47% of Whirlpool's sales.

Of all Sears's bad decisions, the erosion of supplier relationships may be the hardest to turn around. "We historically romanced our vendors," says one former buyer. "But since Telling's tough remarks in 1978, vendors are scrambling for non-Sears business, and Sears ends up with products that are the same as everyone else's. Why should a consumer then buy a Sears product when it could buy a branded product?"

TOP HEAVY

At the root of most of these ill-conceived decisions lies an increasingly ponderous management structure. Sears until recently had an almost schizophrenic approach to management. It gave its field people virtual autonomy on promotional pricing, store size, product selections, and the like, yet it continually beefed up its corporate management staff in futile attempts to coordinate its diverse activities into a coherent whole. While the practice was relatively harmless during the days of unbridled growth, it created an almost knee-jerk reaction to solving problems: that of adding more managers. All through the 1970s, Sears continued to add executives, thus increasing its overhead at the same time it was superimposing a totally unwieldy hierarchy on the company.

For example, in 1976 Sears increased from five to nine its national merchandise groups, which handle buying, market development, promotion, and pricing. It created a new position, senior vice president of field, to coordinate the five territorial management teams that run Sears's vast network of stores and catalog houses. It

even created a national retail sales staff to act as a liaison between headquarters and the field.

"Sears management structures on top of management structures have grown into a hindrance to timely decisions and good execution as well as an enormous cost burden," contends Louis W. Stern, a marketing professor at Northwestern University. Former Sears executives admit they and their colleagues missed the boat. "We kept expecting our sales growth to resume the 10%-to-12% rate that we took for granted in earlier years," admits one high-ranking executive who just took early retirement. "We added more and more people ... and found ourselves with an overhead monster we couldn't control or support."

Making matters worse, while Sears was adding layers of management, its store-level workforce was eroding, and its customer service was going sour along with it. Throughout the 1960s and early 1970s, Sears was able to entice experienced salespeople with lucrative incentive programs based on shares of Sears stock. Once the stock started sinking, however, the incentive evaporated with it, and salespeople began to leave. "With a few exceptions, you just don't find knowledgeable and attentive salespeople at Sears anymore," notes an industry consultant. "When I take something back that doesn't work, the Sears clerks nowadays tend to argue with me instead of readily replacing the item."

Belatedly, but nonetheless forcefully, Sears is grappling with its problems. Early last year, Telling sold his fellow directors on a massive early-retirement program aimed at managers older than 55. By year end, 1,600 of the 2,400 eligible employees took advantage of the plan, which provides three years of half pay in addition to normal pension benefits. The new vice president of field retired, and his job was eliminated. At the same time, Sears consolidated its nine merchandising groups into seven and dropped six of its 41 buying departments and five of its 46 field administrative units. The southwestern territory, which employed more than 300 people, was shut down altogether. Even the national retail sales staff was appreciably reduced. All told, by mid-1980 Sears's merchandising staff decreased to 288,000 employees. According to Telling, the reduction in executive staff will save some $125 million annually, after a write-off of $45 million.

Perhaps most significant, those who were left, combined with those hired to fill vacant positions, are much younger than their predecessors. It is no coincidence. Last year, in an attempt to infuse a more youthful orientation into what had become a stodgy management team, Telling promoted Edward A. Brennan, a 46-year-old territory manager, over the heads of several senior colleagues to become the new chairman and chief executive of the merchandise group. Brennan has, in turn, surrounded himself with a staff that is about 10 years younger than the former manager's. "I think the group will be far less set in beliefs, far more willing to take risks—all the advantages that youth brings will surface," Telling predicts.

PENICILLIN SHOTS

Indeed, the new electronics stores represent a new risk, something that has been markedly absent from Sears. But the group's first priority still remains reducing operating costs. Last fall, for example, it quietly overhauled its time-worn merchandising format in which salespeople rang up sales at as many as 40 different locations in the store. Sears now uses centralized checkout stations in 4–6 clusters per store, an approach it expects will enable it to cut staff and to allow the remaining sales personnel to concentrate on serving customers.

This standardization of Sears stores is typical of what Brennan hopes to accomplish. "I feel very strongly that we need to

approach the business as though we are a single store," he says. Although he insists that he recognizes that different territories do require different approaches, Brennan claims the similarities outweigh the differences. "We're not going to put together a snowblower sales program for Miami," he explains, "but we need consistency. If there is a right way to do something, then that right way should be used in New York, Los Angeles, and Miami."

Despite his protestations, however, Brennan will have to walk a very fine line between standardizing policies and removing decision-making even further from the pulse of the market. Centralized decisions can easily backfire when they are applied across the board to diverse markets and operations. For example, Sears has brutally cut back on promotional programs and trimmed advertising expenses to $532 million in 1979 from $571 million in 1978. The move has cut costs on lagging items but has also made deep inroads into the sales of items that were doing well. "It was like a clinic where the doctor would find the first patient had an infection and immediately order up penicillin shots for 650 other patients in the waiting room," complains one buyer who saw profits evaporate in her department when she cut advertising.

Not surprisingly, morale on the part of formerly autonomous field managers fell to an all-time low. "When I started out working in a store, we could call a lot of the shots and felt a tremendous pressure to perform well," says one Sears veteran. "Now the temptation is to blame someone in the tower if customers don't show up. People tend to get lethargic if they don't have the responsibility for making something work."

CONSOLIDATION

Nonetheless, Brennan's apparent zeal for consolidation is rubbing off in the field, and not all managers are soured on it. William Bass, executive vice president, eastern territory, admits that his organization was a microcosm of the parent in its staffing procedures until 1977. "Then our gross margins started to suffer, and we stopped putting people on the payroll," he says. Instead, last year existing managers for the first time started a formal planning process, coupled with a microscope approach to costs. For example, even store engineers are now expected to prepare detailed plans of how to save energy costs on an item-by-item basis.

What is more, Bass is preparing to mirror Sears's corporate move last month to consolidate two departments—traffic, dealing with retail delivery, and logistics, which handled getting merchandise to stores or warehouses—by combining his own traffic and logistics departments. Similarly, Sears has established a stronger corporate advertising department that Bass hopes will result in his being able to consolidate his own cadre of seven separate advertising staffs into a single, much smaller unit. "We've quit talking about headquarters and field, and now we're talking about Sears, about one program," he says.

Whether all field people will react with Bass's enthusiasm will probably rest on the success of Brennan's communications approach. Last fall Brennan staged a series of two-day meetings that for the first time in 30 years put Sears's top 125 corporate buyers in the same room with more than 1,000 key field people, including every store manager. Brennan himself conducted the meetings and brought along one of Sears's latest "recruits," actress Cheryl Tiegs of the new Sears Cheryl Tiegs signature line. Even some of Sears's crustier veterans claim the meetings generated some badly needed enthusiasm. For employees who could not attend, Brennan had parts of the meetings videotaped. Brennan also taped a separate message in which he made a pitch for salespeople to "act like you're happy the customer is there" and for store manage-

ment to recognize that there is a "whole different world [of competition] out there selling our kinds of goods to our kinds of customers."

POLISHING ITS IMAGE

But the biggest challenge facing Sears is to sharpen its fuzzy and much-tarnished image. Advertising and store displays are a vital route to accomplish this, and Brennan has turned responsibility for unifying them over to Robert E. Wood, II, aged 42, former manager of the home improvements merchandising group and grandson of General Robert Wood, the legendary head of Sears from 1928 to 1957. Wood intends to centralize the planning of local advertising as well as develop integrated national campaigns in Chicago.

Although Wood will make most of the campaign decisions, he insists that store managers will still have reasonable autonomy to promote specific items that sell well in their areas. "We have to integrate national advertising with local plans or run the risk of overkill on certain items and neglect of others," he concedes. In the past, Wood notes, local managers often interpreted plans for a national ad on a given product to mean that it is a high-priority item and should be promoted locally as well. They would thus spend local dollars on a message that was already getting to most customers. "We can't afford to duplicate what we do," he says.

But the jury is still out on whether Brennan will be able to get the proper blend of cost cutting and aggressive image rebuilding, of centralization and decentralization, of youth orientation and experience. Observers are unanimous in saying he faces a Herculean task. "Sears's reason for being was its exclusive products," says Ira Quint, a former Sears merchandising manager. "Expense controls don't give you a reason for being." And they do not attract customers, note other Sears watchers. "The com-

pany has positioned itself in such a nebu-
lous way that I'm not sure the consumer
wants to hear from Sears anymore," suggest Northwestern's Stern. Robert Kahn, a
retailing consultant and director of Wal-
Mart Stores, sums up: "Sears forgot its primary purpose is to please the customer by
stocking the right goods and sticking by its
principle of satisfaction guaranteed. Those
things will be hard to regain."

11

Bennett Association

In mid-October 1981 as Michael Silva reviewed his management plans for the Bennett Association, he wondered about all he needed to accomplish. Having been CEO for less than 2 weeks, he felt he needed to make some significant changes in the companies that formed the Bennett Association. He wanted to have a clear picture of his strategy before he began, because he would need to implement the changes as quickly as possible. Despite having worked with the company for six months as a consultant, Michael was unsure whether the actions he was considering would be sufficient to turn the company around. Developing suggestions as a consultant and implementing them as a CEO were two entirely different things!

Part of the problem, he believed, was the very nature of the company he now ran. A group of traditional, family-owned companies, the Bennett Association had developed a strong, conservative, even paternalistic culture, which could make it resist adapting to changing situations. Several members of the Bennett family still worked at the various Bennett companies, including three as presidents of the paint and glass business, the leasing company, and the car rental agency. Perhaps Michael's most important concern was Wallace F. Bennett, for twenty-four years the U.S. Senator from Utah and current chairman of the Bennett board. Although the Senator had pledged his support to Michael, clearly the Senator's primary allegiance was to the company he had guided for 50 years, and to the 200 family members for whom it provided a source of income.

The Association needed change, however. The banks had made that much evident when they demanded that an outside president be brought in to manage the Association. For the last four years, the Bennett companies had lost money, and this trend was continuing in 1981. Michael's major concern was whether the tradition-bound Bennett family would accept the fundamental changes necessary to save the company.

This material was prepared by Paul McKinnon, Assistant Professor of Business of Business Administration and Elizabeth Bartholomew. All rights reserved, 1983, by the Sponsors of the Colgate Darden Graduate School of Business Administration, University of Virginia, Charlottesville, Virginia.

Another consideration was how many of the changes he should implement before his six week vacation began on December 1. A three-month delay might result in even larger losses. On the other hand, if he wasn't there to push for the changes, staff resistance could undermine implementation of his strategy.

HISTORY OF THE BENNETT ASSOCIATION

The Bennett Association was organized in 1917 as a Massachusetts trust, to function as a holding company responsible for the financial interests of the trust beneficiaries—the more than 200 descendants of John F. Bennett. The decendants received income from the trust according to the number of shares they held, which were similar to stock certificates. The decision-making authority rested with a Board of Trustees composed of family members. No nonfamily member could own shares.

Until 1983, Bennett, Paint and Glass, originally a grain and feed store known as Sears and Liddle, (which dated from 1882) was the primary source of the Association's income. John F. Bennett had joined the company in 1884 and in 1900 he bought out the owners to save the store from bankruptcy and changed the name to Bennett's.

The company soon became profitable and began to manufacture paint in 1904. As profitability continued, the physical plant doubled over the next 20 years. In 1920, John F.'s son, Wallace, a graduate of the University of Utah, joined the growing company. In that year Bennett's also entered the retail glass business.

Wallace was given increasing responsibility for the store's operations. By the mid-1920s he was running the entire manufacturing and sales functions. His brother Harold, two years his junior, saw little opportunity for himself in the family business, and he began a career at ZCMI, a large department store chain in Utah. However,

Harold retained a seat on the Board of Directors.

In 1932 a struggle for control of the company after the death of one of John F. Bennett's brothers ended with John F. narrowly retaining control. However, he became increasingly dependent upon his son Wallace, to make day-to-day decisions. Although John F. Bennett remained president until his death in 1938, Wallace effectively ran the company.

During the next 10 years, under Wallace's guidance, the company not only survived the Depression but opened 4 new branches. During that period, Wallace developed a process that radically changed the paint industry. Until that time, all paint was tinted in the factory, with only 8–12 colors available to consumers. Dealers carried large inventories of the few colors in a variety of sizes. Although some experiments had been made with premeasured tubes of tint that could be added to basic white paint by the dealers to create varied colors, the process had met with limited acceptance.

Expanding on this idea, Wallace hired an interior decorator who created 3,000 distinct colors of paint by mixing tints. In 1935, Wallace decided to distribute 1,320 colors, launching "Colorizer"—the nation's first controlled tinting system. With this new system, paint dealers could carry much lower inventories. Using white paint as a base, dealers could add specific amounts of pigment to create a previously unavailable spectrum of colors. In 1949, Bennett organized Colorizer Associates as group of regional paint manufacturers to promote the system nationally. These companies paid Bennett's royalties in exchange for tints and color cards. In 1981 Bennett's still owned and operated Colorizer Associates, although it represented a small stream of income.

In the late 1930s, Wallace expanded and diversified the association by acquiring a local Ford franchise—Bennett Motor Company—of which he became president.

In 1949, when he became president of the National Association of Manufacturers headquartered in New York, Wallace turned the business over to his brother, Richard (12 years younger than Wallace) who had worked in the company for some time. In 1950, after his stint as NAM president, Wallace returned to Utah to reassume control of Bennett's. Since Richard was reluctant to step down, Wallace, at the urging of several friends, chose to run for the U.S. Senate. He won and held the seat for four terms.

Under Richard's leadership, the Bennett Association continued to grow in profits and revenues. Although the Ford Franchise was sold in 1967, the Association retained two spin-off businesses: Bennett Leasing, which was involved in all types of automotive, truck, and equipment leasing, and a National Car Rental franchise at the Salt Lake City airport. In 1976, an advertising company, Admix was created to meet the promotional requirements of the Bennett Association and other Salt Lake City businesses.

After Richard's unexpected death in 1976, operating control of the Bennett companies fell to Wallace (Wally) G. Bennett, the Senator's oldest son. Although Richard had been formally president only of Bennett's, Paint and Glass, he had exercised strong, if informal, control over the other companies. When Wally assumed control, he focused all his attention on Bennett Paint and Glass, allowing the other company presidents freedom to manage their own operations. Although they still shared a common board of directors, the companies became increasingly independent, and each maintained control of its own finances. (See Exhibit 11–1 for a partial family tree)

Serving with the Senator on the Board of Directors in 1981 were his brother Harold, by then Chairman of the Board of ZCMI, nephews Richard K. Winters and Kenneth Smith, and nephew-in-law Donald Penny. Voting power was unequally distributed with the Senator having three votes, Harold, two, and the others, one each.

FINANCIAL SITUATION

Many internal and external factors contributed to the financial problems that the Bennett companies had faced since 1976. The Arab oil embargo and unprecedented

EXHIBIT 11–1 FAMILY MEMBERS IN THE BENNETT ASSOCIATION

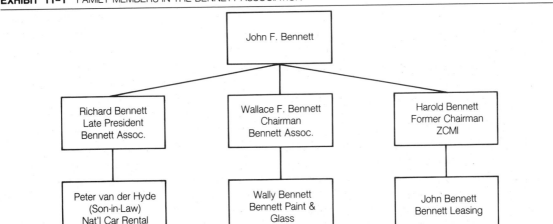

levels of inflation had driven the material costs higher and higher. However, to remain competitive, the paint company for example, could not raise prices at a rate that would compensate for these increases. Compounding this problem was the lack of strong, central financial controls. Richard had been familiar with the financial needs of the various businesses, and had relied on his experience to notice any expenses that appeared out of line. The weakness of this piecemeal control system and lack of centralized budget became painfully apparent, however, only when Wally assumed control. He was inexperienced with financial controls, and could not convince his managers to institute a company-wide budget.

As a result of these and other factors, in 1976 the Bennett Association suffered its first loss in over 100 years, and it had continued to lose increasing amounts in successive years. In 1981 the anticipation of a $3.2 million loss on revenues of $28 million precipitated the bank's demand that an outside CEO be hired.

When Michael Silva became President, the Bennett Association included Bennett Leasing, Bennett Paint and Glass, National Car Rental, and Admix. The first three of these generated the majority of revenues and were headed by a member of the Bennett family. Each of the four was in a different market, however, and faced different challenges. (See Exhibit 11–2)

Despite the five years of operating losses, the Bennett financial situation was not without its bright spots. The Association owned more than $12 million in unencumbered assets, including 8 acres of prime industrial land in Salt Lake City, various stocks and securities, the buildings and manufacturing facilities, and stores in Utah, Nevada and Idaho. In addition, the Bennett name was recognized and respected throughout the region.

EXHIBIT 11–2   ORGANIZATION CHART OF BENNETT ASSOCIATION

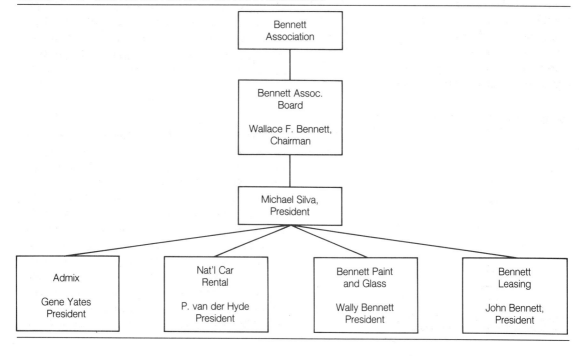

THE BENNETT COMPANIES— INDUSTRY AND COMPANY BACKGROUND

Bennett Paint and Glass

In 1981, the paint and coatings industry was widely dispersed and included nearly 1,200 producers. Half of all the paints, varnishes and lacquers sold covered buildings, predominantly houses. The second largest primary market was automobile and other original equipment manufacturers, which used a third of the coatings produced. The remaining share of the market went to special purpose coatings, which were high performance coverings used to prolong equipment life in such industries as petroleum and chemicals. Forecasts over the next 10 years indicated that this segment would be the fastest growing in the coatings industry.

Building paint sales were seasonal, peaking in the spring and summer, and closely tied to the construction industry. Since 1979 the depressed housing and automobile markets had caused a slump in paint sales (Exhibit 11–3—paint shipments). In addition to the decline in new home construction, the recession had hurt sales in the large "repainting" market, since people could put off painting their homes. Recovery in the paint industry lagged that of the construction industry because coatings are applied toward the end of home building.

Employing a total of 345 people, Bennett's Paint and Glass was the most well-known of the Bennett companies and traditionally, the most successful. Since the advent of the "Colorizer" concept in the 1930s, Bennett's had dominated the paint business in Utah and Idaho. Bennett's original store on First South St. was well remembered by Salt Lake City residents, even though it had long since changed hands and now housed a dress shop. A well-established and prominent Salt Lake City business, Bennett's high visibility within the community nevertheless seemed disproportionate to its size.

As elsewhere, the paint and coatings market in Utah was fragmented and competitive. Neither Bennett's nor any of its major competitors (Fuller-O'Brien, Howells, Pittsburgh Paint & Glass, and Sears) had much more than a 10 percent share of commercial and consumer sales. Estimates indicated that Bennett's, with over $1 million in consumer sales, outsold Sears in this area.

The manufacturing, warehousing, distribution and leasing operations of the Paint and Glass business were located on an 8-acre parcel of land on 23rd South in Salt Lake City. Topped by the Colorizer trademark, a bold spectrum of colors, Bennett's light-green, 9-story warehouse dwarfed all other buildings in the area and was easily visible from the nearby freeway. Under the same roof were the paint-manufacturing and the glass-tempering operations and one of Bennett's 14 retail outlets.

Representative of all the Bennett's stores, the Salt Lake City outlet carried a complete line of Bennett's paints, along with painting supplies, and bathroom and lighting fixtures, and a variety of sample windows. Windows were made to order for both walk-in customers and private contractors. Bennett's also bid on window contracts offered by large, national construction com-

EXHIBIT 11–3 PAINT, VARNISH AND LACQUER TRADE SALES 1971–1981 (millions of gallons)

Year	Sales
1971	431
1972	451.5
1973	424
1974	474.7
1975	451.5
1976	473.5
1977	486.2
1978	512.3
1979	571.3
1980	529.5
1981	504.9

Sources: U.S. Department of Commerce, Bureau of the Census, Kline Guide to the Paint Industry, 1981.

panies, although they had recently had difficulty securing contracts.

Branch and Outlet Sales Each Bennett retail outlet in Utah, Nevada and Idaho employed between 10 and 20 people. Dealers reported to an area manager, who then reported to a sales vice-president in Salt Lake City. In addition to the Bennett owned branches, salesmen visited 200–300 independent hardware stores that stocked Bennett's paint. Only about 20 percent of these stores generated the majority of all sales made through this channel. Salesmen were assigned to a specific geographical district, received a car and an expense account, and were paid on a commission basis.

Captive dealers purchased paint from Bennett at cost and then used a 50 percent markup to determine retail price. The dealers then either sold the paint to customers at full price or applied a variety of trade discounts. For example, depending upon the volume of business, contractors purchased supplies for as little as 10 percent above dealer cost. Each dealer's performance was evaluated by sales volume.

Manufacturing Bennett manufactured a whole line of paints, including both latex and oil-based brands. The manufacturing facility included a research department (experimenting with different additives to improve product quality) and a maintenance staff of three full-time and two part-time people who kept the operation running smoothly. Productivity for the facility was 1969 gallons per man per month in 1981, well below industry average. (See Exhibit 11–4)

As president, Wally Bennett had added both the huge new warehouse and a modern tempering furnace which gave Bennett's state-of-the-art technology. The warehouse on 23rd South measured 80′ × 80′ × 80′, and merchandise was arranged along high corridors serviced by modern forklifts which moved both vertically and horizontally. Thirty-nine employees working in three shifts staffed the warehouse. The morning shift filled the "will call" orders from the previous day, the afternoon shift stored the morning's paint production, and the night shift filled dealer orders.

Three unions represented workers in the plant: the Glaziers, the Allied Glass Workers, and the Steel Workers. In June 1981 the unions called a strike for a wage increase. For several weeks management successfully ran the plant, and many felt that Bennett's was on the verge of winning, but the unions compromised on a contract that provided a 5 percent wage increase each year for three years. Although some managers wanted to hold out, Wally Bennett decided to accept the compromise.

Management Years of profitability had lulled most of Bennett's highly tenured employees into a strong sense of security. Both the managerial and production staffs seemed unresponsive to calls for financial improvement and appeared unaware of the toll the economy was taking on the company's income statement.

A particular problem had been the attitude of Jack Nielson, former executive vice-president of Bennett's. Jack Stevens, vice-president of finance for the Bennett Association, commented on how Nielson's recent retirement had solved some of the problems:

EXHIBIT 11–4 PAINT INDUSTRY PRODUCTIVITY 1970–1980

Year	Average gals. produced/man/month
1970	1737
1971	1931
1972	1946
1973	1959
1974	2030
1975	2154
1976	2132
1977	2184
1978	2144
1979	2371
1980	2260

Source: Kline Guide to the Paint Industry, 1981.

Jack was a V.P. of production and he had been something of a favored son of Richard. He was quite egotistical and difficult to work with at times. Anyone who opposed him created a lot of problems, since this guy would always lose his temper. Because of that and Wally's style, he seemed to exercise more dominance over Wally than any of the other people. Wally always appeared to be rather cautious with this guy and would listen to him more than anyone else. Unfortunately, this guy didn't always have the best business insights. He was an engineer by trade and had been running the production operation, but he was promoted to Executive Vice President and began to have a bigger say in the way the rest of the business was run. As a result it was often very hard to get new ideas into motion.

Jack Stevens had also wanted to get the company to use some form of budgeting.

I know that budgeting is an excellent tool for management, but to others at Bennett's it is just an irritating accounting system. I provide each cost center with a history of their expenses for the current year, so all they have to do is put in a new number. The whole thing falls on deaf ears. When DeVon Johnson (currently VP of Marketing) came on board, he had an interest in it, but he can't implement it. Wally, in fact, came to me one day with a figure that represented the expenses that we would have for the coming year and asked me to calculate the amount of sales we would have to generate to cover those expenses. Jack O'Brien had said that we couldn't cut expenses without adversely affecting our sales function, so that number became our sales target for the year.

Bennett Leasing

The equipment leasing industry dated from the 1950s, when tax credits and accelerated depreciation incentives for investment enhanced the popularity of equipment leasing. The industry experienced explosive growth in the 1960s, particularly in the transportation area (trucks, autos, airplanes, railroad cars), office and information-processing equipment, and industrial equipment and facilities. In 1981 leasing re-mained one of the fastest growing industries in the U.S., with over 1,800 firms writing agreements for billions of dollars of equipment. Not only the number, but the value of transactions had increased substantially, facilitated in part by the development of leveraged leasing. (Exhibit 11–5 describes leasing trends) Inflation, risky business cycles and high interest rates had forced firms of all sizes to turn to leasing.

Firms leased equipment for a variety of reasons, primarily to take advantage of tax credits and to have more flexible financing. Many small firms leased because they lacked sufficient capital to support debt financing of equipment purchases. Leasing companies could take advantage of certain tax benefits resulting from accelerated depreciation and investment tax credits and pass the benefits on, through reduced rates, to firms that couldn't. Differences in capital costs to a leasing company and an operating company encouraged leasing. Operating companies also gained more financial flexibility as leasing extended the length of financing, allowed constant-cost financing, and conserved working capital. Leases could be tailored to the needs of the lessee, such as those in seasonal businesses, and since few or no restrictive covenants were required, as with debt financing, firms could conserve existing lines of credit.

In addition to the numerous quantifiable benefits, leasing reduced the risk of equipment obsolescence, particularly in an era of rapid technological change, and often was simply more convenient than borrow-and-purchase options. The convenience factor

EXHIBIT 11–5   EQUIPMENT LEASING GROWTH

Year	Equipment Cost Added (000's)
1979	8,039,000
1980	10,214,400
1981	13,374,700

Source: American Association of Equipment Lessors 1982 Survey of Accounting and Business Practices World Leasing Yearbook, 1982.

was particularly influential in automobile leasing. While automobile purchases were down throughout the country in 1981, the leasing population remained stable and was expected to grow. Projections indicated that by 1985, over 40 percent of cars purchased would be lease-financed, double the 1981 lease base.

With the growing acceptance of the equipment leasing concept, there arose increasing demand for specialized leases and fast, low-cost maintenance plans. These trends, along with inflationary pressures, were forcing small leasing companies to tighten and streamline operations in order to compete in this highly competitive marketplace.

The Bennett Leasing Company was a holdover from the Bennett Association's expansion into the automobile industry in the 1930s. Senator Bennett retained his role as president of the franchise throughout his presidency of NAM and his Senate terms. He had turned over operating control to a resident manager, and by 1967, when Ford announced that it didn't want absentee franchise owners, Bennett decided to sell. Although it could have resisted Ford's demands, the Association sold the franchise, retaining the car and truck leasing and truck maintenance operations. These operations, headed by John Bennett, Harold's son, constituted the leasing company when Michael Silva arrived.

Management   Tall, laconic, and thoughtful, John Bennett bore a strong physical resemblance to other members of the family, especially his cousin Wally. John liked to explore thoroughly each business decision made by the company. His analytical style and careful consideration of each issue led many around him to observe that he might have been a good college professor. He enjoyed the people with whom he worked and felt that his organization was strong, stable and customer-oriented.

By 1981 Bennett Leasing had 35 employ-

ees and had had as many as 40 at one time. Although willing to lease nearly any type of equipment, automotive and truck leases to major fleet customers, small businesses, and individuals provided the bulk of the revenues. In 1981, 1,800 autos and light trucks were under lease.

Like many leasing companies using floating rate leases, Bennett Leasing lost money between 1979 and 1981 because of sustained high interest levels. Despite the increasing losses, neither the sales staff nor management appeared to be concerned. John Bennett commented:

When Mike (Silva) took over the business, I realized that several changes needed to be made. I know that Michael is looking at the trucking business because it has lost money for us over the past several years, but I have some misgivings about that. I've been here since 1954 and I've noticed that the trucking business is the least interest-sensitive business that we have.

About half of the leasing company's employees worked in the trucking side of the business. The truck leasing segment was growing along with the rest of the leasing industry, increasing the number of units in service by 31% and revenues by 22% in ten years. At Bennett Leasing, many of the employees were experienced mechanics, involved in the maintenance operation. John added:

Mike is wondering what to do with the people in our company. He just doesn't know them as well as I do. There are some of them who might be a bit mediocre, but they have some skills and experience that would be very hard to replace. Many of these people are good friends of mine, and some of them have been here longer than me. We probably need some change in the climate, but you also need stability, experience and knowledge. We don't want to get rid of expertise.

National Car Rental

The car rental industry began in 1916, but the most rapid growth had occurred since 1960. Although 8 to 12 corporate systems could be considered the leading national firms in the business as many as 5,000 independent firms and system licensees operated on a local or regional basis. By 1981, 40 million car rental transactions generated over 3 billion dollars in revenues. The current 19 percent rate of growth was predicted to continue through 1981 because of the high cost of car ownership, the price of gasoline, and increasing reliance on "fly/drive" forms of business and vacation travel (Exhibit 11–6).

The overwhelming majority of rental car service consumers were business travelers, and between 75 and 85 percent of rental car revenues were generated through rentals made at airports. More than 90 percent of car rental fleets were rented to commercial users.

The National Car Rental franchise at the Salt Lake City Airport became part of the Bennett Motor Company in 1959. The franchise had nearly 400 cars, and in a good week, all were rented. Closely tied to tourism and business travel, the business was somewhat cyclical. In 1981 the winter snowfall in the Salt Lake City area had not been plentiful, and there was some concern throughout the area about the impact of this situation on the local economy. In addition, after Budget Rent-A-Car started a premium give-away to increase business in October 1981, the other major rental companies, including National, became involved in a premium war. As a result, National Car Rental Corporation eventually lost $15 million and the local Bennett owned franchise dropped from third to

fourth in its share of the Salt Lake area market.

On the other hand, Salt Lake City had been tabbed the second fastest growing city of the 1980's in the U.S., and Western Airlines had plans to make Salt Lake City its new hub of operations, which would result in expansion of the airport. Many corporations were moving there, which increased the level of business travel. All these developments bode well for the local car rental franchise and the local economy and seemed like positive indicators for the Bennett franchise.

Management   Peter van der Hyde, President of the company, had run the franchise for many years. Born in Holland, he had married one of Richard Bennett's daughters and then come to work for the Bennett Motor Company before it was sold. Peter worked closely with Richard until the latter's death, and many felt that if Richard had outlived his brothers, Peter might have been his successor. Tall and tanned, he still spoke with a slight Dutch accent.

I try to run a tight ship here. I feel a moral obligation to the stockholders and I think it's paid off. Our profit has gone up every year since I took over in 1976. In this business it's very easy to lose customers and hard to get them back. I think you need three things to be successful here: good financing, good luck and common sense.

Peter operated a lean, efficient business with no intermediate levels of supervision. Although concerned about the company as a whole, Peter was proudest of his own operation. Even when the other Bennett companies were losing money, the National franchise was always in the black. As one observer noted, "That company does nothing but generate cash. The nature of the work is relatively routine, so they can pay low wages, and all transactions are in cash or by credit cards."

EXHIBIT 11–6 CAR RENTAL GROWTH —SELECTED YEARS

Year	Units in Service	Revenues (millions)
1970	319,000	936
1972	341,000	1,048
1978	448,000	2,303
1980	512,000	3,349

Source: American Car Rental Association, 1983.

Admix

Admix was the smallest of the Bennett companies, employing only five people. Most of its business was in developing commercials and the operation stayed small by contracting out much of the work. Before coming to Admix, President Gene Yates had worked for several ad agencies managing large accounts, including Western Airlines and Rockwell International. Under his leadership Admix had been profitable since its founding—unaffected by the depressed economy. It was not generally known that Bennett owned Admix; the company had deemphasized the relationship so as not to reduce the number of potential clients.

There was little interaction between Admix and the other companies owned by the Bennett Association. Michael Silva noted, "No one has paid much attention to Gene. He was making money before I came, and he seems to be doing okay now."

BENNETT ASSOCIATION: KEY MANAGEMENT PERSONNEL

Wally Bennett—Paint and Glass

The eldest son of the Senator, Wally Bennett, after serving in the military for 3½ years, had spent his entire career with Bennett's. Like his father, he had attended the University of Utah and had then held a variety of positions at Bennett's Paint and Glass, (most recently director of personnel) before taking control of the company in 1976. As were many family members, he was active in church and civic affairs.

Wally was tall, with greying hair, and had a patrician air about him. In his mid-fifties, he was very popular around the Salt Lake area, and most people who met him found him very agreeable and enjoyed his company. Extremely sensitive to the needs and feelings of others in the business, he would often postpone decisions that might upset his staff until he could contact all the parties involved. He would gather his staff together to try to resolve many of the problems facing the company through consensus decision making. If the group could not arrive at a decision, he would often put the issue off until a later meeting, where it could be discussed more thoroughly.

He had inherited from his father a strong concern for the welfare of the company's employees, and he always tried to act in a way that reflected that concern. Although he maintained a high regard and respect for his father, Wally tended not to consult him on most business decisions. He relied mostly on his 25 years of experience in the company and the expertise of his staff. While he could have exercised more control over the other Bennett companies, as did Richard before him, he chose to devote himself almost exclusively to the Paint and Glass business.

DeVon Johnson—Executive V.P., Bennett's Paint and Glass

DeVon Johnson was relatively new to the company. Immaculately and elegantly dressed, he tended to speak rapidly and directly, generating tremendous energy. Before coming to Bennett's, he spent 35 years in the paint business with Fuller-O'Brien, where he rose from a stockboy to vice-president of the company. Adhering to the management philosophy of "putting in a little more than you expect to get back," DeVon dramatically improved Fuller's sales and profits in each position he had held. He was the youngest branch manager in the history of the company. Eventually, because of the breadth of his sales and operations experience, Fuller began to depend on him to turn around problem areas.

DeVon resigned from Fuller-O'Brien for family reasons and contacted Bennett's about a job shortly thereafter. He had been hired as vice-president of marketing, and by September 1981, he had replaced Jack Nielson, who retired, as executive vice-president of the company.

DeVon had a full slate of objectives for the company. First, he felt it should become more customer-oriented, particularly in responding to complaints more quickly. Second, he was concerned about plant productivity. Although fully staffed, plant output was below industry average. Third, DeVon wanted to increase Bennett's market share:

I'd love to run a company ten times this size. I don't like to sit still. I can't wait to get to work in the morning. I know that I'm impatient, but I've never been a flash in the pan. We're still learning here, and some of the people don't know what they can do yet. In the morning, I get here before 7:30, and I work through the day. I usually don't even leave the office for lunch, because I bring along a bag lunch that I can eat right here at my desk. I got used to that in other jobs and I don't want to change now.

DeVon was concerned about the constraints he felt in meeting the challenges facing the company. Since it was a family-owned, traditional business, led by the son of the chairman, implementing major changes would probably mean going back to the Board repeatedly.

The lack of concern shown by others in the company about the growing losses also puzzled him. Despite all the problems, he didn't believe people were changing their approaches to the problems. Also, although he liked Wally and enjoyed working with him, he wasn't sure whether Wally's deliberate, consensus-oriented style was what Bennett's needed to pull them out of this slide.

The Senator

Senator Wallace F. Bennett was an active Board chairman. Known throughout the company and the family as "The Senator," he provided continuity to a company that had had three presidents in five years. His energy, creativity, and leadership skills served him well, not only in running the companies, but also in his successful ca-

reers as president of NAM and as a U.S. senator. Throughout his terms in Congress, the Senator had kept his post as Chairman of the Board, and had kept abreast of company activities.

Eighty-two at the time Michael Silva became President, the Senator remained physically and mentally active. His daily routine included long walks (up to six-and-a-half miles) and a full schedule of activities at his office on the second story of the original Bennett's building on First South. He was a prominent and respected figure in the city, involved in civic and church affairs.

The Senator was ordinarily modest about his many accomplishments, but exhibited a justifiable pride about the Bennett's early years, under his presidency:

We were bold then. We dominated the paint business in Utah. When we developed the Colorizer concept, everyone told us it wouldn't work. But overnight, we revolutionized the paint business.

I feel very close to Mike because we can give each other ideas. I think I have been able to suggest a few things that Mike has agreed with, and I know that he has come up with a lot of ideas on his own that I thought were great. I think we can be a good team.

I wonder about the future of the Bennett Association. Within the company, there has been a real political struggle for power since Richard's death. I think we needed an outsider.

Michael Silva

Michael grew up in Hawaii and attended Brigham Young University, where he was active in school politics and competed successfully in several intercollegiate and national debate tournaments. Upon graduation, he enrolled in a masters program in Organizational Behavior at BYU, where his quick, analytical mind and remarkable verbal abilities soon distinguished him. Generally, Michael had gotten along well with the faculty and peers, but at times appeared impatient and aloof. In an argument or discussion, Michael's debating prowess made him an intimidating opponent. Therefore, although he had completed 95 percent of the degree requirements and had grades well above the class average, several confrontations with faculty members caused him to leave the program shortly before graduation.

Michael was 30 years old when he took over as President of the Bennett Association, but had a wealth of experience behind him. After leaving BYU, he had been through a series of remarkable job changes, each of which gave him more responsibility. He began as an Assistant to the President of Skaggs Foods, but after a year, moved back to Hawaii to take a staff job as a corporate planner at State Savings and Loan, a large Hawaiian operation with assets of $500 million, 16 branches, and over 300 employees. At the S & L, he worked his way up to a position as Assistant to the Chairman of the Board. After two years with State, he returned to the Intermountain West as manager of Peat, Marwick, Mitchell's bank consulting unit. While Michael was in this position, Warren Pugh, owner of Cummins Intermountain Diesel Company, asked Michael to come straighten out his banking problems, which were costing the company tens of millions of dollars. He was able to put Cummins on a sound financial footing, but only by laying off 70 percent of the work force. Michael then moved to Arthur Young, Inc., as manager of consulting services for the Salt Lake City office.

Michael began to work with the Bennett Association when it engaged the services of Arthur Young in late February 1981. In June 1981, the banks informed Bennett that, because of continued losses, they were going to call in their loans unless the company would agree to an outside CEO—a first in the history of the Association. Bennett then also asked Arthur Young to help them find someone who could make the company profitable once again.

Several candidates with impressive credentials were interviewed by the Senator and the Board. Although each candidate had felt that he could improve Bennett's position, they all agreed a complete turn-around would take at least five years. The Board (in particular, the Senator) were not impressed with the applicants. He finally said, "Gentlemen, I don't think we need to go outside and look for people to help us. I think we have the man right here who is best suited for the job."

In August 1981 Michael was offered the job, and after some negotiation, signed a three-year contract as CEO of what would be called Bennett Enterprises, a central management company that would control the various companies owned by the Bennett Association. He would begin his duties as CEO in early October, 1981.

Management Style Michael's office, located in the Bennett Leasing Company building, was pleasantly, if sparsely, decorated. His office and his secretary's office were separated from the leasing operation by a heavy, black, swinging door, referred to as the "Iron Curtain". Relatively small by executive standards, the office had few of the trappings that one might associate with a CEO. He did have a small computer, one of two he owned. A small, framed quotation immediately caught the eye of any visitor:

There is nothing more difficult to carry out, or more doubtful to success, nor more dangerous to handle, than to initiate a new order of things. For the reformer has enemies in all those who profit by the old order, and lukewarm supporters in all those who would support by the new order.

The existence of the Iron Curtain was significant. Michael was explicit about his non-open door policy. He was protective of his office time and went out of his way to make it difficult for people to find him. He believed that if people knew his time was valuable, and he was difficult to find, they were better prepared than otherwise when they did catch him. Besides, he felt his lack of availability often encouraged people to solve problems themselves.

He managed telephone calls with the same spirit. His secretary Dixie Clark screened all calls. Only those from his family or the Senator were allowed to come through immediately. For all other calls, he was "out of the office" or "in a meeting." Periodically, during the day, Michael would sort through the messages and returned the calls that seemed important. By the end of the day, message slips littered his desk.

When he entered the building, he would greet everyone cheerfully, at times almost playfully. He seemed genuinely pleased with those in the company who would banter with him.

That is something that I encourage. I like the atmosphere of mild sarcasm that we have created here. I encourage people to tease me because I get better information about how people are feeling. It's a type of informal communication.

Schedule   Michael's daily routine as CEO followed one of two patterns. In the first, he arose early, and arrived at the office at 5:00 or 6:00 a.m. He wrote, dictated correspondence, and planned until 8:00 or 9:00 when he began to see people and make calls. After lunch he went home to enjoy the rest of the day with his family. In the second pattern, Michael stayed home in the morning and helped prepare the children for school. He then arrived at the office around 10:00 a.m. and worked until lunch. After lunch he would remain at the office until around 3:00, when he went home to be with his family.

In the evenings, his schedule was less variable. He helped with dinner (he was an accomplished cook) and afterwards put the children to bed. Often he worked (usually on his own writing) from 10:00 p.m. until 1:00 or 2:00 a.m. He seldom needed more than four or five hours of sleep.

I have never worked one Saturday or one Sunday in my career. I don't think I have ever worked an eight hour day. I made a decision when I started to work that my family was always going to come first in my life. This is the first job that has offered me real flexibility. I found that I could easily become too involved with my work, but I don't want to. I work hard at keeping my family #1. I don't want my work to become my life. I really like the freedom that this job could offer me now. I like both the freedom and the money, but I probably wouldn't give up the freedom for the money. I want time to be with my family. Time, in fact, probably drives everything I do. I'm something of a time fanatic. Everything is driven by my time resource. I won't take on anything that will require any more of my time than I already give.

I don't think that it is any big deal to be a good manager. Most anyone could probably be a reasonable manager. The real question is whether you can do it differently. Can you do it in a way that doesn't eat up your life? Can you have an impact in your job, and still maintain a family life?

I think that there are three roles that have to be mastered in management. You need to know strategy, the culture, and the numbers. The problem that you generally find is that few people who are sensitive to issues like culture enjoy working with numbers. You can usually find people who like to do two of those roles, but not all three.

Silva Discusses the Company   After assuming control of Bennett Enterprises on October 1, 1981, Michael felt that he had a good understanding of how the company operated, but was unclear about which problems to attack first, which managers were reliable, and which approach he should take to making changes. He also knew that the six-week vacation he negotiated as a part of his contract was to begin soon, and he was unsure about initiating any major change only to have it sputter and die in his absence. Michael interviewed the key managers from each of the businesses and spent a considerable amount of time with the Senator. He wanted to have as much input as possible before he began to implement a plan.

He talked at length about the situation he faced:

When the company brought in all of the outside applicants for the job, they all took a strictly financial approach and said it would take at least five years to turn the company around. I don't think we have that much time, and I think we can do it in less than that. All of the other people they interviewed for this job said that it was a financial problem. I think the problem is as much cultural as it is financial.

Michael noted that employees at Bennett seemed to have an unwritten expectation that if they had a job with Bennett, they would never be laid off. Even during the Great Depression, no one in Bennett had been let go. Perhaps for this reason, even though the company was having severe financial troubles, there was a noticeable lack of concern among employees and managers about losing their jobs. They had made no special efforts to improve performance or productivity, or even to attract new customers. Some pressure had been put on the sales districts, but with limited response.

Commenting on his goals, Michael stated:

We're going to have a difficult time turning this around. Our biggest businesses are tied directly to the housing and automobile markets, and so we are going to have a hard time if this recession gets any worse.

We need to stress excellence—and making a profit in the long run. It's important to remember that all the variables that insure a profit in the long run are human resource variables. I want people to think they are the best. I will not stand for mediocrity. We should demand the absolute best from our people, but then pay them .

accordingly. Many companies try to pay their people the least amount possible and still keep them. I think that's crazy. I think you should pay them as much as possible to still make a profit. It makes a big difference in the way they think about themselves. More than anything, I think we should be strategy driven. We want to have revenues of $100 million by 1990.

I want to be a leader here. The difference between a leader and a manager is that a manager manages systems and a leader manages values. We need to stress new values, those that emphasize performance. I need to have the confidence of the people here, because when an organization doesn't sense that their leader can get them through a crisis, they lose their incentive.

One factor Michael worried about particularly was the reaction of members of the Bennett family to any changes he might make:

Part of my contract states that the Board cannot counteract my decisions. They can cancel my contract at any time, but I don't have to get their approval for any of my decisions, and they can't counteract what I decide. I don't think I have time for an educational process each time I make a decision. Decisions will have to be made in a hurry, and I don't have the time to go back and forth with the Board. I do stay in close contact with the Senator, though. He has been very helpful so far. I probably see him two times a week, but I talk to him at least once a day.

I like to define culture as the personality of a company, and so I think there are two ways to change that personality. The first is by long-term change, where you gradually work at some of the problem areas in the culture. The second is trauma, where you massively address the company problems.

Given its unique history, Michael was not sure which approach would be best for Bennett's.

12

Midwestern School of Business

Professor David Neal sat quietly in his brightly lit office at Midwestern School of Business. As Chairman of the Computer Committee at MSB, Professor Neal had been asked by the Dean to draft a recommendation outlining the course of action Midwestern should follow with regard to its word processing capability. Amidst recent technological advances, the array of alternatives facing Professor Neal and his committee seemed to be growing rather than shrinking. He knew that pressure was mounting to do something sooner rather than later, but it was not clear to him what the best alternative was. The Christmas holidays were fast approaching, and Professor Neal wanted to have some progress to report before the new year began.

BACKGROUND

Midwestern was part of a state university system that enjoyed a national reputation. The School of Business was a relatively new addition to the university but had it-self developed a growing reputation among applicants and recruiters nationwide. At the time of Professor Neal's concern, the School had been graduating students for 25 years and had grown to a faculty of 70 serving a student-body of about 600. The school maintained a variety of programs including undergraduate, graduate (both Masters and Doctorate), executive education programs, and a few professional institutes of both research and education.

The faculty offices were arranged on two, square floors in a modern-looking structure attached to the classroom wing. Thirty secretaries were dispersed throughout the building, but most of them were stationed in five "bays" situated at the corners of each floor. Some were assigned to specific programs or institutes, but most were assigned to work with from 3 to 5 teaching professors.

As at most academic institutions, the faculty at MSB were charged with a variety of tasks many of which demanded a great deal of writing. Faculty would collect data

This case was prepared by Associate Professor James G. Clawson as a basis for class discussion and not to illustrate effective or ineffective handling of an administrative situation. © 1982 by the Colgate Darden Graduate Business School Sponsors, the University of Virginia, Charlottesville, Virginia.

on a variety of topics, analyze those data, and publish the research in the form of working papers, monographs, articles, and books. The faculty also developed much of their own teaching materials, which included notes describing various managerial techniques, cases, and essays. Administratively, the faculty were often called upon to serve on various committees of the school; in the course of these duties, professors often had to draft reports of committee activities and conclusions. Most of these documents underwent from two to as many as eight to ten rewritings before they were deemed to be finished. These activities, of course, were in addition to the usual, voluminous correspondence.

THE WANG SYSTEM

About five years before Professor Neal's committee began considering the word processing issue, the school had installed a Wang word processing system on a lease basis for about $16,000 per year. The system was composed of one central processing unit, three high-speed letter-quality printers, and six terminals or work stations. One administrator noted:

We asked various departments in the school to identify their current and anticipated needs. We had several vendors come in and show us what they had and make recommendations. At that time we didn't know exactly what uses there would be, so we had lots of questions. The Wang people were most helpful: they talked to the professors and were the most responsive. We were the first school in the university with this kind of word processing system.

At first, not much happened. We assigned one person to work on the machine full-time and encouraged the secretaries to learn it and use it through a sign-up system. Some of them were standoffish, some were excited. Last summer, for instance, we had training scheduled for everyone, but many of them did not attend. But the more they work on it, the more excited they get. Plus, we get more faculty trying to use it. We have put

more materials on it in the last 12 months than we have in the last 5 years.

The Wang system worked well for some people and not so well for others. One professor used the system extensively and could be seen most days typing at one of the terminals or "ports" as they were called. This professor had more than two dozen cases, articles, and notes on the system. Some made no use of the system at all. In between were a number of professors whose secretaries used the system moderately.

The Wang system had some powerful pluses in its favor: It was a "dedicated" system; that is, it only did word processing and, hence, was designed with that function in mind. Its keyboard was arranged conveniently for accomplished typists, and most word processing functions could be executed in one or two keystrokes. The system was also fast; it took an operator no more than 10 to 15 seconds to load a disk and begin editing a particular document.

On the negative side, the system, as it was then configured, required that a secretary leave her office and go to a Wang port. This meant that, when working on large documents, a secretary could be away from her desk for hours at a time. Furthermore, since the number of ports was limited, secretaries had to sign up for terminal time, and ports were not always available when secretaries wanted them. One further problem was that the secretaries were not uniformly interested in working on the Wang or, apparently, any other word processing system. At one point, one secretary was overheard to say that she would rather quit than be forced to work on a word processor.

THE IBM DISPLAYWRITER

About the time that the MSB computer committee was formed and about a year before Professor Neal was asked to consider the word processing problem, the Director of the Executive Education programs was also beginning to feel the backlash from the overload on the Wang system. He had heard about a new dedicated word processor introduced by IBM called the Displaywriter, and he ordered one for use in Executive Programs on a one-year trial lease. The machine arrived, was set up, and was explained to the Executive Program secretaries. Despite repeated encouragement from the administrators of the program, the secretaries refused to use the new machine. They complained that the keystrokes required were cumbersome and difficult to remember. They also said that simple processes like calling up a file to edit took almost three times as long as it did on the Wang. During most of the trial lease period, the Displaywriter collected dust in the teletype room. At the end of the year, the Director asked IBM to remove the machine.

THE APPLE II INVASION

During this same, year-long period, the members of the computer committee were charged with managing the school's computer capabilities. The committee felt that the school should, as a leading school of business, be at or near the front of this rapidly growing and important field of knowledge. The committee split the school's interest in computers into three areas: administrative uses, academic uses, and staff uses. The first pertained to departments like admissions, placement, and executive programs that had particular needs. The second had to do with teaching students how to use and manage computers in a business setting, and with analyzing research data. The third related to secretarial applications like word processing and telecommunications.

After a review of the features and costs of a variety of micro-computer systems, the committee recommended to the Dean in the spring before the word processing mandate that the school purchase 30 Apple II Plus personal computers. This recommendation was carried out. Of the 30, 6 were assigned to float among the faculty for research and course development work. Admissions and placement received 1 each for administrative purposes and the remaining 22 were put into a newly constructed computer room for student use.

The committee recommended and the school purchased several software packages for use in the curriculum. The accepted word processing program was Screen Writer II[tm]. This package was relatively inexpensive ($129.00), as powerful as many dedicated systems, and, unlike several word processing packages, required no additional hardware in order to run on the Apple.

That same year, six faculty members purchased personal computers. Their interest in sharing learning on the computers, the committee's decision, and the low price had convinced all of them to buy Apples. Faculty in other parts of the university had also purchased personal Apples. Several of them formed an "Apple Users' Group," which met regularly to discuss different ways and means of using the Apples and software. As many as 50 people from all over campus attended these meetings. The applications ranged from word processing (in the medical lab) to statistical analysis (in engineering) to personnel reports (in administration).

APPLES AND WORD PROCESSING

With the Apples and Screen Writer in place at the School of Business, it was not long before people began trying them out for secretarial work. Two of the professors encouraged their secretaries to use the Apples for word processing. Professor Neal, himself, used Screen Writer regularly. He noted:

I have my own Apple at home. I can write much faster on the Apple, but I have to maintain the disks and files myself. I have to make the editing changes, and I'd prefer to have my secretary do it.

Initially, I put an Apple in my secretary's office so she could use it when the faculty was not. I spent one hour one day and had her do something. She didn't carry through and lost enthusiasm. She was happy it was moved out.

Another professor, John Arthur, had modified his personal Apple by adding several peripheral devices to the machine and purchased a relatively expensive software package. These modifications, including a Microsoft Z–80 card (which contains a separate 8-bit microprocessor that runs CP/M software), a Videx keyboard enhancer, an 80 column board, and Magic Wand software, cost about $1,000. He spent two days working with his secretary over the course of three weeks helping her learn the system. He said:

When I came here a year ago and realized how much paper we were processing over and over again, I was a little taken aback that we didn't have better systems for handling all of that volume. I felt guilty asking my secretary to type a manuscript for the sixth time. And sometimes there would be more typographical errors on the sixth draft than on the fifth one. It seemed very inefficient to me. I felt like we needed word processing and needed it immediately.

So, I put together this little system and bought a letter-quality printer to hook onto it. The cheapest one I could find then was $1,700, and it was very slow—15 characters per second. It would take 2 hours to print out a 30 page document, but it looked professional.

Since my secretary was working with other professors, I wasn't sure how they would respond to my asking her to learn this new system. I went around and talked about it with them, and they all said go ahead. Before long, the machine was in constant use and was beginning to show signs of wear and tear. I had been pressing everyone I could think of at the school for almost a year by then, trying to get some formal response and a school supported system, but it seemed to be low priority on most people's agendas. I felt constrained, too, because I couldn't use it at

home while it was in the office, so finally I packed it all up and carted it home. My secretary was upset, but I felt the School could see that it worked and that they needed to make a decision. I was tired of asking and getting no response, so I just retreated.

Professor Arthur's secretary later commented:

I had never learned word processing before, but had always been eager to. I thought it would add a lot to my job. And I wanted to learn something about the computers—not just which button to push. First of all, my professor sat down with me and taught me. I had a list of commands from the book; it was a good manual. And from there it was trial and error, more or less. When I had extra time, I would read in the manual about how to do different things. I took the manual home occasionally, too, to read over it.

It was amazing to me what I could do on the Apple; it was also a lot of fun. I really liked it. I found it easier than the Wang; that could have been a function of learning the Apple first, and then trying to go back to the Wang. Both were much better than just the regular typewriters we had, but I really liked the Apple.

For a while I was doing everything on it including cases, articles, book chapters, memos, syllabi, even letters. I would transcribe from dictated audio tapes directly onto the Apple and then edit from there.

I really liked it. I liked it so much that I wish I could afford my own and use it at home.

A few of the other secretaries would stop in to see the two secretaries who had tried the Apple word processors and talk about the systems, but none pressed to have their own. A few of them noted that the Apple was not a good word processor, since it required several keystrokes to do what the Wang could do in one or two. They also mentioned the smaller diskettes. (Apple used 5¼" diskettes that could store about 35 pages of text, while the Wang used 8" diskettes that could store about 120 pages of text.) One was concerned that having a printer in the office would make the workplace very noisy and distracting, especially when trying to talk on the telephone.

THE SECRETARIES

Of the 30 MSB secretaries (all of whom were women) 7 completed an anonymous questionnaire during the fall that Professor Neal's committee began working on the word processing problem. All of the respondents worked with teaching faculty. They had all completed their educations with graduation from high school. Of them, 3 were between 30 and 40 years of age, 2 were over 50. 1 was under 30, and 1 was between 40 and 50. All reported that they used the Wang for a variety of tasks ranging from cases to single draft letters.

Three of the seven reported that their professors had talked to them about word processing, but all reported that no one else had. When asked how they felt about giving up their typewriters for a keyboard and video screen, the secretaries' responses ranged from "Fine, I'd like to have one at home," to "Would not like to see this happen. The 'personal touch' from a typewriter will always be desired." One expressed concern that sitting and looking at a video screen for seven or eight hours a day would be very straining. Two mentioned that "learn it by yourself" approaches were unacceptable.

The secretaries were paid on the regular State wage scale, which was below the wage levels in industry for the same jobs in the area. Consequently, many of the secretaries supplemented their incomes by typing student papers. Although they were not allowed to do this during the regular workday, they did stay late or come in on weekends to use the school's typewriters. Some students had begun using Screen Writer II to type their papers. Others had asked the secretaries to type their papers using Screen Writer. The Screen Writer package had the advantages of working on the Apple without additional hardware modifica-

tion, of having a powerful set of capabilities, and of low cost, but it was seen by some as cumbersome to use, difficult to learn, hard to read on the screen, and not well suited for the Apple keyboard.

OTHER PERSPECTIVES

As Professor Neal pondered the dilemma that faced him, he recalled some conversations he had had with various interested people at the School.

Comments from the Associate Dean

The obstacles that I see include financing, faculty resistance, secretarial resistance, facilities, and institutional inertia. The State budget is down; there are a lot of other demands on our private resources. The current recessionary economy and declining enrollments also make it more difficult to seek additional public funds. Some faculty are either committed to the Wang or are not sure that word processing is necessary; some secretaries may resist trying to use the new technology or changing to a different system since they have already learned one system. The investments (both financial and emotional) that people have in different systems mean that the differences of opinion are hardened. Our building is not designed for the electronic age. We can have a distributed system like the Wang on the same floor, but when we try to change floors, it requires a structural change. We have estimated that those changes would cost about $15,000 per port. The university, for obvious reasons, would like to standardize the systems used on campus, and we want to be responsive to their concerns, but their approved system may not be the best one for us. We also have to deal with the State system, which does not like to explore new alternatives.

It would be nice to have a letter-quality printer with a stand-alone, Apple-compatible unit in each secretarial bay. That way we could utilize the systems as both word processors and as back up micro-computers as needed. The faculty is beginning to accept the microcomputer as far as word processing is concerned, but in many minds the microcomputer approach to word processing is a degraded one, much less acceptable than the dedicated approach.

Professor Arthur is right; we need it. On the other hand, I felt like saying, "Come on. Listen to the other troops. It will take some time to move ahead." He brought some energy to the arena, and I felt frustrated that I could not respond as quickly as I would have liked.

I think we have to ask ourselves, "What really are our baseline, core needs? And then from that develop an approach gradually. There is some ambiguity around how the various needs overlap and where we need more specialized capability. We need to be able to identify the real needs and the real capabilities of the hardware and of the software. That problem is compounded, too, because when you ask people, they can say, "I need this technology" or "that technology," but cannot say for what they need it. I suppose we could bring something in tomorrow, but I wonder if it would really meet the needs. For instance, we tried using the Apples with a particular software package in an administration function and found that it couldn't do 50% of what we wanted it to do. Now, it's been scrapped, and we are starting over with a new package. We need to define better at the outset what we need.

A Conversation with the Associate Dean for Administration

Word processing has become a more important issue the longer I have been here. In all candor, it was not on the top of my list at the outset a year ago. There were a number of other things that I had to learn. We already had some word processing (the Wang) capacity in place that had been introduced in years past and it was gradually getting more use. By the year before last, although it had met with initial resistance, it was clear that the equipment we already had in place was not adequate to meet the demand. Two constituencies were raising questions: faculty who wanted distributed word processing capacity and the secretarial staff who wanted to get more access time on it. We just couldn't keep up with all of the secretarial, research, and administrative staffs trying to use it.

Also, the financial consideration was a concern. Any expenditure would be a heavy one, and we

were already heavy into microcomputers. We needed some way to combine the two needs.

It is high on my agenda now; we can do better. There are conflicting views on which way to go. We have one system, but we are not locked into it. There is considerable material on it; the people are trained to use it, and they have responded positively to it.

In this high technology field, there is a large menu with weekly changes. We need to be careful; we are not able to bring in one system and then switch six months later. We will need to use the next one for at least several years.

The human factors are very important. We will have secretaries assigned to individual faculty members. We will not go the pool route. And with a ratio of three to five professors per secretary, this has to be done very carefully. We have tried to allow the staff to be fully involved, so that it is not a threat to them.

A Conversation with the Assistant Associate Dean

Before installing the Wang, we asked various programs in the school to identify what they needed, and then we had several vendors come in and show us what they had. At that time, we didn't know what uses there would be. The Wang people were the most helpful, talked to the professors, and were the most responsive. So we went with them. We were one of the first universities with this kind of system.

I think that we are going too slowly now. The resistance on the staff has a lot to do with whom they work for. Some senior faculty don't encourage their secretaries because they have to leave the office to work on the Wang. They want their secretaries to be there at the moment when they want them. Any time something is new, people resist change. We need to keep it on a positive note. Some have resisted the whole thing.

PROFESSOR NEAL'S DECISION

As Professor Neal reflected on these conversations, a colleague entered his office. After exchanging pleasantries, Neal began talking about the word processing decision that faced him and the school.

I didn't want to get involved in the administrative side of this thing. There are so many constraints that we need to satisfy: the secretaries, the faculty, admissions, placement, the university, individuals, and the budget. Professor Arthur was continuously pressing me to do something and that was kind of a pain. I wondered if I should get involved. What did he want me to do? I didn't want to, yet I felt like it was a duty. The Dean's office said we had to get approval by the university computer committee, so we let them come in and do their study. Then, the Dean's office decided to try to see if we could get the Apples and the Wang working together. A friend who sells Wangs in town told me there was no way that that could happen. They did get the Wang to print out an Apple file, but that was all. That took six weeks.

One professor says we should let each corner of the building decide what they want and buy it all. He says that would let everyone get what they want, and give the school some additional experience with a variety of packages. But, frankly, that approach surprises me. We would have a hodge-podge of systems then.

We have a great need for distributed word processing. It is not satisfactory to have the secretaries sign up for time in another room. I don't like my secretary to go away to work on the Wang for four hours at a time.

I see three alternatives; though there may be others:

1. We can expand the Wang system. As a group, we rely on it heavily already. It is distributed, and we could put terminals in each secretarial bay and one printer on each floor to get the capacity we need. We have the Wang; though ours are the only ones on campus. That was pushed through by another associate dean, and that was a mammoth job. The university was pushing another computer then.
2. We can go with Apples. We could put one in each secretarial bay and have a high-speed, letter-quality printer to go with it. We would have to decide which hardware configuration we would want and which software package. If we go Apple, do we use the Microsoft Z–80 card and go the CP/M route or do we stick with the Apple's 6502 processor and use something like ScreenWriter?

3. Or we can go with something different. I have been flipping through recent copies of personal computer magazines, and there are literally scores of systems available now. Mini-Micro Systems published a guide to personal desktop computers in its August 1982 issue that listed over 90 different makes with their screen configurations, storage capacities, processor types, software compatibilities, prices, and notes. Desktop Computing published a "Buyer's Guide to Dot Matrix Printers" in their December 1982 issue and a "Buyer's Guide to Letter Quality Printers" in their January 1983 issue. Popular Computing published a "Word-Processing Software Directory" in their February 1982 issue. It is hard to know how to sift through all of that!

The computer committee on the main campus is pushing the NorthStar Advantage for all of the university word and data processing, and they will have to approve our application. Their report (a summary of which appears in Exhibit 12–1) did just what we thought it would—recommend the Advantage.

I know that what I want is not necessarily the best thing for the school. Expanding the Wang would not meet my needs; the Apple does that. The Apple is not too expensive, and it's easy to operate. Personally, I don't care which way we go; I can be just as productive myself. And I am sympathetic to the argument that the Apple was not designed for word processing and probably is not appropriate for primarily word processing tasks. If we go NorthStar, that is no help for me either, but then neither is the Wang. So, I may do my drafts on the Apple and have my secretary retype them on the Wang.

The Associate Dean for Administration has sent me a memo asking the committee to look at the problem. We have met and talked about the issues. The university computer committee has come in and made a study and a report. Now, I need to decide, write a recommendation, and then forward it back to the Dean's office where the final decision is made. Then, we submit a request to the university committee, who will study the application and decide whether or not to grant it. If they do, they send it on to a state government computer committee who reviews that decision to see whether or not they will

EXHIBIT 12–1   SUMMARY OF MIDWESTERN UNIVERSITY COMPUTER COMMITTEE REPORT

In its search for an office automation system that would meet both word and data processing needs in offices throughout the University, the committee identified the following characteristics of the basic system:
— 8 bit microprocessor (upgradeable to 16 bit?)
— CP/M operating system
— Wordstar/Magic Wand or CP/M compatible word processor
— 64K of RAM memory (expandable with 16 bit)
— 5¼″ floppy diskettes for storage
— single user (no shared processing)
— dedicated or shared RS232 compatible printer
— Winchester disk compatible for up to 5mb storage

The committee investigated the following systems and made the attached comments:

System	Comment
Alspa Computer	Little Support outside CA
Apple II	Ltd. keyboard, costly add-ons
Apple III	Hardware problems, bulky wp
Archives	Ideal wp, expensive
Basis 108	6502 and Z–80 but many vendors
Colonial Data Services	Low sales penetration
Commodore	No CP/M, ltd. software
CompuPro	No support outside CA
Cromemco	Uses CDOS not CP/M
Decmate	Low flexibility and high price
Delta	Low sales penetration
Digilog	Poor keyboard feel, noisy
Dynabyte 5200	Low sales penetration
Exxon	Low flexibility
IBM PC	Confusing keyboard, but 16 bit
NEC PC8001	Small keys = errors
NorthStar Advantage	#1 Choice, 16 bit ok, one unit
OSM Zeus	Low sales penetration
Osborne I	64 column screen
Radio Shack TRS–80	Low RAM
Smoke Signal Chieftain	Low sales penetration
Superbrain	Low quality
TeleVideo 802	New, unavailable
Terak	No CP/M
Toshiba	New, unavailable
Wangwriter	Best word processor, bulky
Xerox 820	Expensive
Zenith Z–89	Low disk capacity

allocate funds to support it. Once we have decided and had our decision accepted up the line, we have to be careful about how we introduce the staff to the decision. Implementation will be critical.

We have to choose this year. We can't go another year like this last one. We have got to do something! I suppose that things are proceeding correctly, although not quickly enough.

MIDWESTERN SCHOOL OF BUSINESS STUDY

The school has heavy needs in admissions, registrar's office, and administrative and faculty word processing. The Apple would be an improvement over manual typing, but the committee strongly recommends against adoption as an administrative/word processing microcomputer. These shortcomings include lack of keyboard flexibility, low screen quality, speed and capacity of disk drives, and inherent limits to memory expansion.

There are two viable options: The first is to expand the Wang system to ten workstations. The advantages would be: compatibility with the current disks and comfort of current operators with the system. The disadvantages would be: cost of cabling, cost of hardware and software (including maintenance), and dependence on one source for future enhancements. The cost of purchasing the current system and the recommended enhancements would be about $70,000.

The second option is to purchase stand-alone microcomputers. The advantages of this approach are: low price, flexibility of hardware, availability of industry standard CP/M software and word processing packages, local support and training from our office, portability, no cabling required. The disadvantages would be: required conversion of all existing files and disks, retraining all current operators. The University standard computer is the NorthStar Advantage (as outlined above). Ten machines, six letter quality printers, the software, and maintenance would cost about $53,000.

13

DCI

In early 1979, DCI, a major telecommunications company in the Southwest, faced a shrinking market share in certain of its product lines due to increased competition. Top management at DCI was extremely concerned over this turn of events and was certain that this trend would continue and effect many of its other products. In response, top management at DCI decided to restructure and expand their marketing management division in the hopes of regaining their dominance in the market place.

DCI's new marketing strategy revolved around new product development and technological improvements which could be used to upgrade and modify their existing products. This strategy was prompted because of the rapid influx of many new and smaller competitors into DCI's market as a result of federal deregulation. These companies had some competitive advantages over DCI. They were smaller and could respond more rapidly to changes in the market place. They were also able to exploit new technology by buying state of the art equipment from others and packaging this equipment in their own unique constellations. They were also able to vary price structure more than DCI because of lower capital investment costs.

In June, 1979, the entire Marketing Management Division of DCI was expanded and restructured (see Exhibit 13–1) with many current employees promoted or transferred, and new people hired. Jim Roberts, a former marketing manager with ten years experience at DCI, was designated as Vice President and head of Corporate Marketing. Roberts quickly determined that DCI's diversity of clients required that a market segmentation strategy was necessary in order to understand and serve each major market. Therefore, a unit was created within the division to study and service the hotel/motel industry.

The new manager of the hotel/motel unit was Debbie Drater. Drater was hired from a high technology non-direct competitor with a reputation for sophistication in market strategy.

EXHIBIT 13-1 PARTIAL DCI ORGANIZATION STRUCTURE

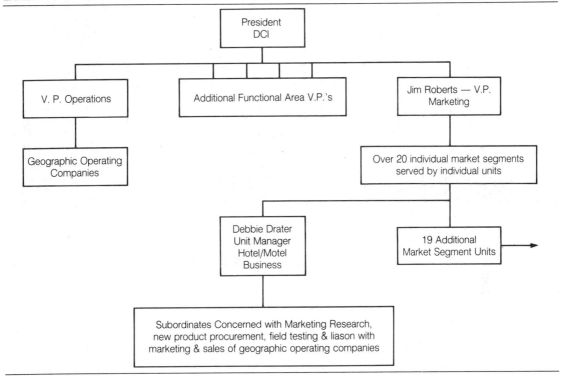

In December of 1979, Debbie Drater and Jim Roberts announced the development of a new product targeted specifically for the hotel/motel industry. The product was a Property Management System (PMS) designed to monitor the usual hotel/motel functions such as check-in, check-out, housekeeping, wake-up, etc., and additionally, to perform novel functions such as local call registration, energy control in all parts of the hotel, and front desk accounting. The corporate objectives of offering such a property management system from Jim Roberts' point of view were:

a. The development of a turn-key concept in communications (i.e., one stop shopping for all of a client's communication needs.)

b. A desire to meet the needs of the hotel/motel industry.

c. An introduction of a technologically advanced product which would broaden the base of DCI's offerings.

Since the Property Management System (PMS) was new, and DCI had no experience along this line, a field trial was set up to "debug" the PMS system. From Debbie Drater's perspective, the field trial would provide the following information:

a. A data base for making appropriate changes in the product and/or the techniques of introduction.

b. The development of a marketing plan for the new system.

c. An identification of the successes and failures associated with the introduction of a new computer system.

d. An assessment of the behavioral impact of a new high technology system on the hotel staff and guests.

The PMS was developed by DCI in collaboration with Techni-Lab, a computer hardware and software manufacturer, as well as one of the world's largest communications organizations. The PMS consisted of a Techni-Lab computer system integrated with standard DCI manufactured equipment.

The field trial began in February, 1980, at The Carlton Hotel in San Antonio, Texas (see Exhibit 13–2). The Carlton was part of the Ripley organization, one of the world's largest hotel chains. The Carlton was chosen by DCI as its test site since The Carlton's existing telecommunications equipment could adapt easily to the new technical hardware. From The Carlton's management point-of-view, the field trial allowed the hotel to test, without financial cost, an innovative system which would give the hotel a marketing edge over its competition as well as save energy at a time when energy costs were skyrocketing. The field trial at The Carlton was to take place

in two phases starting in February, 1980 and ending June, 1980 (see Exhibit 13–3).

The run during Phase I was not uneventful. The most serious problems were the down time during occasional "crashes" of the system and resistance of some of the hotel staff. Nevertheless, the trial was considered to be successful and Phase II began. Unfortunately, the experience with Phase II was even more difficult.

The computer system was often "down", requiring The Carlton to allow guests to leave with bills deferred for later billing because the old manual system for posting the bills had been completely removed, and there was no way to extract them from the new system. Additionally, the hotel staff were not always sufficiently familiar with the operation of the system to use it effectively and the manuals were poorly written and of little help.

Even more serious were the personnel

EXHIBIT 13–2   PARTIAL ORGANIZATION CHART: THE CARLTON

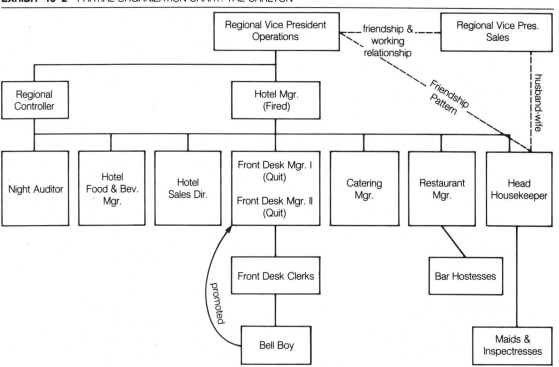

changes at The Carlton during the field trial. At the beginning of Phase II, The Carl-

---

EXHIBIT 13–3   FIELD TRIAL AT THE CARLTON

---

1. Background.
The installation took place in two phases which had the following features:

Phase I Features (February–March)
This part of the Property Management System (PMS) provides a modular computerized data collection and display system integrated with the hotel PBX to perform the following basic hotel/motel functions:

1. *Room Status Management*
   Provides information on the status of each room in the property and assists the hotel personnel in the performance of the room management function.

2. *Housekeeping*
   Updates and displays housekeeping information to provide instantaneous status on the housekeeping conditions of the rooms in the hotel. The system also includes provisions for monitoring the assignment of maids and provides the means for reporting the housekeeping data.

3. *Automatic Wake-up*
   Operating automatically through the telephone lines, this feature will wake guests at a pre-designated time with a pre-recorded wake-up message.

4. *Night Audit*
   Audit displays are available for local telephone charges, wake-up summaries and house summaries to assist the Night Auditor in the performance of his/her functions. The audit can also be printed by the journal printer, providing hard copy.

Phase II Features (March–June)
Expansion is possible through the addition of optional features which enhance the basic system. Each of these features is modular and can be added to the system to provide additional operational and management control of the hotel/motel, such as:

1. *Guest Directory*
   A list of the current guests and their respective rooms occupied at the hotel is provided by this feature.

2. *Guest Ledger*
   The Guest Ledger/Charge Collection feature permits the collection of guest charges at revenue collection areas such as restaurant, pool, pro shop, etc., for allocation to the guest folios. This information is instantly posted electronically on the guest folio.

3. *Energy Control*
   Energy Control consists of a number of remotely located control units under control of the PMS System. The control units can turn off any power-consuming device capable of being electrically controlled. Once certain operating parameters are selected at installation, operation is completely automatic. Intervention is necessary only when the innkeeper elects to alter one of the initial operation conditions.

---

ton's manager, who was supportive and knowledgeable about the PMS was fired. This firing occurred because the hotel was overbooked by 40% and several flight attendants from a large airline were among the many who could not be accommodated. Inasmuch as their airline had booked and paid for these rooms in advance the flight attendants requested help in finding alternative arrangements. Because of a convention in town the hotel found many unaccommodated, grumbling guests milling about the lobby. Since it was also running thin on staff, the hotel was unable to help them. The flight attendants called their airline headquarters in New York for help, reaching the Vice President of Personnel, who in turn called the hotel manager at 7:00 p.m. The hotel manager, who had been harassed and verbally insulted by stranded guests in the lobby, assumed that the Vice President speaking to him was another flight attendant and hung up on her. She, in turn, immediately called the Regional Operations Vice-President of the Ripley chain and demanded that the hotel manager be fired. Within a half an hour of the phone call, the hotel manager was discharged, and was last seen loading his personal furniture on a rental truck the next day. Upon hearing the hotel manager was fired, the front desk manager, who was a friend of the hotel manager and also a supporter of the PMS, quit his job.

The next day, the bell captain was promoted to front desk manager and the Regional Operations Vice-President assumed control of the day to day operations of the hotel. After two days, the newly appointed front desk manager quit citing the pressure of the new job. He took a job in another hotel as a bellhop. One Carlton employee referred to these frequent changes as reflecting "soap opera management."

Other dynamics at The Carlton proved important. The head housekeeper of The Carlton was married to a Vice President of the Ripley organization and lived on the property as did the Regional Operations Vice President who was now running the hotel. During Phase I, the head housekeeper was given a CRT (visual display) to allow her to enter and audit housekeeping data in the system. Noticing that she could also monitor the activity of the front desk on her CRT, she used it in her long standing conflict with front desk personnel. She would call the front desk each time the front desk took an action she did not approve of, especially when a room was rented before she punched in that it had been completely cleaned, even though it was known to be ready. She also stormed the front desk from time to time yelling and berating them for their incompetence.

Due to complaints from the front desk personnel, her CRT was taken away in Phase II and replaced by one with limited ability to monitor non-housekeeping functions. She complained vociferously to her husband and the Regional Operations Vice President. Her full-function CRT was returned the next day.

As a result of her negative feelings, she decided not to inform her maids to leave the fans of the individual room heating/airconditioning units in the "on" position. The computer system required this setting if the heating/airconditioning unit was to be controlled remotely from the front desk and thereby achieve energy savings. Further, the head housekeeper did not make an attempt to maintain the work standards of her maids who had slowed down in anticipation of a "speed up" due to the PMS.

Other problems were also evident. The billing keyboard of the PMS at the front desk was designed the reverse of standard calculator keyboards. This resulted in slowed punching and errors when the front desk was under pressure to speed up at busy times. The night auditor/night manager who was undertrained on the system was hostile to it and bad-mouthed the system because she no longer felt important, as the system would do her auditing job. She also had fears that she might be discharged as no longer being needed. This was not true, but her fears were real to her. No one told her this was a field trial and might be a long time before a system was operational. Nor was she told that the Regional Operations Vice President had made a commitment to DCI to keep her regardless of the systems capability, as she was needed to run the hotel at night and to use the system to prepare daily summary reports for him.

A further difficulty came about because the assignment of responsibility for maintaining the system was not clear. DCI expected their local office to provide training for the hotel staff and maintain the system with the help of Techni-Lab. The local office had received a transfer of funds from the corporate office for this purpose, however, once it was expended the local office refused to commit its own resources to the project. Also, they lacked the expertise to deal with the frequent hardware problems. Techni-Labs was most reluctant to expend any effort to support the system as it was (unknown to DCI) in the process of phasing out of the computer business. The problems became so severe that after contact at the top levels of both companies and the commitment of more funds from DCI the team of Techni-Lab engineers responsible for the development of the system's hardware and software were flown to San Antonio for the remainder of the field trial.

When the Techni-Lab engineers arrived at The Carlton, one hotel employee who had experienced all of the changes associated with the new PMS was heard remarking, "I don't know why everyone is so concerned with this system since it's never going to work here."

14

Acetate Department

The Acetate Department's product consisted of about twenty different kinds of viscous liquid acetate used by another department to manufacture transparent film to be left clear, or coated with photographic emulsion or iron oxide.

Before the change: The Department was located in an old four story building as in Exhibit 14–1. The work flow was as follows:

1. Twenty kinds of powder arrived daily in 50 pound paper bags. In addition, storage tanks of liquid would be filled weekly from tank trucks.
2. Two or three Acetate Helpers would jointly unload pallets of bags into the storage area using a lift truck.
3. Several times a shift, the Helpers would bring the bagged material up the elevator to the third floor where it would be temporarily stored along the walls.
4. Mixing batches was under the direction of the Group Leader and was rather like baking a cake. Following a prescribed formula, the Group Leader, Mixers and Helpers operate valves to feed in the proper solvent and manually dump in the proper weight and mixture of solid material. The glob would be mixed by giant egg beaters and heated according to the recipe.
5. When the batch was completed, it was pumped to a finished product storage tank.
6. After completing each batch, the crew would thoroughly clean the work area of dust and empty bags because cleanliness was extremely important to the finished product.

To accomplish this work, the Department was structured as in Exhibit 14–2.

The Helpers were usually young men 18–25 years of age; the Mixers 25 to 40 and the Group Leaders and Foremen 40 to 60. Foremen were on salary. Group Leaders, Mixers and Helpers on hourly pay.

To produce 20,000,000 pounds of product per year, the Department operated 24 hours a day, 7 days a week. Four crews

From "Redesigning the Acetate Department," by David R. Hampton, Charles E. Summer, and Ross A. Webber, *Organizational Behavior and the Practice of Management* (Glenview, IL: Scott, Foresman and Company, 1982), pp. 751–755. Used with permission.

EXHIBIT 14–1 ELEVATION VIEW OF ACETATE DEPARTMENT BEFORE CHANGE

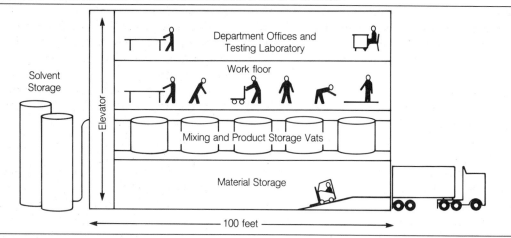

rotated shifts: for example, Shift Foremen A and his two Group Leaders and crews would work two weeks on the day shift 8:00 a.m. to 4:00 p.m., then two weeks on the evening shift 4:00 p.m. to midnight, then two weeks on the night shift midnight to 8:00 a.m. There were two days off between shift changes.

During a typical shift, a Group Leader and his crew would complete two or three batches. A batch would frequently be started on one shift and completed by the next shift crew. There was slightly less work on the evening and night shifts because no deliveries were made, but these crews engaged in a little more cleaning. The Shift Foreman would give instructions to the two Group Leaders at the beginning of each shift as to the status of batches in process, batches to be mixed, what deliveries were

EXHIBIT 14–2 ORGANIZATIONAL CHART OF ACETATE DEPARTMENT BEFORE CHANGE

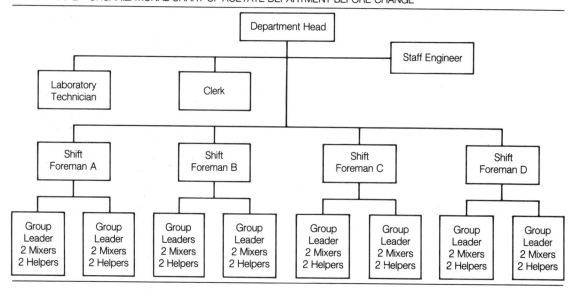

expected and what cleaning was to be done. Periodically throughout the shift, the Foreman would collect samples in small bottles which he would leave at the laboratory technicians' desk for testing.

The management and office staff (Department Head, Staff Engineer, Lab Technician, and Department Clerk) only worked on the day shift, although if an emergency arose on the other shifts, the Foreman might call.

All in all, the Department was a pleasant place in which to work. The work floor was a little warm, but well-lighted, quiet and clean. Substantial banter and horseplay occurred when the crew wasn't actually loading batches, particularly on the non-day shifts. The men had a dartboard in the work area and competition was fierce and loud. Frequently a crew would go bowling right after work, even at 1:00 a.m., for the community's alleys were open 24 hours a day. Department turnover and absenteeism were low. Most employees spent their entire career with the Company, many in one department. The corporation was large, paternalistic, well-paying, and offered attractive fringe benefits including large, virtually

automatic bonuses for all. Then came the change. . . .

The new system: To improve productivity, the Acetate Department was completely redesigned, the technology changed from batches to continuous processing. The basic building was retained, but substantially modified as in Exhibit 14–3. The modified work flow is as follows:

1. Most solid raw materials are delivered via trucks in large aluminum bins holding 500 pounds.
2. One Handler (formerly Helper) is on duty at all times in the first floor to receive raw materials and to dump the bins into the semiautomatic screw feeder.
3. The Head Operator (former Group Leader) directs the mixing operations from his control panel on the fourth floor located along one wall across from the Department Offices. The mixing is virtually an automatic operation once the solid material has been sent up the screw feed; a tape program opens and closes the necessary valves to add solvent, heat, mixing, etc. Sitting at a table before his panel, the Head Operator monitors the

EXHIBIT 14–3   ELEVATION VIEW OF ACETATE DEPARTMENT AFTER CHANGE

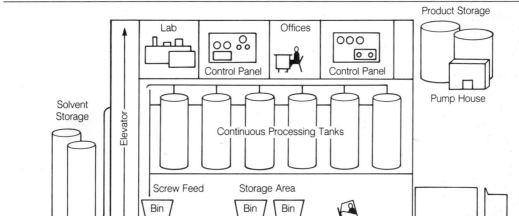

process to see that everything is operating within specified temperatures and pressures.

This technical change allowed the Department to greatly reduce its manpower. The new structure is illustrated in Exhibit 14–4.

One new position was created, that of a pump operator who is located in a small separate shack about 300 feet from the main building. He operates pumps and valves that move the finished product among various storage tanks.

Under the new system, production capacity was increased to 25,000,000 pounds per year. All remaining employees received a 15 percent increase in pay. Former personnel not retained in the Dope Department were transferred to other departments in the company. No one was dismissed.

Unfortunately, actual output has lagged well below capacity in the several months since the construction work and technical training was completed. Actual production is virtually identical with that under the old technology. Absenteeism has increased markedly and several judgmental errors by operators have resulted in substantial losses.

EXHIBIT 14–4   ORGANIZATION CHART OF ACETATE DEPARTMENT AFTER CHANGE

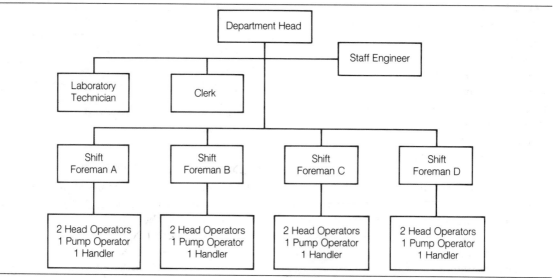

15

Atlas Electronics Corporation (A)

COMPANY HISTORY

Atlas Electronics Corporation was organized by a group of engineers and scientists who pioneered electronic research and development for the Office of Scientific Research and Development during World War II. After the war, members of this group joined together to form a private company to continue their efforts.

From the start, Atlas earned a reputation among government and corporate customers as a leader in advanced electronic techniques and systems. Its present capabilities cover a wide spectrum of electronic applications and skills, including aviation systems, radar, space payloads, communications, and electronic warfare (reconnaissance and counter-measures). Atlas has continued to distinguish itself for advances in the state-of-the-art and for superior quality on numerous prototype and initial operational equipment developed for U.S. government agencies. Fully 95% of its business is on government R & D contracts, whether directly or for prime government contractors.

Atlas's success is largely due to the competence, dedication, and stability of its staff. Of its 3,000 employees, over half have engineering or scientific degrees. Approximately 15% of these have advanced technical or M.B.A. degrees or are working toward them. The primary resource of management is the brainpower of these men, who are professional specialists in diverse fields.

COMPANY ORGANIZATION

Atlas Electronics Corporation is a typical engineering company organized along functional lines. Its Functional Engineering Departments are oriented to various technical disciplines and are staffed with engineers, scientists, and technicians who work on developing advanced techniques and in the support of projects.

The departmental organization structure starts with the department head and goes down the line through the section heads, group leaders, and supervisory engineers, to the scientists, engineers, and technicians who are doing the detail work. The department heads report to John Doan, Executive

This case was developed and prepared by W. R. Lockridge, C. S. Post Center, Long Island University. Reprinted by permission.

Vice-President. Communications, approvals, and directions flow through this organization in an orderly manner. Each level is under the supervision of the level above it and normally will not operate without higher level approval and direction.

Atlas had three Functional Engineering Departments: an Antenna Department, a Receiver Department, and a Data Systems Department. Each of these is responsible for developing advanced techniques, performing engineering, and for giving support to R & D projects in its technical area. The organization of each of these departments is shown in Exhibits 15A–1, 15A–2, and 15A–3.

In addition, Atlas has a Manufacturing Department (Exhibit 15A–4), which does fabrication, assembly, and testing of production units. This department also reports to John Doan. Purchasing, accounting, personnel administration, and other services are performed by various company staff departments not shown in the exhibits.

From time to time, Atlas sets up an ad hoc Project Management to handle a large R & D contract. This is a semiautonomous group consisting of a project manager and other personnel drawn from the functional organizations in the company. It has complete responsibility for meeting all the requirements of the contract, but it gets the

EXHIBIT 15A–1   ATLAS ELECTRONICS
CORPORATION ANTENNA
DEPARTMENT

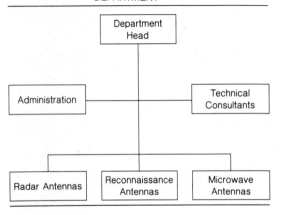

EXHIBIT 15A–2   ATLAS ELECTRONICS
CORPORATION RECEIVER
DEPARTMENT

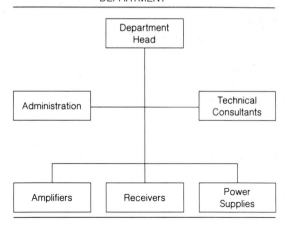

work done in the Functional Departments. At the end of the project it is dissolved.

The Project Management assigns technical tasks to each supporting department to perform. To a limited extent, it is permitted to cut across organizational lines so that it can deal with the people doing the work without having to go through the whole hierarchy of their functional organizations. It handles scheduling and overall cost control; it deals with subcontractors and maintains liaison with customers; and it coordinates all the technical inputs and "hardware" from the supporting organizations into the overall system that is delivered to the customer.

The people who are transferred to the Project Management are mostly of a supervisory or senior category and report directly to the project manager. Their function is to advise him in their respective technical disciplines, to cooperate with him in managing the project, and to give "work direction" * to the personnel in the Functional Departments who are doing the work. The Project Management staff cannot directly supervise the work of the departmental

---

* "Work direction": definition of the goals, specifications, and constraints (budget, schedule, etc.) for a technical task, as distinguished from detailed supervision of the work to perform it; the "what" to do, not the "how" to do it.

personnel because these workers report in line to their department head. The department head may be on the same level or a higher level than the project manager. Consequently, the project manager has the problem of getting the utmost in effort from people who are responsible to someone else for pay raises, promotion, performance, and other aspects of line relationship.

SPYEYE PROJECT

As the result of a successful competitive proposal, the government has awarded Atlas an R & D contract for an airborne reconnaissance system called "Spyeye." The System consists of an antenna, a receiver, an amplifier, and visual read-out equipment. This is an advanced system requiring the development of specific equipment whose performance characteristics are beyond the existing state-of-the-art. Atlas agrees to produce a prototype model in nine months. Following acceptance by the government, it agrees to produce five operational systems within another six months.

The contract is for a firm fixed price of $6 million, of which $5.6 million is the estimated target cost and $400,000 is Atlas's fee. The contract has a profit-sharing incentive whereby the government and the contrac-

EXHIBIT 15A–4 ATLAS ELECTRONICS CORPORATION MANUFACTURING DEPARTMENT

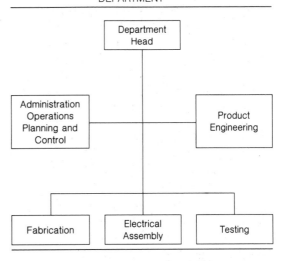

tor share any cost-saving below the $5.6 million on a 90/10% basis. It also provides penalties on the contractor for overrunning the cost, for late delivery, and for failure to meet performance specifications. The government will debit Atlas dollar-for-dollar against its fee for any cost overrun, and will assess it $200 for every day of late delivery. Various penalties, up to 20% of the fee, are provided for failure to meet technical performance specifications.

PROJECT SUPPORT

The Spyeye project requires support from many functional areas throughout the company. It needs technical advice, engineering, and "hardware" from the reconnaissance section of the Antenna Department, the amplifier and receiver sections of the Receiver Department, the visual displays section of the Data Systems Department, and the fabrication, assembly, and testing facilities of the Manufacturing Department. (See Exhibits 15A–1 through 15A–4.)

ALTERNATIVES FOR PROJECT ORGANIZATION

Company management has to decide

EXHIBIT 15A–3 ATLAS ELECTRONICS CORPORATION DATA SYSTEMS DEPARTMENT

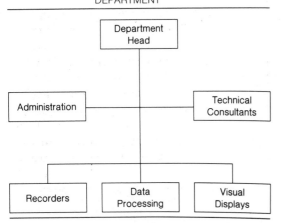

whether to organize Spyeye as an ad hoc Project Management, or to handle it through one of its Functional Departments. Two men are available to lead the project, but the one selected will depend on the choice of organization. These men are Howard Datson and Burt Saunderson.

Howard Datson, 55, is head of the Receiver Department. He has been with the company since its inception and has built his department to the largest in the company. Datson and his group were responsible for numerous innovations in the receiver line and have kept the company ahead of most of its competition in that field.

Datson put in a strong plea to the president, Homer Skillton, to let the Receiver Department manage Spyeye as a project within its functional organization. "My department has been in existence since this company started," he said. "We've a well-trained staff with a lot of managerial and technical know-how. We'll have to do the bulk of the development anyhow. And I'm sure we can handle the interfaces with the other departments without any trouble."

Datson went on to express some of his personal feelings about the alternative of setting up a Project Management. "You must recognize that we've built the reputation of this company on the technical capability and quality performance of its Functional Departments. I personally dislike becoming a 'service' organization to a group who will be here today and gone tomorrow. Also, it'll probably be managed by someone who is not as technically oriented as any of our department heads.

"One thing I want to make particularly clear," he continued, "nobody's going to come into my department and tell my men how they must do their work. They report to me and my supervisors and we're the ones who call the shots."

Burt Saunderson, 45, is a section head in the Antenna Department and has held that position for six years. He started as a pro-

ject engineer 12 years ago and worked up through the group leader level to section head. A year ago he was relieved of his functional assignment and was appointed project manager in an ad hoc Project Management for an R & D project called Moonglow. Moonglow was much smaller than Spyeye, but it had many of the same characteristics, such as the support from several different Functional Departments, a fixed price, and penalties for failure to meet cost, schedule, and performance specifications.

Saunderson and his Project Management group had successfully completed the Moonglow project. They had delivered the system on time, and the performance was satisfactory to the customer, although the equipment deviated slightly from the specification. They also had been able to increase the company's fee 1.5% by bettering the targeted cost. But Moonglow was now over and the people on it had to be reassigned.

While waiting for a new assignment, Saunderson served as bid manager on the Spyeye proposal to the government and was responsible for having come up with the reconnaissance system that the government finally bought. He felt he was the logical one to head up the Spyeye Project, if President Skillton decided to organize it as a Project Management. Accordingly, Saunderson sent a memorandum to Skillton outlining his reasons for this type of organization, which were, in essence, as follows:

1. The project involves four of the company's operating organizations. If management is established in any one of these, the company would have the awkward situation of one Functional Department directing the activities of others who are on a parallel with itself in the company organization structure.

2. The project involves more than mere technical development. Cost, schedule, and technical performance all must be evaluated and balanced to produce the

optimum overall result. A Functional Department, steeped in its own technology and hampered by its organizational structure, would lack the objectivity to view the overall project problem in perspective and to meet the ever-changing operational crises that arise from day to day.

3. The project does not involve pure research. It requires some innovation in the techniques area that can be done by the supporting Functional Departments. But someone will have to develop the overall system and that can best be done by a Project Management.

4. The project will add little to the long-range technical capability of the company. What it needs is an organization to "get the job done"—an organization that can use the technical support of the functional organizations without causing any permanent disruption in the company's organization structure.

President Skillton recognized that both men had good arguments.

Atlas Electronics Corporation (B)

SPYEYE PROJECT MANAGEMENT

President Skillton met with Executive Vice-President John Doan to discuss the Spyeye Project. "John, I've decided to organize Spyeye as a Project Management instead of assigning it to any of the Functional Departments. It's too big and too complex and it'll be in trouble from the start. I don't want to upset the stability of any department by temporarily expanding its personnel and giving it a coordinating job to handle." (See Exhibits 15B–1 and 15B–2.)

PROJECT MANAGER

"But this creates some problems on which I'll need your help," he continued. "The first is the selection of a Project Manager. He's got to be at home in the front office talking about budgets, time schedules, and corporate policies and also at home in the labora-

EXHIBIT 15B–1 ATLAS ELECTRONICS CORPORATION SPYEYE PROJECT MANAGEMENT

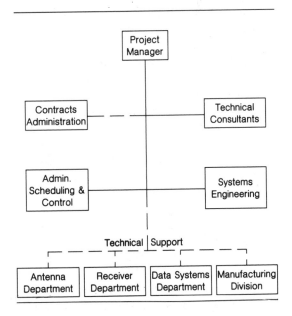

EXHIBIT 15B–2   ATLAS ELECTRONICS CORPORATION SPYEYE PROJECT

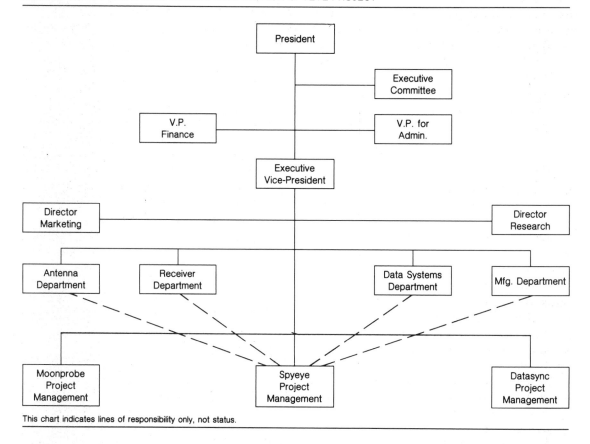

This chart indicates lines of responsibility only, not status.

tory talking about technical research and development problems. Of course, we can't expect him to double as a member of top management and a scientist equally well, but he's got to know what can be done technically and be enough of a business man to get it done within the contract."

"I'm thinking of Burt Saunderson for the job. But I'd like your opinion of him. Burt's a graduate engineer with a B.S. and M.S. in electrical engineering. From his earliest training, he's dealt with scientific analysis. He's accustomed to working objectively with tangible things. But as a Project Manager, he'll have to marshall pieces of preliminary or tentative information, juggle several problems at once, compromise one

requirement for the benefit of another, and make decisions that are often based on experience and judgment rather than on specific knowledge."

"Another thing," Skillton continued, "as a Section Head, Burt's accustomed to having direct-line authority over the people in his department doing the work. They do as he says. But as a Project Manager, he'll have to win the cooperation of the supporting department heads and their staffs to get things done. This kind of management means dealing with human nature, and Burt will have to put a lot of emphasis on human factors to succeed."

"Well, I feel his performance on the Moonglow Project shows he can do the job," Doan replied. "I'd rather have him than one of our department heads. Each of them is a professionally dedicated individual, highly skilled in the techniques of his field. What we need here is a different breed of cat—a manager who can run a business, rather than a professional who is endeavoring to optimize a technical advance."

PROJECT MANAGER AUTHORITY

President Skillton then raised another point. "No matter who we appoint, we've got to give him sufficient authority to get the job done. But we've a delicate situation here. We can't permit him to step in and tell a department head how to run his department. Yet we must give him sufficient status to compel their respect and cooperation. I'll have him report to you. This will place him on the same organizational level as the department heads who are supporting the Project."

"That's OK with me," Doan replied. "After all, I've other Project Managers reporting to me and I try to treat them and the department heads alike."

"Of course, Burt will have overall management of Spyeye and will assign technical tasks to each supporting department," Skillton continued. "But these will be in the nature of subcontracts with budgets and schedules that he'll have to negotiate with each department head and on which he'll obtain their commitment. He can tell them *what* to do, but not *how* to do it. This will keep design development in the Functional Departments where it belongs.

"But I'm not too happy about this arrangement," Skillton reflected, "because it gives the Project Manager little control. When Burt meets with a problem that requires some pressure on a supporting department, he'll have to come to you if he can't reach an agreement with the department head."

"Well, I'll have to assume that as my re-

sponsibility," Doan replied. "All the operations report to me and it's my job to see that any conflicts are resolved in the best interest of the company."

PROJECT STAFF

"Another problem we have to consider," Skillton continued, "is how we'll staff the Spyeye Project Management. Obviously, it should be with supervisory or senior technical people from the departments skilled in the project techniques. But each of these departments needs these people in its own operations. I don't want to step in and direct any department head to transfer people to the Project Management. Burt will have to convince each department head that it's in the best interest of the company and the individual concerned to transfer him. Personally, I feel that it broadens a man's experience and capability to be assigned to a project for a while."

PROJECT SUPPORT

President Skillton meditated for a moment and then continued, "In mulling over the problem, John, it appears to me that if we could induce each department head to set up a Spyeye Support Group as a sub-project within his own department, responsible solely for support to the Spyeye Project Management, it would overcome some of the weakness of the ad hoc organization concept.

"This would, in effect, create a 'project within a project,' headed by a Project Leader who would take his 'work direction' from the Project Management staff rather than from his own departmental supervision. I think this would cut across the organizational lines to implement the interfaces between the Project Management and the supporting groups, and I feel it would inspire a team spirit on the project. At the same time, it would preserve the status of the Functional Department supervision, because detailed supervision of the work would remain with them. I want you to see if the Spyeye support can be organized in this manner," he concluded. (See Exhibit 15B–3.)

EMPLOYEE MORALE

Skillton and Doan had another problem that neither of them had discussed: how to maintain employee morale under the structure of "two bosses" that the Spyeye Project Management created.

Jack Davis was a Group Leader in the Data Systems Department before he was transferred to the Spyeye Project Management. His new assignment required that he be the operational communications link between the project and his "home" department. He gave "work direction" to Abe Marks who was the Project Leader heading up the Spyeye Project group in the Data Systems Department.

Jack and Abe were having lunch together

in the company cafeteria. "I can't keep from wondering what'll happen to me when the project's over," Jack remarked. "Will I be transferred back to the Data Systems Department? If so, will I have lost ground by my temporary absence? Or will they assign me to another project? I don't see anything new coming in and I don't like it. Believe me, I keep looking around."

"I've my problems, too," Abe replied. "While I'm still in the department and report to Joe (his section head), I'm working exclusively on the Spyeye Project. I like the assignment. I feel I'm part of the project team, and when that equipment starts flying out there, I'm sure they'll give me credit for my part. But how does this affect my status and salary?

"When it comes time for rate review," he continued, "will Joe know how I'm doing? Burt knows more about my work than Joe does. Will they talk to each other, or will I be dropped in the crack?

"I'm in another bind," Abe added. "Often I have to decide what's best for the project as against what's best for the department. Should I do what the project needs to meet its contract or be loyal to the department's policies and standards? If I 'bite the hand that feeds me' where'll I wind up?"

"I guess these are some of the risks we have to take," Jack philosophised. "Some guys prefer the challenge of strict technical development. Others want the action of a project. Personally, I feel that this project assignment will broaden my experience, or I wouldn't have taken it. But I can't help but worry about what it'll do to my future."

Burt Saunderson didn't hear this conversation, but he knew that these feelings persisted with personnel working on the project, either on his staff or in the supporting departments. He wondered how he could induce these men to keep their "eye on the ball" and devote their full effort to the project when they were worrying about their personal futures.

EXHIBIT 15B–3 ATLAS ELECTRONICS CORPORATION RECEIVER DEPARTMENT SPYEYE PROJECT SUPPORT

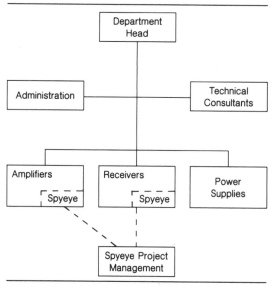

PERFORMANCE PROBLEM

Seven months after the project started, Saunderson noted from his progress reports that the Receiver Department still failed to meet the technical performance specification on the receiver. The specification required a band spread from 1,000–10,000 mc. The breadboard model would only operate at 1,050–9,200 mc.

Time was getting short and he had to take prompt action. Investigation disclosed that it was doubtful if the circuit, as designed by the Receiver Department, would ever meet the specification. Consequently, it did not appear advisable to spend more time on it. Saunderson's technical staff advised him that the addition of another transistor on the lower end and the substitution of a 2QXR tube for a transistor at the upper end would cure the situation. Both of these would increase the cost and the tube would change the configuration of the "black box." His Project Administrator advised him that the project could absorb the cost and the customer said that the slight change in the configuration was not important. But here an obstacle arose. The Receiver Department was not satisfied with the quality of the 2QXR tube and refused to use it.

Saunderson met with Datson to discuss the problem. "Howard, we've got to do something to get that receiver up to spec. Time's getting short. We'll get socked $200 a day for late delivery and they'll take a slice of our fee for failure to perform. Now, I know you hate to use the 2QXR, but it'll do the job long enough to meet the life requirements and will satisfy the customer. We've got to give somewhere or we'll be in serious trouble."

"Yeah, I know how you feel," Datson replied, "but I've got to preserve the quality reputation of the company. After all, we obtained Spyeye because of our reputation for quality as much as for our technical competence and favorable price. If I do anything to impair that image it'll only hurt us in the long run."

16

Calgary Police Department

The function of the Calgary Police Department is to protect the life and property of the citizens and visitors to Calgary. To achieve this goal we must effectively prevent crimes, make arrests and carry out the other related aspects of police work.

Chief Rousseau (1980)

RECENT HISTORY

James T. Rousseau was elected Chief of Police on February 2, 1962. He inaugurated a permanent recruit school. New types of radio equipment were purchased. The officers were given a much deserved day off each week. The headquarters building was redecorated to make working conditions better. The Detective Department was reorganized by division into robbery, larceny, burglary, homicide, vice, and miscellaneous squads. A wrecker was purchased to impound cars illegally parked, and a parking lot for these impounded cars was built.

In 1965 the first traffic policewomen were sworn in and given special training.

In 1966 the entire Calgary Police Department was reorganized into four divisions. These were Services, Uniform, Traffic, and Detective. Training and Detention were made separate divisions later. There was a superintendent in charge of each division.

In 1967 the County Police Department was absorbed into the Calgary Police Department. Police protection was extended to parts of the county outside the city that formerly had depended on the county police. The police department was now responsible for a geographical area almost twice as large.

Space problems were severely felt in 1971 and several departments had to be moved from headquarters. These problems were relieved in 1974 with the completion of a new headquarters building.

In 1973 there was a rise in racial and religious agitation. A Jewish temple was bombed and attacks against persons grew in frequency. The black civil rights and racial problem also became more significant.

THE COMMUNITY ENVIRONMENT

In 1980, the Calgary Crime Commission completed a study of the city's needs for police department services. The following are excerpts from the Crime Commission report.

Calgary's Youth

There is a serious need to focus the city's resources on the problem of preventing and controlling juvenile delinquency. We therefore recommend that the Calgary Youth Council be created as an official agency for this purpose. Membership would include the Superintendent of the Calgary Public Schools, the head of the Parks Department, the Chief of Police, a full-time executive director, a lay chairperson, and six lay members, for a total membership of 11.

The police department should be actively involved in the formulation and implementation of a community program of delinquency prevention and control. All available public and private resources should be fully used in such a program. It also should work with the public, private, and religious agencies devoted in whole or in part to delinquency prevention and coordinate the activities of these agencies to the extent desirable. Finally, it would collect, correlate, and disseminate information, statistics, and data on the subject of juvenile delinquency and make this information available to all agencies that might benefit from it.

Police in Low-Income Areas

There is a serious lack of understanding between residents of low-income areas and the police. All available means should be used to inform every citizen of the fact that the police serve not only to arrest and punish the lawbreaker, but also to protect the average citizen in his or her day-to-day life. The Calgary Police Department should send police counselors into problem areas to hold meetings and generally to inform the public of the protective role of the police. Neighborhood committees that include a police officer trained in social problem areas should be established. Existing independent neighborhood civic associations should also be used and a police counselor stationed in each Economic Opportunity Calgary neighborhood center.

Parks

One of Calgary's most serious problems with regard to juvenile delinquency and crime is that the most congested areas of the city have the fewest recreation facilities. Parks should be built in congested high crime areas of the city. Trained supervisory personnel must be provided. Equipment should be modern. More park police should be provided so that Calgary's people can enjoy their parks. Community centers should be kept open longer during the week and on weekends, particularly during the summer.

Organized Crime

The Commission has found that organized crime exists in Calgary on a local basis. More members of the Calgary Police Department should be trained to deal with the problems of organized crime. All law enforcement agencies in the Calgary area must constantly be on the alert for encroachments of organized crime on a local or national basis.

Care of the Alcoholic

Alcoholic offenders should be identified and a concerted effort should be made to remedy their addiction, thus eliminating the expense of their continued apprehension by the police, their imprisonment, and their trial before the Municipal Court. The Commission feels that this responsibility should belong to the City of Calgary.

Advancement

Police officers must be made secure in their jobs by an appropriate type of merit system. A cadet school for qualified high school graduates should be created, and there should be continued police training for recruit and veteran alike.

Modernization

The police department itself needs considerable modernization. The department should use all modern developments and law enforcement techniques, including such crime-fighting equipment as computers.

Police Department Study

The police department should be studied thoroughly by an independent professional agency to determine its present capabilities and its need for the immediate future. This study should evaluate and estimate Calgary's police requirements; it should appraise its organizational structure, personnel, equipment, and promotion system. On the basis of this study, there should be proposed a detailed plan of improvement to give the city and its citizens a modern police organization second to none.

Community Diversity

Different areas of the city have unique problems that do not seem to be recognized within the department. Similar services are provided throughout the city.

PRESENT ORGANIZATION STRUCTURE

In early 1980, the Calgary Police Department consisted of six divisions, each headed by a superintendent reporting to Chief Rousseau. The six divisions were: Service, Detective, Traffic, Uniform, Detention, and Training. The organization chart is shown in Exhibit 16–1.

Service Division

The Service Division, under the command of Superintendent Milton, is responsible for all the administrative aspects of the department. Superintendent Milton joined the department in 1950 and was named superintendent in 1975.

Specifically the division is charged with the compilation of criminal records (including the Royal Canadian Mounted Police reports), the transmitting and receiving of radio communications, and the telephone switchboard. The division is also responsible for all monies received by the department as well as the department's inventories, purchases, and maintenance.

The Service Division consists of the Crime Report Bureau, including Missing Persons Bureau, the Tabulation Room, and Communications. In addition, the division includes the Custodian's Office, Arsenal, and Maintenance Crew.

Detective Division

The Detective Division is headed by Superintendent Raymond Hill. Superintendent Hill joined the department in 1962 and was named Superintendent of the Detective Division in 1979.

The Detective Division is charged with the prevention of crime, the investigation of criminal offenses, the detection and arrest of criminals, and the recovery of stolen or lost property. The division consists of ten squads: Auto, Burglary, Homicide, Larceny, Robbery, Vice (includes Narcotic Investigations), Fugitive, Juvenile, Security, and Lottery. In addition, the Division includes the Identification Bureau and the General and Criminal Investigation Bureaus.

The most recent additions to the Detective Division are the Juvenile, Security, and Fugitive Squads.

The Juvenile Squad was formed in 1975 following rapid increase in the number of juveniles involved in illegal acts. The squad

EXHIBIT 16–1 ORGANIZATIONAL CHART FOR THE CALGARY POLICE DEPARTMENT

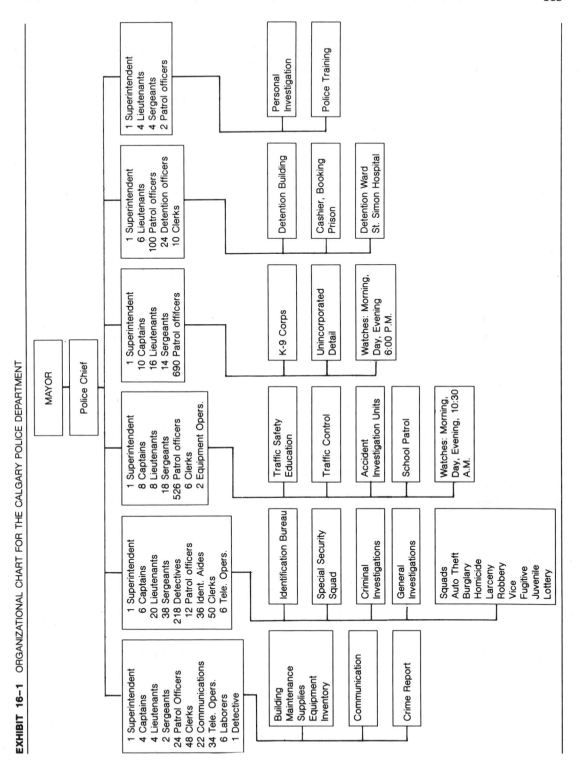

investigates cases in which children under 17 years of age are involved and assists other detective squads (when needed) to investigate crimes by juveniles. The division also works with the Juvenile Court authorities in the prevention of crime and rehabilitation of wayward children.

Sergeant Croy, who joined the department in 1962, heads the Juvenile Squad. Reporting to Sergeant Croy are nine persons.

The Security Squad consists of 12 officers and was formed in 1975. It operates under direct orders from the Chief of Police and the Superintendent of Detectives. The squad is charged with maintaining a constant check on the activities of subversive groups as well as keeping a check on any section of the city where racial tension exists or may start. The squad is also responsible for the safety of any visiting dignitaries (which includes working closely with other governmental agencies), investigating bombings, investigating internal problems that may arise within the department, and any other special assignments given by the Chief.

Lieutenant Madaline Barnett heads the Security Squad. Lieutenant Barnett is 32 years old. She joined the department eight years earlier as a uniformed officer patrolling a footbeat.

The Fugitive Squad was created in 1970. This squad specializes in the apprehension and prosecution of fugitives from penitentiary and justice. Lieutenant Benson heads this squad of 15 officers from Calgary plus 10 from other local jurisdictions.

Traffic Division

The Traffic Division promotes street and highway safety and the enforcement of vehicular traffic laws and regulations. In addition, the division is charged with handling large crowds who attend sports events, conventions, parades, circuses, and funerals. The Traffic Division consists of

the following groups: Motorcycle, Accident Investigation, Foot Traffic, Parking Control, Radar Speed Control, and Helicopter Traffic Control. The division also includes School Police Officers, School Patrols, and the police wrecker.

Superintendent Spencer J. Lloyd heads the Traffic Division. He joined the department in 1952 and was named superintendent in 1980.

According to Chief Rousseau, if the Traffic Division can keep the number of fatalities low, the other traffic accident statistics will be reduced also. In pursuit of this goal, Chief Rousseau and Superintendent Lloyd meet weekly to discuss the current and projected traffic situation with representatives of the city, county, and provincial government agencies responsible for highways, the Calgary Safety Council, and several prominent citizens.

Uniform Division

The Uniform Division is charged with the protection of life and property, the prevention of crime, the detection and arrest of offenders, and the preservation of the public peace. Superintendent Samuel Locke is the commanding officer. He joined the department in 1949 and was named superintendent in 1966. Superintendent Locke's division consists of the following squads and bureaus: Radio Patrol; Motorcycle (nontraffic); K–9 Corps; Unincorporated Detail (see below); and Foot Patrols.

The Calgary Police Department furnishes, through the Uniform Division, services to the unincorporated area of Fulton County under a contract between the City of Calgary and Fulton County. The personnel and equipment comprising the Unincorporated Detail includes 4 captains; 2 lieutenants; 60 patrol officers; 16 patrol cars; 22 school traffic officers; and 8 motorcycles.

Detention Division

The Detention Division was established in

1973. Previously it was part of the service division. According to Chief Rousseau, during the racial problems of the early 1970's, 400 to 500 persons might be jailed at any one time. This created numerous problems that he believed could best be handled by a separate division.

Superintendent Jack Marston heads the Detention Division, which is responsible for the operations of the adjoining headquarters building and the detention ward at the Saint Simon Hospital, a large downtown public hospital. During 1980 about 155,000 people were processed by the Detention Division.

Superintendent Marston joined the department in 1955 and was named superintendent in 1966.

Training Division

The Training Division was created in 1974. Formerly it was part of the service division. The Training Division is responsible for police training and the investigation of applicants seeking to join the department. The division's commanding officer is Superintendent T. N. Danvers. He joined the force in 1950 and was appointed superintendent in 1973.

The division's principal training activity is a six-week school for new recruits conducted at least three times a year. Between 40 and 55 people attend each session, which is set up along the same lines as the RCMP's National Academy. Each session usually includes several officers from other departments, such as the airport or park police. These officers attend free of charge.

Other training activities include bimonthly discussion by each squad of the training keys prepared by the International Association of Chiefs of Police. These meetings are conducted by lieutenants and sergeants for the officers in their squads. Periodically, written examinations are given to all officers. These papers are graded and the results recorded in each officer's personnel file.

Watch System

The Police Department operates on the watch (shift) system. The watches are:

11 P.M.-7 A.M.	Morning Watch	Traffic
7 A.M.-3 P.M.	Day Watch	Division
3 P.M.-11 P.M.	Night Watch	
10 A.M.-6 P.M.	Traffic Watch	(intersection control)
8-9 A.M. & 2-4 P.M.	School Patrol	
8 A.M.-4 P.M.	Office Personnel	
12 P.M.-8 A.M.		Uniform &
8 A.M.-4 P.M.		Detective
4 P.M.-12 P.M.		

Each watch is covered by a captain from either the Uniform or Traffic Divisions, depending upon which one happens to be on duty at the time. "In this way," Chief Rousseau said, "I am able to have a superior officer responsible for whatever happens during the watch."

Districts

For patrol duty purposes, the City of Calgary is divided into four districts. Either 10 or 11 two-person patrol cars are assigned to each district during each watch. These cars are in constant radio communication with the central radio room located in the police headquarters building. Chief Rousseau referred to these patrol cars as his "mobile precincts." He believed it would take more funds to operate his department if it were organized on a precinct basis.

STRENGTHS AND WEAKNESSES OF THE CURRENT ORGANIZATION

Interview with Chief Rousseau:

Changes in Formal Structure At the time I took over as chief, the service office operated out of the chief's office. In line with my desire to delegate authority, I created the Service Division and moved to the service and other divisions many of the management tasks formerly carried on by the chief's office. In the process I also abolished the two Deputy Chief of Police positions. Now, in my absence, the Superintendent of the Service Division acts as Chief.

Selection and Training When I became Chief, I took action in two areas. First, I wanted to improve the training of police officers. I realized a number of officers did not fully realize what was demanded or expected of them. Second, I wanted to strengthen the moral courage and integrity of the department. While it is not always manifest, police officers are always under scrutiny and open to accusation. It appeared to me a number of officers were overly fearful of making mistakes or being falsely accused. I set out to correct this situation through training and clear-cut policies.

Our personnel department will accept applications only if our training division says that in their opinion the applicant will make a good police officer. Once the applicant is accepted and joins the force, s/he is assigned a counselor who is either a lieutenant or sergeant. The officers are encouraged to discuss with their counselor their problems. Also, we have squad meetings periodically to discuss the things on the officers' minds. I've told the counselors that if I get any reports of misconduct involving their advisees, I want to see the counselor. I want results.

The improvements over the last 10 years have been remarkable. We now have procedures and facilities for selection, training, and continuous officer testing and development. The ability of our officers is high.

Referring to the Crime Commission Report Now the Crime Commission has recommended we get more involved in prevention activities for juvenile and organized crime. The Mayor has told me to follow up these recommendations, but not to go over my budget allocation. In a sense our 6 P.M. detail has functioned as our crime prevention detail. Moreover, the Commission report seems to be calling for more than the normal concept of a police officer's function. How should I organize for crime prevention? How many officers should I assign to this task? What kind of officers should they be? What are some of the things these officers should be doing? These are all questions I must resolve quickly.

Other Problems The police department is becoming very large. Size is a problem. Police officers get lost in the bureaucracy. They have trouble identifying with the purpose of the organization. I wonder if a "precinct" form of organization (self-contained area police units) would be better? In addition we have so much paperwork. Millions of pieces of paper are processed each year. No one likes it.

Coordination between divisions is poor. Each division is becoming a separate organization, doing its own business. For example, one division doesn't know what another is doing when working in schools or low-income areas. They don't communicate with one another. Other examples: a patrol officer will write up a burglary, and never hear back from the detective division. Job openings are usually filled from within the same division. Personnel rotation is poor. Police officers can spend their careers in one activity.

We would like to install a large centralized computer in the Service Division to handle paperwork and do statistical analyses. We are afraid it may be unreliable, and that it will make the Police Department more bureaucratic and impersonal. Could computers be installed in each division?

17

Club Méditerranée

Sipping a cognac and smoking one of his favorite cigars on his way back to Paris from New York on the Concorde, Serge Trigano was reviewing the new organization structure that was to be effective November 1981. In the process, he was listing the operational problems and issues that were yet to be resolved. Son of the chief executive of the "Club Med," Serge Trigano was one of the joint managing directors and he had just been promoted from director of operations to general manager of the American zone, i.e., responsible for operations and marketing for the whole American market. Having experienced a regional organization structure that was abandoned some four years ago, he wanted to make sure that this time the new structure would better fit the objectives of Club Med and allow its further development in a harmonious way.

COMPANY BACKGROUND AND HISTORY

Club Med was founded in 1950 by a group of friends led by Gérard Blitz. Initially, it was a non-profit organization, set up for the purpose of going on vacation together in some odd place. The initial members were essentially young people who liked sports and especially the sea. The first "village," a tent village, was a camping site in the Balearic Isles. After four years of activities, Gilbert Trigano was appointed the new managing director. Gilbert Trigano came to Club Med from a family business involved in the manufacture of tents in France, a major supplier to Club Med. With this move, and in the same year, the holiday village concept was expanded beyond tent villages to straw hut villages, the first of which was opened in 1954. Further expanding its activities, in 1956 Club Med opened its first ski resort at Leysin, Switzerland. In 1965, its first bungalow village was opened, and in 1968 the first village started its operation in the American zone. Club Med's main activity, which it still is today, was to operate a vacation site for tourists who would pay a fixed sum (package) to go on vacation for a week, two weeks, or a month and for whom all the facilities were

This case was prepared by Professor Jacques Horovitz as a basis for class discussion rather than to illuminate either effective or ineffective handling of an administrative situation. Copyright © 1981 by IMEDE (International Management Development Institute), Lausanne, Switzerland. Not to be used or reproduced without permission.

provided in the village. Club Med has always had the reputation of finding beautiful sites that were fairly new to tourists (for instance, Moroccan tourism was "discovered" by Club Med) and that offered many activities, especially sports activities, to its members.* In 1981, Club Med operated 90 villages in 40 different countries on five continents. In addition to its main activity, it had extended to other sectors of tourism in order to be able to offer a wider range of services. In 1976, Club Med acquired a 45% interest in an Italian company (Valtur) that had holiday villages in Italy, Greece, and Tunisia, mainly for the Italian market. In 1977 Club Med took over Club Hotel, which had built up a reputation over the last 12 years as a leader in the seasonal ownership time-sharing market. The result of this expansion had been such than in 1980 more than 770,000 people had stayed in the villages of Club Med or its Italian subsidiary, whereas there were 2,300 in 1950. Most members were French in 1950, and in 1980 only 45% were French. See Exhibit 17–1. In addition, 110,000 people had stayed in the apartments or hotels managed by its time-sharing activity. In 1980, Club Med sales were actually about 2.5 billion French francs and its cash flow around 170 million French francs. The present case focuses exclusively on the organization structure of the holiday village operations and not on the time-sharing activities of the company.

SALES AND MARKETING

In 1981 Club Med was international with vacation sites all over the world, and so were its customers. They came from different continents, backgrounds, market segments, and did not look for the same thing in the vacation package. Club Med offered different types of villages, a wide range of activities to accommodate all the people who chose to go on a package deal. The

---

* When going on vacation to any of Club Med's villages, one becomes a "member" of Club Med.

EXHIBIT 17–1   MEMBERS OF CLUB MED ACCORDING TO COUNTRY OF ORIGIN (1979) (EXCLUDING VALTUR)

France	301,000	43.1%
USA/Canada	124,000	17.8%
Belgium	41,600	6 %
Italy	34,400	4.9%
W. Germany	34,100	4.9%
Switzerland	18,500	2.6%
Austria	6,800	1 %
Australia	18,400	2.6%
Others	84,900	12.1%
Conference & seminars*	34,700	5 %*
	698,500	100 %

*Most seminars are in France for French customers.

Club offered ski villages, i.e., hotels in ski resorts for those who liked to ski; straw-hut villages with a very Spartan comfort on the Mediterranean, mainly for young bachelors; hotel and bungalow resort villages with all comfort open throughout the year, some with special facilities for families and young children. An average client who went to a straw-hut village on the Mediterranean usually did not go to a plush village at Cap Skirring in Senegal (and the price was different too), although the same type of person might go to both.

A family with two or three children who could afford the time and money needed to travel to a relatively nearby village with a baby club was less likely to go to a village in Malaysia due to the long journey and the cost of transportation. Broadly speaking, a whole range of holiday makers were represented among the Club's customers. However, there was a larger proportion of office workers, executives, and professional people and a small proportion of workers and top management. The sales and marketing of the Club, which began in Europe, had expanded to include two other important markets: the American zone, including the U.S., Canada, and South America, and the Far Eastern zone, including Japan and Australia. The Club's sales network covered 29 countries; sales were either direct through the club-owned offices, 23 of which existed at the moment (see Exhibit 17–2 for coun-

EXHIBIT 17-2   COUNTRIES OF OPERATIONS (BEFORE NEW STRUCTURE)

Country	Separate Commercial Office	Country Manager	Country Manager Supervising Commercial Operations	Villages
Germany	X			
Switzerland	X	X		X
Turkey			X	X
Italy	X	X		X
Venezuela	X			
Belgium	X			X
Mexico			X	X
USA	X	X		
Bahamas		X	same as U.S.	X
Haiti		X	same as U.S.	X
Brazil			X	X
Japan	X			
Great Britain	X			
Tunisia			X	X
Morocco		X		X
Holland	X			
Greece	X	X		X
Israel			X	X
Malaysia	X	X		X
France	X	X		
New Zealand	X			
Australia	X			X
Egypt		X		X
Singapore	X			
Canada	X			
Tahiti		X		X
South Africa	X			
Spain	X	X		X
Senegal		X	same	X
Ivory Coast		X		
Mauritius		X	same as Reunion	X
Sri Lanka		X	same as Mauritius	X
Guadeloupe		X	same as U.S.	X
Martinique		X	same as U.S.	X
Reunion Island		X		X
Dominican Republic		X	same as U.S.	X
United Arab Emirates				X

tries where the Club owns commercial offices as well as villages and operations) or indirect through travel agencies (in France Havas was the main retailer). Originally, all the villages were aimed at the European market; in 1968 with the opening of its first village in America, the Club broke into the American market and opened an office in New York. Since then, the American market had grown more or less independently. Some 80% of the beds in the villages located in the American geographical area were sold to Club members in the United States and Canada; 65% of French sales, which represent 47% of the Club's turnover, were direct by personal visits to the office, by telephone or letter. However, in the U.S., direct sales accounted for only 5% of the total, the remaining 95% being sold through travel agencies. These differences were partly explained by national preferences, but also by a deliberate choice on the part of the Club. Until the appointment of Serge Trigano to lead the U.S. zone, all sales and marketing offices reported to a single world-wide marketing director.

THE VILLAGE

Club Med had around 90 villages and it was growing fast. In the next three years (1981–84) about 20 new villages were scheduled to open. At Club Med a village was typically either a hotel, bungalows, or huts, usually in a very nice area offering vacationers such activities as swimming, tennis, sailing, water skiing, windsurfing, archery, gymnastics, snorkling, deep sea diving, horseback riding, applied arts, yoga, golf, boating, soccer, circuits, excursions, bike riding, and skiing. There were also usually on site a shop, a hairdresser, even some cash changing, car renting, etc., and a baby or mini club in many places. Club Med was well known for having chosen sites that were the best in any country where they were, not only from a geographical point of view, but also from an architectural point of view and the facilities provided. Exhibit 17–3 shows the number of villages that were open during the winter or summer season by type.

Essentially, there were three types of villages. The hut villages, which were the cheapest, open only during the summer season, and which started Club Med, and which were on the Mediterranean did not offer all the comfort that the wealthy traveler was used to (they had common showers, for example). Then there were bunga-

EXHIBIT 17-3   NUMBER OF VILLAGES BY TYPE
                   AND SEASON*

		Sea		Mountain	Total
	Huts	Bungalows	Hotels		
Summer season	14	31	26	10	81
Winter season	0	19	11	23	53

Source: *Club Méditerranée Trident N123/124 Winter 80-81,
            Summer 81.*

lows or hotels or "hard type" villages, which were more comfortable with private bathrooms. Most were still double-bedded, which meant that two single men or women would have to share the same bedroom. In a village, there were two types of people. The GMs, or "gentils membres," who were the customers, usually came for one, two, three, or four weeks on a package deal to enjoy all the facilities and activities of any village. The GOs, or "gentils organisateurs," helped people make this vacation the best; there were GOs for sports, for applied arts, for excursions, for food, for the bar, as disk jockeys, as dancing instructors, for the children or babies in the miniclubs, for maintenance, for traffic, for accounting, for receptions, etc. [Although the GOs were specialized by function, they also had to be simply "gentils organisateurs," i.e., making the GM's life easy and participating in common activities, such as arrival cocktails,

shows, games, etc.] On average, there were 80 to 100 GOs per village.

There was a third category of people who were behind the scene: the service people, usually local people hired to maintain the facilities, the garden, to clean up, etc. (about 150 service people per village). They could also be promoted to GOs.

Every season, i.e., either after the summer season from May to September and winter season in April, or every six months, all the GOs would be moved from one village to another; that was one of the principles of the Club since its inception, so that nobody would stay for more than six months in any particular site. The village chief of maintenance was an exception. He stayed one full year; if a village was closed in the winter, he remained for the painting, the repair, etc. The service people (local people) were there all year around or for six months, if the village was only open in the summer (or winter for ski resorts). Exhibit 17-4 shows a typical organization structure of a village from the GO's point of view.

Under the chief of the village there were several coordinators: one for entertainment, responsible for all the day and night activities (shows, music, night club, plays, games, etc.); the sports chief who coordinated all the sports activities in any particular village; the maintenance chief who would see to the maintenance of the vil-

EXHIBIT 17-4   ORGANIZATION CHART OF A TYPICAL VILLAGE

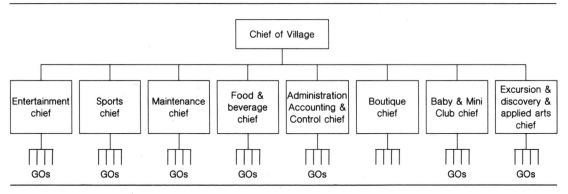

lage, either when there was a breakdown or just to repaint the village or keep the garden clean, grow new flowers, etc., and who was assisted by the local service people; the food and beverage chief who coordinated the cooking in the different restaurants and was responsible for the bar. Usually there was a bazaar for miscellaneous, a garment boutique, and a hairdresser under a boutique's coordinator. There was a coordinator for the baby club (if existent) within the village to provide the children with some special activities; this coordinator was also responsible for the medical part of the village (nurses and doctor). Many times there was a doctor on site, especially when a village was far from a big town. There was a coordinator of excursions and applied arts. Its services would help the GM to go somewhere or propose accompanied excursions (one, two, three days) for those who wanted it, or try with the help of a GO to make a silk scarf or pottery. There was a coordinator of administration, accounting, and control who dealt with cash, telephone, traffic, planning

and reception, basic accounting, salaries for GOs and service personnel, taxes, etc. The services of food and beverages and the maintenance were the heaviest users of local service personnel.

COMPANY ORGANIZATION STRUCTURE

Exhibit 17–5 shows the organization structure of Club Med's holiday village activity just before Serge Trigano's appointment as Director of the U.S. zone. (The rest—time-sharing activities—are additional product-market subsidiaries.)

There were several joint managing directors who participated in the Management Committee. Essentially, the structure was a functional one with a joint managing director for marketing and sales, another one for operations, and several other function heads for accounting, finance and tax. Exhibit 17–6 shows how the operations part of the organization was structured.

Essentially the structure was composed of three parts. As there was an entertain-

EXHIBIT 17–5   ORGANIZATION CHART—BEFORE NOVEMBER 1981
HOLIDAY VILLAGES ACTIVITY ONLY

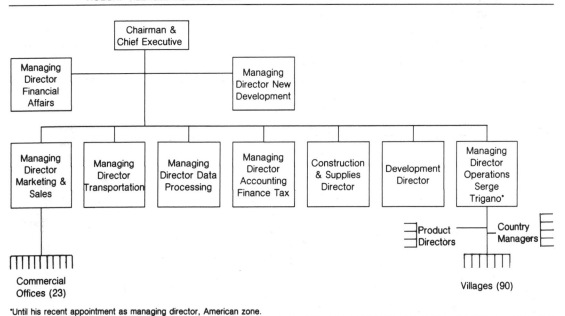

*Until his recent appointment as managing director, American zone.

EXHIBIT 17-6   ORGANIZATION CHART—JUST BEFORE THE NEW MOVE (NOV. 1981)

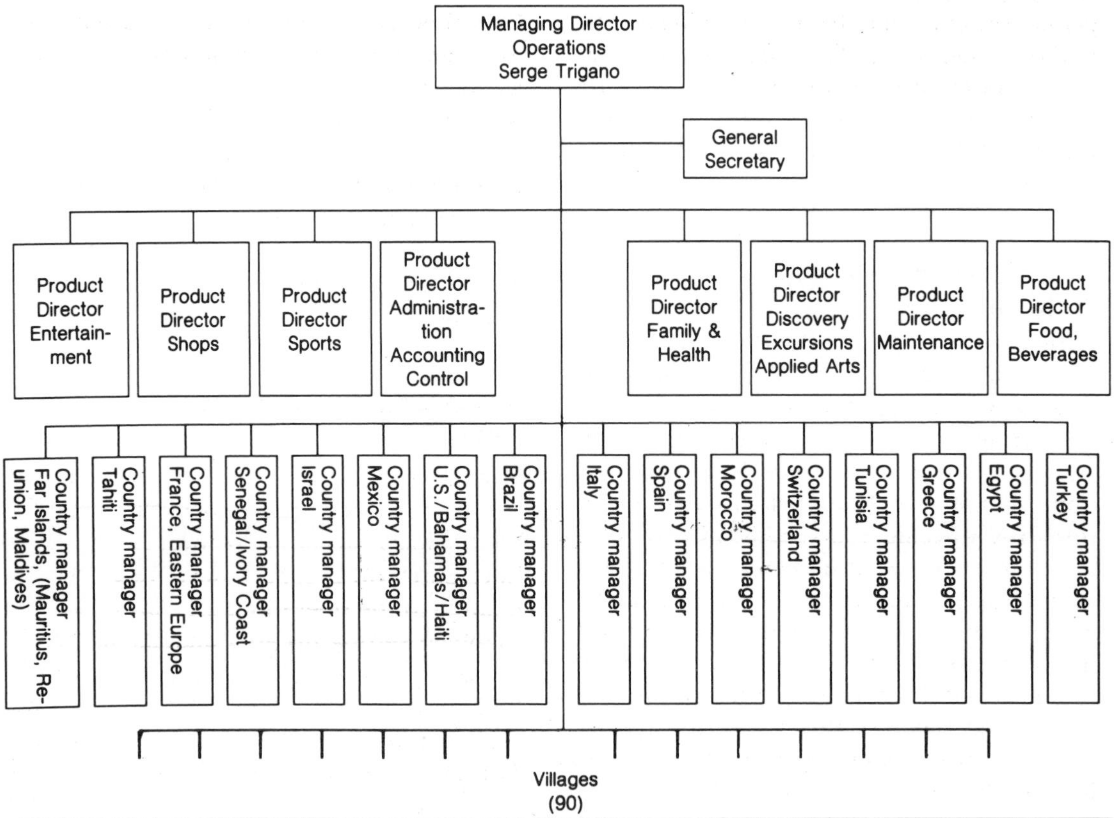

```
                          ┌─────────────────────┐
                          │  Managing Director  │
                          │     Operations      │
                          │    Serge Trigano    │
                          └─────────────────────┘
                                    │
                                    │        ┌──────────────┐
                                    │        │   General    │
                                    │        │  Secretary   │
                                    │        └──────────────┘
```

| Product Director Entertainment | Product Director Shops | Product Director Sports | Product Director Administration Accounting Control | Product Director Family & Health | Product Director Discovery Excursions Applied Arts | Product Director Maintenance | Product Director Food, Beverages |

Country manager Far Islands, (Mauritius, Reunion, Maldives) · Country manager Tahiti · Country manager France, Eastern Europe · Country manager Senegal/Ivory Coast · Country manager Israel · Country manager Mexico · Country manager U.S./Bahamas/Haiti · Country manager Brazil · Country manager Italy · Country manager Spain · Country manager Morocco · Country manager Switzerland · Country manager Tunisia · Country manager Greece · Country manager Egypt · Country manager Turkey

Villages
(90)

ment chief in the village, there was a director of entertainment at head office; the same was true of sports. There were several product directors who mirrored the structure of the village. There were country managers in certain countries where the Club had several villages in operation, and then there were the 90 villages. All reported to Serge Trigano.

THE ROLE OF THE PRODUCT DIRECTORS

Product directors were responsible for the product policy. They made decisions with respect to the policy of Club Med in all the villages, such as the type of activities that should be in each village, and the maintenance that should be done. They recruited and trained the various GOs needed for their domain (i.e., sports GOs, entertainment GOs, administration GOs, cooks, etc.). They staffed the villages by deciding with the director of operations which chief of village would go where and how many people would go with him. They made investment proposals for each village either for maintenance, new activities, extension, or renovation purposes. They also assumed the task of preparing the budgets and controlling application of policies in the villages by traveling extensively as "ambassadors" of the head office to the villages. Each one of them was assigned a certain number of villages. When visiting the village, he would go there representing not his particular product but Club Med's product as a whole. Also, each of them, including the director of operations, was assigned on a rotating basis the task of answering emergency phone calls from any village and making emergency decisions, or taking action if necessary. Exhibit 17–7 presents examples of product organization. In the new regional structure, their role and place were questioned.

THE ROLE OF THE COUNTRY MANAGER

Country managers were mainly the ambassadors of Club Med in the countries where Club Med had village(s). Usually they were located in countries with more than one village. They would handle political relations themselves, maintaining lasting relationships with elected bodies, mayors, civil servants, regional offices, etc. They would introduce to the new team coming every six months what the country had to offer, its constraints, local mores, the local people to be invited, local artists to be invited, the traps to be avoided, the types of suppliers, the type of local events that might be of interest for the village (so that the village would not forget, for instance, national holidays, etc.). They would try to get Club Med more integrated politically and socially in the host country, in particular in less developed countries where there was a gap between the abundance and richness of the Club compared to its immediate environment. They also had an assistance role such as getting work permits for GOs and also finding suppliers; sometimes, in fact, the country manager had a buyer attached to his staff who would purchase locally for the different villages to get economies of scale. In addition, the country managers personally recruited and maintained lists of the service personnel available to Club Med. They would negotiate the salaries, wages, and working conditions of the service personnel with the unions so that the village wasn't involved every six months in a renegotiation. Also, they might have an economic

role by helping develop local production or culture as the Club was a heavy buyer of local food and products. They could also act as a development antenna looking for new sites or receiving proposals from local investors and submit them to head office. They would handle legal and tax problems when Club Med had a local legal entity, and maintain relationships with the owners of the land, hotels, or bungalows when Club Med—as was often the case—was only renting the premises.

PROBLEMS WITH THE CURRENT STRUCTURE

The current structure had been set up about four years ago. It had also been the Club Med's structure before 1971, but in between (1971–1976) there had been a change in the operations side only that had involved setting up area managers; instead of having one director of operations, there had been five directors who had under their control several countries and villages. From 1971 to 1976, there had been no country managers and each of the area managers had had about 10 or 15 villages under his supervision. This structure was changed in 1976 because it seemed to have created several Club Meds in one. The area managers had started to try to get the best chiefs of village and people for their area. As a result, GOs were not moving around every six months from one area of the world to another as was the policy, and area managers started giving different types of services to their customers so that, for instance, a Frenchman going to one of the zones one year and to another the next year would find a different Club Med. These reasons had led to the structure presented in Exhibit 17–6 for the operations. But until now marketing had always been world-wide.

Of course, the structure in operation until now had created the reverse problem: it

EXHIBIT 17–7 EXAMPLES OF PRODUCT MANAGEMENT

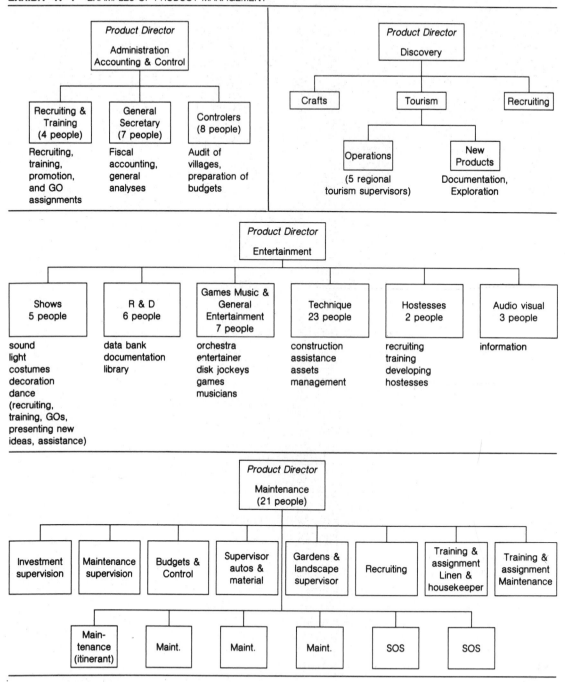

seemed to Serge Trigano and others that it was too centralized. In fact, Serge Trigano had a span of control (which is rarely achieved in industry) of 90 chiefs of village plus 8 product directors and 14 country managers, all reporting to him from all over the world. There was an overload of information, too much detail and too many issues being entrusted to him, which would be worse as time would go by since Club Med was growing and doubling its capacity every five years. Besides the problem of centralization and information overload, another problem seemed to appear because Club Med's operations had not adapted enough to the international character of its customers. Most of the GOs were still recruited in France whereas now 15–20% of the customers came from the American zone. France was not even the best location to find GOs, who often needed to speak at least one other language. They had to be unmarried, under 30, they had to change countries every six months, and they had to work long hours and be accessible 24 hours a day, seven days a week, for a relatively low salary. The feeling was that maybe one could find happier and more enthusiastic people in Australia or Brazil than in France. Too much centralization, information overload, and lack of internationalization in operations were among the big problems in the current structure. Also, there was a feeling that a closer local coordination between marketing and operations could give better results since customers seemed to concentrate on one zone (American in the U.S., European in Europe) because of transportation costs, and a coordination might lead to a better grasp of customer needs, price, product, offices, etc. For example, when Club Med was smaller and operating only in Europe, departure to its villages was possible only once a week. As a result, reception at the village, welcome, and departure was also once a week. Lack of local coordination between operations and marketing had created arrivals and departures almost every day in certain villages, overburdening GO smiles and organization of activities. As another illustration, the American customer was used to standard hotel services (such as bathroom, towels, etc.), which may differ from European services. Closer local ties might help the Club respond better to local needs.

Centralization had also created bottlenecks in assignments and supervision of people. Every six months everybody—all GOs—was coming back to Paris from all over the world to be assigned to another village. Five or ten years ago, this was in fact a great happening that allowed everybody to discuss with the product people, see headquarters, and find friends who had been in other villages. But now with 5,000 GOs coming almost at the same time—and wanting to speak to the product directors—reassigning them was becoming somewhat hectic. It was likely to be even worse in the future because of the growth of the company.

PLANNING AND CONTROL

The planning cycle could be divided into two main parts: first, there was a three-year plan started two years ago, which involved the product directors and the country managers. Each product director would define his objectives for the next three years, the action programs that would go with it, and propose investments that he would like to make for his product in each of the 90 villages. All the product directors would meet to look at the villages one by one and see how the investment fitted together as well as consider the staffing number of GOs and service personnel in broad terms for the next three years. Of course, the big chunk of the investment program was the maintenance of the facilities since 55% of the investment program concerned such maintenance programs. The rest was concerned with additions or modifications of the villages, such as new tennis courts, a new theater, restaurant, revamping a boutique, etc. The country managers were involved in that same three-year plan. First of all they would give the product directors their feelings and suggestions for investments as well as for staffing the villages. In addition, they would provide some objectives and action programs in the way they would try to handle personnel problems, political problems, economic problems, cultural and social integration, sales of Club Med in their country, and development.

Besides this three-year operational plan, there was the one-year plan that was divided into two six-month plans. For each season a budget was prepared for each of the villages. This budget was mostly prepared by the product director for administration accounting, and it concerned the different costs, such as goods consumed, personnel charges, rents, etc. This budget was given to the chief of the village when he left with his team. In addition to this operational budget, there was an investment budget every six months that was more detailed than the three-year plan. This investment budget was prepared by the maintenance director under the guidance of and proposals from the different product directors. It was submitted to the operations director and then went directly to the chief executive of the company. It had not been unusual before the three-year plan had been controlled that the proposals that product directors were making to the maintenance director were three times as high as what would be in fact given and allowed by the chief executive.

On the control side, there was a controller in each of the villages (administrator chief of accounting and control) as well as central controllers who would be assigned a region and would travel from one village to the other. But the local controller and his team in fact were GOs like any others and they were changing from one village to another every six months. There was a kind of "fact and rule book" that was left in the village so that the next team would understand the particular ways and procedures of the village. But, generally speaking, each new team would start all over again each time with a new budget and standard, rules, and procedures from central head office as well as with the help of the fact and rule book. These two tools—the three-year plan and the six-month (a season) budgets—were the main planning and control tools used.

OBJECTIVES AND POLICIES

Five objectives seemed to be important to Serge Trigano when reviewing the structure.

One was that the Club wanted to continue to grow and double its capacity every five years, either by adding new villages or increasing the size of the current ones.

The second objective, which had always guided Club Med, was that it would continue to innovate, not to be a hotel chain but to be something different as it had always been and to continue to respond to the changing needs of the customers.

A third objective stemmed from the fact that Club Med was no longer essentially French; the majority of its customers did not in fact come from France. As a result, it would have to continue to internationalize its employees, its structure, its way of thinking, training, etc.

The fourth objective was economic. Costs were increasing, but not all these costs could be passed on to the *gentils membres* unless the Club wanted to stop its growth. One way of not passing all costs to the customer was to increase productivity by standardization and by better methods and procedures.

The fifth objective was to retain the basic philosophy of Club Med: to keep the village concept an entity protected as much as possible from the outside world, but integrated in the country in which it was; to keep the package concept for GMs; and finally to retain the social mixing. Whatever your job, your social position, etc., at Club Med you were only recognized by two things: the color of your bathing suit and the beads you wore around your neck that allowed you to pay for your scotch, orange juice, etc., at the bar. Part of the philosophy, in addition, was to make sure that the GO's nomadism would continue: change every season.

THE PROPOSED NEW STRUCTURE

With these objectives in mind, the new structure to be effective November 1981 had just been sketched as shown in Exhibit 17–8.

The idea would be to move the operations and marketing closer together in three zones. One would be America (North and South), another Europe and Africa, and the third (in the long run when this market would be more developed) the Far East. In each area, a director would manage the operations side (the villages) and the marketing side (promotion, selling, pricing, distributing Club Med's concept). In fact, most of the American GMs were going to the American zone villages, most of the European GMs to the European zone, and most of the Asian GMs to the Asian zone. As the cost of transportation from one zone to another was increasing, people could not afford to go very far.

This was the general idea and now it had to be pushed further. Among the main interesting and troublesome aspects of the new structure were the following: how to keep the Club Med from separating into three different entities with three different types of products with this structure? Should such an occurrence be avoided? It seemed that this should not be allowed; that's why the structure that had been there four years ago with five regions failed. It had transformed Club Med into

EXHIBIT 17–8   THE PROPOSED STRUCTURE

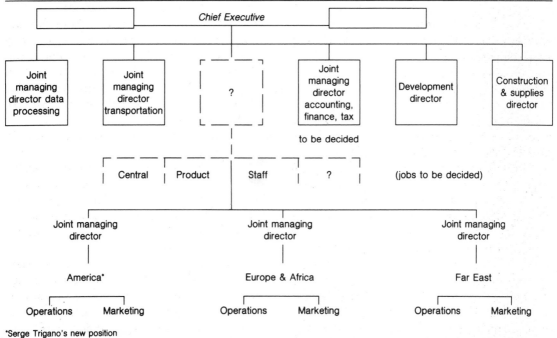

*Serge Trigano's new position

five mini Club Meds, although even at that time the five area managers did not have marketing and sales responsibility. In addition to this major issue of how to preserve the unity and uniqueness of Club Med with a geographic structure, several other questions were of great importance:

- Who would decide what activities would take place in a village?
- Who would decide the investments to be made in a village?
- Who would staff a village?
- Would there be a central hiring and training of all GOs or only some of them?
- How would the geographic managers be evaluated in terms of performance?
- If they wanted to continue with the GOs and give them the right and the opportunity to move every six months from one part of the world to another, how would the transfer of GOs be done?
- How should the transfer of GOs be coordinated?

- Should there be some common basic procedures, like accounting, reporting, etc., and in that case, who would design and enforce those procedures?
- How could there be some coordination and allocation of resources among the three regions? Who would do it? How would it be done?

Also of importance was the problem of transition.

- What would happen to the country managers?
- What would happen to the product directors?
- What would happen to central marketing and sales?

These were some of the questions that bothered Serge Trigano on the flight to Paris from New York.

18

C & C Grocery Stores, Inc.

The first C & C grocery store was started in 1947 by Doug Cummins and his brother Bob. Both were veterans who wanted to run their own business, so they used their savings to start the small grocery store in Charlotte, North Carolina. The store was immediately successful. The location was good, and Doug Cummins had a winning personality. Store employees adopted Doug's informal style and "serve the customer" attitude. C & C's increasing circle of customers enjoyed an abundance of good meats and produce.

By 1984, C & C had over 200 stores. A standard physical layout was used for new stores. Company headquarters moved from Charlotte to Atlanta in 1975. The organization chart for C & C is shown in Exhibit 18–1. The central offices in Atlanta handled personnel, merchandising, financial, purchasing, real estate, and legal affairs for the entire chain. For management of individual stores, the organization was divided by regions. The southern, southeastern, and northeastern regions each had about seventy stores. Each region was divided into five districts of ten to fifteen stores each. A district director was responsible for supervision and coordination of activities for the ten to fifteen district stores.

Each district was divided into four lines of authority based upon functional specialty. Three of these lines reached into the stores. The produce department manager within each store reported directly to the produce specialist for the division, and the same was true for the meat department manager, who reported directly to the district meat specialist. The meat and produce managers were responsible for all activities associated with the acquisition and sale of perishable products. The store manager's responsibility included the grocery line, front-end departments, and store operations. The store manager was responsible for appearance of personnel, cleanliness, adequate check-out service, and price accuracy. A grocery manager reported to the store manager and maintained inventories and restocked shelves for grocery items.

Prepared by Richard L. Daft. From: *Organizations: A Micro/Macro Approach* by Richard L. Daft and Richard Steers. Copyright © 1986 by Scott, Foresman and Company. Reprinted by permission.

The district merchandising office was responsible for promotional campaigns, advertising circulars, district advertising, and for attracting customers into the stores. The grocery merchandisers were expected to coordinate their activities with each store in the district.

During the recession in 1980–81, business for the C & C chain dropped off in all regions and did not increase with improved economic times in 1983–84. This caused concern among senior executives. They also were aware that other supermarket chains were adopting a trend toward one-stop shopping, which meant the emergence of super stores that included a pharmacy, dry goods, and groceries—almost like a department store. Executives wondered whether C & C should move in this direction and how such changes could be assimilated into the current store organization. However, the most pressing problem was how to improve business with the grocery stores they now had. A consulting team from a major university was hired to investigate store structure and operations.

The consultants visited several stores in each region, talking to about fifty managers

EXHIBIT 18–1   ORGANIZATION STRUCTURE FOR C & C GROCERY STORES, INC.

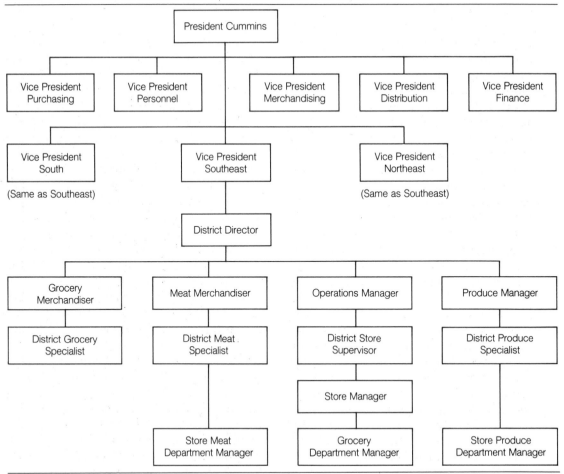

and employees. The consultants wrote a report that pinpointed four problem areas to be addressed by store executives.

1. The chain is slow to adapt to change. Store layout and structure were the same as had been designed fifteen years ago. Each store did things the same way even though some stores were in low-income areas and other stores in suburban areas. A new grocery management system for ordering and stocking had been developed, but after two years was only partially implemented in the stores.

2. Roles of the district store supervisor and the store manager were causing dissatisfaction. The store managers wanted to learn general management skills for potential promotion into district or regional management positions. However, their jobs restricted them to operational activities and they learned little about merchandising, meat, and produce. Moreover, district store supervisors used store visits to inspect for cleanliness and adherence to operating standards rather than to train the store manager and help coordinate operations with perishable departments. Close supervision on the operational details had become the focus of operations management rather than development, training, and coordination.

3. Cooperation within stores was low and morale was poor. The informal, friendly atmosphere originally created by Doug Cummins was gone. One example of this problem occurred when the grocery merchandiser and store manager in a Louisiana store decided to promote Coke and Diet Coke as a loss leader. Thousands of cartons of Coke were brought in for the sale, but the stockroom was not prepared and did not have room. The store manager wanted to use floor area in the meat and produce sections to display Coke cartons, but those managers refused. The pro-

duce department manager said that Diet Coke did not help his sales and it was okay with him if there was no promotion at all.

4. Long-term growth and development of the stores chain would probably require reevaluation of long-term strategy. The percent of market share going to traditional grocery stores was declining nationwide due to competition from large super stores and convenience stores. In the future, C & C might need to introduce non-food items into the stores for one-stop shopping, and add specialty sections within stores. Some stores could be limited to grocery items, but store location and marketing techniques should take advantage of the grocery emphasis.

To solve the first three problems, the consultants recommended reorganizing the district and the store structure as illustrated in Exhibit 18–2. Under this reorganization, the meat, grocery, and produce department managers would all report to the store manager. The store manager would have complete store control and would be responsible for coordination of all store activities. The district supervisor's role would be changed from supervision to training and development. The district supervisor would head a team that included himself and several meat, produce, and merchandise specialists who would visit area stores as a team to provide advice and help for the store managers and other employees. The team would act in a liaison capacity between district specialists and the stores.

The consultants were enthusiastic about the proposed structure. By removing one level of district operational supervision, store managers would have more freedom and responsibility. The district liaison team would establish a cooperative team approach to management that could be adopted within stores. The focus of store responsibility on a single manager would

EXHIBIT 18-2 PROPOSED REORGANIZATION OF C & C GROCERY STORES, INC.

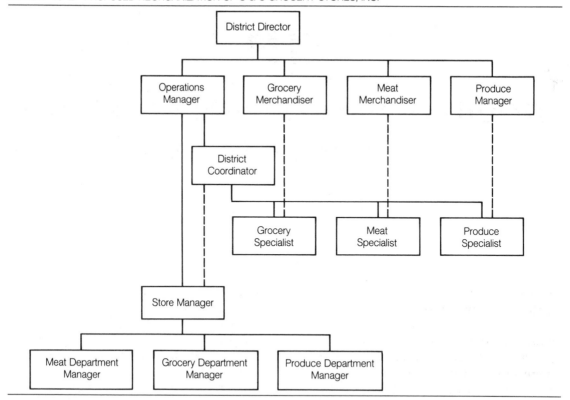

encourage coordination within stores, adaptation to local conditions, and provide a focus of responsibility for store-wide administrative changes.

The consultants also believe that the proposed structure could be expanded to accommodate non-grocery lines if enlarged stores were to be developed in the future.

Within each store, a new department manager could be added for pharmacy, dry goods, or other major departments. The district team could be expanded to include specialists in these departments who would act as liaison for stores in the district.

19

Dennison Manufacturing Company: A Proposed Reorganization

Top management at the Dennison Manu-facturing Company was considering a plan to reorganize the marketing division. This plan was intended to fix responsibility for profits by product lines at the top manage-ment level of the company. The president and other executives believed there was a trend for companies to organize along product lines to gain benefits of specializa-tion and to fix profit responsibility. The di-rector of marketing felt that the "intensifi-cation of competition" was forcing this change on Dennison. He stated, "While dis-trict sales managers are generally well in-formed, they are not getting the answers they need to meet competition on all the company's lines. In this period of intense competition they need strong home office backing on each of our lines."

BACKGROUND

The Dennison Manufacturing Company, a paper converter, sold more than 6,000 stock items plus thousands of made-to-order products used by millions of people in homes, schools, offices, factories, stores, professions, and service enterprises. "Mak-ing paper more useful to more people" was the basic Dennison policy for success. The company utilized materials produced by others and added value to these materials through creative and productive tech-niques. The home office and main factory was located in Framingham, Massachu-setts. Five other manufacturing plants were also maintained by Marlboro and Maynard, Massachusetts; Chicago, Illinois; Drum-mondville, Quebec; and in England.

Dennison produced and sold boxes, crepe papers, gift wrappings, gummed pa-pers, labels, packages, party decorations, school and office supplies, tags, tapes, tick-ets, seals, specialties, and machine systems. The set-up paper box line which included made-to-order and stock boxes and cases was sold primarily to jewelers, department stores, and manufacturers. Stock merchan-dise for home, school, and business use such as crepe paper, marking tags, ship-ping tags, gummed labels, gummed papers, gift wrapping papers, decorations, diaper

By Fred Kniffen, Professor of Marketing, University of Connecticut, in *Administering the Going Concern* by Leslie Waters, Wayne Broehl, Charles H. Spencer, and Ray M. Powell, *Administering the Going Concern*, Prentice-Hall, Inc., Englewood Cliffs, N.J., 1962. Reprinted by permission.

liners, pin tickets and holiday merchandise was sold by Dennison salesmen to wholesalers and retailers. Also, some stock merchandise was sold to manufacturers in lines such as novelties and artificial flowers. Made-to-order merchandise such as printed tags, labels, and seals, printed crepe and price marking equipment and tickets were marketed primarily to manufacturers, transportation companies and large-scale distributors for packaging, production control, product identification, informative labeling, price marking, and shipping.

Both sales and net earnings for the past ten years had approximately doubled.

ORGANIZATION OF THE MARKETING DIVISION

The organization charts in Exhibits 19–1, 19–2, and 19–3 show the company's current marketing organization. Reporting to the director of marketing were the general merchandise manager and publicity director. R. S. Thomson, the director of marketing, also held the position of general sales manager and in this capacity the four division sales managers reported to him. The duties and responsibilities of the four division sales managers and twenty-four district sales managers are shown in Exhibit 19–4. The selling organization is shown in Exhibit 19–2. Each sales district number denoted the product line or lines under the supervision of the district manager. In districts numbered less than one hundred, district managers had reporting to them salesmen who were selling all the company's product lines. Depending upon the market, individual salesmen in these districts may have sold the entire Dennison product line or have specialized in certain products. However, all of them reported to a non-specialized (by product line) district manager. In districts numbered in the one hundreds, the district managers were responsible only for resale product lines

which included dealer-crepe, gummed and coated papers, holiday, and box lines. Most one-hundred district salesmen were strictly resale product salesmen. In districts with two-hundred numbers, the manager and salesmen specialized exclusively on machine systems, while in the three-hundred numbered districts they specialized exclusively on industrial products. Salesmen in the four-hundred district in New York sold box merchandise only.

The six merchandise managers reported to the general merchandise manager through the assistant general merchandise manager, as shown in Exhibit 19–3. Each of the six managers was responsible for the sales volume and gross profit of his line. (Gross profit was the difference between selling price and finished goods factory cost.) The functions of the merchandise division are shown in Exhibit 19–5.

Relations were excellent between the field sales organization and the merchandising division. Merchandise managers kept themselves informed by traveling with salesmen to call on customers from time to time. Salesmen called on the merchandise divisions for technical and specialized information on their problems. Merchandise managers kept salesmen informed on sales problems and market information by sending out "sales letters."

The director of marketing used a pricing problem to illustrate the working relationship between the selling and merchandising organizations. He reported that if a competitor offered goods at a lower price than Dennison, the salesman reported this to his district manager, who in turn referred the matter to the division manager. Division managers had some discretion over prices, depending upon the limits set by the merchandise manager for the particular product line. This leeway ranged from 5 to 10 per cent depending upon the product. If the salesman's request for a special price was within this discretionary range,

EXHIBIT 19-1 DENNISON MANUFACTURING CO. GENERAL ORGANIZATION

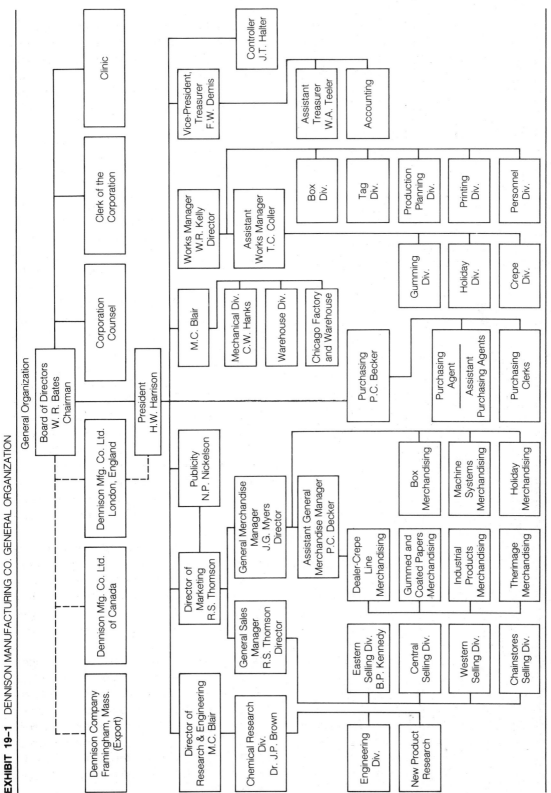

EXHIBIT 19-2 DENNISON MANUFACTURING CO. SELLING ORGANIZATION

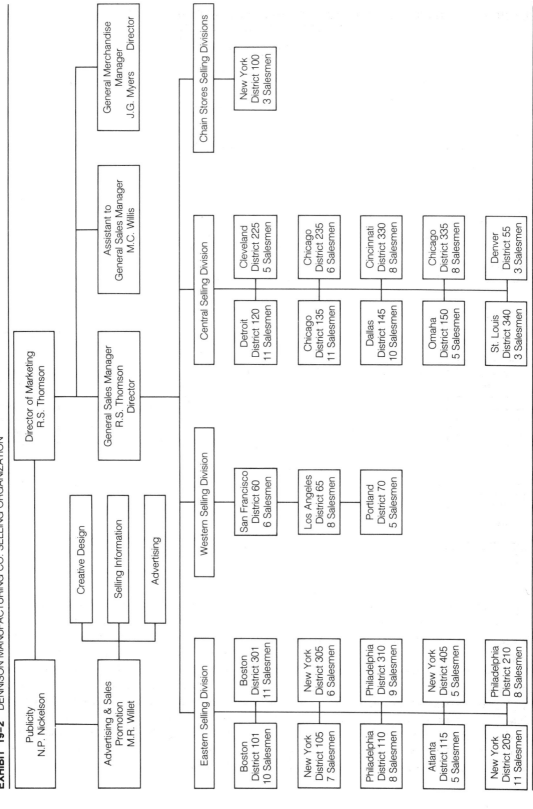

EXHIBIT 19–3 DENNISON MANUFACTURING CO. MERCHANDISING ORGANIZATION

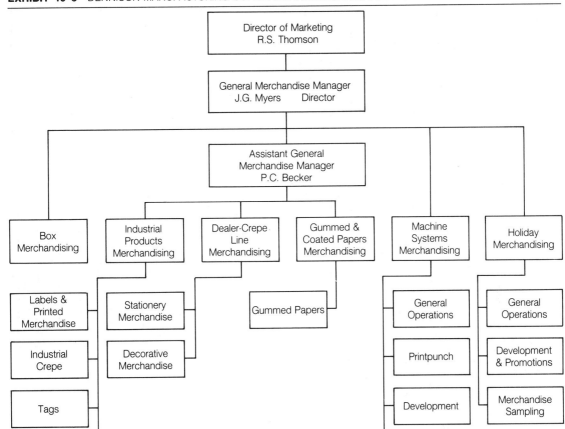

the division manager made the decision. If the request was for a price outside of the discretionary range, an "estimate call" was placed to the merchandise manager who then decided whether or not to meet the competitor's price.

The merchandising division was responsible for the marketing research activities of the firm. Merchandise managers assigned marketing research on their products to assistants or initiated projects themselves. In recent years the company had expanded its marketing research activities by hiring two market researchers to work on long-range problems in the new product research division under M. C. Blair, director of research and engineering. Also, the merchandise managers retained outside marketing research consultants who often were assigned projects which merchandise managers had submitted to the marketing committee.

EXHIBIT 19–4   DENNISON MANUFACTURING
                   COMPANY

DUTIES AND RESPONSIBILITIES OF THE DIVISION MANAGER

The Division Manager is responsible for the over-all sales in his division and for seeing to it that all Sales Managers carry out their duties.

He will be responsible for carrying out the company policies in respect to sales personnel and expense control.

He will be responsible for maintaining records and providing reports of orders received and sales by commodities as required by the Director of Sales.

Selling Functions

He will be responsible for the following selling functions:

1.   Determination and fulfillment of commodity sales quotas for each district.

2.   Making sure that each District Manager establishes and carries out an adequate system of coverage planning.

3.   Securing technical assistance from other divisions of the company whenever necessary and with the approval of the Director of Sales.

4.   The Division Manager will not be directly responsible for order getting and order handling negotiations with customers and the Framingham, Marlboro, and Chicago Plants.

Product Functions

The Division Manager will be responsible for the following product functions:

1.   Estimates of commodity sales for budget purposes.

2.   Reporting competitor activities and progress to the Director of Sales.

3.   Reporting the need for changes in policies to meet competition or to maintain good customer relations.

Personnel

1.   The Division Manager will exercise the final control of all personnel within his division for hiring, training, assignment and discharge.

2.   He will make salary budget recommendations to the Director of Sales for all the personnel in his division.

3.   He will consult with Sales Managers and Service Managers as a basis for making salary change recommendations.

4.   In offices where there is more than one Product Sales Manager, the Division Manager will appoint one Senior Manager to resolve office problems which cannot be settled by the Service Manager.

Expense Control

1.   The Division Manager will be responsible for administering the expense budgets established by the Director of Sales.

2.   He will be responsible for the negotiation of office leases subject to the approval of the Director of Sales, delegating to the Resident Sales Manager in question the preliminary negotiations.

DUTIES AND RESPONSIBILITIES OF DISTRICT SALES MANAGERS

The Sales Manager will report to the Division Manager. The Sales Manager will be directly responsible for the following:

1.   Planning for and carrying out the plans to secure sales in accordance with the established quotas by commodity groups and in accordance with sales budgets.

2.   The direction and supervision of the salesmen and any other personnel under his jurisdiction.

3.   Order-getting and order-handling negotiations with customers, and if necessary to call for aid on the Framingham, Marlboro, and Chicago Plants.

4.   Informing his Division Manager of any important large volume business negotiations that are not proceeding satisfactorily.

5.   Securing proper distribution of sales in relation to the market in his district.

6.   Keeping Merchandise Division Managers informed of new product requirements and needs for changes in established commodities. In case of written reports, copies should be sent to his Division Manager.

7.   Making personal contacts with the principal accounts in his district, becoming well acquainted with their key personnel, and seeing that these accounts are properly served.

8.   Maintaining a complete and accurate knowledge of competitor activities, and reporting anything of interest to Merchandise Managers and his Selling Division Manager.

9.   Controlling expense in accordance with the budget and policies laid down by the Division Manager.

10.   Properly maintaining automobiles and selling and sampling equipment.

11.   Preparing estimates of district sales for budgeting purposes as required by the Division Manager.

12.   Properly maintaining furniture and fixtures, except in those offices where there is a Service Manager who will be responsible for this function.

13.   Cooperating with Sales Managers and salesmen of other product lines to the best interest of the company.

Each Sales Manager will be directly responsible for the sales of his line of merchandise within his district; he will not be responsible for any other line of merchandise.

When a salesman is responsible for the sale of two or more lines he will consult his Sales Manager about any nonselling problems. Selling problems are to be referred to the Sales Manager of the line concerned.

When a Sales Manager notes any improper conduct on the part of a salesman in an office where the man's Sales Manager does not reside, the matter should be referred to the salesman's Manager for whatever action is advisable.

It is inevitable that some salesmen will look to the resident Sales Manager for advice on problems which are beyond that Sales Manager's jurisdiction. If the question is of such nature that it should be referred to the salesman's own Sales Manager, the salesman should be so advised by the resident Sales Manager.

In offices where there is no Service Manager the clerical staff will report to the Sales Manager, who will be responsible for the hiring, training, and direction of clerical staff; and for the proper division of their time between the respective lines. Any conflicts arising are to be referred to the Division Manager.

EXHIBIT 19–5   DENNISON MANUFACTURING COMPANY

FUNCTIONS OF MERCHANDISING DIVISION
General Definition: To develop, package, price, and provide merchandise for sale that can be produced at a profit by the factory.

Functions:

Market and Product Research and Development:
New products
Maintenance of old products
Market conditions
Competitive activity and position
Product analysis
Control of products:
Pricing, terms, conditions, and permitted costs
Timing and channels of distribution
Additions and eliminations
Sales estimating and budgeting
Finished goods inventory in cooperation with production planning department.
Advisory:
Sales letters
Sampling department
Advertising and promotion department
Purchasing department on special material requirements
Sales management on policies pertinent to merchandising
Sales organization upon request for assistance in customer contacts and relations.
Chemical, methods, and mechanical engineering departments on developments, cost reductions and product maintenance.
Trade Association and Trade Shows
Government Regulations and Laws

THE MARKETING COMMITTEE

The marketing committee had been established three months ago to replace and enlarge on the activities of the product policy committee. Top management agreed that this latter committee generally had lost its effectiveness. Exhibit 19–6 is a statement of the activities of the product policy committee that was superseded by the new marketing committee, for which no statement of duties had been written as yet. Membership of the marketing committee included H. W. Harrison, M. C. Blair, J. T. Halter, R. S. Thomson, and J. G. Myers. These five men were also directors of the company. The other three directors of the company were the chairman of the board of directors, works manager, and vice president-treasurer. The president of the company was chairman of the marketing committee and the controller was the secretary.

The marketing committee was established because top management believed that marketing would be the area with the greatest number of problems directly related to the profitability of the firm in the immediate years ahead. The committee assignment was a broad one, i.e., to chart the course of the company in the years ahead. The members of the committee looked upon attendance at meetings as compulsory, or relatively as important as attendance at meetings of the board of directors. The committee met the second and fourth Mondays of each month, and during the first few months of operation it had met every Monday. Much of the time of these meetings was devoted to reports from the merchandise managers of the six product lines and discussion of the proposed organization plan.

THE PROPOSED ORGANIZATION PLAN

The president and other members of top management were considering the following organization plan which they hoped would achieve a more meaningful profit responsibility for each of the six product lines and thus place the company in a better competitive position. This plan was to have Myers, Thomson, and Becker report directly to the president with each of these three men responsible for two of the six product lines. The president thought highly of these three men who had proven their abilities over many years with the company. Myers was to assume responsibilities for machine systems and industrial products. Thomson was to take over the box and the holiday divisions. Becker was to be in charge of the dealer-crepe line and

EXHIBIT 19–6   DENNISON MANUFACTURING COMPANY

DEFINITION OF RESPONSIBILITY OF PRODUCT POLICY COMMITTEE

Membership: J. G. Myers, Chairman; R. S. Thomson, W. R. Kelly, M. C. Blair, J. T. Halter; I. C. Dodds, Secretary

Definition

The Product Policy Committee will examine the nature and character of Dennison's merchandise in relation to its abilities of manufacturing and distribution. It will define the areas of interest, the objectives and the appropriate direction of development for new products and expansion of existing product lines.

It will search for, screen, evaluate and recommend to the Executive Vice-President on major product developments for profitable investment and expansion.

Technique of Operation

The Committee represents Merchandising, Sales, Manufacturing, Financial, and Research. It will meet regularly under the chairmanship of the General Merchandise Manager.

It will focus its attention primarily on projects in which an investment of over $100,000 is involved.

It will apply an appraisal technique to new product developments and review and update where necessary the evaluation of major projects that are under way.

In order to form objective judgments of existing products or product proposals, the Committee shall analyze the financial and market strengths and weaknesses of Dennison's merchandise, and shall explore the reasons for Dennison's successful existence in each of its many businesses.

Some time during the course of any sizable research project, preferably as early as possible, the Committee will make a comprehensive appraisal to indicate whether the project should be continued, how much attention it is worth, and how it rates in relation to other projects.

Upon request, the Committee will recommend, through the Executive Vice-President, the order or priority in which research, development and other staff groups should proceed with selected projects.

In the process of reckoning the quality of projects, policy conflicts will be ironed out, and marketing and manufacturing difficulties anticipated and resolved. A calendar will be set up which will integrate the operations with the various branches of the business in bringing the adoption of a new product line to fruition.

The Committee will assist Research in the examination of the implications of technical developments and scientific discoveries on current merchandise and marketing programs.

Over-all Objective

The Committee will integrate scientific research, engineering, market research and merchandising with "management." It will provide guidance to exploratory research and thinking. The record of its deliberations should be an authoritative statement of Dennison's merchandise prospectus. It will be the vehicle by which "top management" specifies, based on considered marketing intentions, the broad fields within which all parts of the Company should operate.

gummed and coated papers. With this change, Becker would have what might be called the "stock merchandise" lines; Thomson, the holiday and box merchandise lines; and Myers the "specialty merchandise" lines. With two product lines, each man would be responsible for approximately one-third of the company's domestic sales, based on the record of recent years.

With these new job assignments, the coordination of merchandising, selling, and production of each product line would be fixed on one of the three men. Responsibility for profits on his lines also would rest with Myers, Thomson, and Becker.

Top management felt that the new plan would be quite a drastic shift from the former organization. They believed patience would be required on the part of all those involved during the transition period and some time would be needed before all the details could be worked out. For example, there was to be no immediate change in the activities of the division and district sales managers or the merchandise managers for each of the product lines. However, under the proposed plan, merchandise managers would report directly to Myers, Thomson, or Becker, whoever was responsible for the line. Also, each of the persons involved in the change would retain his present title. New titles would be worked out sometime in the future. During the transitional period, the marketing committee of the company would assume some powers of final decision over marketing policies and operations. Thomson would continue to manage the sales force and Becker would continue in purchasing until a replacement could be trained. Under the proposed plan Myers and Becker would have "direct line authority for getting orders" for their products over division and district sales managers and salesmen. Although this arrangement would not be in writing, it meant that problems such as pricing, order handling, customer relations and the like, having to do with the lines of merchandise assigned to Myers and Becker, were to be referred to them.

Under the proposed plan each of the four division sales managers would report to Myers, Thomson, or Becker for aid on merchandising problems concerning their lines. The division managers were to report to Thomson, the general sales manager, on administrative sales problems such as recruiting and selecting sales personnel, sales budgets, and supervision of district managers.

Management thought that relations with district sales managers would be less of a problem under the proposed plan than relations with division sales managers, since 70 per cent to 80 per cent of the districts already were specialized by product line. For example, in 200- and 300-numbered sales districts, managers would be responsible through their division managers to Myers. The 400-numbered district sales managers would be responsible to Thomson. The 100-numbered district managers would be responsible to Thomson and Becker and district managers with a number less than one hundred would be responsible through their respective division managers to Myers, Thomson, and Becker.

Management realized that the proposed plan might aggravate a number of difficult problems. For example, what should be done in the Denver district where the market was too thin to support a specialized sales force? What should be done with the holiday line which was seasonal and did not have enough market potential to support a separate selling organization?

The two activities of publicity-advertising and sales promotion would continue reporting to Mr. Thomson under the proposed plan. Management hoped that with time the personnel in the advertising department would specialize by product lines. For example, one or two people in the advertising department would work only on "resale" lines which would be Becker's responsibility. In this way, personnel in the advertising department would be directly under Willet, but would work closely with the merchandising staffs of Myers, Thomson, and Becker. No changes were contemplated in marketing research activities under the proposed organization plan.

If the new plan were adopted, the president thought that possibly the best way to introduce the plan would be for himself and the director of marketing to announce it to division and district sales managers at meetings in Chicago and New York. He believed it would be wise to explain the plan to them verbally and offer it as an "experiment" to aid the sales force "in meeting competition." In addition to wondering about the difficulties which might be encountered in communicating the plan and its purposes to the sales force and other parts of the company, and the problems of transition which he believed might arise, he was trying to evaluate whether the proposed plan could be expected to accomplish its long-run purposes.

INTRODUCTION TO THE ACTIVITY

One of the important skills that a manager must have is that of determining appropriate relationships among the various components of his organization. If organized properly, all subunits should be contributing effectively to the overall goals of the organization.

While this is the ideal, in practice, it rarely seems to work this way. Individual parts of the organization develop specific goals and objectives that are different from or even in opposition to the goals and objectives of the total organization. Organization theorists call this process "suboptimization," and in this situation when goals are in conflict the total organization is performing at less than optimal capacity.

And, even though the boxes and lines on the charts may look good, an organization rarely functions the way the chart says it is supposed to. An organization chart is simply a picture of the organization at any given point in time, and does not reflect the dynamics of the organization. While it is possible to construct a picture (chart) of the *real* functioning of an organization, most organizations don't bother to do so. If they do, however, this chart will usually look much different than the formal organization chart.

The formal organization chart has many uses, but it doesn't accurately reflect the living organization. Most managers know this, yet when the talk about organizing or reorganizing ends and they take action, they shuffle around the boxes on the formal chart. This shuffling usually has very little effect on the way the organization really works, although it may satisfy the needs of the manager for "reorganization."

The Dennison Manufacturing Company is a good example of this phenomenon. A rather extensive reorganization is planned, and it is difficult to predict the ramifications of the new organization and how it will function, although obviously there will be some drastic changes in the way the organization will look on paper.

PROCEDURE

Working individually, construct an organization chart reflecting the proposed organization for the Dennison Manufacturing Company. It should be useful to carefully study the organization charts in the case as they now exist. All the information you need to construct a new chart is contained in the case under the heading, "The Proposed Organization Plan."

In devising the chart it may be useful to use the following form to enumerate the various functions to be performed by the three primary executives involved in the

Executive Responsibilities

Function or responsibility	Becker	Thomson	Myers
1. Coordination of merchandise, selling *and production* of respective product lines			
2. Responsibility for profit			
3. Merchandising managers of respective lines			
4. "Manage the sales force"			
5. Purchasing			
6. "Direct line authority for getting orders" over division and district sales managers and salesmen			
7. Pricing, order handling, customer relations, etc., for each line			
8. Merchandising problems (via merchandise managers)			
9. Administrative sales problems—budgets, recruiting, supervision			
10. 200 and 300 # districts (through managers)			
11. 400 # districts			
12. 100 # districts			
13. Under 100 # districts			
14. Market research			
15. Advertising			

proposal and the responsibilities that these three men will assume. You will find that in some instances two or even three of these executives share responsibility for the same activity. This part of the exercise should take you about 45 minute to 1 hour.

After you have done this, use the partially completed chart of the proposed reorganization (Exhibit 19–7) to help you devise a complete chart of the organization. In addition to the activities outlined, you must be certain the following organizational units are included on the completed chart:

Dealer crepe

Box

Holiday

Machine systems

Purchasing

Gummed and coated paper

Publicity and advertising

Market research

Industrial products

All of the numbered sales districts in each of the four major sales divisions

STEP 1: *Individual Analysis* (**suggested time 30 minutes**)

Considering your completed chart and the listing of functions and responsibilities, identify the significant characteristics of the organization. For example, is responsibility well defined? Are communications facilitated? Does everyone know to whom he is accountable? Is the total organization clear and simple? Do important functions receive appropriate emphasis?

STEP 2:

In your judgment, will the proposed organization accomplish the stated purpose of the reorganization?

EXHIBIT 19–7   PARTIAL OUTLINE OF PROPOSED ORGANIZATION (OBJECTIVE: TO FIX RESPONSIBILITY BY PRODUCT LINES AT THE TOP MANAGEMENT LEVEL OF THE COMPANY)

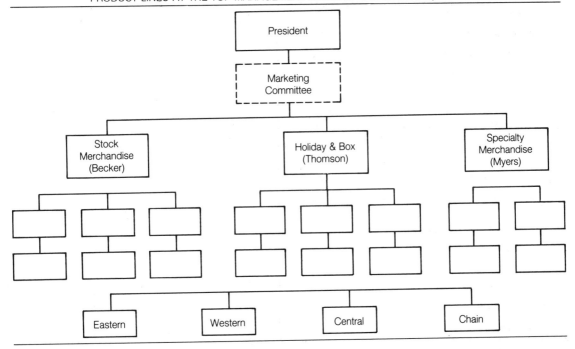

PURPOSE: "To fix responsibility for profits by product lines at the top management level of the company."

STEP 3:

What kinds of problems do you predict will arise in the reorganization?

What strengths does the proposed plan have?

STEP 4: *Group Project* (**suggested time 45 minutes**)

Form in groups of five or six persons.

Review your reactions to the proposed reorganization.

Devise a more effective way to organizing the marketing activities of the Dennison Manufacturing Company to achieve the desired objective.

OBJECTIVE: "To fix responsibility for profits by product lines at the top management level of the company."

Draw a chart of your group's proposed plan on a separate sheet.

Discuss how your group's plan differs from the reorganization plan proposed by the Dennison Company. What characteristics of your plan led you to believe it is better?

What kinds of problems do you expect?

How would you implement such a plan?

What kind of system would you use to determine if the organization was actually functioning according to your plan? How would you install such a system?

Optional

If you have time, share the conclusions of your group with another group.

SUMMARY

One of the obvious conclusions to be drawn from this exercise is that structuring an organization, and the relationships among people in the organization is a most difficult task. Most groups find that it is quite easy to find fault with the organization proposed by the Dennison Company, but that developing an organization that will achieve the desired objective is very difficult. This difficulty is great at just the theoretical level—the level of moving the boxes on the chart around to find the best structure. The challenges of actually implementing an organizational change are even greater because of the dynamics involved.

How, then, does a manager go about structuring or restructuring his organization to achieve the most effective relationships?

Management theory suggests that there are several factors that should be considered. One approach suggests the following steps as a constructive approach to organization:

1. Identify key operating departments that fit the goals—consider balance and emphasis among departments.
2. Decide on the level at which operating decisions can be made most effectively.
3. Consider the nature and location of auxiliary and staff units which are needed.
4. Adjust the parts to make optimum use of structural forms.

Further some additional features of total structure—the use of committees, the number of persons reporting to one supervisor, the desirability of having parallel departments in different parts of the organization, and the like—must be considered. William Newman suggested the following organizational features that are likely to vary with the strategy of the organization.[1]

The amount of centralization or decentralization

---

[1] William H. Newman, "Strategy and Management Structure," *Proceedings of the 31st Annual Meeting of the Academy of Management*, copyright 1972 by the Academy of Management.

The degree of division of labor

The size of self-sufficient operating units

The kinds of mechanisms for coordination

The nature and location of staff

The kind of management information system

The kinds of control systems used

The kinds of planning systems

The characteristics desired in key personnel

Both of these approaches suggest areas in which the manager should make some decisions, but leave the main responsibility for identifying the trade offs involved in these decisions to the manager himself.

A somewhat different approach that features the concept of organizational overlays is taken by Pfiffner and Sherwood. In their view of organizations, the basic organization is a job-task pyramid—a structure derived from the relationships of the jobs/tasks to be performed. This is the "official" version of the organization as the people in the organization believe that it is and should be.[2]

The official organization is modified by several factors which they conceive of as "overlays," i.e., each factor is considered to be a transparent overlay upon the basic structure. Using this approach, they contend that the manager can get a more accurate picture of the real functioning of his organization.

The overlays that they consider are:

The sociometric network in the organization—the relationships among people that are purely social in nature.

The system of functional contacts—the contacts that occur when a person of specialized skill or knowledge exerts his influence upon operations for which he does not have direct responsibility.

The pattern of decision-making centers—the flow of significant decisions in the organization. Where the important decisions are really made.

The pattern of power—location of the centers of power in the organization.

Channels of communication—the way that communication really flows in the organization.

By analyzing the basic structure *and* the impact of these overlays, the manager will get a better idea of the dynamics of his organization that do not appear on the official chart.

Each of these varied approaches is useful and the elements which they contain should be given consideration by the manager. On a less theoretical level, however, organization is simply one tool that the manager has available to him to help him achieve his objectives. The objectives that he has will have great impact upon the way that he will structure relationships and moreover, on how he designs the organization.

Let us ignore for the moment any personal objectives that a manager might have and concentrate upon organizational objectives. If, for example, he is concerned about control of operations, he will probably develop an organization with a high control orientation. This organization would probably have very explicit lines of accountability and responsibility, emphasize standardization and uniformity, have very clear and frequent measures of output, and have predetermined methods of conflict resolution.

If a manager has high concern for being able to solve complex problems effectively, he will design an organization that will provide for quickly getting the best resources working on the problem, have high flexibility of structure, be capable of fast responses to new situations, and be very adaptable to change.

If a manager places high priority on de-

[2] John M. Pfiffner and Frank P. Sherwood, *Administrative Organization*, Prentice-Hall, Inc., Englewood Cliffs, N.J., 1960.

velopment of human resources in the organization, he will design an organization that has opportunities for individual growth, provides for meaningful job assignments, and is concerned about people getting satisfactions from their activities. Thus, depending upon what he wants his organization to emphasize, a manager might come up with some very different organizational structures and relationships.

As we consider any personal objectives that a manager might have, the situation becomes even more complex. Look at the situation in which a weak manager may be fearful about protecting his job. He may design an organization which will district attention from himself and locate decision making primarily in committees so that he can avoid responsibility for those decisions.

Or, consider the manager who is concerned about being cut off from communication. Instead of appointing one assistant, he appoints two, just so he has more than one communication channel into the organization. Other examples are easy to visualize. The important point is that a manager's personal objectives as well as his organizational objectives will have a strong impact upon his thinking regarding the kind of organizational relationships that he desires in his situation.

Probably no other area of management is as susceptible to the preferences of the manager as the area of organization. Many value judgments are inherent in any organization structure, and these judgments reflect the assumptions, priorities and goals of the manager. While it is important to consider valid organizational theory in designing an organization, the manager should recognize that there is no "best" organization and that his organization will be determined primarily by *his* feelings, *his* attitudes, and *his* personal and organizational objectives.

III

Internal Organizational Processes

20

The University Art Museum

Visitors to the campus were always shown the University Art Museum, of which the large and distinguished university was very proud. A photograph of the handsome neo-classical building that housed the Museum had long been used by the university for the cover of its brochures and catalogues.

The building, together with a substantial endowment, was given to the university around 1912 by an alumnus, the son of the university's first president, who had become very wealthy as an investment banker. He also gave the university his own small, but high quality, collections—one of Etruscan figurines, and one, unique in America, of English pre-Raphaelite paintings. He then served as the Museum's unpaid director until his death. During his tenure he brought a few additional collections to the museum, largely from other alumni of the university. Only rarely did the museum purchase anything. As a result, the museum housed several small collections of uneven quality. As long as the founder ran the museum, none of the collections was ever shown to anybody except

a few members of the university's art history faculty, who were admitted as the founder's private guests.

After the founder's death, in the late 1920s, the university intended to bring in a professional museum director. Indeed, this had been part of the agreement under which the founder had given the museum. A search committee was to be appointed, but in the meantime a graduate student in art history who had shown interest in the museum and who had spent a good many hours in it, took over temporarily. At first, she did not even have a title, let alone a salary. But she stayed on acting as the museum's director and over the next 30 years was promoted in stages to that title. But from the first day, whatever her title, she was in charge. She immediately set about changing the museum altogether. She catalogued the collections. She pursued new gifts, again primarily small collections from alumni and other friends of the university. She organized fund raising for the museum. But, above all, she began to integrate the museum into the work of the universi-

Case #3, "The University Art Museum: Defining Purpose and Mission" (pp. 28–35), from *Management Cases* by Peter F. Drucker. Copyright © 1977 by Peter F. Drucker. Reprinted by permission of Harper & Row, Publishers, Inc.

ty. When a space problem arose in the years immediately following World War II, Miss Kirkhoff offered the third floor of the museum to the art history faculty, which moved its offices there. She remodeled the building to include classrooms and a modern and well-appointed auditorium. She raised funds to build one of the best research and reference libraries in art history in the country. She also began to organize a series of special exhibitions built around one of the museum's own collections, complemented by loans from outside collections. For each of these exhibitions she had a distinguished member of the university's art faculty write a catalogue. These catalogues speedily became the leading scholarly texts in the fields.

Miss Kirkhoff ran the University Art Museum for almost half a century. But old age ultimately defeated her. At the age of 68 after suffering a severe stroke, she had to retire. In her letter of resignation she proudly pointed to the museum's growth and accomplishment under her stewardship. "Our endowment," she wrote, "now compares favorably with museums several times our size. We never have had to ask the university for any money other than for our share of the university's insurance policies. Our collections in the areas of our strength, while small, are of first-rate quality and importance. Above all, we are being used by more people than any museum of our size. Our lecture series, in which members of the university's art history faculty present a major subject to a university audience of students and faculty, attracts regularly 300–500 people; and if we had the seating capacity, we could easily have a larger audience. Our exhibitions are seen and studied by more visitors, most of them members of the university community, than all but the most highly publicized exhibitions in the very big museums ever draw. Above all, the courses and seminars offered in the museum have become one of the most popular and most rapidly grow-

ing educational features of the university. No other museum in this country or anywhere else," concluded Miss Kirkhoff, "has so successfully integrated art into the life of a major university and a major university into the work of a museum."

Miss Kirkhoff strongly recommended that the university bring in a professional museum director as her successor. "The museum is much too big and much too important to be entrusted to another amateur such as I was 45 years ago," she wrote. "And it needs careful thinking regarding its direction, its basis of support, and its future relationship with the university."

The university took Miss Kirkhoff's advice. A search committee was duly appointed and, after one year's work, it produced a candidate whom everybody approved. The candidate was himself a graduate of the university who had then obtained his Ph.D. in art history and in museum work from the university. Both his teaching and administrative record were sound, leading to his present museum directorship in a medium-sized city. There he converted an old, well-known, but rather sleepy museum to a lively, community-oriented museum whose exhibitions were well publicized and attracted large crowds.

The new museum director took over with great fanfare in September, 1971. Less than three years later he left—with less fanfare, but still with considerable noise. Whether he resigned or was fired was not quite clear. But that there was bitterness on both sides was only too obvious.

The new director, upon his arrival, had announced that he looked upon the museum as a "major community resource" and intended to "make the tremendous artistic and scholarly resources of the Museum fully available to the academic community as well as to the public." When he said these things in an interview with the college newspaper, everybody nodded in approval. It soon became clear that what he meant by "community resource" and what the faculty and students understood by these words were not the same. The museum had always been "open to the public" but, in practice, it was members of the college community who used the museum and attended its lectures, its exhibitions, and its frequent seminars.

The first thing the new director did, however, was to promote visits from the public schools in the area. He soon began to change the exhibition policy. Instead of organizing small shows, focused on a major collection of the museum and built around a scholarly catalogue, he began to organize "popular exhibitions" around "topics of general interest" such as "Women Artists through the Ages." He promoted these exhibitions vigorously in the newspapers, in radio and television interviews, and, above all, in the local schools. As a result, what had been a busy but quiet place was soon knee-deep in school children, taken to the museum in special buses that cluttered the access roads around the museum and throughout the campus. The faculty, which was not particularly happy with the resulting noise and confusion, became thoroughly upset when the scholarly old chairman of the art history department was mobbed by fourth-graders who sprayed him with their water pistols as he tried to push his way through the main hall to his office.

Increasingly, the new director did not design his own shows, but brought in traveling exhibitions from major museums, importing their catalogue as well rather than have his own faculty produce one.

The students too were apparently unenthusiastic after the first six or eight months, during which the new director had been somewhat of a campus hero. Attendance at the classes and seminars held in the art museum fell off sharply, as did attendance at the evening lectures. When the editor of the campus newspaper interviewed students for a story on the museum, he was told again and again that the museum had become too noisy and too "sensational" for students to enjoy the classes and to have a chance to learn.

What brought all this to a head was an Islamic art exhibit in late 1973. Since the museum had little Islamic art, nobody criticized the showing of a traveling exhibit, offered on very advantageous terms with generous financial assistance from some of the Arab governments. But then, instead of inviting one of the University's own faculty members to deliver the customary talk at the opening of the exhibit, the director brought in a cultural attache of one of the Arab embassies in Washington. The speaker, it was reported, used the occasion to deliver a violent attack on Israel and on the American policy of supporting Israel against the Arabs. A week later, the university senate decided to appoint an advisory committee, drawn mostly from members of the art history faculty, which, in the future, would have to approve all plans for exhibits and lectures. The director thereupon, in an interview with the campus newspaper, sharply attacked the faculty as "elitist" and "snobbish" and as believing that "art belongs to the rich." Six months later, in June 1974, his resignation was announced.

Under the bylaws of the university, the academic senate appoints a search committee. Normally, this is pure formality. The chairperson of the appropriate department submits the department's nominees for the committee who are approved and appointed, usually without debate. But when the academic senate early the following semester was asked to appoint the search committee, things were far from "normal". The dean who presided, sensing the tempers in the room, tried to smooth over things by saying, "Clearly, we picked the wrong person the last time. We will have to try very hard to find the right one this time."

He was immediately interrupted by an economist, known for his populism, who broke in and said, "I admit that the late director was probably not the right personality. But I strongly believe that his personality was not at the root of the problem. He tried to do what needs doing and this got him in trouble with the faculty. He tried to make our museum a community resource, to bring in the community and to make art accessible to broad masses of people, to the blacks and the Puerto Ricans, to the kids from the ghetto schools and to a lay public. And this is what we really resented. Maybe his methods were not the most tactful ones—I admit I could have done without those interviews he gave. But what he tried to do was right. We had better commit ourselves to the policy he wanted to put into effect, or else we will have deserved his attacks on us as 'elitist' and 'snobbish.' "

"This is nonsense," cut in the usually silent and polite senate member from the art history faculty. "It makes absolutely no sense for our museum to try to become the kind of community resource our late director and my distinguished colleague want it to be. First there is no need. The city has one of the world's finest and biggest museums and it does exactly that and does it very well. Secondly, we here have neither the artistic resources nor the financial resources to serve the community at large. We can do something different but equally important and indeed unique. Ours is the only museum in the country, and perhaps in the world, that is fully integrated with an academic community and truly a teaching institution. We are using it, or at least we used to until the last few unfortunate years, as a major educational resource for all our students. No other museum in the country, and as far as I know in the world, is bringing undergraduates into art the way we do. All of us, in addition to our scholarly and graduate work, teach undergraduate courses for people who are not going to be art majors or art historians. We work with the engineering students and show them what we do in our conservation and restoration work. We work with architecture students and show them the development of architecture through the ages. Above all, we work with liberal arts students, who often have had no exposure to art before they came here and who enjoy our courses all the more because they are scholarly and not just 'art appreciation.' This is unique and this is what our museum can do and should do."

"I doubt that this is really what we should be doing," commented the chairman of the mathematics department. "The museum, as far as I know, is part of the graduate faculty. It should concentrate on training art historians in its Ph.D. program, on its scholarly work, and on its research. I would strongly urge that the museum be considered an adjunct to graduate and especially to Ph.D. education, confine itself to this work, and stay out of all attempts to be 'popular,' on both campus and outside of it. The glory of the museum is the scholarly catalogues produced by our faculty, and our Ph.D. graduates who are sought after by art history faculties throughout the country. This is the museum's mission, which can only be impaired by the attempt to be 'popular,' whether with students or with the public."

"These are very interesting and important comments," said the dean, still trying to pacify. "But I think this can wait until we know who the new director is going to be. Then we should raise these questions with him."

"I beg to differ, Mr. Dean," said one of the elder statesmen of the faculty. "During the summer months, I discussed this question with an old friend and neighbor of mine in the country, the director of one of the nation's great museums. He said to me: 'You do not have a personality problem, you have a *management* problem. You have not, as a university, taken responsibility for the mission, the direction, and the objectives of your museum. Until you do this, no director can succeed. And this is *your* decision. In fact, you cannot hope to get a good man until you can tell him what your basic objectives are. If your late director is to blame—I know him and I know that he is abrasive—it is for being willing to take on a job when you, the university, had not faced up to the basic management decisions. There is no point talking about *who* should manage until it is clear *what* it is that has to be managed and for what.' ''

At this point the dean realized that he had to adjourn the discussion unless he wanted the meeting to degenerate into a brawl. But he also realized that he had to identify the issues and possible decisions before the next faculty meeting a month later. Here is the list of questions he put down on paper later that evening:

1. What are the possible purposes of the University Museum:

   ■ to serve as a laboratory for the graduate art-history faculty and the doctoral students in the field?
   ■ to serve as major "enrichment" for the undergraduate who is not an art-history student but wants both a "liberal education" and a counter-weight to the highly bookish diet fed to him in most of our courses?
   ■ to serve the metropolitan community—and especially its schools—outside the campus gates?

2. Who are or should be its customers?

   ■ the graduate students in professional training to be teachers of art history?
   ■ the undergraduate community—or rather, the entire college community?
   ■ the metropolitan community and especially the teachers and youngsters in the public schools?
   ■ any others?

3. Which of these purposes are compatible and could be served simultaneously? Which are mutually exclusive or at the very least are likely to get in each other's way?
4. What implications for the structure of the museum, the qualifications of its director, and its relationship to the university follow from each of the above purposes?
5. Do we need to find out more about the needs and wants of our various potential customers to make an intelligent policy decision? How could we go about it?

The dean distributed these questions to the members of the faculty with the request that they think them through and discuss them before the next meeting of the academic senate.

21

Measuring Organizational Effectiveness

Organizational effectiveness is the degree to which an organization realizes its goals. Various approaches to assessing effectiveness include whether the organization achieves its goals in terms of desired levels of output; whether the organization obtains the resources necessary for high performance; and whether the internal activities and processes of the organization reflect an internal health and efficient use of resources.

The organizations listed below operate with different goals in mind and assess their effectiveness at meeting these goals in different ways. The purpose of this exercise is to illustrate the relationship between goals and effectiveness and methods for measuring effectiveness.

STEP 1: *Determining Goals and Assessing Effectiveness (20 min.)*

For each organization below list two possible goals and the approach which might be used to assess the organization's effectiveness at meeting these goals.

STEP 2: *Small-Group Discussion (15 min.)*

Working in groups of three, discuss the goals you have identified and the measures necessary to determine the effectiveness of the organization in meeting these goals.

STEP 3: *Group Presentation (10 min.)*

Each group should select from the list one organization and corresponding set of goals and effectiveness measures to share with the class. In explaining your choice, indicate why other types of measures would or would not be just as useful in measuring organizational effectiveness.

STEP 4: *Class Discussion (15 min.)*

Review and discuss the goals and measures identified by the members of the class. The following questions may be helpful in integrating this exercise with previous class discussions regarding goals and effectiveness.

DISCUSSION QUESTIONS

1. Did the goals and measures of effectiveness tend to be stated in quantitative or qualitative terms? Which is easier to observe?

2. Is it possible to have multiple measures for

one goal? If so, give an example. Do multiple measures guarantee a better assessment of achieving goals?

3. How does efficiency relate to the goals and effectiveness measures identified by the exercise? Are there different determinations for efficiency? Such as?

4. When determining measures of effectiveness, who did you decide would be applying such measures? Top management? Employees? Customers? Does it matter?

5. In which domain is each goal? How does this translate into the measurements you selected?

	Goals	*Effectiveness Measures*
1. Automobile Manufacturer		
2. Post Office		
3. Professional Hockey Team		
4. Local Newspaper		
5. Farmer		
6. High School		
7. Labor Union		
8. Community Theater Group		
9. Local Chamber of Commerce		

22

Layoff at Old College

Memorandum: Office of the College President

To: College Budget Committee

Subject: Next Year's Budget Preparation

In my continuing effort to hold down the costs of running the college, I am ordering you to identify existing academic programs that will be subject to reduction or elimination. In order to support the academic programs that have proven to be effective and cost beneficial I am asking you to identify the five departments/programs/activities (D/P/A) of the lowest priority in the college. Elimination or reduction of these activities should result in a reduction of no less than 10% of your budget for this past year as a base. If the five D/P/A of the lowest priority do not amount to a 10% reduction in your budget, continue listing D/P/A until the 10% reduction is achieved.

The following criteria will be used in developing your reductions:

1. No across-the-board reduction (i.e., 10% from each D/P/A).
2. Assume that statutes and regulations can be changed to achieve the reduction (i.e., faculty can be dismissed despite tenure status).
3. Identify exactly which D/P/As are to be reduced.
4. Identify the number of Faculty and Clerical/Technical (C/T) positions that would be eliminated/abolished.
5. Submit the information to my office immediately.

The proposed changes may result in radical changes in the character and objectives of the college. Consider carefully whether a program is absolutely essential for a well-rounded college experience. Maintain the basic integrity of the college but at the same time carry out your duty. Whatever reductions you impose must be determined by a well-reasoned, thorough, and sensitive assessment of the potential implication of such reduction. There should be no illusion, however, that the required cuts can be accomplished in a painless or popular way.

Signed /S/ the College President

Attachment

Reprinted with permission of Allen J. Schuh, Professor, California State University at Hayward.

REASON FOR THE BUDGET REDUCTION

The College President's memorandum ordering the reduction in personnel is a result of the tremendous recent and sustained drop in student enrollments, while at the same time the costs to maintain departments/programs/activities have substantially increased. The President has decided that not every college can be all things to all people and Old College simply can't provide every course or major that the faculty and students might like. There is a need to increase the efficiency of the college and now is the time to make the required reductions. It should be noted that personnel salaries compose over 80% of the total cost of running the college. The staffing pattern of Old College is detailed in Exhibit 22–1. Exhibit 22–2 at the end of the case presents a variety of statistics about each department that could be helpful in making the layoff decision.

TIMEFRAME

The President will allow the reduction to be phased in over a three-year period if necessary to allow the laid-off people an opportunity to secure other employment. Also, each college job generates approximately a half position in the local community. The college is a major employer in the local geographical area. A phase-in over several years would also allow students in the affected areas to complete current graduation requirements. Appropriate admissions policies and criteria would be revised to limit access of new students to the threatened departments/programs/activities.

ORIGINAL MISSION OF THE COLLEGE

Upon its founding, Old College was expected to provide: (a) a general education for undergraduates, primarily in the first two years of college, (b) a wide range of academic majors and minors for students pursuing a baccalaureate degree, and (c) job-related education for potential teachers and other students seeking a variety of public and private employment. It was hoped that masters degrees might also be offered in a limited number of fields. The most prestigious occupational training programs such as dentistry, medicine, engineering, and law would never be attempted. Also, no programs in agriculture or natural resources, architecture and environmental design, or home economics would ever be offered.

At the founding ceremony, the trustees declared:

Students selecting Old College for their major educational experience will know and feel the spirit, imagination, and traumas of mankind, they should be able to understand and apply the method of scientific inquiry, they should know man as he is, and they should discover, develop, and practice their talents and interests through original expression. Thus, an array of offerings in Humanities, Physical and Life Sciences, Social Sciences, and Expressive Arts would be presented and retained for the enrichment of students at least for their first two years of college experience.

Job-related courses and programs should be offered to strengthen and extend the occupational opportunities of students in school-based services, client-oriented professions, management of public and private organizations, and quantitative data-processing occupations.

Upper division and graduate programs should be offered and sustained that will lead to an academic major or minor or to a master's degree, to prepare students for doctoral programs in other universities, proceed to teaching positions in secondary schools and community colleges, proceed to advanced occupational training programs in fields such as law, engineering, dentistry, and medicine elsewhere.

Specialized academic training is to be offered in ways that enrich the lives of the students and/or serve their communities.

LOCATION, HISTORY, AND PHYSICAL FACILITIES

Old College is located in a picturesque setting with rolling hills. Trees, grass, and flowering shrubs abound on the campus. The college strives to maintain a friendly atmosphere with close student-faculty relations, an emphasis on student self-government, and community involvement. The college has been in existence for 20 years. The peak enrollment occurred eight years ago and has since dropped 20%.

The physical facilities include large modern buildings for instruction, a bookstore, library, administration building, student health center, cafeteria, athletic stadium, theater and television facility, a foreign language laboratory, a computer center, and an on-campus ecological field station.

The educational emphasis stresses small class size and easy student access to professors. The curriculum presents a balanced approach of liberal arts and applied degrees in undergraduate and graduate programs. There are extension and summer sessions, and late afternoon and evening classes. The college operates on the quarter system. The programs of the college are accredited by the appropriate associations.

CHARACTERISTICS OF THE STUDENTS

The total enrollment is 9,800 students—49% men and 51% women. Only about 1% of the students are from foreign countries. The undergraduates make up 70% of the students while the remaining 30% are graduate students. The average student age is 27 years. Undergraduate courses are 90% of the curriculum (many graduate students take undergraduate courses to meet the prerequisites for graduate study in a field other than that for which they hold an undergraduate degree). Fifty-five percent of the students carry 12 or more units per

term, which is considered full time attendance. The ethnicity breakdown has been estimated at approximately: 72% Caucasian, 14% Black, 6% Oriental, 4% Chicano, 1% Filipino, 1% Central-Latin-South American, 1% Native American, 1% Other.

EXHIBIT 22–1 STAFF ORGANIZATION CHART FOR OLD COLLEGE

Area		Number of Positions
I.	Instructional Administration	36
	School (Administrative unit above the department level) Offices Clerical/Technical	
	Assistance to Administration	25
	Faculty Teaching Courses	403
	Clerical/Technical Assistance to Teaching	
	Faculty	94
	Subtotal	558
II.	Academic Support	
	Library	63
	Audio-Visual	14
	Computer Center	33
	Subtotal	110
III.	Student Services	
	Social and Cultural Development	9
	Counseling	13
	Testing	3
	Placement	7
	Housing	2
	Disabled Students	2
	Equal Opportunity Program	15
	Financial Aids	13
	Health Services	21
	Subtotal	85
IV.	Institutional Support	
	Executive Management	26
	Financial Operations	35
	Personnel	7
	Logistical Services	
	Business Management	20
	Security	13
	Motor Pool	4
	Admissions and Records	48
	Plant Operations	165
	Community Relations	5
	Subtotal	323
	Total College Personnel	1,076

Comment: Approximately $30 million is required to meet this payroll. These salaries account for over 80% of the total cost of running the college for one year.

EXHIBIT 22–2 RELEVANT STATISTICS BY DEPARTMENT

Department	A	B	C	D	E	F	G	H	I	J	K	L	M	N	O	P	Q
Black Studies	1	1	0	4.4	2.0	.5	.0	1.56	130	0	14.0	0	0	211.4	113.7	21.5	18.6
English	18	0	.3	18.2	18.3	2.0	.0	4.15	312	46	18.8	0	1	202.2	115.3	16.3	18.0
Foreign Languages	19	1	0	13.7	20.0	1.75	1.0	3.50	155	10	11.5	9	0	198.4	135.2	14.0	12.8
History	21	0	0	17.2	21.0	2.0	.0	4.31	284	44	16.6	1	0	196.6	119.1	19.9	20.5
Philosophy	9	0	0	6.2	9.0	1.0	.0	1.45	65	0	10.8	2	1	196.4	105.3	20.9	16.4
Speech	9	0	1	9.5	10.0	3.0	.0	2.4	63	26	33.4	2	0	195.1	113.7	17.7	15.9
Biology	15	0	.7	16.1	15.7	3.0	5.5	4.11	534	71	42.9	5	4	212.2	128.7	14.7	16.6
Chemistry	11	0	.3	11.4	11.3	2.0	5.5	2.83	106	15	17.6	6	3	220.3	147.4	14.8	14.9
Geology	6	0	0	5.8	6.0	1.0	1.5	1.33	47	0	39.8	2	4	217.9	151.9	14.2	17.1
Health Sciences	1	0	0	1.3	1.0	0	0	.25	15	0	54.0	0	8	—	—	24.6	16.4
Mathematics	27	0	0	27.1	27.0	3.0	0	6.62	215	37	11.1	15	0	204.0	127.7	18.8	19.3
Nursing	4	3	.7	6.3	7.7	1.0	0	1.4	342	0	93.9	0	7	213.1	123.7	8.9	8.9
Physical Science	1	0	0	.5	1.0	0	0	.1	3	0	0	0	5	—	—	19.9	14.3
Physics	4	0	0	5.3	4.0	1.0	2.0	1.19	31	7	21.0	6	2	199.2	88.7	17.3	17.7
Statistics	8	2	.3	11.4	10.3	1.5	.5	2.78	48	26	9.8	16	1	199.4	132.6	19.3	19.6
Anthropology	8	0	.7	6.2	8.7	1.25	.25	1.76	100	33	19.5	1	5	196.7	157.2	18.6	17.3
Geography	7	0	.7	4.3	7.7	1.0	.5	1.25	123	18	46.2	0	3	201.3	130.4	18.7	14.2
Human Development	4	0	0	6.8	4.0	1.75	0	1.98	517	0	69.7	1	0	195.5	115.6	19.3	20.1
Mass Communication	3	0	.3	6.4	3.3	1.0	.75	1.61	84	0	54.6	0	2	196.1	120.6	20.9	17.1
Mexican-American Studies	1	0	0	.6	1.0	0	0	.13	18	0	6.2	0	2	196.7	112.1	19.6	11.3
Native-American Studies	0	1	0	.7	1.0	0	0	.15	0	0	0	0	0	—	—	17.0	10.4
Political Science	10	0	.7	7.9	10.7	1.75	0	1.98	343	18	38.1	1	3	195.6	114.3	21.3	14.5
Psychology	18	0	0	16.6	18.0	3.0	1.0	4.07	527	0	40.0	7	2	194.9	114.5	23.8	19.2
Sociology	13	0	0	16.0	13.0	2.5	.5	3.89	491	29	36.2	3	3	197.7	109.9	20.0	21.2
Art	15	0	0	11.6	15.0	2.0	4.5	3.02	457	0	53.9	0	0	201.1	110.7	15.6	13.4
Drama	3	0	.3	3.8	3.3	1.0	3.5	.83	10	0	42.8	0	1	217.5	120.6	16.4	13.5
Music	22	0	0	13.6	22.0	2.5	4.5	3.45	228	42	64.8	0	0	208.6	139.8	13.5	10.1
Accounting	11	0	.3	27.7	11.3	2.0	0	6.13	696	139	75.6	3	4	205.6	129.2	20.3	22.3
Management Sciences	14	4	0	28.5	18.0	1.5	0	6.31	717	143	86.3	3	4	205.6	129.2	21.0	21.6
Marketing	4	0	.3	6.3	4.3	0	0	1.19	135	26	86.7	3	4	205.6	129.2	23.7	21.8
Criminal Justice	1	0	1	4.9	2.0	0	0	.77	0	0	50.8	0	4	—	—	25.8	28.1
Economics	9	1	.7	17.5	10.7	1.0	0	3.88	99	19	7.1	3	3	201.2	111.2	22.7	24.6
Educational Psychology	20	0	0	15.0	20.0	3.0	0	3.67	0	556	85.9	0	0	—	—	13.0	12.5
Physical Education	21	0	.7	26.5	21.7	3.5	3.7	5.26	348	37	38.9	1	4	205.3	126.9	14.8	14.3
Public Administration	2	3	2	7.7	7.0	1.0	0	2.10	0.	291	69.0	0	0	—	—	14.6	17.1
Recreation	1	1	0	3.1	2.0	1.5	0	.79	356	0	66.1	0	2	196.5	116.2	19.7	16.3
School Administration	5	0	0	2.0	5.0	.5	0	.59	0	0	56.5	0	0	—	—	11.2	7.8
Teacher Education	28	0	.7	19.0	28.7	4.0	.5	5.83	0	471	16.8	0	0	—	—	15.7	12.8
General Studies	0	0	0	2.5	0	0	0	.99	0	0	—	0	0	—	—	18.4	12.9
Women's Studies	0	0	0	.2	0	0	0	.05	0	0	—	0	0	—	—	22.3	14.2

Titles for Column Headings A to Q:

A Number of tenured faculty in the department. Tenure is not permanent employment in a university. Tenure is only in a department or teaching service area. Professors have tenure only if there is work and they commit no illegal, immoral, or incompetent act. If the teaching service area or department is eliminated, faculty lose all job rights.

B Number of faculty seeking tenure in the department. Typically a few members of the teaching faculty are new to the college and are seeking a tenured position. These faculty are evaluated for a period of up to seven years and are subject to yearly evaluation on their publications, teaching, committee work, and work in the community.

C Number of temporary faculty who teach in the department (not tenure track). These are lecturers or temporary faculty who are usually Ph.D. candidates at other local universities.

D Number of faculty positions that should exist in the department if all departments were held to a standard student-faculty ratio of 18:1. Since the college receives its money from the State Legislature on a ratio of one full-time faculty position for each 18 full-time equivalent students (usually expressed as 18:1) it could be a rough justice practice to require all departments to meet that ratio. Departments should use this ratio as a reference each year as they consider their teaching load. Classes that are small should be combined. A professor might even view his/her own contribution from this perspective. If one course has only 10 students, another class better have at least 26 to offset the smaller expensive offering. Any department that consistently falls below 18:1 is simply not paying its share.

E Total number of faculty in the department (the sum of A, B, and C)—the total number of full-time teaching positions in the department now. No provision is made here to alert the reader of pending retirements or separations. These data are just as they appear on the course control computer printout.

F Number of clerical positions in support of teaching faculty who work in the department. Clerical employees receive permanency after one year in their job. A clerical's permanency is to the whole college. Thus, if a particular clerical position is eliminated, the person would not necessarily separate from the university. Possibly that person would bump a person of less seniority in another part of the campus. Typing is the same anywhere on campus, thus the situation is not the same as with faculty. With faculty, a sociologist can't always teach biology or accounting. But clerical duties are essentially the same everywhere.

G Number of technical positions working in the department. Technical support to faculty positions are glass blowers in chemistry, specimen preparers in biology, or piano tuners in music. Thus, while they have permanency rather than tenure, a highly skilled technician has fewer transferable skills to an entirely new area. We have no experience record to suggest what exactly will happen with the technical support positions in a layoff.

H Percentage of courses taken by students in comparison to the college as a whole. This is a popularity ratio arrived at by counting the number of students taking a course in the department and expressing it as a ratio to the total enrollments in the college.

I Number of undergraduate degrees awarded in the past five years. Self explanatory. What isn't here is whether this number is increasing, steady, or declining over the years.

J Number of graduate degrees awarded in the past five years. Self explanatory. See I above.

K Percentage of courses taken by students who major in the department. This is a concentration ratio that counts all students taking courses in a department and then checks their college major. A department with a low percentage is essentially a service department to other majors. To some extent, such service to others insures one's own survival. A high ratio shows that the majority of students taking courses there are their majors. A department with a high ratio could be eliminated without affecting many people other than those being eliminated.

L Number of other departments that require students in their major to take courses in the department. Some departments offer courses highly regarded by the other departments. For example, a course in statistics is required by over a third of the departments on the campus, but no one but geographers are required to take a geography course. Obviously, any department with a zero in this column is more vulnerable to elimination than those with a higher number.

M Number of other departments where a student in this major will have to take at least one course. This octopus variable shows how broad a background in other departments the major in this department is required to have for graduation. Health Sciences is well wired politically because it requires their students to have courses in eight other departments. These other departments are apt to come to their assistance if anyone would suggest they be eliminated.

N Number of units a student in this major takes on the average before graduating (186 quarter units are required for graduation). Frequently students transfer from another college or change majors and so accumulate a larger number of units than needed before graduating.

O Number of units a student takes here at Old College who majors in this department before graduating with an undergraduate degree (i.e., units not transfered in from another college). Self explanatory.

P The average student-faculty ratio for this major at 18 comparable institutions. Self explanatory.

Q The approximate student-faculty ratio for this department last academic year. These data were calculated for three regular academic quarters plus the summer session. No information is available on whether the ratio is raising, stable, or falling over the last five years.

23

Denver Department Stores

In the early spring of 1974 Jim Barton was evaluating the decline in sales volume experienced by the four departments he supervised in the main store of Denver Department Stores, a Colorado retail chain. Barton was at a loss as to how to improve sales. He attributed the slowdown in sales to the current economic downturn affecting the entire nation. However, Barton's supervisor, Mr. Cornwall, pointed out that some of the other departments in the store had experienced a 15% gain over the previous year. Cornwall added that Barton was expected to have his departments up to par with the others in a short period of time.

BACKGROUND

Jim Barton had been supervisor of the sporting goods, hardware, housewares, and toy departments in the main store of Denver Department Stores for three of the 10 years he had worked for the chain. The four departments were situated adjacent to each other on the ground floor of the store. Each department had a head salesclerk who reported to Mr. Barton on merchandise storage and presentation, special orders, and general department upkeep. The head salesclerks were all full-time, long-term employees of Denver Department Stores, having an average of about eight years' experience with the chain. The head clerks were also expected to train the people in the department they supervised. The rest of the staff in each department was made up of part-time employees who lived in or near Denver. Most of the part-time people were students at nearby universities who worked to finance their education. In addition there were two or three housewives who worked about 10 hours a week in the evenings.

All sales personnel at Denver Department Stores were paid strictly on an hourly basis. Beginning pay was just slightly over the minimum wage and raises were given based on length of employment and work performance evaluations. The salespeople in the housewares and sporting goods departments were paid about 40¢ an hour more than the clerks in the other departments because it was thought that more sales ability and experience were needed in dealing with the people who shopped for items found in those departments.

As a general rule the head salesclerk in each department did not actively sell, but kept the department well stocked and presentable, and trained and evaluated sales personnel. The part-time employees did most of the clerk and sales work. The role of the salesclerk was seen as one of answering customer questions and ringing up the sale rather than actively selling the merchandise, except in the two departments previously mentioned where a little more active selling was done.

The salesclerks in Barton's departments seemed to get along well with each other. The four department heads usually ate lunch together. If business was brisk in one department and slow in another, the salespeople in the slower area would assist in the busy department. Men clerks often helped the women clerks in unloading heavy merchandise carts. Store procedure was that whenever a cash register was low on change a clerk would go to a master till

in the stationery department to get more. Barton's departments, however, usually supplied each other with change, thus avoiding the longer walk to the master till.

Barton's immediate supervisor, Mr. Cornwall, had the reputation of being a skilled merchandiser and in the past had initiated many ideas to increase the sales volume of the store. Some of the longer-term employees said that Mr. Cornwall was very impatient and that he sometimes was rude to his subordinates while discussing merchandising problems with them.

The store manager, Mr. Blanding, had been with Denver Department Stores for 20 years and would be retiring in a few years. Earlier in his career Mr. Blanding had taken an active part in the merchandising aspect of the store, but recently he had delegated most of the merchandising and sales responsibilities to Mr. Cornwall. (Exhibit 23–1 is an organizational chart of the store.)

SITUATION

Because of Mr. Cornwall's concern, Barton consulted with his department supervisors

EXHIBIT 23–1 DENVER DEPARTMENT STORES ORGANIZATIONAL CHART

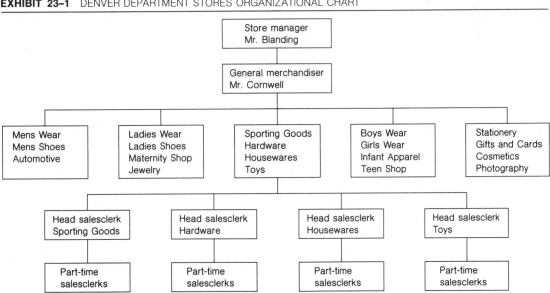

about the reason for the declining sales volume. The consensus reached was that the level of customer traffic had not been adequate to allow the departments to achieve a high sales volume. When Barton presented this problem to Mr. Cornwall, Cornwall concluded that since customer traffic could not be controlled and since the departments had been adequately stocked throughout the year, the improvement in sales would have to be a result of increased effort on the part of the clerks in each department. Cornwall added that if sales didn't improve soon the hours of both the full- and part-time salesclerks would have to be cut back. Later Barton found out that Cornwall had sent a letter around to each department informing employees of the possibility of fewer hours if sales didn't improve.

A few days after Barton received the assignment to increase sales in his department Mr. Cornwall called him into his office again and suggested that each salesperson carry a personal tally card to record his daily sales. Each clerk would record the sales he made and at the end of the day the personal sales tally card would be totaled. Cornwall said that by reviewing the cards over a period of time he would be able to determine who were the "dead wood" and who were the real producers. The clerks were to be told about the purpose of the tally card and that those clerks who had low sales tallies would have their hours cut back.

Barton told Cornwall he wanted to consider this program and also discuss it with the head salespeople before implementing it. He told Mr. Cornwall that the next day was his day off but that when he returned to work the day after he would discuss this proposal with the head salesclerks.

Upon returning to the store after his day off, Mr. Barton was surprised to see each of his salespeople carrying a daily tally sheet. When he asked Mr. Cornwall why the program had been adopted so quickly, Cornwall replied that when it came to improvement of sales, no delay could be tolerated. Barton wondered what effect the new program would have on the personnel in each of his departments.

When Mr. Cornwall issued the tally cards to Barton's salespeople, the head salesclerks failed to fill them out. Two of the head clerks had lost their tally cards when Cornwall came by later in the day to see how the program was progressing. Cornwall issued the two head clerks new cards and told them that if they didn't "shape up" he would see some "new faces" in the departments.

The part-time salespeople filled out the cards completely, writing down every sale. The rumor that those clerks who had low sales tallies would have their hours cut spread rapidly. Soon the clerks became much more active and aggressive in their sales efforts. Customers were often approached more than once by different clerks in each department. One elderly lady complained that while making her way to the restroom in the back of the hardware department she was asked by four clerks if she needed assistance in making a selection.

When Barton returned the day after the institution of the program the head salesclerks asked him about the new program. Barton replied that they had no alternative but to follow Cornwall's orders or quit. Later that afternoon the head clerks were seen discussing the situation on their regular break. After the break the head clerks began waiting on customers and filling out their sales tally cards.

Not long after the adoption of the program, the stock rooms began to look cluttered. Unloaded carts lined the aisles of the stock room. The shelves on the sales floor were slowly emptied and remained poorly stocked. Sales of items that had a large retail value were especially sought after and the head salesclerks were often seen dusting and rearranging these more expensive items. The head clerk's tally sheets always had the greatest amount of sales when the clerks compared sheets at the end of each day. (Barton collected them daily and delivered them to Cornwall.) The friendly conversations among salespeople and between clerks and customers were shortened and sales were rung up on the cash register and completed in a much shorter time. Breaks were no longer taken as groups and when they were taken they seemed to be much shorter than before.

When sales activity was slow in one department, clerks would migrate to other departments where there were more customers. Sometimes conflicts between clerks arose because of competition for sales. In one instance the head clerk of the hardware department interrupted a part-time clerk from the toy department who was demonstrating a large and expensive table saw to a customer. The head clerk of the hardware department introduced himself as the hardware specialist and sent the toy clerk back to his own department.

Often customers asked for items that were not on the shelves of the sales floor. When the clerk looked for the item it was found on the carts that jammed the stock room aisles. Some customers were told the item they desired wasn't in stock and later the clerk would find it on a cart in the stock room.

When Barton reported his observations of the foregoing situations to Mr. Cornwall, he was told that it was a result of the clerks adjusting to the new program and to not worry about it. Cornwall pointed out, however, that sales volume had still not improved. He further noted that the sum of all sales reported on the tally sheets was often $500 to $600 more than total department sales according to the cash register.

A few weeks after the instigation of the tally card system Cornwall walked through the hardware department and stopped beside three carts of merchandise left in the aisle of the stock room from the morning of the day before. He talked to the head clerk in an impatient tone and asked him why the carts weren't unloaded. The clerk replied that if Mr. Cornwall had any questions about the department he should ask Mr. Barton. Cornwall picked up the telephone and angrily dialed Barton's office. Barton told him that the handling of merchandise had been preempted by the emphasis on the tally card system of recording sales. Cornwall slammed down the receiver and stormed out of the department.

That afternoon, as a result of a request from Barton, Blanding, Cornwall, and Barton visited the four departments. After talking with some of the salespeople, Mr. Blanding sent a memo announcing that the tally card program would be discontinued immediately.

After the program had been terminated, salesclerks still took their breaks separately and conversations seemed to be limited to only the essential topics needed to run the department. Barton and the head salesclerks didn't talk as freely as they had before and some of the head clerks said that Mr. Barton had failed to represent their best interests to Cornwall. Some of the clerks said that they thought that the tally card system was Barton's idea. The part-time people resumed the major portion of the sales and clerking job and the head clerks returned to merchandising. Sales volume in the departments didn't improve.

24

A New Division

At the Craig Company, a new division was formed that would be responsible for the corporate mining investments overseas. The objectives were to oversee mining investments in Africa; protect the company's interests in mining investments under construction in South America; and market iron ore thoughout the world, especially in the Far East and in Europe. The long-term organizational goals were to maintain or augment dividend income from the African investments that were under increasing African political pressure to reduce dividends or reinvest in Africa; to handle all legal, financial, and managerial responsibilities involved in an iron-mine investment under construction in South America; to continue to market iron ore, and to develop new markets for the ore.

Senior management decided to locate the division headquarters at the main office, in a 30-story building located in a major international capital. The corporate offices were on floors from the sixth through the sixteenth, but because of shortage of office space, a decision was made to locate the new division on the second floor. The existing offices of the president and vice-president were on the fourteenth floor. The offices of the Market Research section, composed of five people, were on the eleventh floor; part of the Commercial staff (four people) was on the sixth floor; the Engineers (five people) and the Financial group (six individuals) were quickly moved to the second floor. The subgroups of the division were separated from each other physically by location on different floors of the building.

Since the new division was crucial to the operations of the total organization, the president was to be the chief executive officer with his vice-president assisting him. Each of the new division's separate activities was to be headed by a managing executive who would supervise the people under him. Each of these executives was to report directly to the president or, in his absence, to the vice-president.

The president determined that the prime short-term goals of the new division were to concentrate on marketing iron ore and

Robert E. C. Wegner/Leonard Sayles, *Cases in Organizational and Administrative Behavitor,* copyright © 1972, pp. 197–204. Reprinted by permission of Prentice-Hall, Inc., Englewood Cliffs, NJ.

to handle all details for the mine under construction. Management determined that a total work force of about 25 people would be adequate to accomplish all the work.

Before discussing the actual operation of the new division, it is necessary to make a few comments about the jobs of the president and vice-president of Craig Company. Because of the international operations of the company, both these men spent less than half their working time in their offices at corporate headquarters.

During the periods when the president and vice-president were in the office they were diligently preparing reports on their previous trips, catching up with correspondence that had accumulated during their absence, and making plans for the next trip. The periods spent in the office were short, two weeks at most, therefore both men tried to accomplish as much work as possible by giving dictation not only to their own secretaries but also to the supervisors' secretaries. The supervisors resented having their secretaries involved in this way because their own work fell behind. In order to complete the work, some overtime was required by the secretaries. The typing quality of the work for the executives was poor, because the secretaries who were enlisted often did not understand the dictation given by the officers and therefore did not type letters up to the quality standards expected by these men. The low-quality work was returned to the secretaries for retyping. Letters and reports were retyped two or three times, and occasionally some work was redone four or five times.

The executives as well as the secretaries became irritated, and such irritation manifested itself among the girls by crying, grumbling, and refusing to work overtime, and by the executives in vocal outbursts. After a few months, one excellent secretary requested a transfer. Her reason for this request was that she had never before been a secretary to several people simultaneously, and she did not intend to begin now!

All groups should have moved to the new offices in September, but the offices on the second floor required major renovation before they could be occupied. From September until January no decision was taken on the floor-plan arrangement of the new offices. The president wanted to be consulted on all phases of the layout planning. But during those months he was away on business trips about 60% of the time, so there was little opportunity to discuss with him the details of the floor plan. The vice-president traveled with the president; consequently he could not be apprised of the layout planning being done by the engineers. No other group was requested to help with the layout, or make any decision on the plan, although all groups made suggestions.

At the time the division was formed, all employees were asked by the president whether a transfer would be acceptable. If anyone refused to leave his or her existing job, no penalty was assessed. Some who were invited did not accept because they believed—or so they said—that the new organization would not afford them the best opportunities. These people were not questioned further as to the reasons for their decision. Among those who joined the group were certain individuals who were dissatisfied with their present positions and had requested transfers. There were also others who had been suggested for transfer by their superiors because of unsatisfactory performance in their present positions. A few of these were accepted because they had the talents required, even though they had not done acceptable work in other positions. One or two had a long history with the company and previously had done fine work.

One transferee, a Market Research analyst, had been transferred from two other divisions prior to joining the Overseas Investment group. In the past he had done some superb analyses, but developed a reputation for being difficult to work with. He preferred to work alone, producing volumes of work some of which proved difficult to read because of unusual grammar and syntax. His approach to a job was imaginative and considered brilliant by his co-workers. He had never been promoted to a supervisory position when younger people around him were moved up. He claimed that the other employees had taken advantage of his special knowledge and used his work to advance their own interests. After a short period of time in each division, say three months, he became increasingly close-mouthed about the work he was doing and sent progress reports and final reports of his work not to his immediate supervisor for inspection, but to the senior man of the division.

Often the supervisor objected; but the analyst continued the practice. Resentful of his behavior, the supervisor refused salary increases or job promotions for this analyst. This had been his typical history prior to entering the new division. It was hoped that by transferring him, he would find satisfaction in the job and the company would benefit from his work. In the new division he was to report to the president. His job was analyzing and reporting on potential markets. Since the president was often absent, the analyst was subjected to little supervision and was soon working on pet projects unrelated to the work of the division.

From September to January he did almost no work that could have been useful to the president, and continually irritated the Marketing personnel who requested assistance from him and were refused; moreover, he constantly criticized the work of others. Eventually there was little conversation between the analyst and the others in the division. He claimed that his reason for not complying with their requests was that the work had not been initiated by the president who was, in fact, his boss.

OPERATIONS OF THE NEW DIVISION
Work efficiency in the new division was not high when the group was formed. Output was far less than expected. Most of the employees had not previously worked under the direction of executives; neither had the subgroups worked with their supervisors before. For some people, the type of work was different from what they had done previously. Also, employees were located on four separate floors.

Primarily the work involved calculation and accumulation of engineering, financial, and marketing data, and writing reports for the division executives and for the senior management. Advice on decisions approved or actions initiated by the division executives was relayed to the other workers vocally; however, when these men were out of the city, communication was in writing or by telephone. Frequently the executives made overseas telephone calls to keep the chief accountant, chief engineer, or other employees fully apprised of their activities.

Reports from subordinates were mailed to the executives when the latter were absent from the city. Reports from corporate headquarters were also mailed to the executives. Reports written by subordinates, however, were sent to the president and vice-president upon request and without approval of the traveling executives. Conflicts resulted when the travelers did not accept the conclusions in the reports, and in several instances subordinates were asked to retrieve the reports from the senior management so that they could be altered. The subordinates were greatly embarrassed on these occasions.

Communication between the offices in the building was accomplished almost entirely by telephone. A memorandum of instruction for normal day-to-day activity was time-wasting and unnecessary. Excessive time was consumed by the president, vice-president, and the division executives in traveling by elevator to the appropriate floors to give instructions, comment on work in process, provide trade-offs, or simply to observe what was going on. Often several trips each day were necessary for these purposes. In addition, employees were constantly traveling from floor to floor to pass on information, provide trade-offs, gossip, and report to the executives.

Telephones provided the most convenient way to communicate, but confusion and misunderstanding persisted. Errors in office correspondence and in reports to the president and vice-president became common. The uncovering of these errors resulted in anger or a feeling of frustration among the employees. Arguments between the subgroups that had cooperated to produce the reports became more frequent. Eventually the president and vice-president lost confidence in the work of the subordinates, and consequently also in the work of the division executives.

All groups attempted to take extra care to catch errors before the work left the office; yet, regardless of the amount of time devoted to eliminating errors, the instances of such errors did not diminish to any great extent. The total amount of work that would normally be expected ebbed as the writers and editors slowed in their output. Reports were produced late. A general lack of confidence in the work pervaded the entire office. The executives did not trust the subordinates, and the subordinates believed that the executives were exaggerating small errors. High-quality work, a goal of the executives and senior management, was not being produced.

Corporate management (the chairman of the board and some of the directors) also began to doubt the quality of work and pressured the president to insist on better performance from the new division. The result of this was that the president and vice-president became vocally abusive to division executives and employees, and to each other. Naturally enough, the problems continued.

As September passed into October, then November, there was a steady deterioration in work quantity and quality. Many employees spent considerable time just grousing together. The length of time spent traveling between floors to pass on information increased. One division executive began to arrive at work late and to leave early. His subordinates eased up on their work until he arrived, then slowed up again after he left. He began complaining to almost everyone who would listen. Some of his comments were, "The company has been unfair to me before on my job, and now they have shifted me to a new position where I won't be able to use my knowledge effectively." Or, "Now that I have this new job, which is a promotion, I expected to get a pay raise." Or, "The boss isn't here, and I don't know what I am supposed to do. He won't be back for a week."

In the four months that the division continued working on the four floors, morale among the employees disintegrated. A divisional esprit de corps had not developed. The few groups of three to five people who worked together on one floor developed strong subgroup strengths. They worked together all day, and even had lunch together as often as possible. Each group was composed of people who did similar work. A kind of professionalism developed among the groups, especially in their supervised relationship with the division executives.

The president was absent from the office because he had to travel, but he was also "absent" from the employees because he believed that a certain distance should be kept between the supervisor and subordinates. He disliked administrative and personnel work, and avoided these activities as often as possible. It was his intention to have the vice-president handle these functions. The vice-president had a reputation for getting along with most people and tended to supervise using the "be good" approach, but he was not in the office enough to be effective. The president was autocratic in his dealings with subordinates and disdainful of the assistantshiptype function of some groups, such as the corporate Personnel Department.

At the time the new division was formed, the vice-president was requested to fill out a job description of his work in the new division. The request emanated from the corporate Personnel Department. After completing the job description form, he asked the president to evaluate it. The president signed the form with the comment that the description of work was too elaborate, but that he would sign it anyway. Some months later, when the vice-president took an action with which the president disagreed, the latter questioned why the action had been taken without requesting permission. The reply was that the decision area for that work lay with the vice-president. The vice-president reminded the president of the job description. The president then remarked that what was on the description form was for the Personnel Department, but that the form had nothing to do with what his job in the division was, so "forget the job description!"

The subgroups began to operate almost as separate companies with their own goals and objectives. After a few months, the differentiated groups increased the inter-group conflicts as trade-offs became difficult because of the physical barrier imposed by work done on separate floors. The flow of work, insufficient from the outset, decreased as conflicts increased and confusion between the groups arose. No cohesion between the subgroups existed, and inner subgroup cohesion developed to an excessive degree as the supervisors of each subgroup tended to represent only their subordinates' interests.

As this unhappy and unproductive situation wore on, top corporate management began to wonder whether the forming of the new division had been such a good idea in the first place. There was more and more talk that a complete reorganization of the new division was in the cards and, as rumor had it, "heads would roll." The president, vice-president, and division executives, feeling insecure about their jobs, were even more irritable and thus also inefficient.

25

The Bank of Boston

INTRODUCTION

The chilly February morning became colder as Bostonians heard the news reports and read the headlines: "Bank of Boston Guilty in Cash Transfer Case." In a plea bargaining arrangement with the Financial Investigation Task Force unit of the Justice Department, the Bank agreed to pay a $500,000 fine after pleading guilty to federal charges of "willfully and knowingly" failing to report $1.2 billion in cash transfers with nine foreign banks. The Bank had violated the Bank Secrecy Act which stipulates that all cash transfers over $10,000 made through financial institutions be reported to the Internal Revenue Service. The allegations came quickly:

- The Bank was involved in businesses with criminal overtones.
- The Bank laundered drug money.
- Bank employees were "on the take."

Less than one week later, one of the allegations appeared to be true. The Bank had placed two companies controlled by a reputed organized crime figure on a list which exempted their cash transactions from being reported to the Fed.

That information started an avalanche of events. Two local communities withdrew their funds from the Bank and, of greater magnitude, the City of Boston was considering withdrawing its funds. Bills to remove state money from the Bank were filed in the state legislature. Both houses of Congress scheduled hearings, and approval of two pending mergers of out-of-state banks was deferred.

Stories about the Bank dominated the news media until early March, when two events signified a turning point:

- Two other Boston banks disclosed reporting violations.
- Merrill Lynch announced that the Bank would retain its quality rating.

Meanwhile the Congressional hearings continued; and at the Bank's annual meeting, the stockholders were told that an addi-

This case was prepared by David Breyer, PhD. Assistant Professor of Management, Suffolk University, as the basis for class discussion rather than to illustrate either effective or ineffective handling of an administrative situation. Copyright 1986.

tional $110 million transfer had not been reported. This time the cash was transported from the Bank's international banking subsidiary in Miami to banks in Haiti. Despite all the troubles, the Chairman of the Board, William L. Brown was able to announce to the stockholders a 70 percent projected increase in earnings.

NARRATIVE OF EVENTS

In an effort to aid law enforcement officials in the detection of criminal, tax, and regulatory violations, Congress passed the Bank Secrecy Act in 1970. By requiring that banks report large cash transactions to the IRS, Congress intended that "money laundering" (a method by which criminals attempt to funnel illegal funds through a legal institution) be abated. Banks were given until July 1, 1972, to establish a list of customers who, in the normal course of business, have currency transactions in excess of $10,000. This "exempt" list precluded the necessity for those customers to file large currency reports. The Bank complied with this request and submitted its exempt list to the government, thereby alerting the authorities to those customers normally dealing in large amounts of cash.

In 1976, the branch manager of the North End branch of the Bank placed Huntington Realty Co. on the exempt list, and in 1979 added Federal Investments, Inc. These companies were owned and operated by the Angiulo family, customers of the bank since 1964 and allegedly involved in organized crime in New England. The Bank's records show that between 1979 and 1983 representatives of the Angiulo companies purchased with cash 163 cashier's checks totaling $2,163,457.50.

In 1980 new regulations narrowed the scope of the exempt list to operators of retail-type businesses, such as supermarkets and restaurants, whose receipts involved substantial amounts of cash. But when the Bank submitted a new list, Huntington Re-

alty and Federal Investments were still included.

In 1982, the Department of the Treasury, with help from the Organized Crime Strike Force, began investigating organized crime activities in Massachusetts. This investigation brought to light the Bank's unreported overseas currency transactions completed. On June 8, 1982, investigators asked the Banking Offices Administration unit of the Bank to provide additional information concerning certain customers on the exempt list. With that request, the Treasury enclosed a copy of the Bank's exempt list with two types of notations:

1. check marks beside customer names requiring additional information (taxpayer number, address, etc.).
2. an X beside names of depositors that did not appear to be types of establishments that a bank is permitted to put on its exemption list without prior approval of the Treasury Department.

Because the Bank's Coin and Currency Department was responsible for its own exempt list of customers (some of whom the Treasury was investigating) Banking Offices Administration referred the June letter to that department. The Coin and Currency Department did not respond to the Treasury's request until several months later.

After reviewing the information provided by the Bank, the Treasury announced that several items on the list did not meet the requirements of the regulations. The Treasury requested further information which the Bank supplied. Because the Treasury's request was interpreted by the Bank as a request for information rather than as a request to remove the questionable customers from the list, the list remained intact at that time. However, in May 1983 the Bank received subpoenas relating to its lack of compliance with the Act. At that time the Bank conducted a more thorough review of the exempt list and removed the Huntington and Federal companies.

In 1984 a grand jury probe into organized crime activities was begun in Boston. That same year, action was initiated by the Justice Department's newly formed Financial Investigative Task Force, comprised of representatives from U.S. Customs, the IRS, and the Organized Crime Strike Force. As a result of both investigations, Bank of Boston, on February 2, 1985, pleaded guilty to large currency reporting violations. The specific charge focused on cash transfers of $1.2 billion to Swiss banks without the filing of large currency reports. A $500,000 fine was assessed. However, given the nature of the plea, criminal overtones were unavoidable; and on February 13 local papers reported that the Angiulo businesses had been on the exempt list, thereby loosely linking the foreign cash transfers to money laundering. An onslaught of accusations followed.

William L. Brown, Chairman of the Bank's board of directors, called a press conference at which he blamed the violations on "systems failure" and made the point that the international money transfer business is a legitimate banking function.

Another damaging report was released on February 27: the Treasury announced that Federal bank examiners had informed the Bank of international reporting failures in 1982, at which time the Bank had promised to take corrective action. The Bank issued a swift denial, stating that the 1982 report had referred only to domestic violations, which the Bank had corrected. The Treasury later retracted its statement and admitted it was mistaken. This strengthened the Bank's assertion that it did not know of the international reporting violations until the summer of 1984. Nonetheless, by the end of February five independent investigations had been initiated by the following groups: the United States Senate, the United States House of Representatives, the Securities and Exchange Commis-

sion, the New England Organized Crime Strike Force, and the Bank's special committee (comprised of five outside directors). The probe into reporting compliance extended even to brokerage houses, as reported in a *Boston Globe* spotlight report on money laundering channels.

Throughout this period, Chairman Brown asserted that criminal activities had not occurred at the Bank; he emphasized that international transfers were legitimate and entirely unrelated to the Angiulo exemptions. He acknowledged, however, that the Bank used "poor judgment" in placing the Angiulo companies on the exempt list. To restore confidence in the bank, he charged the special committee to evaluate the Bank's overall state of compliance, not only with the Act, but with other regulations, including Regulation E which governs electronic funds transfers, and Truth-in-Lending.

Over the next several months, the Bank continued to be the target of a highly critical media barrage which included coverage of banking activities well beyond the scope of the reporting failures. In one case, as a result of a negative news report, a pending merger with Rhode Island Hospital Trust was called into question and put on hold by the state legislature. The news media also questioned the Bank's decision to relocate its credit card operation to New Hampshire.

The reporting violations became a national issue as other banks came forward with admissions of similar failures. On March 9, the Shawmut Bank of Boston made public its failure to report over $200 million of large currency transactions. Shortly thereafter, similar reports were released by Wells Fargo Bank, Chemical Bank, Bank of America, Manufacturers Hanover Bank, Irving Trust, and the Bank of New England. In all cases, officials at these banks claimed that the reporting failures were unintentional, due either to a failure to note the changes in the Bank Secrecy

Act, or to a misinterpretation of those changes. The Bank was the only one to plead guilty to "willfully and knowingly" violating the regulations.

The special committee appointed by the Bank's directors to conduct an internal investigation made its findings public on July 25, 1985. The report acknowledged that the "level of noncompliance at the bank with the [Bank Secrecy] Act was extensive" and that Bank employees exhibited "widespread laxity and poor judgment." The committee concluded, however, that no one had profited from the reporting violations.

On July 28, 1985, the *Boston Globe* ran an editorial entitled "Finale at the First." The closing sentence captured the prevailing feeling among many bank employees and customers: "The First's world will never be the same as before, but it has won the right to get back to its main line of work."

THE SPECIAL COMMITTEE

On February 25, 1985, the Board of Directors appointed a special committee to review the Bank's efforts to comply with the Act. The special committee consisted of five outside directors: George R. West (Chairman), Chairman of the Board, Allendale Mutual Insurance Company; Samuel Huntington (Vice Chairman), President and CEO, New England Electric System; Martin R. Allen, Chairman of the Board, Computervision Corporation; Thomas A. Galligan, Jr., Chairman of the Board, Boston Edison Company; and J. Donald Monan, S.J., President, Boston College.

The mandate of the special committee was to review the adequacy of the record compiled by management on matters relating to the reporting of large currency transactions as required by the Act; to determine who was responsible for the failures of the Bank to comply with the Act; to recommend disciplinary action if deemed appropriate; and to review management's policies, procedures, and systems to ensure future regulatory compliance.

During the next four months the committee conducted a rigorous investigation which included holding over 100 interviews, reviewing files, consulting legal experts, and conducting audit tests.

The committee's findings were reported to the Board of Directors on June 27, 1985. The report confirmed that the level of noncompliance at the Bank was extensive. Failure to comply with the Act went beyond the immediate situation and extended into other operations of the Bank and its affiliates. Further, when the Government began its investigation, management failed to realize the seriousness of the situation or to take corrective action.

The investigation uncovered the fact that, although the requirements of the Act received widespread distribution throughout the Bank, there was no concerted follow-through to see that the new reporting requirements were implemented. As a result, no one caught the mistake for four years. The Coin and Currency Department which handled the cash transfers misunderstood, and therefore neglected to implement, the amended regulations. At the same time, many personnel in other departments and divisions, including Staff Services (Corporate HRD), the Law Office, and the Internal Audit Department, failed in their staff responsibilities. (Exhibit 25–1 shows the organization of the bank.) The committee found no evidence that the cash transfers involved "tainted" money.

The problems at the North End branch concerned a modification in the Act which narrowed the circumstances under which domestic transactions must be reported. Prior to July 1980, the regulations provided that transactions with established customers whose business regularly involved large currency transactions could be exempted from reporting. Therefore, having the Angiulo's real estate businesses on the Bank's exempt list prior to 1980 did not violate any

EXHIBIT 25-1 BANK OF BOSTON CORPORATION, 1984–85

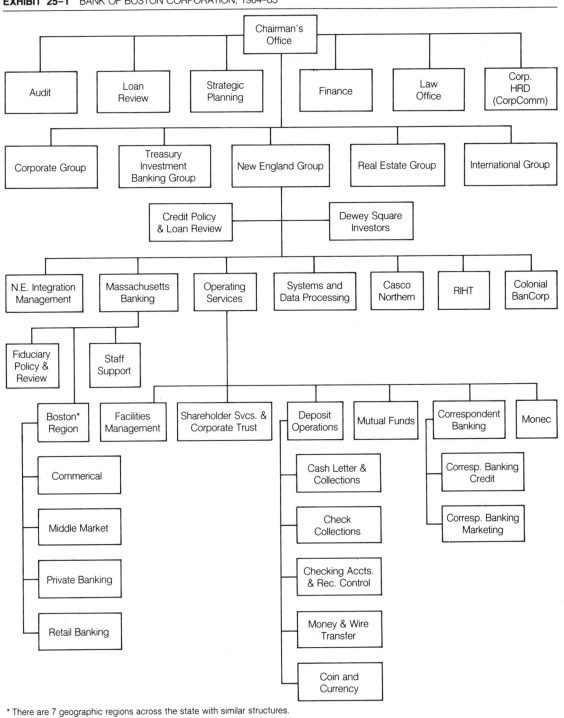

* There are 7 geographic regions across the state with similar structures.

express provision of the regulations. The amendment clearly disqualified the Angiulo businesses from the exempt list, but the manager of the North End branch kept them on the list. Although the decision to do so was questioned by the Banking Offices Administration (Retail Banking Division), it was not overruled.

Although numerous transactions went unreported and personnel in the North End branch were aware of the Angiulos' reputed ties to organized crime, there was no evidence of collusion between any employee of the Bank and the Angiulos to violate any requirement of the Act. The Angiulos, like some other customers, occasionally gave small gifts to branch personnel. There was no evidence, however, that such gifts were related to the improper maintenance of their accounts on the exempt list.

Much more serious was the Bank's failure to respond promptly when a Treasury official questioned the appropriateness of certain customers on the list, including the Angiulos. Some 13 months passed before the Bank responded to the Treasury, during which time the Bank's Coin and Currency Department failed to report transactions for those customers.

In concluding the findings, the special committee found an unsatisfactory overall level of compliance with the Act by the seven independent banks which the Bank of Boston Corporation had acquired during 1974 through 1981. Also, there was evidence of unsatisfactory compliance by the Bank's Suffolk County branches and by certain branches of the Casco Northern Bank, a Maine based affiliate acquired by the Bank in 1984.

CONCLUSION

After careful review of the special committee's report, on July 24, 1985, the Bank's Board of Directors made public its conclusions in a news release:

The policy of the Bank is and always has been to comply with all governmental regulations. Thus, the Bank had written procedures regarding the Treasury Department's currency reporting requirements since their inception in 1972. However, the Bank failed to put in place systems and controls adequate to ensure that regulatory changes would be incorporated promptly and correctly into that policy, and to ensure that the policy would be understood and fully implemented throughout the organization. These failures led to widespread misunderstanding, and misapplication of the currency reporting requirements, especially after the change in the regulations in 1980 ...

The Staff Services Department circulated to a number of the Bank's other departments the Bulletin received by the Bank in July 1980 from the Office of the Comptroller of the Currency. Neither Staff Services nor any of the recipients of the Bulletin, however, requested appropriate action by Information Systems and Services, the department which prepares and publishes the Bank's operating procedures. As a consequence, the operating procedure on currency reporting which the Bank had had in place since 1972 was not amended to reflect the new requirement of reporting transactions with foreign banks and the new standards for exemption for retail customers.

Even those units of the Bank's operations which were in fact informed of the 1980 changes did not in all cases properly interpret and apply them. Although Banking Offices Administration sent a detailed memorandum to all branches under its jurisdiction explaining the changed standards for exempting Bank customers from reporting, it did not exercise sufficient supervisory control over the exempt list to remove the ineligible customers from the list.

Similarly, as previously noted, the Coin and Currency Department of the Bank received notice of the 1980 regulatory changes but failed to understand them to require reporting of transactions with foreign banks. Because the 1980 changes were not highlighted in any subsequent operating procedure or other directives to Coin & Currency, this serious error of interpretation went uncorrected until it was discovered in mid-1984.

In addition, the Bank failed to adequately audit

its operating units for compliance with the Act's requirements. As a result, opportunities were missed to correct the misapplication and violation of those requirements which in fact occurred. Although the Bank's internal auditors conducted periodic branch audits, which included a cursory review of compliance on a periodic basis, neither the North End Branch nor Coin & Currency was audited for compliance after the change in the regulations in 1980. Moreover, even prior to 1980, the Internal Audit Department failed adequately to test the Bank's administrative controls relating to compliance with currency requirements.

26

Elling Bros. Got Costs Under Control

Back, in 1974, Clifford Elling discovered his company had sprung a leak. Tiny cost overruns on a $2.3-million contract were beginning to drain money out of Elling Brothers Mechanical Contractors at a rate that threatened to put the 53-year-old Somerville, N.J., firm out of business.

As Elling watched in dismay, a carefully budgeted 15-month job to install industrial piping turned into a financial nightmare. Day by day, design specifications changed, the price of materials shot up, and unexpected delays increased payroll costs. By 1975, when Elling Bros. closed its books on the contract, 30 months had elapsed, and the trickle of tiny overruns had become a flood. Elling's company was out $250,000 on the job—half of the privately owned company's total net worth of $500,000.

Cliff Elling decided it was time to plug the leaks on costs. He'd always taken estimates and budgets seriously; every bid was based on a meticulously prepared estimate of the materials and manpower each job would require. But budgets alone weren't enough to keep costs under control. Like any business, Elling Bros. functioned in a world of constant change. If budgets weren't updated promptly to reflect these changes, even tiny errors could multiply until they wiped out the company's profits altogether.

The problem was particularly acute in the construction industry, in which even the strongest firms typically operated with narrow profit margins and very little net worth to cushion the business against mistakes. One thing Elling did know was that there weren't any easy solutions to cost control problems, no magic wand he or a consultant could wave.

Elling Bros. wasn't prone to sloppy bookkeeping or risky ventures. The firm had been launched in 1921 by Elling's father and uncle, hardworking sons of a German immigrant farmer, who began by using the family barn as a small plumbing shop. Cliff joined the company in 1950, at age 26, after a stint in the Army and an M.B.A. degree from Wharton. For his first three years, he worked in the field, doing heating and

Prepared By Matthew Berke. Reprinted with the permission of *INC.* Magazine, January 1982.
Copyright © 1983 by INC. Publishing Company, 38 Commercial Wharf, Boston, MA 02110.

plumbing work as an apprentice to the journeymen.

That fieldwork proved invaluable in giving Elling a sense of how to estimate costs and figure schedules. "Back in the '50s," he says, "there was a great lack of professionalism and training in the management aspect of construction. There was no way to become an estimator except to get a feel for the practice in the field. There was no school you could go to, no course you could take, no book you could read, to find out how long it takes to install a toilet, for instance."

As Elling worked his way up through the ranks of the family company (he became president in 1969), he learned that cost control was a subject most contractors paid lip service to, but felt very little urgency about. The 1960s in particular were "lush, plush days" for contractors, with plenty of highly profitable jobs for everyone. "If you have a budget of $850,000 for a job that pays a million," he says, "well, it's very difficult to lose money. You say, 'Why worry about all this detail? So what if I go over budget a little? I know I'm going to make money anyhow.' You worry about budgeting only when things are tight and competitive."

By the mid-1970s, Elling realized that conditions in the construction industry were changing dramatically. Competition was increasing and margins were becoming tighter. Elling's own company, moreover, found itself involved in far more complex projects. Instead of standardized piping for schools and government buildings, the company was now bidding on industrial jobs that often required innovative piping systems for moving liquids and gases. "If you make 10,000 Chevies you know how much the next one will cost and how long it will take," Elling explains. "It will be pretty much like the 10,000 before it. But in these kinds of construction projects you don't have that same degree of repetition. Each job is unique."

That lesson was hammered home by the disastrous cost overruns Elling Bros. experienced on its 1973–75 contract. The budget for the job predicted a modest but acceptable gross profit for Elling Bros. But very little went according to plan. The Nixon price control program first created critical shortages of materials, then caused prices to soar after controls were lifted. The work force, supervised by unfamiliar foremen in a relatively distant part of New Jersey, was performing at only about two-thirds of expected efficiency. And dozens of changes ordered by the customer often went unbilled and unrecorded. "We weren't yet sophisticated enough to keep detailed account of them all," Elling concedes. "We didn't have the mechanism to price and record them, so we didn't get the extra money in time."

Just to survive, Elling Bros. had to cut costs quickly, and scrounge for every penny. Purchasing was rationed; only urgently needed deliveries were accepted, and only when there was money to pay for them. The top six company executives, including Elling, all took salary cuts. Bonuses and profit sharing disappeared for everyone in the office and warehouse. Though the company cut its volume of work and trimmed its fixed overhead, Elling and other stockholders had to pledge their homes and personal assets to the bank to raise operating capital. "I've always prayed a few times a day," says Elling, "but I had never prayed for the company. For the first time I started to."

Elling knew he had to go beyond emergency survival measures if he wanted to stay in business over the long haul. His financially shaky firm would have to do something more drastic than slashing overhead. Elling would have to develop a budgeting and cost-monitoring system that would blow the whistle on costs early enough to do something about them before they escalated. Most of the problems of the 1975 fiasco, he realized, could have been minimized if he'd had accurate, up-to-date information—instead of reports that were months old.

Elling huddled with his accountants and pored over books by cost-control experts. Just getting more information, he quickly realized, wasn't the answer. Elling Bros. had three purchasing agents who handled hundreds of daily transactions and a labor force of 75 that might be employed in 15 different locations at one time. Elling couldn't hope to keep track of the details of all this activity without drastically expanding his office staff and overhead.

Elling found the nucleus of an answer in a manual written by Jack Baker and a committee of the national Mechanical Contractors Association of America (MCAA). Baker, a contractor himself, pointed out that large, complex budgets can't be properly monitored by checking individual line items or by comparing current expenditures against the overall progress of the job. Instead, Baker suggested that budgets can be monitored by subdividing them into small, easily evaluated units and by focusing attention on those items on which costs are most likely to get out of hand.

The new cost-monitoring system Elling established for the company drew heavily on Baker's principles. Each week, a foreman and a site manager report to Elling about the progress made on well-defined stages of work at each site. Progress is measured by man-hours expended and the amount of work completed. (Most units involve fewer than 100 hours of labor; none exceed 1,000.) Elling has his foremen and site managers send him separate opinions on each stage so he can compare reports: "You can measure a roof in square feet or a road in cubic yards of concrete. But I defy anyone to walk through a system of pipe or

EXHIBIT 26-1   ELLING BROS. COST-CONTROL HISTORY

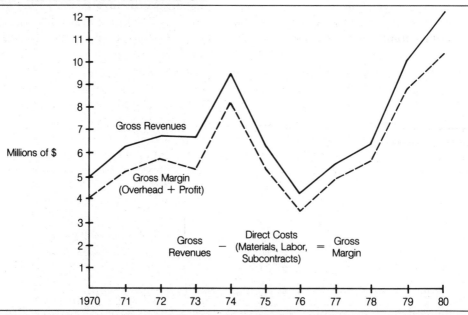

Over the last 10 years, Elling Bros. has experienced wide fluctuations in its revenues from large-scale mechanical contracting projects. Most of the company's revenues are turned over quickly to pay for job-related materials, labor, and subcontracting, leaving only a narrow margin after costs to cover overhead and profit. In the early 1970s, when high-profit jobs were more plentiful, the company's gross margins were wide enough to absorb small cost overruns. But a major contract in 1973–75 almost put Elling Bros. out of business and forced the company to retrench considerably. To deal with the crisis, Cliff Elling introduced a stricter cost-monitoring system—and today, revenues and profits are both once again growing rapidly.

electrical conduits and say the job is half done or three-quarters done."

At the same time, Elling gets reports on the most cost-volatile materials that go into the job, chiefly pipe valves and fittings, small $5 to $20 items that add up to a major proportion of job costs. Overruns are more likely to occur here, he points out, and will have the greatest long-term effect, even though individual dollar amounts are small. "You concentrate your energy where the danger is," says Elling, "as any good general will tell you."

The information from these reports goes into a small Nixdorf computer the company acquired in 1974. The computer then prints out an analysis of where Elling Bros. stands in its projections for each job—man-hours budgeted against man-hours actually spent, work accomplished, man-hours spent as a percentage of both the whole job and work accomplished, and finally, deviation from expectations, with a figure for man-hours over or under budget.

With the new monitoring system in place, Elling finally felt that he had the company's costs under control. Yet the system did not work any immediate profit magic: Elling Bros. continued to lose money. In fiscal 1971, the company had shown a respectable pretax profit of 5.5% on $4.8 million in revenues. By 1974, in the middle of the contract morass that taught Elling that he needed to monitor costs more carefully, pretax profit was down to 2.2% and, by 1975, to .9%. In 1977 Elling Bros. actually lost money. "It was," Elling says, "a rather bleak picture of marginal earnings." (See Exhibit 26–1).

Yet small gains slowly began to offset the losses, and none of the losses developed into catastrophes—because they were caught early. In November 1979, for example, Elling Bros. started a job for a chemical manufacturer. By January Elling's reports showed that he was losing $1,000 a month. The reports also pinpointed the source of the losses: major overruns in labor at several job sites. Elling hopped in his car with a foreman and drove to one job site. Here he found union jurisdiction disputes over certain tasks, combined with late deliveries of

EXHIBIT 26–2   SMALL SAVINGS ON COSTS ADD UP TO MAJOR PROFITS

1980 Income Statement	Elling Bros.			The Industry	
	($000)	(%)		($000)	(%)
GROSS REVENUES		12,174	100.0		10,590	100.0
Materials & equipment	3,358		27.6	3,310		31.3
Subcontracts	4,125		33.9	1,907		18.0
Job-related wages	2,100		17.2	2,929		27.6
Payroll taxes, job insurance, union benefits	680		5.6	807		7.6
Misc. direct job costs	96		0.8	290		2.7
DIRECT JOB COSTS		10,359	85.1		9,242	87.3
GROSS PROFIT		1,815	14.9		1,348	12.7
G&A expenses	999		8.2	1,186		11.2
NET INCOME (LOSS) BEFORE TAXES		726	6.0		162	1.5

In 1980, when an intensive cost-monitoring program was finally beginning to pay off for Elling Bros., the company had gross revenues of $12,174,000. An industrywide survey by the Mechanical Contractors Association of America (MCAA), published in 1980, showed that average construction revenues for member firms were about the same—$10,590,000. Elling Bros. also spent similar amounts on direct costs—85.1% of revenues compared to an industry average of 87.3% —and on G&A costs—8.2% compared to an average of 11.2%. Yet small cost savings had a dramatic effect on overall profitability. The average mechanical contracting firm earned 1.5% on its construction revenues; Elling Bros. earned four times as much, with 6.0% in pretax profits.

critical materials. The problems were relatively easy to solve—and by the time the job was finished, in August, Elling had come out well below budget, despite his early losses.

In dozens of jobs, the cost-monitoring system brought problems to Elling's attention promptly, when dollar amounts were still small and dramatic solutions unnecessary. Says Elling, "It's really a story of what didn't happen rather than what did happen. The triumph is that we survived. It may sound ho-hum, but not if you compare it to years of losses, frustration, and cliffhanging."

Eventually, as economic conditions in the contracting industry brightened and the company recovered its lost volume of work, Elling didn't have to be satisfied with just breaking even. In fiscal 1979 Elling Bros. turned a 2.5% pretax profit on $6.6 million in revenues. In 1980, revenues jumped to $10.3 million and pretax profits

were 5.1%. And last year the company hit $12.2 million in revenues, with a 6.0% pretax profit—at a time when the industry average for mechanical contractors was only 1.5% profitability on revenues of $10.6 million. (See Exhibit 26–2).

"We're making more money than ever before," says Elling, "not because of fatter markups or less competition, but because we know in a timely way about any problems. The essence of good budgeting is having *timely* accounting and monitoring of changes. We have found it is critical to know where we stand, and the only way to do this is by having reasonable control over the budget and schedule.

"What you have done is constant," he adds, "but what you have to do is constantly changing. If you can imagine a football game where the goal line is changing as often as the line of scrimmage, then you can understand the kind of game we're playing."

27

Making of a Bad Cop

What makes a policeman go sour? I can tell you. I was a Denver policeman until not so long ago. Then I quit so I could hold my head up.

Don't get me wrong. I'm not trying to shift the burden of responsibility for the burglaries, break-ins, safe jobs and that sort of thing. That is bad, very bad. But I will leave it to the big shots and the newspapers and the courts to say and do what needs to be said and done about that.

My concern is about the individual officer, the ordinary, hard-working, basically honest but awfully hard-pressed guy who is really suffering now.

Young fellows don't put on those blue uniforms to be crooks. There are a lot of reasons, but for most of the guys it adds up to the fact they thought it was an honorable, decent way of making a living.

Somewhere along the line a guy's disillusioned. Along the way the pressures mount up. Somewhere along the way he may decide to quit fighting them and make the conscious decisions to try to "beat" society instead.

But long before he gets to that point, almost as soon as he dons the uniform, in fact, he is taking the first little steps down the road that does, for some, eventually lead to the penitentiary.

Let me back up a little. I want to talk about how you get to be a policeman, because this is where the trouble really starts.

Almost any able-bodied man can become a policeman in Denver. If he is within the age brackets, if he is a high school graduate, if he has no criminal record, he is a cinch.

There isn't much to getting through the screening, and some bad ones do get through. There are the usual examinations and questionnaires. Then there is the interview. A few command officers ask questions. There is a representative of civil service and a psychiatrist present.

They ask the predictable questions and just about everybody gives the predictable answers: "Why do you want to become a policeman?" "I've always wanted to be a policeman. I want to help people." Five or ten minutes and it is over.

Reprinted by permission of *The Denver Post*.

Five or ten minutes to spot the sadist, the psychopath—or the guy with an eye for an easy buck. I guess they weed some out. Some others they get at the Police Academy. But some get through.

Along with those few bad ones, there are more good ones, and a lot of average, ordinary human beings who have this in common: They want to be policemen.

The job has (or had) some glamour for the young man who likes authority, who finds appeal in making a career of public service, who is extroverted or aggressive.

Before you knock those qualities, remember two things: First, they are the same qualities we admire in a business executive. Second, if it weren't for men with these qualities, you wouldn't have any police protection.

The Police Academy is point No. 2 in my bill of particulars. It is a fine thing in a way. You meet the cream of the Police Department. Your expectations soar. You know you are going to make the grade and be a good officer. But how well are you really prepared?

There are six weeks at the academy—four weeks in my time. Six hectic weeks in which to learn all about the criminal laws you have sworn to enforce, to assimilate the rules of evidence, methods of arbitration, use of firearms, mob and riot control, first aid (including, if you please, some basic obstetrics), public relations, and so on.

There is an intangible something else that is not on the formal agenda. You begin to learn that this is a fraternity into which you are not automatically accepted by your fellows. You have to earn your way in; you have to establish that you are "all right."

And even this early there is a slight sour note. You knew, of course that you had to provide your own uniforms, your own hat, shoes, shirts, pistol and bullets out of your $393 a month.

You knew the city would generously provide you with the cloth for two pair of trousers and a uniform blouse.

What you didn't know was that you don't just choose a tailor shop for price and get the job done.

You are sent to a place by the Police Department to get the tailoring done. You pay the price even though the work may be ill-fitting. It seems a little odd to you that it is always the same establishment. But it is a small point and you have other things on your mind.

So the rookie, full of pride and high spirit, his head full of partly learned information, is turned over to a more experienced man for breaking in. He is on "probation" for six months.

The rookie knows he is being watched by all the older hands around him. He is eager to be accepted. He accepts advice gratefully.

Then he gets little signs that he has been making a good impression. It may happen like this: The older man stops at a bar, comes out with some packages of cigarets. He does this several times. He explains that this is part of the job, getting cigarets free from proprietors to resell, and that as a part of the rookie's training it is his turn to "make the butts."

So he goes into a skid-road bar and stands uncomfortably at the end waiting for the bartender to acknowledge his presence and disdainfully toss him two packages of butts.

The feeling of pride slips away and a hint of shame takes hold. But he tells himself this is unusual, that he will say nothing that will upset his probation standing. In six months, after he gets his commission, he will be the upright officer he meant to be.

One thing leads to another for the rookies. After six months they have become conditioned to accept free meals, a few packages of cigarets, turkeys at Thanksgiving, and liquor at Christmas from the respectable people in their district.

The rule book forbids all this. But it isn't enforced. It is winked at on all levels.

So the rookies say to themselves that this is OK, that this is a far cry from stealing and they still can be good policemen. Besides, they are becoming accepted as "good guys" by their fellow officers.

This becomes more and more important as the young policeman begins to sense a hostility toward him in the community. This is fostered to a degree by some of the saltier old hands in the department. But the public plays its part.

Americans are funny. They have a resentment for authority. And the policeman is authority in person. The respectable person may soon forget that a policeman found his lost youngster in the park, but he remembers that a policeman gave him a traffic ticket.

The negative aspect of the job builds up. The majority of the people he comes in contact with during his working hours are thieves, con men, narcotics addicts, and out and out nuts.

Off the job his associations narrow. Part of the time when he isn't working, he is sleeping. His waking, off-duty hours do not make him much of a neighbor. And then he wants to spend as much time as he can with his family.

Sometimes, when he tries to mix with his neighbors, he senses a kind of strain. When he is introduced to someone, it is not likely to be, "This is John Jones, my friend," or "my neighbor"; it is more likely to be, "This is John Jones. He's a policeman."

And the other fellow, he takes it up, too. He is likely to tell you that he has always supported pay increases for policemen, that he likes policemen as a whole, but that there are just a few guys in uniform he hates.

No wonder the officer begins to think of himself as a member of the smallest minority group in the community. The idea gradually sinks into him that the only people who understand him, that he can be close to, are his fellow officers.

It is in this kind of atmosphere that you can find the young policeman trying to make the grade in the fraternity. But that is not the whole story.

A policeman lives with tensions, and with fears.

Part of the tensions come from the incredible monotony. He is cooped up with another man, day after day, doing routine things over and over. The excitement that most people think of as the constant occupation of policemen is so infrequent as to come as a relief.

Part of the tensions come from the manifold fears. I don't mean that these men are cowards. This is no place for cowards. But they are human beings. And fears work on all human beings.

Paramount is the physical fear that he will get hurt to the point where he can't go on working, or the fear that he will be killed. The fear for his family.

There is the fear that he will make a wrong decision in a crucial moment, a life-and-death decision. A man has been in a fight. Should he call the paddy wagon or the ambulance? A man aims a pistol at him. Should he try to talk to him, or shoot him?

But the biggest fear he has is that he will show fear to some of his fellow officers. This is the reason he will rush heedlessly in on a cornered burglar or armed maniac if a couple of officers are present—something he wouldn't do if he were alone. He is tormented by his fears and he doesn't dare show them. He knows he has to present a cool, calm front to the public.

As a group, policemen have a very high rate of ulcers, heart attacks, suicides, and divorces. These things torment him, too. Divorce is a big problem to policemen. A man can't be a policeman for eight hours and then just turn it off and go home and be a loving father and husband—particularly if he has just had somebody die in the back of his police car.

So once again, the pressure is on him to belong, to be accepted and welcomed into the only group that knows what is going on inside him.

If the influences aren't right, he can be hooked.

So he is at the stage where he wants to be one of the guys. And then this kind of thing may happen: One night his car is sent to check on a "Code 26"—a silent burglar alarm.

The officer and his partner go in to investigate. The burglar is gone. They call the proprietor. He comes down to look things over. And maybe he says, "Boys, this is covered by insurance, so why don't you take a jacket for your wife, or a pair of shoes?" And maybe he does, maybe just because his partner does, and he says to himself, "What the hell, who has been hurt?"

Or maybe the proprietor didn't come down. But after they get back in the car his partner pulls out four $10 bills and hands him two. "Burglar got careless," says the partner.

The young officer who isn't involved soon learns that this kind of thing goes on. He even may find himself checking on a burglary call, say to a drugstore, and see some officers there eyeing him peculiarly.

Maybe at this point the young officer feels the pressure to belong so strongly that he reaches over and picks up something, cigars perhaps. Then he is "in," and the others can do what they wish.

Mind you, not all officers will do this.

Somewhere along the line all of them have to make a decision, and it is at that point where the stuff they are made of shows through. But the past experience of the handouts, the official indifference to them, and the pressures and tensions of the job don't make the decision any easier.

And neither he nor the department has had any advance warning, such as might come from thorough psychiatric screening, as to what his decision will be.

Some men may go this far and no further. They might rationalize that they have not done anything that isn't really accepted by smart people in society.

This is no doubt where the hard-core guy, the one who is a thief already, steps in. A policeman is a trained observer and he is smart in back-alley psychology. This is especially true of the hard-core guy and he has been watching the young fellows come along.

When he and his cronies in a burglary ring spot a guy who may have what it takes to be one of them, they may approach him and try him out as a lookout. From then on it is just short steps to the actual participation in and planning of crimes.

Bear in mind that by this stage we have left all but a few policemen behind. But all of them figure in the story at one stage or another. And what has happened to a few could happen to others. I suppose that is the main point I am trying to make.

28

University Control Graph

The purpose of this exercise is to develop control graphs for the participants' university. The control graph illustrates the concepts of both amount and distribution of control in organizations. The questions are worded in exactly the same way as control graph research. For use with non-university organizations, titles in the question should be replaced with titles appropriate to the organization under consideration.

STEP 1: *Answer Control Graph Questions (5 minutes)*

Each student in the class and the instructor should complete the control graph questions below.

1. In general, how much influence would you say each of the following persons or groups *actually have* on what happens in your university?

	Almost no influence	A little influence	Moderate influence	Quite a lot of influence	A great deal of influence
The President	1	2	3	4	5
Deans	1	2	3	4	5
Department Heads	1	2	3	4	5
Professors	1	2	3	4	5
Students	1	2	3	4	5

2. In general, how much influence would you say each of the following persons or groups *should have* on what happens in your university?

	Almost no influence	A little influence	Moderate influence	Quite a lot of influence	A great deal of influence
The President	1	2	3	4	5
Deans	1	2	3	4	5
Department Heads	1	2	3	4	5
Professors	1	2	3	4	5
Students	1	2	3	4	5

STEP 2: *Calculate Influence Scores (10 minutes)*

Volunteers from the class should gather information from all students about their scores. The scores may be written on a piece of paper or the volunteers may wish to have a show of hands. From this information the average score for each hierarchical level for each question can be calculated.

The instructor's response should be kept separate from student responses in these calculations.

STEP 3: *Draw Control Graphs (5 minutes)*

Students' average scores for the "actually

191

have" and "should have" curves should be drawn on the chalkboard as illustrated in the graph below. The vertical axis reflects the amount of influence and the horizontal axis shows the hierarchy levels. The "actual" control should be written as a solid line and the "should have" as a dashed line. A separate graph should be used for the instructor's scores.

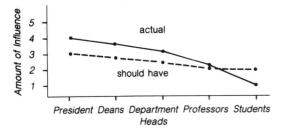

STEP 4: *Discussion (15 minutes)*

At this time the class should discuss and interpret the results of the control graph. The following questions may facilitate discussion.

1. Does the slope of the curves indicate a democratic or autocratic organization?
2. Are the slopes the same as would be expected in manufacturing organizations, in municipal governments, or other organizations?
3. Does the instructor's perception of control differ from the students'? Why would this be? Which is more accurate?

4. Which curve reflects the most total control for the university? What does greater total control mean for university functioning?
5. Which of the curves reflects the most skewed distribution of control? The most even distribution of control? What does distribution of control mean for university functioning performance?
6. Would the university be more effective if it conformed to the amount of control that students think each hierarchical level "should have?"

STEP 5: *Variation (20 minutes)*

Variations of the above exercise can be repeated to illustrate that overall control is not a unidimensional phenomenon in organizations. Influence and control may differ considerably depending on specific issues. For example, administrative versus academic domains of control may produce wide variation in perceived influence. The above questions (Step 1) can be changed to ask how much influence each of the following persons or groups have on the content of courses taught in this university? This would reflect the academic domain. Questions could also be asked with respect to pay raises, or changes in organization structure that are in the administrative domain. These variations would help participants map influence throughout the university for specific issue areas.

29

The Queen Elizabeth Hospital

The Queen Elizabeth Hospital was founded in 1894 under the name of the Montreal Homeopathic Hospital (the name was changed in 1951). The hospital has been at its present location in the west end of Montreal since 1927. The catchment area consists of approximately 200,000 persons, the majority of whom live in middle-class residential districts. There are over 250 beds in the hospital and the number has grown only very slightly over the past 10 years *.

The hospital is classified as an acute general hospital center. Most types of surgery are performed and the institution is considered to have a first-class psychiatric staff. In recent years there has been a shortage of nursing staff and psychiatric beds. The public demand for outpatient services has grown much more quickly than the hospital resources available to deal with it. For example, the total nursing staff has grown from 221 in 1972 to 232 in 1973 whereas in the same period emergency admissions

have increased over 10%, and the percentage increases in ambulatory visits, diagnostic radiology services, laboratory units, and social service contracts were 10%, 22%, 17%, and 16% respectively.

Of the 102 full-time members of the medical staff, 46 are directly associated with the Faculty of Medicine at McGill University as Associate Professors, Assistant Professors, Lecturers, or Demonstrators. The Queen Elizabeth's institutional affiliations are numerous.

In 1973 the Queen Elizabeth was requested by the provincial government to close its obstetric facilities. This case looks at the decision-making process involved in the termination of obstetric care and the conversion of facilities to other uses.

KEY PARTICIPANTS AND ADMINISTRATIVE BODIES

The discussion of administrative structure will be limited to a consideration of the key entities involved in the decisions to close and transform the obstetric facilities at the hospital. The organization chart (Exhibit

---

* "The Hospital's aspirations are not directed to expansion but toward higher standards of performances within our resources." From *Presentation to McGill Teaching Hospital Council*, June 18, 1974, p.4.

Written by Danny Miller. Reprinted with permission of the author.

29–1) illustrates many of the important formal interrelationships in authority and accountability amongst these bodies.

The key participants in this case include:

1. *The Department of Social Affairs* of the Province of Quebec issued directives concerning the consolidation of obstetric services and the closing of facilities at the Queen Elizabeth. The resulting changes in function and budget had to be approved by this government ministry.
2. Several members of the *McGill University Faculty of Medicine* played an adviso-

ry role in the reorganization of obstetric resources among seven English-speaking hospitals in the Montreal area (including the Queen Elizabeth). Dr. Lee, the Associate Dean of Community Medicine, was particularly active in helping the various hospitals assess their obstetric facilities.

3. *The Board of Directors* and the *Executive Committee of the Council of Physicians and Dentists* in the Queen Elizabeth were responsible for ratifying the key decisions made regarding obstetrics by the committees within the hospital, within the framework, of course, of the government's directives.

EXHIBIT 29–1   QUEEN ELIZABETH HOSPITAL OF MONTREAL CENTRE, ORGANIZATION & OPERATIONS CHART

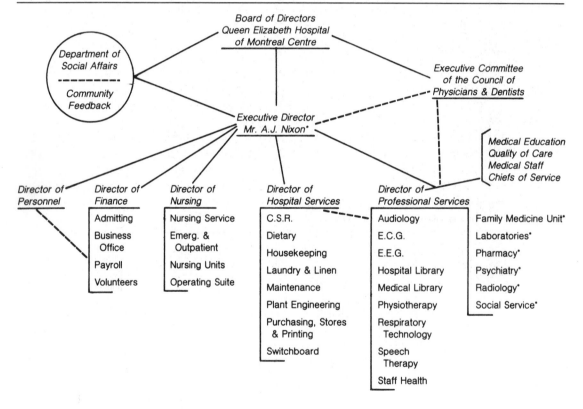

June 3, 1974.

Solid line ——————— denotes direct accountability.

Broken line — — — — — denotes staff relationship (communications and advisory capacity) with no direct accountability.

*Departments that report to Executive Director for administrative matters.

4. *The Executive Director* of the hospital, Mr. Nixon, coordinated the various decision-making bodies, was influential in suggesting administrative procedures and committees to facilitate decision-making, and was instrumental in helping devise solutions to the transition problem. Mr. Nixon sat on the committees mentioned in (3) and (5) and reported to the Board.

5. *The Property, Space Utilization, and Equipment Committee* (not shown on the organization chart) reported to both the Executive Committee of the Council of Physicians and Dentists and to the Board of Directors of the hospital. This committee was the most important decision-making body to deal with the problem of what to do with the obstetric facilities. The members of the committee included: the Executive Director (Mr. Nixon), the Director of Professional Services (Dr. Nancekivell), the Chairman of the Executive Committee of the Council of Physicians and Dentists, the Physician in Chief (Dr. Palmer), the Chief of Obstetrics and Gynecology (Dr. Catterill), the chiefs of the other medical departments (e.g., surgery, radiology, psychiatry), the Director of Nursing (Miss Bryant), the Nurse Coordinator of the Family Medicine Unit, and the Maintenance Supervisor. Because he had the greatest amount of relevant expertise, Dr. Catterill was particularly active on this committee.

THE DECISION–MAKING CLIMATE

Mr. Nixon was convinced that the decision-making approach in hospital centers should be as participative as possible and that the advice of experts was essential in making complex decisions. He maintained that because decisions in one area influence many other departments in the hospital, it was mandatory for many people to be consulted before taking action. Mr. Nixon's belief in participative decision-making set the climate in which the closing of the Obstetric Unit was carried out.

Mr. Nixon also stressed his interest in rationalizing the planning, decision-making, and transition processes in the hospital. As a senior executive with much management experience, Mr. Nixon had evolved guidelines for drafting proposals and resolving issues. He encouraged the use of cost benefit analysis, clear objectives, longer time horizons, and the generation of alternative solutions in decision-making. He also emphasized the importance of the practicality of solutions, the need to pay attention to details and potential problems in implementation, and the importance of social psychology in organizational behavior.

THE DECISION TO CLOSE THE OBSTETRICS DEPARTMENT

The Department of Social Affairs had become increasingly concerned about the effectiveness of the obstetric units within the Province. It appeared that there was an excess number of maternity beds and that infant and maternal mortality rates were unduly high. A subsequent study by the Department revealed that hospitals with small obstetric units (less than 1,000 deliveries per annum) had by far the highest mortality rates and were less efficient financially. The conclusion was reached that 3,000 deliveries per unit would be the minimum acceptable number to yield better quality care at a lower cost. The Department decided to consolidate the 26 obstetric units in Greater Montreal into 9 to 12 centers, each having a neonatal intensive care unit.

The process was well under way by February 1973 when the Deputy Minister of Social Affairs requested the help of McGill University in examining the obstetric units of hospitals associated with McGill. Dr. Lee, the Associate Dean of Community Medicine at McGill, was asked to submit his recommendations on how to consolidate obstetric facilities. Seven English-language hospitals were subsequently visited and appraised by Dr. Lee, who had considerable familiarity with the problem.

Because their obstetric unit was relatively small, the Queen Elizabeth Hospital was one of the seven to be affected by the plans of the Department. The number of deliveries there had declined from 1,267 to 1,182 between 1969 and 1972, and approximately 30 of the 44 beds in the Obstetrics and Gynecology area were devoted to obstetrics.

Early in March, Mr. Nixon attended a meeting with members of the McGill Faculty of Medicine (including Dr. Lee) and the administrators of the other six hospitals. The government's consolidation plans were discussed and the hospital representatives were informed that only about half of the seven hospitals would be allowed to retain their obstetric units (no names were mentioned). None of the seven hospitals handled the minimum 3,000 deliveries. The reactions of the administrators were diverse; some were much against closing their units while others were receptive to the idea. Mr. Nixon adopted the latter posture.

On March 20, the bi-weekly meeting of the Property, Space Utilization, and Equipment (P.S.E.) Committee took place. Mr. Nixon discussed his meeting with the representatives of McGill and the other hospitals and mentioned the Department's proposed plan to close the obstetric facilities. Dr. Catterill, the Chief of Obstetrics and Gynecology, was asked to head a committee with Mr. Nixon, Miss Bryant (the Director of Nursing), and Dr. Palmer (the Physician in Chief). The committee was to prepare recommendations on the issue for presentation to the Council of Physicians and Dentists, the Hospital Board, and McGill.

The Executive Director, most of the medical staff, and the nursing staff had long known the government's plans to consolidate obstetric facilities in the province. Thus, although no formal plans had been considered before the setting up of this committee, the hospital administration and medical personnel were aware that changes were in the wind.

On March 29 Dr. Catterill submitted a report to Mr. Nixon summarizing two options that he felt were open to the Queen Elizabeth in response to the government's directives. Exhibit 29–2 shows this report.

In late March, Dr. Catterill met with representatives from the McGill Faculty of Medicine. His impression of the obstetrics situation is recorded in the minutes of the April 2nd meeting of the P.S.E. Committee as follows:

Obstetric Beds. Dr. Catterill stated that four obstetric units of the seven in the English sector will be closed. The names of these four are not known. He was not sure whether they will be closed 3 + 1, or all four at once. The final decision will be made in July. It looks as if we will be asked to close our unit since our facilities do not seem adequate for the required number of deliveries. However, Dr. Catterill felt we could reach the minimum requirement with cramping and some reconstruction. It is undecided as to what will happen to the beds that are closed. Should this happen, gynecology may be closed out elsewhere and we then might have to increase our gynecology beds. Dr. Catterill will be meeting with Dr. Lee shortly, and will report further at our next meeting.

Discussions with Dr. Lee in early April confirmed Dr. Catterill's conclusion that the appropriate action to take would be the closure of obstetric facilities at the hospital. The Board of Directors were informed of this development during the month and so was the Executive Committee of the Council of Physicians and Dentists. Each of these bodies voiced some complaints regarding the potential loss of obstetric facilities (so did the Director of Nursing) but by and large they accepted the development as a

EXHIBIT 29–2 DR. CATTERILL'S REPORT

RETAIN QUEEN ELIZABETH HOSPITAL OBSTETRICAL UNIT
Utilizations of at least 40 of the 44 beds on the present obstetrical floor at an ideal 85% occupancy rate, thus handling approximately 3,000 deliveries annually. This Unit would serve the west end of the city and could remain associated with clinics in St. Henri and Pte. St. Charles as well as Elizabeth House for unmarried girls. Neonatal problems would be handled in the Neonatal Unit of the Montreal Children's Hospital.

Difficulties:
1. There are only three delivery rooms; four would be necessary to handle this volume.
2. There are only four labor rooms; would need to increase to six or eight.
3. Lack of Recovery Room.
4. Nursery area is barely adequate.
5. Loss of present gynecology beds that are now an integral part of the obstetrical floor. This would necessitate providing gynecology facilities elsewhere.

Impression:
Our present obstetrical volume (1,200 deliveries annually) could be increased to 2,000 without major changes becoming necessary, but beyond that, the above deficiencies could create extreme problems.

DISBAND QUEEN ELIZABETH HOSPITAL OBSTETRICAL UNIT
At present there are 44 beds on the obstetrical floor, of which 15 to 18 are used for gynecology. With the loss of the Obstetrical Unit, 26 beds would be effectively freed.
Without capital outlay, the obstetrical area on the third floor could be used for:

1. *A Complete Gynecology Unit*
The 26 beds could be available as replacements for gynecology beds closed or displaced in other hospitals as the result of enlarged obstetric units.

2. *Combined Gynecology-Surgical Specialty Unit*
The specialty beds now on the second floor could be relocated on the obstetrical floor, thus releasing beds for the ICU and Coronary Care areas.

3. *Combined Gynecology-Urology Unit*
Urology Unit could be relocated on the third floor, with an increase in the number of beds now allocated to Urology. This would provide a more functional Urology Unit in close association with Gynecology and provide sufficient beds for residency training in Urology.

In the above plans, the present delivery rooms would be available for minor surgical and gynecological procedures, particularly on an outpatient basis. Nurseries could be used for holding areas (Surgical Day Center).

Difficulties:
Staffing problems (Nursing and Anesthesia).

Impression:
The loss of the Obstetrical Unit would seem to be the more practical and economical plan of the two. In this way a pressing need for a Surgical Day Center area would be realized, long on the list of priorities at the Queen Elizabeth Hospital.

Respectfully submitted,
T.B. Catterill, F.R.C.O.G., F.R.C.S.(C)
Obstetrician and Gynecologist-in-Chief

fait accompli. Only token resistance was offered.

On May 3, the Deputy Minister of the Department of Social Affairs sent a letter to the President of the Board of Directors of the Queen Elizabeth requesting the hospital to close their obstetric services. (See Exhibit 29–3.)

The decision process up to this point was fairly clear cut. The government decided that obstetric resources could be more effectively allocated. McGill Faculty of Medicine personnel and several key people in the Queen Elizabeth Hospital agreed with this decision. Only a small amount of resistance to the potential closing facilities at the Queen Elizabeth was expressed by the Board and the Council of Physicians and Dentists. Then a directive came from the Deputy Minister of Social Affairs instructing the hospital to terminate its obstetric services. Thus, although the final decision came from outside the hospital, the key parties concerned—the Executive Director and the Obstetrician and Gynecologist-in-Chief—were receptive to such a decision on the basis of their own analysis. The entire sequence of events took place in less than two months.

THE DECISION ON RESOURCE REALLOCATION

The key issues after May 3 were how and when to phase out obstetrics and more importantly, how to reallocate the resources set free. Mr. Nixon stated that the key criteria were the beds of the community, and the hospital's ability to use existing (or retrained) personnel in the new undertaking. That is, it was agreed that any new service would have to both satisfy pressing social needs and assure complete utilization of idle resources—staff, space, beds and equipment. The facilities to be vacated upon the elimination of obstetric services consisted of 3 delivery rooms, 4 labour rooms, 3 nurseries, and about 30 beds.

EXHIBIT 29–3 RECOMMENDATION TO CLOSE
QUEEN ELIZABETH HOSPITAL
OBSTETRIC SERVICE

Mr. J.R. Houghton
President
Board of Governors
Queen Elizabeth Hospital
2100 Marlowe Avenue
Montreal, Quebec

Mr. President:

As you no doubt know, the Ministry of Social Affairs has just completed the analysis of the needs in obstetrics and postnatal sector. Following this study, the Ministry does not deem it desirable, from an economics and medical level, to maintain small obstetrics departments such as yours.

Consequently, we request you to take the necessary measures, in view of the closing of your obstetrics department around October 15, 1973.

We appreciate the quality of services rendered the population during many years and we request you to increase your services in the spheres where the needs appear to increase rapidly.

Please note that the Ministry has requested the following Hospital Centres in your region to increase the capacity of their obstetrics services: St. Mary's, Jewish General.

The Ministry is presently studying a project aimed at developing obstetrics services of the Royal Victoria Hospital. In view of the considerable time necessary for the full realization of this project, the Montreal General Hospital will continue to offer obstetrics services until it is possible for the Royal Victoria to receive a larger number of patients, in more modern quarters.

The Ministry trusts your institution will contribute important assistance to Physicians and other groups concerned, in order to facilitate the putting into effect of the changes involved by these decisions.

The Ministry personnel is disposed to meet with you to discuss dispositions relative to these changes. Dr. Stanly Knox has been assigned to act as representative of the programmation with your Board of Governors.

Please accept, Mr. President, the expression of my best regards.

JACQUES BRUNET, M.D.
Deputy Minister
cc: Dr. A. F. Nancekivell
Dr. T. B. Catterill

Around the middle of May, the P.S.E. Committee began to tentatively discuss the mechanics of the phasing-out process and various suggestions were received on the alternative uses of facilities. Problems of staff training and space and bed utilization were mentioned. Since it was agreed that the committee should develop concrete plans to present to the government, all Chiefs of Service were asked to study the

problem to present their perspectives at the next P.S.E. meeting.

At that meeting, which took place on May 28, Dr. Catterill suggested that since the Obstetrics and Gynecology issue had not been completely settled in *all* seven hospitals, plans for the reallocation of facilities on the 3rd floor (the area of the Obstetrics Department) should be postponed until the needs of the community became better known. Dr. Palmer, Physician-in-Chief, thought it would be best to have a plan ready to present to the Department of Social Affairs as soon as possible.

Mr. Nixon suggested that the 3rd floor would lend itself to surgery procedures and a Day Care Center. (This idea had been discussed several times over the past few years by surgical representatives on the Council of Physicians and Dentists.) The need for such facilities had become increasingly evident with growth of emergency and outpatient services.

Dr. Catterill suggested having Gynecology on one floor—the 3rd—and giving up present Gynecology beds on the 6th floor to other services. He also stated that there could be room left over for a Urology ward on the 3rd floor. The possiblity of relocating Psychiatry on the 3rd floor was considered but since this would increase its capacity by only two beds some felt such a move would not justify the cost of the relocation. The option was kept open, however.

More suggestions were offered at this meeting of May 28th but they were essentially in the same vein as above. The meeting closed without reaching any firm conclusions on the issue, although the various proposals were not fundamentally different. The P.S.E. Committee stated that it would remain open to further suggestions.

In early June the Committee decided on a closing date for Obstetric Services. October 19th was chosen after considering existing commitments to patients.

By mid July the P.S.E. Committee had

refined its ideas on the proposed use of the Obstetric facilities. Dr. Catterill's submission outlines the proposed changes in Exhibit 29–4.

On July 20th, the P.S.E. Committee met to make a final decision on the matter. The resolution varied only slightly from Dr. Catterill's July 16 proposal in that it was decided to move E.N.T. (Ear, Nose and Throat, a surgical sub-specialty) to the third floor. Delivery rooms were to be used for the Surgical Day Center and 30 beds were to be devoted to Gynecology.

Mr. Nixon informed the Board of these recommendations and Dr. Nancekivell (Director of Professional Services) called a meeting of the Executive of the Council of Physicians and Dentists before the end of the month to discuss the recommendations and seek ratification.

The final decisions concerning the use of vacated obstetric services fulfilled the two original requirements: the hospital would be better able to meet community needs for emergency and outpatient surgery services, and the facilities could be adapted to this new service with minimal cost. The Day Care Center would also reduce operating costs by eliminating the need for overnight hospital stays. Further, the additional 15 to 30 gynecology beds would help meet the increased demand that would occur with the closing of services elsewhere.

IMPLEMENTATION

Late in the summer, Mr. Nixon began planning the implementation of the new facilities. At the P.S.E. Committee meeting of September 10, it was recommended that a committee be formed to organize the Surgical Day Care Center. The committee was comprised of the professionals most familiar with the medical requisites of such a unit.

While some members of the nursing staff were a little reluctant to change their work areas, retraining of Nursing personnel in O.R. procedure went very smoothly. The Director of Nursing supported the changes not only because she approved of the rationalization of the city's obstetric resources but also because she felt that the nursing services in the Queen Elizabeth's obstetric unit had been uneconomical because of the spatial layout of facilities. She suggested that the nursing staff in general were receptive to the changes because they had been advised of events at an early stage (before the government's edict arrived) and

---

EXHIBIT 29–4 PROPOSED REQUIREMENTS AND CHANGES FOR THE 3rd FLOOR

1. Delivery Room Area to be used as follows:		*C*	Infertility Center - hopefully to move to larger quarters in out-patient area
Delivery Room No. 1	Minor Out-Patient surgery under general anaesthesia (gynecology, general surgery, etc.) cystoscopies excluded	4. *Obs-Gyn Bed Changes*	
Delivery Room No. 2	Recovery Room	1.	Loss of 6 Gyn beds on 6th Floor
Delivery Room No. 3	Out-patient surgery under local anaesthesia (Cases presently being done in Emergency Area)	*2.	35 gynecology limit on 3rd Floor
		*3.	Remaining 10 beds for Urology (male and female)
2. *Labor Rooms (4)*	Admission Area for out-patient surgery		
3. *Nurseries*			
A or B	Out-Patient surgical admission and late recovery area to replace Room 237 when 2nd Floor O.R. changes are made and to relieve eventual congestion in labor room area (#2 above)		

*The present complement of gynecology beds is 21, with frequent overflow to the Obstetrical area.

After October 15, there will be three further Staff members requiring gynecology facilities. If one considers that 3.5 beds are required per gynecologist, we will then have to supply 9 staff members and the Infertility Center; thus the need for 35 beds.

T. B. Catterill, M.D.
July 16, 1973

EXHIBIT 29–5 NIXON'S REPORT

October 22, 1973.

Dr. Jacques Brunet
Deputy Minister
Ministry of Social Affairs

Dear Sir:

In accordance with your letter of May 3, the Queen Elizabeth Hospital of Montreal Center Obstetrics Department closed at 12:00 noon October 19, 1973.

The phasing-out of this Department has moved ahead as planned. The delivery room area will be used as a Day Center for elective Medical/Surgical minor procedures.

The Gynecology Department will have access to 30 beds and the sub-specialties of Surgery will have access to the balance of 15 beds. The only expense that we will incur in this change will be the purchase of Medical/Surgical supplies

for the Day Care Center, at approximate cost of $9,000.00

All our Nursing Staff and other employees have been relocated satisfactorily without any disruption to their service.

The projected 1973 operating cost of our third floor including the Case Room and Delivery Room area is $427,441.00.

The 1974 budget estimate for the third floor including the Day Care Center is $350,225.00; a net saving of approximately $77,216.00.

We are constantly reviewing the need for beds in our Family Medicine Unit and Department of Psychiatry. Presently we are able to meet both these Departments' bed requirements, although pressure is mounting from Psychiatry for more beds.

We would appreciate receiving confirmation of these changes from your Department.

Albert J. Nixon
Executive Director

---

were assured in a series of group discussions (which had taken place from April to October) that individual skills and preferences would be considered in the relocation of staff.

Most of the medical specialists in Obstetrics and Gynecology were to maintain their affiliation with the Queen Elizabeth with respect to their Gynecology practices but were to start to perform deliveries at two other major hospital centers (The Royal Victoria and St. Mary's). Some of these physicians expressed remorse at having to leave the hospital for their obstetrics practice but it is believed that most did not feel seriously inconvenienced at having to do so.

On September 25, the P.S.E. Committee discussed some of the specific details which had to be settled before the Day Care Center could open in early November. The points raised centered on the disposal of old equipment, the oxygen and suction to be installed, the precise staffing requirements, the surgical supplies required, the scheduling of personnel resources, and so forth. It was suggested that a committee be formed to look after any problems in implementing the Surgical Day Care Center. The Chiefs of Services were asked to nominate representatives of their departments to sit on this committee.

On October 19, 1973 the Obstetrics Department was closed. On October 22, Mr. Nixon sought confirmation for the changes from the Department of Social Affairs. (See Exhibit 29–5.)

The Day Care Center opened, as planned, in early November, 1973.

30

Memorial Hospital

The purpose of this role-playing exercise is to illustrate and reinforce concepts relating to organizational decision-making processes. Organization decision-making may follow several models depending on the organizational situation. The following exercise will challenge you to analyze the organization setting, determine the goals of the organization and the path for achieving those goals, identify the problem, and propose a solution. Upon completion of the role-playing exercise the class will discuss the decision-making models as they relate to the situation presented.

STEP 1:   *Volunteers (5 min.)*

The instructor will ask for six volunteers from the class to be the "actors" in this role-playing exercise.

STEP 2:   *Introduction of Background Material (5–10 min.)*

The volunteers will leave the room and re-ceive descriptions of their individual roles. They will not be able to discuss their roles with each other. While the volunteers are reading their roles the rest of the class should read the background material below.

STEP 3:   *Committee Meeting (15 min.)*

Returning to the front of the classroom, the volunteers will meet as the Pediatric Ward Administrative Committee, with the nurse and social worker as guests. The group will attempt to reach a decision on the issue presented by Mrs. Mills and Mr. Brown while the remainder of the class observes the decision-making process.

STEP 4:   *Class Discussion (20 min.)*

In reviewing the group role-playing session as a class, consider the following discussion questions as they relate to material previously presented in classroom lectures.

This exercise is based on "Strategies of Changing: A Multiple-Role Play" in *The 1973 Annual Handbook for Group Facilitators*, John E. Jones and J. W. Pfeiffer, editors, LaJolla, CA: University Associates, Inc., 1973, and "You Are Bob Waters, Assistant Administrator at Unity Hospital," distributed by the Intercollegiate Case Clearing House, Soldiers Field, Boston, MA 02163.

DISCUSSION QUESTIONS

1. What are the goals of the hospital? Does each person involved in the decision-making process agree on one set of goals? On how to meet these goals?
2. What is the problem the hospital is facing? What are the possible solutions? How was the committee meeting influenced by each person's interpretation of the problem and solution?
3. How would you analyze the hospital's problem situation in terms of social factors, political factors, uncertainty, constituencies?
4. Which model of organization decision-making did you see operating in your group? Would another model have been more appropriate based on the organization's situation? Why or why not?
5. Did you see evidence of coalition building taking place? When can this be effective in decision-making? When is it harmful to the process?
6. If this problem were to be presented to Dr. Peterson for him to solve as an individual, what process would you suggest he use for reaching a decision? Would his solution be an organizational decision even though he is responsible for the final recommendation?

The Pediatric Ward, Memorial Hospital

The Pediatric Ward Administrative Committee meeting will start in a few moments. The Administrative Committee consists of Dr. Peterson, Chief Resident in Pediatrics, Mr. Perez, Assistant Administrator of the hospital, Mrs. Axel, Head Nurse of the Pediatric Ward, and Mr. Jones, Assistant Head Nurse of the ward. Two additional people will be present at today's meeting, Mrs. Mills, a nurse on the ward, and Mr. Brown, a social worker.

Memorial Hospital is located on the near west side of a large city in Ohio. Over the last 10 years, the neighborhood has changed to predominantly blue-collar and minority residents, and the economic status of the neighborhood has decreased. Local residents are the primary clientele of the hospital.

The pediatric ward, along with other wards, faces a continuing shortage of financial resources. The hospital is supported by county taxes, but resources never seem adequate to provide all the services needed. The pediatric ward has adopted techniques that enable staff to accomplish more work. Older children are typically harnessed to little chairs in front of TV sets or placed in cribs to watch TV. Infants lie in cribs with bottles tied to the side of the crib. The bottles can be popped into the children's mouths without having to take them out of the crib. The nurses are kept busy filling out reports in the nursing station, which is closed from the wards, although they do make regular tours through the ward every 30 minutes or so. Nurses aides check on the children and do the routine tasks of sweeping the floor and making beds.

The nurse and social worker who have asked to attend today's administrative committee meeting are concerned about the changing conditions on the ward. They have asked for an opportunity to express these concerns. (Information for specific roles will be distributed by the instructor.)

31

Company A: The CIM Decision Process

THE RESURGENCE OF TECHNOLOGY

Company A is a large mature corporation with several business units, all of which operate in a basic industry. In the late 1970's, a number of people within Company A began to feel that technology was not being taken seriously by the corporation. While this idea was expressed in different ways by different people, it centered around the perception that the company was overly concerned with finance and marketing, and that these disciplines had replaced technology as the driving force within the firm. ''Technologists'' were not occupying key vice-presidential positions, their statements were discounted, and technologically risky decisions were not being made. In the period between 1978 and 1982, a number of efforts arose spontaneously, in disparate parts of the corporation, to try to combat this trend.

Steven Robinson, at the Corporate Research Center (CRC), had become increasingly frustrated with the type of R & D planning that was going on in the business units. R & D projects were funded by the business units, and the General Managers of the business units also chaired the committees that allocated funds to research projects. Over time, it became clear that long-range, fundamental, ''blue sky'' projects were not getting funded. Instead, the business units were funding research which would generate quick returns in terms of existing product lines.

Robinson and others became concerned about the long-term effects of this type of planning on the corporation. In order to address the problem, an R&D planning group was formed at CRC. The focus of this group was to assist the committees in developing long-range R&D plans. They experienced some success in getting the business units to think in a more long-term and strategic manner about research.

At about the same time, Thomas Kidwell was transferred from CRC into corporate planning. He soon became concerned about the harm done to technology by the strategic planning process. He expressed it as follows:

Corporations, not just this one, but corporations as a whole are getting increasingly into

---

Prepared by James Dean Jr., The Pennsylvania State University. Reprinted with permission from James W. Dean's *Deciding to Innovate: Decision Processes in the Adoption of Advanced Technology,* Copyright 1987, Ballinger Publishing Company.

technological and business problems because there's an inordinate financial emphasis in the strategic planning process. Strategy is more than finance. Strategy expresses itself ultimately in finance, but it does not capture technology unless it asks for a moment "What could technology substantively do for us?" You do that in the language of technology, and then, you can fold it into a financial plan. But if you don't do that carefully, you'll miss it.

While Kidwell tried to express this problem to the top management, he was unsuccessful in doing so, at least during this period. He was hampered by his place within the financial organizations, and the fact that he had three new bosses in the two years he was in the position. As Kidwell tells it, "Each time I got some awareness in the Vice President, he moved and I got a new boss." So Kidwell's message limitedly got beyond corporate planning.

The third, and probably the most significant, initiative in the resurgence of technology at Company A began in the hills outside the city where Company A's headquarters are located, on a Sunday afternoon in 1982. Geoffrey Munson, who had one year to go before retirement as Vice Chairman of Company A, was having dinner with his daughter-in-law at a local country club. He noticed at a nearby table a man who was a former vice president for a steel company. Something clicked for Munson. He said, "You know it's beginning to haunt me that those men, instead of being able to enjoy this country club, should be punished for the way they've destroyed an industry." He wondered if the management of Company A could be guilty of this as well. At that moment, he made a vow to himself that he would not be in a position to be accused of the same thing after he retired.

As a result of this experience, Munson felt that he really needed to do a better job of incorporating technology into the business plans than was being done at the time. He was thus instrumental in creating a new entity within Company A: the Strategic

Technology Group. Thomas Kidwell was named Director of Strategic Technology and reported to Munson. As Kidwell describes it:

[Munson] knew he had to make it so that technology could rise to the top of the corporation without passing through finance. That meant that corporate planning and technology planning had to be parallel. I could not report into corporate planning. It had to rise to the top of the corporation in parallel.

The R&D Planning group that Robinson had started at CRC now reported to Kidwell, and their scope was broadened from R&D to include the whole corporation.

The main task of the Strategic Technology Group was to assist the business units in preparing their plans, so that they would seriously include technology. Nate Charles, who had worked in the R&D Planning group and then in Strategic Technology described the impact of the group:

It's reached a point that in the forthcoming planning cycle, when the businesses bring in their annual five year plans . . . they have been instructed by the President that they must deal explicitly with technology . . . [they must] give explicit examples of what their targets are, how much it's going to be worth once they reach those targets, and how they are going to get there. No broad brushed stuff any more. No more glib words like "we're going to put in robots" . . . He said that you've got to be much more explicit than that.

Shortly after the formation of the Strategic Technology Group, Company A's "Office of the Chairman" changed *en masse*. The former chairman retired, and was replaced as Chairman and CEO by Peter Chandler, who had been President. Geoffrey Munson also retired, and Howard Ruskin assumed roughly similar duties under the title of Executive Vice President of Science and Technology. Chandler was replaced as President by Ralph Fredericks. Paul Jamison remained as Vice Chairman, with the financial organization reporting to him.

Howard Ruskin, the new Executive Vice President for Science and Technology, had the following comment on the situation at that time:

I would suspect that the technical effort wasn't getting the proper coordination or push; it would be pretty easy for whatever came up to be washed away.

I suggest that [when the top level changes] is the best time for change ... It is certainly a time in which you can make changes that the top guys won't block. Whether the rest of the organization will block it or not depends on how good the top guys are.

Also, it's a time that creates an awful lot of turmoil. Folks are jockeying for position ... Everyone is nervous.

Many aspects of Ruskin's sentiment were in fact borne out by subsequent developments at Company A.

With the creation of the Strategic Technology Group, and the turnover of the senior officers, the seeds which Munson and others had planted began to grow and bear fruit. First, the new Executive Committee drafted a Statement of Direction for Company A. The process by which the statement was drafted was significant because both Corporate Planning and Strategic Technology were involved. The content of the document also provided some direction for technology within the corporation:

We will strengthen our core by focusing our resources where Company A can improve our competitive advantage ... enter new areas and expand existing businesses that build upon our strengths ... In all our endeavors we will continue to be an innovative technological leader ...

While such statements can be dismissed as boilerplate, this one was taken as a serious statement about technology and competition by people within Company A. As Bruce Lindsay, the Director of Management Information Systems (MIS) put it:

I think there's a total commitment at the policy level of this company to have a rallying point ...

we are going to plant a flag, we're not going to abdicate our business to foreign competition, and we're not going to sit and atrophy the way steel did. Here's where we stand and fight. That implies we're going to do things differently, because [what steel did] was a formula for disaster.

One school of thought would be that basic industry is a lousy business ... we should get out of it, let the third world have it, and start building semi-conductors or something. We've said no, we'll change, this is our business. It's going to be our business ten years from now. Instead of looking for an easy solution, we'll do what we've got to do, to be here ten years from now, and hand off a healthy company to somebody else.

Subsequent to the executive turnover and the Statement of Objectives, a number of tangible outcomes of the resurgence of technology emerged. The budget for CRC was increased, with the expectation that it would not be the first thing cut back in the event of an economic downturn. A science advisory group, consisting of top people in various fields, was formed, and its reports are presented to the Board of Directors. Another new group, called the Technology Council, was formed with Howard Ruskin as Chairman. This group includes the Director of CRC, the Vice President of Engineering, the Vice Presidents of the business units, and Kidwell. Its mission is to oversee the total portfolio of technology activity.

Thus, there have been a number of outcomes of the resurgence of technology at Company A. The outcome on which the rest of this case report will focus, however, is the development of Computer Integrated Manufacturing (CIM).

THE APRIL 1983 MEETING

The Strategic Technology Group was formed in the fall of 1982. As indicated above, its primary role was to assist the businesses in developing a technological context and strategy as an integral part of their business plans. In addition to coordinating this activity, Thomas Kidwell had taken on another task. With input from the executive level, he had developed a list of words or terms, each of which denoted a technological option which might be open to Company A. As he started his new job, he began to explore the words on his list. The word that quickly rose to the top of the list was "computer".

Kidwell had not had a great deal of prior involvement with computers and he was immediately fascinated with them. While most of the technologies he was exploring had price/performance ratios growing at a yearly rate of two or three percent, computers were growing at 25 to 100 percent, with no limit in sight.

In order to explore this technology, Kidwell and Helen Evans, a member of his group, spent the early months of 1983 visiting other firms. Many of the firms they visited, such as IBM, DEC, and GE, were both producers and users of computer equipment. Kidwell and Evans quickly noted that the emphasis on computers in the firms they visited was quite different than the emphasis at Company A: while Company A was emphasizing business applications (e.g., accounting, payroll), others were emphasizing manufacturing applications (e.g., process control), and the integration of manufacturing and business systems. They were quite struck by this discrepancy.

In order to further Company A's involvement in the technology of computers (which Kidwell had dubbed "low-cost information management"), he decided to have a meeting of those people within the firm who were most involved with computers. Three groups would be involed: MIS which is in the financial organization, the process computing group, which at this time reported to the Chief Electrical Engineer, and CRC which reported to Ruskin. The meeting was planned for April 1983.

In discussing his plans for the upcoming meeting, Kidwell indicated that he had gathered data on the wisest use of low-cost information. This broke down into two areas: the technology itself, and the organizational arrangements necessary to support it. On this latter point, he noted that, for example, Company A would need a higher ratio of engineers to accountants than was currently the case.

At this point Kidwell began what was to become a long and frustrating campaign to keep consideration of computer technology from being overwhelmed by organizational or "turf" considerations. It soon became clear that at Company A, the notion of computers, and particularly of computer integration, was intricately entangled with the notion of what organizational arrangements would support this technology.

The initial impact of this entanglement was that Kidwell was explicitly directed to exclude discussion of organization from the meeting. As Kidwell put it:

They told me "How can you even bring up the subject? Don't you know how sensitive it is in the organization?" So this part got killed off. Organization was illegal ... We narrowed the subject area to say that even though we've learned some things about how the human system responds to computerization, that's not going to be dealt with in those three days at all.

As the meeting approached, Kidwell and Evans decided that it should be limited to high-level people in the three computer-related areas. Bruce Lindsay, who had recently become Director of MIS, but had an extensive background in operations, represented the MIS group. Sanford Turner, the Chief Electrical Engineer, represented process computing. Donald Joyce, an Assistant Director at CRC, represented the computer-oriented research part of the company. Each of the three was accompanied by two others from their area. Finally, two people from the business units were present, and Kidwell and Evans participated as facilitators.

It was amazing to many in the company that the meeting could be held at all, given the fact that MIS and the process computing group had a long history of ignoring one another. They were located in two different buildings separated by a river, which was seldom crossed:

Our human system began as completely separated. Four hundred and fifty MIS people degreed in business, accounting, and computer science. One hundred fifty [in process computing] with electrical engineering degrees, and no mobility between them. Nobody from here ever went there, and nobody from there ever came here. They don't even know who each other is ... they've never met each other before, it's a human problem. (Kidwell).

The meeting was held on April 11–13, 1983. As promised, the guidelines distributed to the participants were to "deal with what Company A should do with computers, not what organization best enables us to do it." The Company A participants spent the first one and a half days of the meeting listening to presentations made by representatives from IBM, Digital Equipment Corporation, Arthur D. Little, and General Electric. These representatives were asked to say what use a manufacturing company like Company A should be making of computers. The mechanism for doing this was to distribute 100 points among the various types of potential computer applications: business computing, office automation, CAD, process computing, and so on. Kidwell and Evans did this to allow the participants to experience directly the gap they had perceived in their visits, between Company A's (de facto) computer strategy and the thrust of state-of-the-art computing. All of the presenters stressed the need for Company A to emphasize process computing and computer integration, or CIM.

The agenda item that followed the consultants' presentations was a description of Company A's current deployment of computer resources. This presentation was made by Helen Evans, who had spent several months performing an audit of Company A's use of computers. This completed the picture of a problem with Company A's current strategy that had been begun by the consultants: while they had advised that Company A emphasize process computing and integration, Company A was placing two-thirds of its resources on business computing, one-third on manufacturing/process computing, and virtually no resources on the integration of the two.

Faced with this information, the meeting participants were next asked to enumerate potential computer strategies for Company A in the next decade, and to arrive at a consensus as to which strategies were most appropriate, and would therefore be pursued by the group. The three strategies around which consensus emerged were the idea of using computers as a tool to differentiate Company A from the competition, the need to increase computer literacy within Company A, and CIM, which quickly rose to the top of the list. The draft of the key strategies arrived at by the group at the meeting went beyond mere endorsement of CIM to advocating the immediate selection of a demonstration site:

- Formulate/implement an integrated information system for Company A ...
- Select a location and immediately implement the integrated system (including CIM) at a plant or business unit of manageable size, such that feasibility and benefits can be effectively demonstrated.
- Recommend that the upcoming modernization embody state-of-the-art CIM ...

So in the space of a three-day meeting, the top computer professionals within Company A came to an agreement as to computer strategies for the next decade, and how they could be initially implemented. All the participants agreed that there was a high degree of consensus on these strategies. The next major step would be to obtain approval for these strategies from the Executive Committee of the corporation.

What actually happened at the April meeting? First of all, what apparently *did not* happen is that the Company A participants learned about CIM:

Tom felt more strongly than the rest of us about the consultants being there. They didn't say anything that anyone who reads Datamation wouldn't know themselves . . . a lot of hype, no real insights (Lindsay).

Sanford Turner also noted that everyone pretty much knew what the experts were going to say. Lindsay, Turner, and Tony Joseph (a member of Turner's group) all had some previous interest/experience with CIM.

If the meeting was not primarily an educational experience for the participants, why was it universally seen as important? Several things were apparently accomplished. Sanford Turner felt that the big contributions of the meeting were the buffering of the participants from their pressing day-to-day concerns, and the establishment of a direction:

In an operating entity, the problem is today's business, and that's where you gravitate all the time. You have to get off and think about new and innovative things, which is very difficult. So we were looking for approval of a direction that would allow us to go off and worry about CIM . . . keep ourselves out of the mainstream of daily problems.

In addition, while the ideas that were presented by the consultants were not seen as a big revelation, the fact that several respected outside sources would agree did seem to have an impact. As Lindsay put it:

What they lent is a catalyst. Four different perspectives, all with a common theme, without rehearsing . . . made people feel a little bit better . . . Any one of a dozen [Company A people] could have gotten up and said it, but I don't think it would have carried the same weight.

Finally, in spite of, or perhaps because of, the proscription against discussion of organization, some organizational barriers were overcome. Bruce Lindsay commented:

I think Tom really threw a spotlight on the need to work together. You've got four computing communities in Company A: the research group, the business computing group (MIS), the process computing group, and the plants. To get anything done, those four end up having to coordinate and work together. The overlap had been minimal, and the interfacing had been only when necessary. The thing that's getting increasingly apparent to everyone is that . . . we've all got a vested interest in [CIM], let's work on it together.

Perhaps the real significance of the April meeting can best be captured by an exchange that took place between Helen Evans and Thomas Kidwell when the meeting was over. Evans told Kidwell that she was disappointed with the outcome of the meeting, because the strategies that had been adopted were obvious before the meeting took place. Kidwell responded:

Wait a minute, there's a difference between you having made up your mind [on the strategies] as a result of spending four months outside, and the corporation forming consensus and commitment around this word computers. In a sense, the meeting was to develop the backdrop, the common commitments, and the working relationships to do something about it.

Evans, after reflecting on the meeting, concluded:

Out of everything that happened out of this meeting, this was the most valuable thing. These guys closed ranks. They put away politics for a while, and said, "Hey, there's a technology out there that we ought to be grasping."

As subsequent events would show, the closed ranks, common commitments, and working relationships would be absolutely necessary to survive the challenges ahead.

THE EXECUTIVE COMMITTEE

Following the April meeting, the team of

Sanford Turner and Bruce Lindsay, with the help of Tom Kidwell, tried to schedule a presentation before the Executive Committee, so as to obtain top-level corporate support for the computer strategies they had devised. However, the Secretary of the Committee did not feel that this was an appropriate agenda item for the committee, so the presentation was made to only some of its members, as well as other key individuals in the senior management of Company A.

The presentation was not very well received. Descriptions of the reaction to it included "a bloody nightmare," "great abuse," "blown out of the water," and "thrown out." In fact, it did not even end with the presentation itself. As one of the presenters mentioned, "we were beat up all week long."

Why this reaction? The participants were unanimous in concluding that, once again, technology had been defeated by organization. At a time when Company A was undergoing a major push toward decentralization and business unit autonomy, the officers thought that Lindsay, Turner, and Kidwell were advocating recentralization through computers. The timing, the wording and even the identity of the presenters were all problems:

The first thing that happened was that it was a political thing. It was not a technological argument, it was an organizational argument, and this kind of slowed things down a lot. It was turf: who was going to do what ... I think that just clouded things ... At the time, we were doing all of this reorganization ... and the word organization came up, and it kind of worried them (Ruskin).

The subject of centralization/decentralization had gotten confused with the subject of networking and architecture. Those of us who had considered computerization had never dealt with the question of whether or not computers should be used in a centralized or decentralized corporation ... You can draw the corporate lines either way ... But when we were talking about words like architecture and networking and so on, people thought that meant centralization at a time when they were trying to be decentralized (Kidwell).

At the time we did this, we were in the throes of decentralizing ... they wanted no inference whatsoever that the integration effort was going to centralize [the corporation]. They had just committed their souls and a lot of people's livelihood [to decentralization], and they couldn't segregate the two. Maybe, if we would have had a representative from the two or three major business units with us as presenters, the officers would not have read what they read into it. But here were Bruce and I ... both of us corporate, making this presentation on computer strategy ... It came across that these strategies were going to be corporate mandated (Turner).

The computer spokesmen did not back down in the face of this reaction, a fact which did not go unnoticed by the senior management. They (Turner et al.) felt that there was nothing substantive in what they had heard that would change their minds, and they concluded that the problem was "basically semantics." Thus, they tried a number of related tacks to recover from the presentation debacle.

First, anything that even hinted at organizational issues was deleted. Second, they removed any language in the strategies that sounded, even remotely, like computer jargon. They were concerned that the uncertainty created by this language may have been threatening to the officers, none of whom were experienced in computing. Third, the strategies got "softened" a little.

In order to defuse any further misinterpretation of what they had in mind, Turner, Lindsay, and Kidwell held a number of one-on-one meetings with the senior officers. Kidwell met with Ruskin, his boss, as well as Jamison and Fredericks. Turner spent an hour with Chandler, at Chandler's request. Lindsay talked with his boss, Warren Ernest, Company A's Controller.

After a week or two of this sort of activity, the officers were convinced that at least

Kidwell et al., did not think of this as an organizational issue. With this in mind, another meeting was scheduled to discuss the strategies. The revised strategies were explicit in their recognition of business unit autonomy:

Emphasize the technological importance of the following key elements in business unit computer strategies . . . CIM

Work with the business unit managers to select a location of manageable size and immediately begin implementing a computer integrated manufacturing system . . .

The wording changes and explanations in one-on-one meetings had the combined effect of swaying the officers: at the second meeting, the strategies were approved. With this approval, however, came more evidence of the officers' commitment to decentralization. The computer spokesmen were directed to go to the business units, and try to sell them on the strategies: "Get your story together and then go talk to the businesses. If they support it, then we support it."

THE BUSINESS UNITS—ISSUES

The arena for the CIM initiative had now shifted to the business units. Rather than soliciting corporate consensus on broad strategies for computer utilization, the computer spokesmen would now have to convince the Vice Presidents/General Managers of Company A's three major business units to spend money on CIM. The next hurdle would be funding for demonstration sites, which presented a new set of issues.

One set of related issues was the long time it would take for the business unit managers to see any return, the intangibility of the short-term products of their investment, and the large amounts of money that would need to be spent. As Bruce Lindsay put it:

What's just alien to a lot of management is that

we [want to spend] at one location a million and half dollars to do nothing but a general design. That still hasn't dawned on the operating folks. They expect to spend a million and a half dollars and get a 50% ROI next year . . . It's just how we are conditioned to go at things. I think that's one of the more fragile dimensions of the whole process. Some folks are going to spend a million and a half dollars, and what they are going to get is four thousand sheets of paper that tell them they have a real bear to take on, versus a product.

Then, you say to carry it through the detail designs, it's going to take ten years and $20 million or whatever it is. When you get into those kind of numbers, rather than being a nicety in the corner, it is going to be center stage, because now you are starting to compete with major capital. There's going to be a lot of people saying "Wait a minute. When I buy a cold mill, I know what I get. When I buy this, all I know is I got a bunch of computer types running around saying this is the right thing to do. I don't grow up with it, I don't understand it, and I'm not really sure what the hell I'm going to get out of it." I think we still have to cross that bridge before we are really off and running.

Another issue that would have to be addressed is the criteria to be used in evaluating investments in CIM. Due to intense competition for corporate capital, Company A's hurdle rate for cost reduction projects (which would include computer projects) had been increased from 50 to 100%. It became clear that CIM would have a very difficult time meeting these hurdle rates, so there was something of a mismatch between the computer strategy and the finance policy. It was perhaps another sign of Company A's technological resurgence that the issue was resolved in a way generally favorable to CIM:

These projects have to be justified to some extent, but there's a little bit of the rigor removed from the intensity of the justification . . . Once the corporation begins to lean toward computer integrated manufacturing, then the individual proposals have a better chance of passing the guidelines (Kidwell).

[Years ago] the technical people said we don't really need computers. You can't justify them ... They held back the development of the computer for a long time. In these kinds of technologies, you have to get ahead, and do some degree of testing it out. Get it out of the conversational stage, get a critical mass in there, move it ... There's hardly any way you can IE it or MBA it to really find out. You've just got to try it (Ruskin).

I'm financial and quantitative and analytical by nature, and I don't think that [ROI] is the right question to be asking. I think the question is, "Do you want to be in the business?". What does it take to be successful at that? If this is one of the things that it takes, I don't think you have an option not to do it ...

Our controllers today have a very heavy [operations] kind of background. They use accounting as ... one of many tools ... It's usually false precision when you start reducing things to columns and rows anyway. They'll run through that to make sure they're in the general ballpark, but within that I think they agonize with the general manager about the market and the risk, and the technology ... Ultimately, I don't see [the numbers] driving our decisions. I think that's very healthy (Lindsay).

A third issue that had to be addressed before CIM could proceed was, inevitably, organization. Put simply, who would do the work? The reorganization had included a substantial downsizing of corporate engineering, in which a large number of engineers had been relocated to the plants, given early retirements, or had quit. Thus, corporate handling of the projects was made difficult by a lack of engineering resources, as well as the obvious clash with the pervading spirit of decentralization.

Many felt, however, that the plants did not possess the resources to do CIM either. And, even if they did, could a truly "integrated" system be created by a set of autonomous plant-level groups? If corporate were to develop an architecture at one plant that would then be used at others, who would pay for it? And so on. Perhaps the most daunting organizational issue was

the likelihood that to "create" CIM at Company A would require some combination of technical support from Electrical Engineering, MIS and CRC. This was a coalition which simply had never before existed in Company A.

To emphasize the importance of the CIM initiative, the process computing group was elevated one step in the corporation. Rather than reporting to the Chief Electrical Engineer, it now reported to the Vice President of Engineering. Sanford Turner was chosen to head this group, and, to underline the move, was given the title of General Manager.

In spite of the difficulties to be overcome, Bruce Lindsay was optimistic about the business units' response. He felt that what was most necessary was an initial success with CIM:

I would guarantee that the business and plant managers, if you demonstrate to them the ability to meaningfully change their ability to compete, they'll go through the hammers of hell with you. Their staying power is greater than that of a functional person when they believe there is something at the end of the road.

In the second half of 1983, Turner, Lindsay, and Kidwell began to approach the business units to talk about CIM.

THE BUSINESS UNITS' RESPONSE

The Northwestern plant, which is part of the Midstream business group, had been mentioned by name in the strategies adopted at the April meeting. Those attending that meeting had felt that the size of the plant was appropriate for a demonstration project, and there was also some interest from the technologists within the plant.

In July 1984, Scott Varano, VP/GM for Midstream, approved $900 thousand to be spent on a requirements definition for CIM. This work was to be done by Sanford Turner's group, with the help of some MIS personnel, and was to be completed by late 1985 or early 1986. To date, there has been good support and enthusiasm from personnel at Northwestern. Some have credited Tony Joseph, a member of Turner's group with responsibility for Northwestern, with solidifying process computing's relationship with that plant's production management.

The response of the Downstream business unit has been more problematic. When CIM emerged from the April meeting and the Executive Committee as an area of emphasis for Company A, Downstream was already in the midst of a complete modernization effort involving three plants. The Midwestern plant was chosen as a demonstration site for CIM over the Southern plant (the other likely candidate), both because it was smaller, and because there was a greater volume of technical skill present within the plant.

Once personnel at Midwestern began to talk to Sanford Turner about how the job would be done, however, tensions arose. Midwestern has always seen themselves as an independent plant, and they felt that Turner was telling them that it would be done his way. A falling out occurred between the plant and the process computing group. The type of bond that had been formed between the corporate group and Northwestern never materialized, and the relationship came to be characterized by "a fair degree of animosity."

The culmination of this was that Midwestern decided that, rather than utilizing corporate services, they would engage an outside consultant, and hired one to begin work. This firm had never done a CIM job outside of their own facilities, and most corporate computer personnel were convinced that their approach to the Midwestern project was much too narrow. This effort is still in process at Midwestern.

The third and final business unit which

showed interest in CIM was Upstream. Following the April meeting, Kidwell, Patrick Broadbent from CRC, and Michael King, the Chief EE for the business unit held a similar meeting in October, just for personnel from the business unit. Some of the same outside presenters were used. Broadbent and King both had some prior interest in CIM, and Broadbent had participated in the April meeting.

As a result of these efforts, the Upstream group approved $350 thousand for the development of some CIM capacity for the Foreign plant. This project was also to be undertaken by an outside group. Turner and others were again disappointed with the scope of the Foreign effort. It was, however, clear that the corporate group did not have the resources to pursue this project.

Ironically, the Foreign initiative in CIM had to be discontinued altogether. There was such a world oversupply of its product that, in early 1985, the Foreign plant was shut down.

POSTSCRIPT

In the early months of 1985, the Science Advisory Board, which had been formed by Howard Ruskin, began to look at Company A's computer strategies. In their feedback to the company, they stressed the fragmented nature of Company A's computer initiatives, and the unevenness of the progress being made toward CIM. They described the company as "fragmented," "a set of baronies," and "lacking focus." Thomas Kidwell, who substantially agreed with the Advisory Board, said that the situation reminded him of a passage from scripture: "In those days there was no king in Israel; every man did that which was right in his own eyes" (Judges 21:25).

32

Atlantic Store Furniture

Atlantic Store Furniture (ASF) is a manufacturing operation in Moncton, New Brunswick. The company is located in the Industrial Park and employs about 20–25 people with annual sales of about $2 million. Modern shelving systems are the main products and these units are distributed throughout the Maritimes. Metal library shelving, display cases, acoustical screens, and work benches are a few of the products available at ASF. The products are classified by two distinct manufacturing procedures that form separate sections of the plant, as illustrated in Exhibit 32–1.

THE METAL–WORKING OPERATION

In the metal-working part of the plant sheet metal is cut and formed into shelving for assembly. The procedure is quite simple and organized in an assembly-line method. Six or eight stations are used to cut the metal to the appropriate length, drill press, shape, spotweld, and paint the final ready-to-assemble product. The equipment used in the operation is both modern and costly, but the technology is quite simple.

EXHIBIT 32–1 ORGANIZATIONAL CHART FOR ATLANTIC STORE FURNITURE

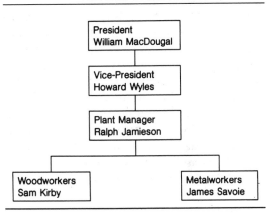

The metal-working operation employs on average about eight or ten workers located along the line of assembly. The men range in age from 22 to 54 and are typically of French Canadian background. Most have high school education or have graduated from a technical program. The men as metalworkers are united by their common identity in the plant and have formed two or three subgroups based on common in-

---

Reprinted with permission of Peter McGrady, Assistant Professor, Lakehead University, Thunder Bay, Ontario.

terests. One group, for example, comprising the foreman and three other workers has season tickets to the New Brunswick Hawks home games. Another group bowls together in the winter and attends horse races in the summer months.

The foreman's group is the most influential among the workers. The men in this group joined the company at the same time and James Savoie, the foreman, was once a worker with the three other men in the group. The group characteristically gets to the lunch counter first, sits together in the most comfortable chairs, and punches the time clock first on the way out of work. Conrad LeBlanc, another group member, has a brother who plays professional hockey in the NHL and he frequently describes the success of the team and the large home his brother lives in.

The metalworkers as a group operate on one side of the plant and work at a very steady pace. The demand for products in this section is high and the production is usually constant. The group adjusts well to changes in the order requests and the occasional overtime pressures. The salespeople on the road provide a constant flow of orders to the point where there is a small backlog of requisitions to be filled. The products vary in size and style but for the most part they are standardized items. A small amount of work is performed on a customized basis.

WOODWORKING OPERATIONS

The woodworking operation differs considerably from the metal-working operation. It is a new addition to the plant and has had some success. It is separated from the metal production unit by a sliding door.

The organization of the wood shop is haphazard. Some areas are organized to produce standard products like screening, but the majority of the woodworking section is organized around a particular project. Typically tools, equipment, and supplies are left in the area of the partially completed projects.

Custom cabinets and display cases are made for large department and retail stores. A small line of products is produced as a regular line while the rest of the products are custom designed. The flow of work is basically steady in the shop, but there are stages when the work orders become intermittent. Though the appearance of the woodworking shop is quite disorganized and messy, reflecting the nature of the work, the workers in this section of the plant see themselves as real craftsmen and take considerable pride in their work. Typically two or three projects are in progress simultaneously along with the normal run of standard products. The metal workers store some of their completed units in the woodworking area to the dislike of the woodworkers and to the disorganization of the section.

Unlike the metalworkers the woodworkers have a distinct hierarchy based on seniority and ability. The apprenticeship program within the company has produced a number of good carpenters. This section of the company, though still relatively young, has produced good work and has a reputation for quality craftsmanship.

The morning coffee break for the woodworkers follows that of the metalworkers. Lunch hour is staggered by 20 minutes as well. Only a minimal amount of interaction occurs between the woodworkers and metalworkers as there tends to be rivalry and competition between the two groups.

The supervisor who oversees the two sections of the plant (plant manager) is Ralph Jamieson, a production engineer from a local university. As plant manager he reports to the vice-president. He is responsible for the plant operation, which includes the metal and woodworking shops. At the time of his hiring ASF had not developed the woodworking section of the plant. Jamieson's work at the University became integrated into the production line when he discovered a method of galvanizing the product in final stages of production. He spends a good deal of his time in the metal-working operation, planning and discussing problems in production with the foreman, James Savoie. Laboratory research is another occupation assigned to Jamieson who enjoys experimentation with new methods and techniques in design and fabrication of metal products. Jamieson and Savoie are friends and they spend a good deal of time together both on and off the job. James Savoie is quite happy with the way his operation is running. He has good rapport with his men and absenteeism is minimal.

A recent personnel change within ASF is the addition of two new salesmen who are on the road in New Brunswick and Nova Scotia. Their contribution to the company is most notable in the metal work area. They have placed many orders for the company. The new sales incentive program has motivated these people to produce, and their efforts are being recognized.

Sam Kirby, the woodworking supervisor, blew up at the plant manager the other day after the metalworkers had pushed open the sliding door with an interest in storing more excess shelving units in the woodworking area. Sam is a hothead sometimes and has become quite annoyed recently with all the intergroup rivalry between the metalworkers and the woodworkers. Storage space has been a sore point between the groups for the last six months or so, ever since the metalworkers became very busy. Jamieson and Howard Wylie, the vice-president, were asked to settle the problem between the two shops. They decided that the metalworkers were to access the woodworking shop only if absolutely necessary and with consent of the foreman or supervisor.

This latest incident really upset the employees in the woodworking shop. The woodworkers feel intimidated by the metalworkers who are taking space and interrupting their work.

In a later conversation Kirby and Jamieson smoothed things over somewhat. It was explained to Kirby that it was the metalworkers who were really turning out the work and that they needed the space. The area that metalworkers want to use is not really needed by the woodworkers. It is simply an area around the perimeter of the room by the walls.

Kirby did not like Jamieson's response, knowing full well his commitment to the metal-working operations. With this decision the metalworkers proceeded to use the area in the woodworking shop and never missed an opportunity to insult or criticize the woodworkers. The effect of the situation on the respective groups became quite obvious. The metalworkers became increasingly more jocular and irritating in their interactions with the woodworkers.

The fighting continued and became of more concern to the president and vice-president. For example, the large sliding doors separating the shops were hastily closed one afternoon on a metalworker who was retreating from a practical joke he was playing on a woodworker. The resulting injury was not serious but it did interrupt a long series of accident-free days the company had been building up. This incident further divided the two groups. Meetings and threats by management were not enough to curtail the problems.

The woodworkers were now withdrawing all efforts to communicate. They ate lunch separately and took coffee breaks away from the regular room. Kirby became quite impatient to complete new products and to acquire new contracts. He urged management to hire personnel and to solicit new business. The climate changed considerably in the woodworking shop as the workers lost their satisfying work experience. Much of the friendly interaction that had gone on previously had ceased. Kirby's temper flared more frequently as small incidents seemed to upset him more than before. After work get-togethers at the tavern were no longer of much appeal to the men.

The metalworkers were feeling quite good about their jobs as the weeks passed. Their orders remained strong as demand continued to grow for their products. The metalworkers complained about the woodworkers and demanded more space for their inventory. The metalworkers were becoming more cohesive and constantly ridiculed the woodworkers. Their concern for the job decreased somewhat as back orders filled up and talk of expansion developed for the metal-work operation.

Just as the metal shop became more confident there were more difficulties with the woodworking shop. The woodworkers were completing the final stages of an elaborate cabinet system when information came regarding a shipping delay. The new store for which the product was being built was experiencing problems, causing a two- or three-month delay before it could accept the new cabinet system. Kirby was very disturbed by this news as the woodworkers needed to see the completion of their project and the beginning of a new one.

The predicament was compounded somewhat by the attitude of the metalworkers who heard of the frustration of the woodworkers and added only more jeers and smart remarks. Morale at this stage was at an all-time low. The chief carpenter, and integral member of the woodworkers, was looking for a new job. One or two of the casual workers were drifting into new work or not showing up for work. Contracts and orders for new products were arriving but in fewer numbers, and casual workers had to be laid off. Defective work was beginning to increase, to the embarrassment of the company.

Management was upset with the conditions of the two operations and threatened the foreman and supervisors. Kirby was disturbed at the situation and was bitter about the deteriorating state of the woodworking plant. Despite many interviews he was unable to replace the head carpenter who had left the company, attracted by a new job prospect. Efforts to reduce the intergroup conflict were made but without success.

The president of ASF, William MacDougal, was alarmed with the situation. He recognized some of the problems with the different operations. One operation was more active and busy while the other section worked primarily on project work, i.e., building a custom display cabinet for a retail company. The organization was designed with the normal structure in mind. The men in the company, he thought to himself, were very much of the same background, and what little diversity there was should not have accounted for this animosity. As president, he had not developed a climate of competition or pressure in the company.

The disorganization and chaos in the woodworking plant was alarming, and there was very little that could be done about it. Kirby had been discussing the problem with the president trying to identify some of the alternatives. This had been the third meeting in as many days and each time the conversation drifted into a discussion about current developments in Jamieson's metal-working pursuits. James Savoie felt that there was too much worrying going on "over there"!!!

Plans for expanding the building at ASF were developing at a rapid pace. The president felt that more room might alleviate some of the problems, particularly with respect to inventory, warehousing, and storage.

Kirby became enthusiastic about the prospects of some relief for his side of the operation. He was very much aware of the fact that the performance of his operation was quite low. The president of the company felt satisfied that the woodworking concern was going to improve its performance. One or two new contracts with large department stores inspired the effort to improve the operation.

The men in the woodworking section became relaxed. A few positive interactions between the woodworkers and metalworkers became evident. One afternoon about two weeks after the disclosure by the president of the new plant development Kirby observed blueprints for the new expansion. The plans had been left on Jamieson's desk inadvertently and to Kirby's surprise revealed full details of the expansion for the new building.

Examining the details more carefully, Kirby recognized that the woodworking area was not to be included in the expansion plans. Kirby left the office in a rage, stormed into the president's office, and demanded an explanation.

Kirby shouted that he had changed things around in the woodworking shop on the promise of more room and the possibility of expansion. The president shook his head and apologized and explained he was going to be told but nothing could be done. The demand was simply just not that great for wood products. Kirby left the office and went straight for his car and drove off.

33

Space Support Systems, Incorporated

Space Support Systems, Incorporated (SSS) is a small but growing corporation located in Houston, Texas, adjacent to NASA's Manned Spacecraft Center. The corporation was founded four years ago with the objective of obtaining government contracts for research studies, for preliminary development in space suit technology, and for studies in other areas of environmental systems connected with space flight. At present, 25 people are associated with Space Support Systems.

The company was founded by its current president, Robert Samuelson, for the specific purpose of bidding on a study contract for an extravehicular hard suit (a special type of space suit) with lunar, and possibly Mars, capabilities. At the time of the company's inception, Samuelson, James R. Stone, and William Jennings comprised the entire Space Support Systems company.

Mr. Samuelson, the President, is 47 years old, holds a B.S.E.E. degree from a large southern state university, and prior to forming Space Support Systems, was a senior engineer with North American. He has worked

for several large aircraft corporations since his graduation from college 25 years ago. The present venture, however, represented a technologically new slant for him.

James R. Stone, Vice-president and director of Technological Research, is 38 years old. He has a Ph.D. in physiology from a leading West Coast university and had, prior to the inception of Space Support Systems, taught for six years at a leading university. He also has degrees in the field of aeronautical engineering. He worked for two years in the aeronautics industry before returning to school to work toward his doctorate in aerospace applications. Dr. Stone's reputation among his colleagues in both the theoretical and creative aspects of aerospace environmental control is quite good.

William Jennings, Vice-president and Director of Technology Applications, is 42 years old. After graduating from high school, he attended college for three years before a shortage of funds forced him to quit school and seek employment in the then-lucrative aircraft industry. While in college, he majored in mechanical enginer-

Chapter 13, "Space Support Systems, Incorporated" (pp. 59–67) from *Organizational Behavior: Cases and Situations* by B. J. Hodge, Herbert J. Johnson, and Raymond L. Read, copyright © 1974 by Harper & Row, Publishers, Inc.

ing. For three years prior to joining SSS, Mr. Jennings worked on an air force contract that involved the development of high-altitude flight suits. His particular specialty was in the development and construction of functional flight suits for initial testing, but he also showed considerable insight in new developments and changes in designs that were submitted to him prior to final construction. His reputation was such that Mr. Samuelson had been prompted to seek him out to join SSS four years ago.

The current organization chart for Space Support Systems is shown in Exhibit 33–1. There are two branches under Dr. Stone, the Environmental Studies Team and the Space Suit Studies Team. The Environmental Studies Team is primarily concerned with studies on environmental and physiological systems in spacecraft and modular structures for lunar (and other planetary) habitation. At present, there is no hardware output from the company along these lines. The team leader is Roger Swanson, and there are four men under him. Roger is 33 years old and has a master's degree in biology. He is highly respected by his peers and well thought of by Dr. Stone.

The Space Suit Studies Team works on

study contracts investigating either hard or soft space suits used primarily for extravehicular use. Its members have also worked on suits for wear within the spacecraft. Composed of bright men, the Team is led by Don Hammond, who is 28 years old and has a master's degree in physiology. He has had many opportunities to return to school to work on a Ph.D. but has elected to stay with the company each time. He is considered extremely bright and, while not as old as most of the men on his team, he is unanimously accepted as the leader. On occasion, Don and Dr. Stone have had differences of opinion and, while the two do not seem to like each other personally, they respect each other's professional abilities and qualifications.

Much of the actual management and leadership of both these teams comes from Dr. Stone. The team leaders serve as depositories for information and as spokesmen for their groups, rather than as centers of responsibility and authority. These teams are, for the most part, college-educated and well qualified technically. The average age of the 14 men under Dr. Stone is 31 years, and the average number of college degrees per man is 1.6.

Bill Jennings's area is responsible for actually developing and building suits for testing and presentation to NASA. This function is a logical extension of the work of the Space Suit Studies Team and requires a close coordination between the two groups. The five men under Jennings are all skilled technicians who are actually the craftsmen who build the technological systems. None of them has a college degree, although two of the men completed junior college. The average age of these men is 43 years. They work together well and have formed a close-knit work unit. Jennings may often be found in the middle of the group working on some aspect of building mockups of functional space suits. The group is quite autonomous and functions with little direction from Mr. Samuelson.

EXHIBIT 33–1 ORGANIZATION CHART OF SPACE SUPPORT SYSTEMS, INCORPORATED

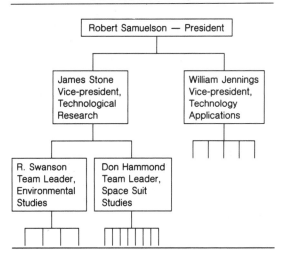

Mr. Samuelson had never had any managerial problems in SSS that he knew of. The work had always run along fairly smoothly and, being very project-oriented, the company's employees seemed to be constantly busy with one job or another. Mr. Samuelson had to be engaged in the work of obtaining contracts and serving as a liaison with the government once a contract was secured. As a result, he knew that he might not have as thorough knowledge as he should regarding the inner workings of the SSS organization. He particularly realized that he had little feedback from personnel in the firm, but since he had experienced no apparent difficulties, he felt that all must be going well.

One afternoon, Jennings came in to see Mr. Samuelson. Jennings seemed upset and it was apparent that something was on his mind.

Samuelson: What's on your mind, Bill?

Jennings: Bob, I have worked for you for four years and I have always enjoyed my work and, in particular, working under you. But I don't think I can continue to function much longer with Jim Stone's group hanging like an albatross around my neck.

Samuelson: I don't understand. What kind of problem are we talking about?

Jennings: Well, my group does its job, and does it well; now, we could do it much better if Don Hammond, in particular, would keep his nose out and let us work once a plan is submitted to us for building. I mean—that crew from Space Suit Studies think they are supposed to supervise our work. My men are proud of their jobs and of their work. But we are going to lose some of our best guys pretty soon if this meddling isn't stopped.

Samuelson: Have you discussed this with Stone?

Jennings: No. Jim's difficult to talk to. He looks down his nose at my group because we are not eggheads. One other thing—whenever I make a change that improves the suit,

Hammond's crew gets upset, particularly when it is an obvious improvement.

Samuelson: We'll straighten this problem out, Bill, I promise. But what bothers me is that your group and Don's are supposed to work together.

Jennings: Yes, I know. But it has never worked out that way. They simply look over our shoulders and don't think we are competent to work with their precious designs— even when we can make them better—which is almost always.

The conversation was terminated when Samuelson told Bill that he would look into the problem thoroughly. Bill seemed relieved that Samuelson was taking action.

The first thing the next morning, Mr. Samuelson asked Dr. Stone if he would drop by for a chat. Upon Dr. Stone's arrival Mr. Samuelson asked him to be seated and opened the conversation.

Samuelson: Jim, how are things in your area? Any problems with the X–2B suit design?

Stone: No, we are working primarily on the breastplate design right now. I think we are ahead of our target schedule.

Samuelson: Bill mentioned some friction between his men and Don Hammond's group.

Stone: [Thinking a moment] Well—you know we have never gotten the support and cooperation from Bill's team that we need to do our job. Don's team has to have a significant amount of cooperation from Applications in order to do its job. We need to be able to work with Bill's group, to be there to make changes and alterations as needed. Their job is to build to our specifications and let them go from there. We have to provide continuing guidance, and Bill just won't accept it. On top of all this, Bill seems intent on putting his personal touch on each piece of hardware they build.

Samuelson: I don't understand.

Stone: He makes changes on his own, which alter the specs. His group often comes up with a different product from what we asked for. We can't do anything about it because he won't allow cooperation between our groups.

Samuelson: Are his changes worthwhile?

Stone: Oh, I suppose he has some good ideas. Yes, some of his changes were very imaginative and worthwhile. But the point is that his function is to build and ours is to create designs. His suggestions are sometimes worthwhile, but he should consult me before making any changes. That's why he is there and we are here. Otherwise, why don't we simply change the structure of the organization?

Samuelson: Are there any other problems that you have experienced?

Stone: No, otherwise things are fine. All in all, we don't really have any major problems. As long as everybody does his job and stays within bounds, everything functions fine. As I said before, only when someone usurps another's authority does a problem arise.

Samuelson: Well, thanks, Jim, you've been very helpful. Do you mind if I talk with Don about this problem?

Stone: No, go right ahead.

Mr. Samuelson immediately called in Don Hammond and opened the conversation.

Samuelson: Don, I'll get right to the point. How is the working relationship between your areas and Bill's?

Hammond: What relationship? Those guys won't do anything we say. We don't get along at all.

Samuelson: Why is this?

Hammond: I don't know. Maybe it's a defense mechanism.

Samuelson: Meaning what?

Hammond: Well, Mr. Samuelson, I think they resent us because we are educated. They want to do our jobs and don't seem to realize that they are not qualified. They want to do more than build suits, they seem to want to do our design function. They just aren't qualified. I really think they resent our superior knowledge. I have tried to get Dr. Stone to talk to them or you about this, but he seemed somewhat indifferent. I guess he finally did something though. Anyway, something has got to be done. We can't do our jobs if we can't give them guidance in the building of our suits.

Samuelson: Are their changes ever worthwhile?

Hammond: No.

Samuelson: Never?

Hammond: Oh, I suppose so . . . sometimes. *[Hesitation.]* But that's not the point. It's not their job. They just aren't qualified to tinker with our designs. Don't they realize that is why we spent all those years getting our degrees? Did I waste my time? If a bunch of guys with no education can do my job, maybe I'd be better off uneducated.

Samuelson: Of course not, Don. You and your team are top notch. But you must, by the very nature of the work, have a working relationship with Bill's group. If they can suggest improvements, all the better.

Hammond: Yes, I guess so. But we can't seem to work together. They don't clear their changes through me or Dr. Stone.

Samuelson: Well, we've never made a definite statement about the arrangement for changes, as far as I can remember.

Hammond: Mr. Samuelson, I think all their recommendations should come through me. I can then study their merits and decide on which ones should be accepted. However, they just are not qualified to design this type of equipment. They should stick to their jobs of building.

Mr. Samuelson closed the conversation by thanking Don for his frankness and promising to take action when he had all the facts.

Left alone, Robert Samuelson pondered this new turn of events. He had thought everything was just fine. The work seemed to be getting done—and now this.

He realized that after four years of the successful operation of Space Support Systems, he was faced with the first real test of his managerial abilities.

34

Omega Aerospace Corporation

INTRODUCTION

The Omega Aerospace Corporation is a multidivisional organization with production facilities throughout the western and southern parts of the United States. Each division is an autonomous organization and is established on a product-orientation basis. Thus, all research, design, engineering, and production for aircraft, for example, are organized in the aircraft division, while all activities relating to space research and space vehicles are organized in the space division. There are four primary divisions—namely, space, aircraft, weapons systems, and commercial products. Each division is functionally independent; that is, each has its own research, engineering, production, marketing, accounting, and personnel departments. Policy determination, however, in terms of corporate policy, is originated and administered by the "headquarters division," which functions as the policymaking and control agency for the corporation. Within the framework of this corporate policy structure, each division operates as an independent "profit center," accountable only to the corporation president and the board of directors.

This particular study is concerned with two department-level organizations which are part of the weapons systems division and are located in a large West Coast city. These two organizations are the Management Analysis Department and the Data Processing Department. To familiarize the reader with the general purpose of these departments, we are offering below a brief description of their functions.

Both organizations are concerned with the analysis, design, and implementation of "management systems." The term *management system*, in this context, refers to any set of activities directed toward achieving improved control of the operations of the corporation in general and the individual division in particular. Closely associated with "control," in this sense, is the notion of improved profitability resulting from more efficient operations, improved communication for management decision making, more timely reporting of financial and

Prepared by Professor Rolf E. Rogers, California Polytechnic State University at San Luis Obispo. Copyright © 1979 by Rolf E. Rogers. From Rolf E. Rogers and Robert H. McIntire, *Organization and Management Theory*, Wiley, 1983. Used by permission of the author.

operating data, and the ability to predict the results of various operating alternatives (decisions) in a timely and scientific fashion. Thus, the majority of management systems are viewed as requiring "computerization" in order to achieve the quick response time and the ability to manipulate and calculate large quantities of data.

In a more specific sense, the concept of a management system, from a developmental point of view, includes the following general steps:

1. Analysis of management problems and requirements.
2. Evaluation of alternatives for the solution of these problems and requirements.
3. Selection of the "optimum" solution.
4. Design of the appropriate management system based on the "optimum" solution.
5. The implementation of the system— both technically and organizationally.
6. The maintenance of the system (i.e., its continual operation).
7. The evaluation of the system's performance and effectiveness.

The responsibility for developing and operating a management system at the Weapons Systems Division of Omega Aerospace Corporation was divided between two organizations—the Management Analysis Department and the Data Processing Department. The Management Analysis Department reported to the vice president for administration; the Data Processing Department reported to the chief financial officer—the controller. Both executives reported to the president of the division who, in turn, reported to the corporation president and the board of directors. Exhibits 34–1 and 34–2 reflect the formal organization of these two departments.

The division of tasks relating to management systems between these two departments was, theoretically, as follows:

An operating or management problem was presented to the Management Analysis Department for study. This could be by executive direction (for example, by the president) or by formal request from an operating or staff manager who felt that he had such a problem. Upon receipt of the request, the director of management analysis would assign the study project to the appropriate manager in his department for scheduling and appointment of an analyst or a team of analysts. The scheduling and appointment were based on the perceived or assigned priority of the problem, the availability of analysts, and the complexity of the required study approach. Upon completion of the study, a formal report would be issued by the Management Analysis Department to the "client" describing the problem, the evaluation of alternative solutions, and the recommended solution. If the solution was a data processing computer system, the system would be described in the report in terms of a conceptual design along with recommended standards, data criteria, input-output specifications, reporting formats, and so on. If the "client" organization accepted this recommended solution, the report would be turned over to the Data Processing Department for detailed computer systems design, programming, implementation, and sustaining operating maintenance responsibility. A coordinator from the Management Analysis Department was assigned to data processing, if requested, for purposes of coordinating the development of the system.

It is apparent that this organization of tasks into specialized activities and into defined areas of responsibility follows the postulates of F. W. Taylor and is inherent in Max Weber's bureaucratic ideal type. As such, this arrangement should, in theory, accomplish an "efficient" solution to the implementation of management systems. The logic of organization design to accomplish this end is demonstrated by first staffing the Management Analysis Department with specialists in various disciplines, which assures the qualification for performing diagnostic analyses of management problems along with the development of conceptual solutions. Secondly, once the solution was identified as being a computer system, the Data Processing Department possessed the expertise to design, program, implement, and operate the system. Unfortunately, as will become apparent later, the practical operation of this process worked quite differently from the intended organization design.

THE CASE

The profitability of the Weapons Systems Division of Omega Aerospace Corporation was solely based on its ability to obtain military contracts for the study, design, and production of weapons systems. The division was one of several enterprises in this field and the award of contracts by the respective government agency was based on competitive bids. The preparation of a bid is an involved, complex process, which was performed by a separate organization in the division known as the Estimating Staff. This staff, headed by a chief estimator, reported directly to the division president. Estimates for bidding were prepared by this staff based on the data furnished by the various departments of the division, such as engineering, production, quality control, accounting, and personnel.

At the beginning of our survey in June 1967, the corporate profit contribution of this division had been showing a substantial decline for some time, which had resulted in considerable concern at both the

EXHIBIT 34–1   ORGANIZATION OF MANAGEMENT ANALYSIS DEPARTMENT

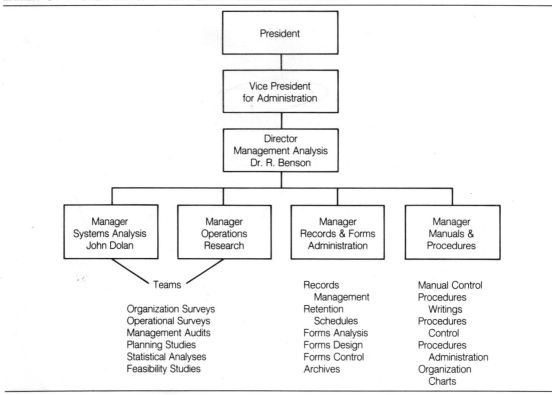

corporate and divisional executive levels. The division had been unable to obtain any new contracts, having been consistently underbid by competitors. To identify the cause of this problem and to develop a solution to it, the president of the division directed Dr. Robert Benson, the director of management analysis, to conduct a study of the estimating system to determine its effectiveness for providing accurate cost factors for bidding. The project was assigned top priority; a letter signed by the president was sent to all department heads soliciting their cooperation and directing that all possible assistance be provided to the study team. The study team was organized under the general direction of John Dolan, the manager of systems analysis, and headed by a project chief, Carl Abel. The team consisted of four specialists: Vernon Mitchel, an accountant; Bill Ward, a computer expert; Joe Paloze, an operations research analyst; and Ralph Bingham, an industrial engineer. Exhibit 34–3 depicts the organization of the project team.

The team spent three months examining the estimating system and related procedures and, at the end of that period, wrote a report outlining the problem, various alternative solutions, and recommending the solution considered optimum by the team.

The essence of the conclusions resulting from the survey was that the present procedures of accumulating data relating to labor, material, and overhead costs were cumbersome, inaccurate, and too time-consuming to be of maximum value for estimating purposes. The time factor, especial-

EXHIBIT 34–2   ORGANIZATION OF DATA PROCESSING DEPARTMENT

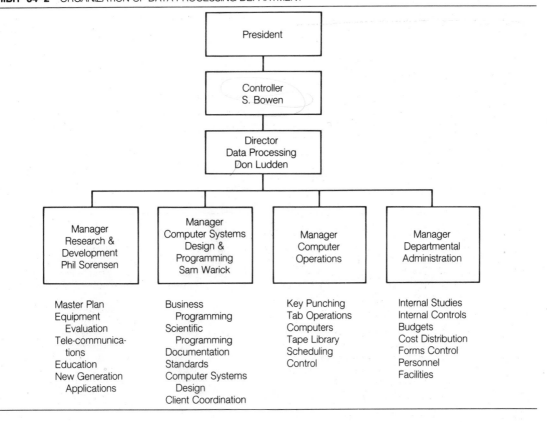

ly, was singled out by the team as being a major problem in providing up-to-date cost data to the Estimating Staff when required for preparation of estimates. A second factor, considered equally important, was the inability to efficiently manipulate and integrate the various cost categories (i.e., labor, material, and overhead) to arrive at usable cost figures. To provide these capabilities, the report recommended as the optimum solution, the immediate development of a computer-based estimating system that would utilize the already automated data from the accounting and production systems to integrate these data and produce "estimating cost factors" as a regular output feature of the new computer system. In addition, the new system would furnish "management control reports" reflecting cost and estimate variances, as well as predicted profitability factors for each contract.

The report was presented by Mr. Dolan on September 15, 1967, at the division president's monthly staff meeting (attended by all department heads of the division) and was enthusiastically received by all present—including the chief estimator. The president directed Dr. Benson to submit the report immediately to the Data Processing Department for design, programming, and implementation of the system. He asked Mr. Dolan to express his appreciation to the project team for "a job well done." He further instructed Mr. S. Bowen, the controller, to direct his director of data processing to move with the utmost speed in the implementation of the new system. In addition, the president requested that he be furnished with monthly progress reports by data processing, reflecting the status of the development of the system.

At the president's monthly staff meeting on October 15, the following discussion took place:

President: Mr. Bowen, I have not received a progress report from your organization on the status of the new estimating system. Why not?

Mr. Bowen: I don't know, sir, but I'll check on it immediately.

President: Please do.

(Mr. Bowen leaves the room to call Don Ludden, the director of data processing.)

Mr. Bowen (on the phone): Don, where is the progress report to the president on the new estimating system? I told you that this report is due every month in my office on the 10th and in the president's office on the 12th.

Don Ludden: We are having problems making sense out of the system proposed by management analysis [department]. I tried to reach Carl Abel but he is out of town.

EXHIBIT 34–3 ORGANIZATION OF A PROJECT TEAM

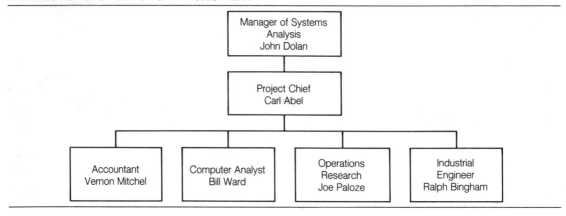

Mr. Bowen: O.K., but I want action on this project immediately. I'll talk to Dr. Benson about Abel.

(Mr. Bowen returns to the staff meeting.)

President: Well, Mr. Bowen?

Mr. Bowen: My data processing people tell me that they can't make sense out of the management analysis report and they have not been able to reach the project chief, Carl Abel.

President: Dr. Benson?

Dr. Benson: Well, I don't know why there should be any problem in understanding the proposal. Mr. Abel is out of town on another assignment but they could have talked to Mr. Dolan or any one of the team members.

President: I suggest that you two gentlemen get together on this and get the show on the road. I should have been informed immediately of any problems, Mr. Bowen, instead of me bringing the subject to your attention. I suggest that you personally keep track of this project from now on.

Mr. Bowen: Yes, sir.

After the staff meeting, Dr. Benson and Mr. Bowen agreed to schedule a meeting for October 18, in one of the conference rooms, to discuss the apparent problems associated with the proposed system. Dr. Benson agreed to have Carl Abel present at that meeting.

At the October 18 meeting the following were present: Management Analysis Department—Dr. Benson, John Dolan, and Carl Abel; Data Processing Department—Mr. Bowen, Don Ludden, Sam Warick, the manager of computer systems design and programming, and Phillip Sorensen, the manager of research and development.

Dr. Benson: Well, what's the problem in your shop with getting this new system off the ground?

Mr. Bowen: I'll let Sam [Warick] describe some of the initial problems.

Sam Warick: Well, to begin with, your proposal is too vague for us to do any detail design work. None of my systems people can make

sense out of the interface model in the system. Secondly, your proposal calls for the use of the XL2 programming language: we have never used that language here and I don't have anyone who can program in it.

Phillip Sorensen: Yes, that's right. The XL2 is so new that nobody has had any experience with it. I called several computer manufacturers and none of them have used it; they are still testing whether the language can be used at all.

John Dolan: To answer your first point, it is not our responsibility to do detail design work; that is your job and you are supposed to have the people to do it. If you don't, that's your problem not ours. Secondly, on the XL2 language, I'll ask Carl to answer that.

Carl Abel: I don't know who you have been talking to, Phil, but that language is used by the computer center at the state university and they tell me it's the best approach to the type of computation required in our proposed system.

Phillip Sorensen: That's just great. Who do you think we have for programmers here? Ph. D.'s in computer science? We are lucky if we can get people with bachelor's degrees. If you people would check your high-level solutions with us practical people instead of writing all this theoretical, we wouldn't have half of the problems we have now.

Don Ludden: That's right. We are handed the dirty work without being consulted and then told it's our problem.

Dr. Benson: Now let's not get personal. It seems to me that we have two problems. First, there is some problem in understanding the proposed system; second, there is a problem with the programming language. Now I suggest that Carl, Sam, and Phil sit down together and work these problems out. We will meet again, as a group, one week from today at the same time to discuss what solutions you three have come up with. Is that OK with you, Sam [Bowen]?

Mr. Bowen: OK.

During the ensuing week the trio met several times to discuss and attempt to resolve the design and programming language problems, but without apparent success. According to our informants, the relationship between the two factions became progressively more hostile and unyielding; accusations of incompetence and related implications were apparently frequent. As a result of these developments, which were reported by the three participants to their superiors, Mr. Bowen canceled the agreed-upon meeting, and on October 26 scheduled a personal meeting for him and Don Ludden with the division president. According to secondary sources (none of our informants were present at that meeting), the discussion, in essence, went as follows:

President: Well, Sam, you asked for this meeting. What's the problem?

Mr. Bowen: A real problem has developed with Dr. Benson's people over this proposed estimating system. I feel that this is no longer a technical disagreement but a problem of who tells whom what to do. Now my people resent being stuck with the responsibility for developing systems without having had the opportunity to be in from the ground floor. In other words, Benson's people dream up some theoretical system without consulting us and then we are supposed to make the thing work. If it doesn't work, we are the scapegoats while they sit back and call us incompetent.

President: Have they used the term *incompetent?*

Mr. Bowen: Yes, sir. My people feel like second-class citizens around here.

Don Ludden: I am beginning to have real morale problems in data processing as a result of the recent meetings between our people and Carl Abel. I feel that my people are the specialists in computer systems and languages, not Dr. Benson's group. His people are diagnostic consultants and primarily trained for identifying problems. But when it comes to computer systems, my people are the experts and they don't care to be told by somebody with less knowledge what's practical or how to do their job.

President: I was not aware of these feelings. What brought all this about?

Mr. Bowen: I think it's primarily the implication that whenever something goes wrong with the development of a new computer system—it's our fault. The management analysis people write a report and sell their proposed solution to the client organization. If the client accepts it, it's turned over to us and they wash their hands of the whole thing. Anything that goes wrong after that is blamed on us—even though the problem lies more often with the proposal which is frequently impractical from an operational standpoint. Yet, if we try to make changes they object immediately and put pressure on us through the client.

Don Ludden: In addition to this, they also recommend an implementation time schedule for their proposed systems right in the report. We are never consulted about this and the client organization expects us to comply with it. That simply doesn't make sense. We are the only ones who can and should determine our own work schedules. We have standard operating systems, such as payroll, which must be run at certain times and we certainly object to having some staff outfit telling us how to run our own shop.

President: I was not aware of this situation. There is, apparently, a very undesirable conflict developing between your people and Benson's group. I will think it over and let you know what my decision is.

The next day, Dr. Benson was called into the division president's office. We were not able to obtain any reliable information on what happened in that meeting, however, it is reasonable to assume that the president was attempting to obtain Dr. Benson's point of view on the conflict between the two organizations.

During the next divisional staff meeting on November 15, the president made the following announcement:

President: After due consideration of the current problems between the Management Analysis Department and the Data Processing Department, I have retained the services of an outside consulting firm to advise me of the best solution to the present intolerable situation. I have discussed this problem with members of the corporate staff and they concur in my appointment of an external consultant. I will inform you of my final disposition of the present situation after I have received the consultant's recommendations.

The firm of outside consultants arrived within a few days of this announcement and spent several weeks examining the task structures, organization structures, personnel qualifications, and related aspects of the two organizations. The consultants obtained much of their information through interviews with the various participants involved in the conflict. We were fortunate to obtain a recount from one of our informants who was present in a meeting between the senior consultant and Dr. Benson.

According to this recount, the interview went, essentially, as follows:

Consultant: Dr. Benson, how do you view the differentiation in authority and responsibility between your group and data processing?

Dr. Benson: Well, as you probably know, our primary purpose is to function as internal consultants, so to speak, to the management of this division. Our charter gives us the authority to conduct studies of divisional problems in any and all departments of the division. Of course, our authority is advisory in the sense that we cannot order another department to accept our recommendations. Of course, we can use informal methods if they don't accept them.

In terms of responsibility we are responsible for the accuracy of our analytical methods and the evaluation of alternative solutions. In other words, we have to be able to prove that our proposed solution is the best solution, considering all relevant variables.

Now, as to the differentiation between the two departments, we are responsible to develop a computer-based solution, which is the only time we get involved with data processing, to the conceptual point. This means, that the system's framework must be sufficiently defined for them [data processing] to do the detail work in design, programming, and so forth. We are not responsible for leading them by the hand or doing their work for them.

Consultant: I see. Would you explain what you mean by "informal methods" to assure acceptance of your recommendations?

Dr. Benson: Well, if an organization does not accept our recommendations, I have to explain in the staff meeting to the division president, who receives a copy of all our reports, why the recommendation was rejected. I feel that my people are the experts and therefore are in a superior position, collectively, to solve any problem better than the individual organization. By "informal" I mean, that if our recommendation is not accepted, I make the client prove—right in the staff meeting—why his solution, if he has one, is better than ours.

Consultant: Are there many such cases?

Dr. Benson: There were a couple when I first assumed my present position. After I got through with those people in the staff meetings—well, there have not been any problems since.

Consultant: What about the claim by Mr. Bowen's people that your proposed estimating system is inadequately developed and the programming language technically unacceptable?

Dr. Benson: You, of all people, should realize that the issue here has nothing to do with technical aspects. This is simply a convenient means for Bowen to satisfy his power complex. When the Management Analysis Department was set up, Bowen felt that it should have been placed under his jurisdiction. He wrote memos to everybody in the home office [headquarters corporate staff], using the most infantile arguments. When the group was set up as a separate department and I was appointed director, he became almost paranoid about it. I had been hired from the state university to fill this position, but Bowen would not even talk to me for the first few months after I came here. I think the man needs help.

Consultant: Are you a psychologist, sir?

Dr. Benson: No. My degrees are in statistics.

During the period of the consultants' study little, if any, apparent interaction took place between the personnel of the two organizations. The consultants' report, which was classified "confidential" was presented by the senior consultant to the division president and a select group of corporate executives on January 12, 1968, in a closed meeting. On January 14, the division president called a special meeting of his staff (which included Dr. Benson and Mr. Bowen) at which he made the following announcement:

President: We have received the report from the consulting firm which had been retained to study the recent problems between the Management Analysis and Data Processing Departments. The recommendations have been reviewed by me and members of the corporate staff. Accordingly, the following reorganization will take place, effective February 1.

A new department known as the "Management Systems Department" will be established and will report directly to me. The head of this new department, known as "director of management systems," will be Mr. O'Connel from our corporate management audit staff. The new department will consist of the present Management Analysis Department and the present Data Processing Department. Data processing will be removed from the controller's organization. Management analysis will be integrated into the new department and cease to exist as a separate organization. (See Exhibit 34–4).

The staffing and appointment of managers

EXHIBIT 34–4   MANAGEMENT SYSTEMS DEPARTMENT

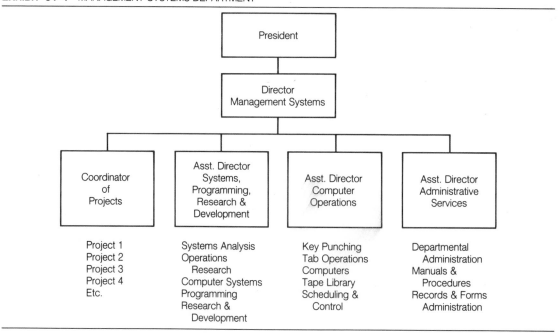

will be the responsibility of Mr. O'Connel, assisted by the directors of personnel both here and at headquarters. Some recommendations as to personnel are also contained in the consultants' report which will be made available to Mr. O'Connel.

It is my considered expectation that this integration of tasks and responsibilities under one organization will eliminate the present jurisdictional disputes and enable a more efficient performance of systems and data processing activities within the division. To this end, I expect all personnel involved to cooperate fully with Mr. O'Connel in effecting an orderly transition of responsibilities. Any questions of a personal nature should be directed to Mr. Schwenger [the director of personnel for the Weapons Systems Division].

Between the time of this announcement and February 1, the following developments took place:

1. Dr. Benson submitted his resignation on January 15, the day after the announcement.

2. Mr. Bowen, through his "functional" superior—the corporate vice president of finance—requested a transfer to the Commercial Products Division which had an opening for a controller. No action had been taken on his request at the time our own survey ended in February 1968.

3. Messrs. Abel, Ludden, Dolan, and Warick had separate meetings with Mr. O'Connel. Within one week of these meetings, Messrs. Abel and Dolan submitted their resignations. Mr. Sorensen requested a transfer to another division of the company.

4. There was no abnormal turnover reaction in the lower echelons of the two departments.

35

Bridging the Information Gap at Three Mile Island: Radiation Monitoring by Citizens

INTRODUCTION

Public interest in policy decisions of a complex, technical nature has grown in recent years. Formal provisions for disseminating information to the public about proposed policies are now commonplace. Because of the National Environmental Policy Act (1969) and other federal legislation, public hearings, public comment periods, and environmental impact statements have become widely adopted mechanisms for introducing and gaining public acceptance of new plans.

This paper, however, examines a situation in which these existing mechanisms for information exchange between government officials and the public were neither functional nor adequate. The issue under review was the purging of radioactive Krypton from the disabled reactor at the Three Mile Island Nuclear Generating Station (TMI), which had been the site of a serious accident one year earlier. In this case the normal public information process did not address the depth of public concern over the proposed purge and did not

facilitate public understanding or acceptance of the proposed plans. Instead, the process was hampered by substantial public resistance.

In response to these circumstances, the U.S. Department of Energy (DOE) sponsored a unique project to provide citizens with information about radiation exposures and to rebuild public confidence in information supplied by government agencies. The Citizen Radiation Monitoring Program (CRMP) trained citizens to monitor, interpret, and publicize radiation levels in the community. This paper analyzes why such an intensive effort to involve citizens in disseminating public information was necessary, describes the program and its outcomes, and reflects on implications for disseminating public information on similar, complex social and technological issues in other settings.

PUBLIC CONCERN ABOUT THE RISKS OF RADIATION EXPOSURE

The accident at TMI in March 1979 released small but significant levels of radioactivity

Written by Barbara Gray Gricar and Anthony J. Baratta. Used by permission of JAI Press.

into the atmosphere, exposing the public to a maximum exposure of twice that of average yearly background levels. While subsequent studies identified no immediate or expected long-term physical health effects from the accident (Kemeny, 1979), they did point to both social and psychological consequences (Scranton, Note 1; Brunn, Johnson & Ziegler, Note 2; Kemeny, 1979). Overall, the personal impact of the accident, according to self-report, was moderate (Brunn, Johnson & Ziegler, Note 2).

Removal of large quantities of radionuclides that remained after the accident requires extensive clean-up and decontamination over several years. The first major step in the clean-up was the proposed purge of the reactor building that was expected to release radioactive Krypton-85 into the atmosphere. Many residents became concerned about the risks associated with the purge. The staff of the Nuclear Regulatory Commission (NRC) had determined that the purge would increase the average yearly radiation exposure for an individual by about 1% and that this increase would not endanger the health and safety of the public (TMI Support Staff, Note 3). The public, however, did not totally accept this conclusion. Their concerns were exacerbated by their lack of scientific and technical knowledge about radiation and by the widely held belief that initial public reports about radiation levels during the accident were deliberately misleading. The Governor's Commission on TMI (Scranton, Note 1) attributed the psychological stress associated with the accident to the lack of credible scientific information on which residents could rely. The NRC's own special inquiry into the accident reached similar conclusions,

... the public misconceptions about risks ... has [sic] been due to a failure to convey credible information regarding the actual risks in an understandable fashion to the public. (Rogovin, Note 4)

Even before the announcement of the purge, some communities near TMI had initiated inquiries about methods for monitoring radiation levels. In mid-1979, officials of Lancaster County (directly east of TMI) explored the possibility of measuring radiation levels independently of the NRC and Metropolitan Edison (the utility that operates TMI) but abandoned their efforts because costs were prohibitive. Residents of Middletown (just north of TMI) appealed to their congressman and directly to President Carter for an independent source of information about radiation levels. And another community approached the governor of Pennsylvania about a community monitoring program. Moreover, the governor's own commission (Scranton, Note 1) specifically recommended that the Pennsylvania Department of Environmental Resources (DER) design, implement, and supervise a pilot community radiation monitoring program to ensure local officials and residents quick access to information on radiation levels.

When the NRC, the EPA, and DER held public meetings to discuss the purge and its anticipated environmental impact, public opposition was fierce. Several explosive public meetings showed the serious information gap that existed, the lack of information about radiation levels and their effects, and the erosion of public confidence in information provided by the government.

Two excerpts from these meetings are illustrative:

Citizen A: I would like to ask you gentlemen personally to put a monitoring device in my yard so I can read it and we know what is going on around our neighborhood.

NRC Official: But I must also point out that there is a monitor right at the observation tower the EPA has there.

Citizen A: I don't know what it says. Nobody informs us what is going on or what the readings are.

NRC Official: Well, we will certainly provide you that information. (Three Mile Island Public Meeting, March 1980)

Citizen B: Why should we believe you when you've made such collossal mistakes already?

Citizen C: There are questions here and there are problems here that have not been faced elsewhere.... I've tried to believe the NRC. I've tried to believe Met Ed as best possible. When is the bottom line going to be that there will be one person that ... won't pass the buck? When are we going to get some credibility? I want to believe you, but I do not believe you. (Three Mile Island Public Meeting, March 1980)

Ironically, communication between government officials and the public was so poor that an announcement by the NRC at one public meeting that the state and federal agencies were already pursuing a community monitoring program fell on deaf ears.

THE CITIZEN RADIATION MONITORING PROGRAM

The primary purpose of the Citizen Radiation Monitoring Program was to provide a source of accurate and credible information about radiation levels to communities within a five-mile radius of TMI. This information would permit citizens to make informed and independent judgments about the safety of radiation levels in their community and to verify radiation levels measured by existing state and federal agencies. The program was, in essence, an independent, routine surveillance program operated by local communities.

Since this program was the first of its kind, there was no precedent to follow for its design. A conceptual rationale for the design, however, was based on the premise that citizens are more likely to believe information generated by themselves or by their neighbors (subject to the same poten-

tial risks) than by government officials whose credibility is questionable, at best.

In early March 1980 the sponsoring organizations (hereafter referred to as the technical working group [TWG]) approached officials of 12 municipalities and three counties that fell within a five-mile radius of TMI to solicit their reaction to and input into the design of the program. They were asked how the program could be useful to them and how it could best be designed to ensure that timely and credible information was available to citizens. Officials were then invited to nominate four citizens from each municipality to serve as monitors. This was the first step in establishing local responsibility for the program.

The next step was to put the 51 citizens who were nominated through a comprehensive three-week training program. The training program was designed to provide sufficient technical background so the residents could use selected radiation detection equipment to obtain the necessary data and interpret the results. Nominees had little or no formal training in nuclear science or radiation detection. The typical individual was a high school graduate with an average of one year of college. The nominees ranged in age from early twenties to senior citizens and included teachers, secretaries, engineers, housewives, police officers, and retirees. The course included information about sources of radioactivity, how radiation affects the body, and methods of radiation detection as well as hands-on training in how to operate the monitors they would later use in the townships.

The lack of knowledge and understanding about radiation among the participants was clearly demonstrated on a number of occasions. During the first class, basic nuclear terminology related to radiation and radioactive material was defined along with the fundamentals of atomic and nuclear science. When asked by the instructor what the basic unit of activity was, less than half of the 51 participants knew the correct answer (a curie). Of those, only two or three demonstrated any understanding of the magnitude of one curie of activity. During another class, many of the citizens were surprised to find that commonplace household objects emitted low but measureable radiation levels.

One could argue that such comprehensive training was not required for simply taking readings. The program included enough fundamentals, however, that the participants would be conversant about radiation and could interpret their measurements to fellow citizens.

Once the training was completed, the monitors began to collect data on a regular basis using radiation detectors installed by the TWG at community-selected sites. The radiation levels were recorded on strip-chart recorders. Each day the monitors examined the charts and recorded the high, low, and average for the completed 24-hour period on forms developed specifically for use with the program.

The citizen monitors immediately posted a public copy of the report in their townships and reported any abnormal readings to the TWG. Later, a courier collected the reports and tapes and transmitted them to DER, who verified the readings, summarized the data from all 12 communities, and disseminated the results to the press, NRC, EPA, the local townships, and other state and federal agencies.

Reactions of the monitors and local officials and input on procedural details were continually sought during the preparatory phase through informal conversations and formally scheduled review sessions. This give and take among the TWG, the monitors, and local officials created rapport among those involved, provided input to improve the program's operation, and transferred more responsibility for the program to the communities. For example, once installation of all the monitors was completed, the class was expressly convened to critically review the procedures.

Based on their first-hand experience with the system, the citizens provided a number of suggestions that led to revisions in the operating procedures. At another meeting, each community was asked to draw up and present a schedule for monitoring during and after the venting period. One community requested that a second monitoring site be established at the opposite end of their township to quell fears of residents in that area. Others agreed to exchange and compare their results. Some made tentative plans to reduce the frequency of monitoring once the venting had subsided. By mid-June, when the NRC officially approved Met Ed's request and the actual venting began, the monitors had already had one month of official monitoring experience.

OUTCOMES

Results of the Monitoring

When initially queried about the program, most community leaders reacted favorably to the concept, but some were skeptical about whether it could really be done. They feared that citizens could not be adequately trained to make accurate readings, that the data would be misused or reported incorrectly, and that the program would generate data that contradicted government reports. This indeed was not the case.

The citizens' readings were comparable to and in agreement with the independent measurements made by EPA. Exhibit 35–1 lists the total dose from Krypton-85 measured by the citizens. For three monitoring sites, the EPA measurements are provided for comparison.

In addition to being posted at the local monitoring sites, the citizens' data were published by the EPA concurrently with their own. Additionally, the local newspapers and TV stations carried the results during the initial days of the purge. DER and EPA received many calls from local citizens inquiring about radiation levels.

EXHIBIT 35–1 SUMMARY OF CITIZEN RADIATION MONITORING PROGRAM (CMP) DATA FOR THE REACTOR BUILDING PURGE (6/28/80–7/11/80)

CMP Station Locations

Municipality	Azimuth	Distance from TMI (mi)	CMP-Measured Skin Dose from Kr–85 Venting (mrem) [a]	EPA-Measured Skin Dose from Kr–85 Venting (mrem)
Londonberry	40°	1	0.105	
Elizabethtown	90°	6.5	0.015	
West Donegal	100°	7	0.011	
Conoy	160°	2	0.036	0.042 [b]
East Manchester	170°	7	ND	
York Haven	175°	3	0.041	
Newberry	245°	4.5	0.003	
Goldsboro	270°	1.5	0.004	0.001 [b]
Fairview	285°	7	ND	
Lower Swatara	335°	2.5	0.006	
Middletown	350°	2	0.030	0.039 [b]
Royalton	355°	2	0.087	

[a] The radiation units are millirem. The millirem (mrem) is a unit of radiation dose that takes into account the type of radiation, its intensity, and its biological effect. In comparison, a person receives an average skin dose of 80 mrem per year from natural background radiation.

[b] The variations shown between CMP and EPA measurements are within statistical errors.

Survey of Citizen Monitors

An effort was made at the beginning and later in the program to obtain the citizens' perceptions about their own safety and about the credibility of the information they received. A 10-question survey administered on the first day of class (t_1) and again on the last day (t_2) revealed some significant differences in the citizens' attitudes.

The following sample question illustrates the format: "I feel well-informed about the progress of the clean-up activities at TMI." Responses were recorded on a 5-point Likert scale varying from strongly disagree to strongly agree. Mean responses were compared using a t-test. (See Exhibit 35–2.)

Generally, the results demonstrate improvements in how informed and how safe the citizen monitors felt. While the mean values of the responses to these questions only indicated they had neutral to slightly positive feelings about safety, this did represent a significant change for three questions. The responses indicated that the monitors felt better equipped to judge their own safety at the end of the course than they did when it began.

The citizens were also asked to rate (on a 5-point scale ranging from 1 = excellent to 5 = bad) the quality of the information they received from 11 sources, including the NRC, Met Ed, the governor's office, the Pennsylvania Emergency Management Agency, their county officials, and the agencies represented in the TWG. The citizens rated the quality of information from Met Ed and the NRC as poor (3.6 and 3.5, respectively) and that from The Pennsylvania State University as good (1.8), with ratings of other agencies falling somewhere in between. (See Exhibit 35–3.) No significant changes in these ratings were observed from the beginning (t_1) to the end of the course (t_2) with the exception of those for EPA, which improved from 2.7 to 2.2. Several explanations for this change are possible. EPA provided and serviced some of the citizens' monitors and maintained a public information center during the purge.

On the second survey an additional 10 questions were asked specifically about the citizen monitoring program and about the

EXHIBIT 35–2   ATTITUDE SURVEY RESULTS

Attitude Items	t_1		t_2		
	Mean	S.D.	Mean	S.D.	p [a]
1. My community is a safe place in which to live.	3.3	1.1	3.5	1.0	n.s.
2. I feel well-informed about the progress of the clean-up activities at Three Mile Island.	2.5	1.3	2.7	1.2	n.s.
3. I receive a minimum exposure to radiation every day which does not pose any hazard to my health.	3.6	1.0	3.7	1.0	n.s.
4. I have access to sufficient information from existing public and private sources to make a judgment about my safety with respect to radiation.	2.9	1.3	3.4	1.0	.01
5. Metropolitan Edison should proceed with the clean-up activities at Three Mile Island as quickly as possible, even if it means venting the Krypton gas to the atmosphere.	3.2	1.6	3.5	1.4	n.s.
6. I feel well-informed about what to do in case of an emergency.	2.9	1.3	3.3	1.2	n.s.
7. Radiation-levels in my community are currently above safe levels.	2.6	.9	2.2	1.1	.02
8. The Nuclear Regulatory Commission (NRC) should not permit Metropolitan Edison to re-open reactor #1.	3.1	1.4	2.7	1.6	n.s.
9. I currently can get accurate information about radiation levels in my community.	2.5	1.2	2.9	1.2	.03
10. Most of my friends and neighbors in my community are well-informed about radiation and its effects.	1.9	.8	1.7	.8	n.s.

Note: Attitudes were measured along this continuum: 1: strongly disagree; 2: disagree; 3: neutral; 4: agree; 5: strongly agree.

[a] Significance values for two-tailed t-test.

course itself. (See Exhibit 35–4.) The responses reveal that the citizens received needed information from the course and trusted those who provided the information. Moreover, they indicate that the citizens did not feel the course influenced them to either accept or reject nuclear power. This was important since the instructors took great care to guard against propaganda for or against nuclear power in order to preserve their own credibility as reasonably unbiased experts.

In open-ended questions about what they liked best and least about the course, many participants indicated that the course responded to the communities' need for information, and most believed that the material was presented objectively, as these comments by one participant suggest:

EXHIBIT 35–3   CREDIBILITY OF INFORMATION SOURCES

Information Sources	t_1		t_2		
	Mean	S.D.	Mean	S.D.	p [a]
Pennsylvania State University (PSU)	2.0	.8	1.8	.5	n.s.
Pennsylvania Dept. of Environmental Resources (DER)	2.6	.8	2.2	1.0	n.s.
Environmental Protection Agency (EPA)	2.7	.7	2.2	.8	.05
Township Officials	2.3	1.1	2.4	.9	n.s.
County Emergency Preparedness Agency	2.6	1.2	2.7	1.0	n.s.
Department of Energy (DOE)	3.0	.7	2.8	1.1	n.s.
Pennsylvania Emergency Preparedness Agency (PEMA)	2.5	1.1	2.9	.9	n.s.
County Officials	2.8	1.0	3.0	1.0	n.s.
Gov. Thornburgh's Office	3.0	1.2	3.3	.7	n.s.
Nuclear Regulatory Commission (NRC)	3.3	1.2	3.5	1.2	n.s.
Metropolitan Edison	3.9	1.2	3.6	1.3	n.s.

Note: Respondents were asked to use this scale to rate the quality of the information that is available from each of the following sources: 1: Excellent. I trust it completely. 2: Good. I trust it most of the time. 3: Sometimes good sometimes bad. I trust it 50% of the time. 4: Poor. I don't trust it much. 5: Bad. I never trust it.

[a] Significance values for two-tailed t-test.

EXHIBIT 35–4   COURSE EVALUATION

	Mean	S.D.
1. I did not learn anything in this course that I didn't already know.	1.5	.8
2. I feel better equipped to explain radiation and its effects to my neighbors than I did before the course began.	4.1	.9
3. This course provided far too much information.	2.3	1.0
4. I am well prepared to begin my job as a citizen radiation monitor in my community.	3.7	.8
5. Most of the material covered in this course was not relevant.	2.1	1.0
6. I received accurate information from the course instructors.	4.2	.6
7. This program will provide needed information to people in my community.	4.1	.6
8. My feelings about being a citizen radiation monitor are generally positive.	4.1	.6
9. I feel less secure now living near TMI than before I began the course.	2.2	1.1
10. I have been brainwashed in this course.	1.8	.83

Note: Attitudes were measured along this continuum: 1: strongly disagree; 2: disagree; 3: neutral; 4: agree; 5: strongly agree.

The instructors were impartial and did their best to take scientific data and bring it to the layman. I felt they did not try to influence anyone's opinion whether they were anti- or pro-nuke . . . I can live with the truth, but lies do create fear and strong distrust.

Other comments by the citizens suggest that their appetite for information about TMI and nuclear energy in general was barely whetted by the course. Many were eager for additional classes for themselves and for others in the community. One participant asserted, "Most of this material presented to the general public in a proper manner would definitely enlighten them, increase their confidence, and improve the general sense of security."

Overall, the survey results indicate that the program was at least moderately successful in meeting its purpose—providing an accurate and credible source of information about radiation levels to citizens around TMI. Judging the program's impact on the community at large is a difficult task for which concrete data (e.g., the number of residents who left the area during the

purge) are not available. Both DER and EPA received calls from citizens either inquiring about radiation levels or expressing their support for the local monitors. In addition, the mayor of Middletown publicly credited the Citizen Monitoring Program as one of the major reasons for public acceptance of the purge.

REFERENCE NOTES

1. Scranton, W. W. *Report on the governor's commission on Three Mile Island.* Commonwealth of Pennsylvania, February 26, 1980.
2. Brunn, S. D., Johnson, J. H., & Ziegler, D. J. *Final report on a social survey of Three Mile Island area residents.* East Lansing, Mich.: Michigan State University, Department of Geography, August 1979.
3. TMI Support Staff. *Environmental assessment for decontamination of the Three Mile Island unit 2 reactor building atmosphere* (NUREG–0662). Washington, D.C.: Office of Nuclear Reactor Regulation, U.S. Nuclear Regulatory Commission, March 1980.
4. Rogovin, M. *Three Mile Island. Report to the commissioners and to the public.* Washington, D.C.: Nuclear Regulatory Commission Special Inquiry Group, January 24, 1980.
5. Trist, E. *Referent organizations and development of interorganizational domains.* Distinguished lecture presented to the Academy of Management, Atlanta, August 9, 1979.

36

Datatrak: Dealing With Organizational Conflict

Goals

I. To illustrate the types of conflict that can arise within a work group.

II. To provide the participants with an opportunity to experience and deal with organizational conflict.

III. To help the participants to identify effective and ineffective methods of resolving conflict.

Group Size

Twenty-six to thirty participants.

Time Required

Two to two and one-half hours.

Materials

I. One copy of the Datatrak Background Sheet for each participant.

II. Seven or eight copies of the Datatrak Accounting Department Sheet (one for each of the six department members and one for each of the department's observers).

III. Six or seven copies of the Datatrak Purchasing Department Sheet (one for each of the five department members and one for each of the department's observers).

IV. Six or seven copies of the Datatrak Operations Department Sheet (one for each of the five department members and one for each of the department's observers).

V. Seven or eight copies of the Datatrak Marketing Department Sheet (one for each of the six department members and one for each of the department's observers).

VI. One copy each of the following role sheets (a different sheet for each of the twenty-two participants who are designated as department members):

1. Datatrak Accounting Role Sheets 1 through 6;

2. Datatrak Purchasing Role Sheets 1 through 5;

3. Datatrak Operations Role Sheets 1 through 5; and

4. Datatrak Marketing Role Sheets 1 through 6.

VII. One copy of the Datatrak Observer Sheet for each observer.

Prepared by David J. Foscue and Kenneth L. Murrell. Reprinted from: J. William Pfeiffer and Leonard D. Goodstein, (Eds.), *The 1984 Annual: Developing Human Resources*, San Diego, CA: University Associates, Inc., 1984. Used with permission.

VIII. A name tag for each participant. Prior to conducting the activity, the facilitator completes twenty-two of these tags with the job titles appearing on the role sheets and each of the four to eight remaining tags with the word "Observer."

Physical Setting

A room with movable chairs and plenty of space to accommodate four separate groups as well as a group-on-group configuration (see Process, Step VII).

Process

STEP I: *Assigning Roles*

After announcing that the participants are to be involved in an activity that deals with organizational conflict, the instructor forms four groups and designates them as follows:

1. The Accounting Department (seven or eight participants);
2. The Purchasing Department (six or seven participants);
3. The Operations Department (six or seven participants); and
4. The Marketing Department (seven or eight participants).

Each group is seated at a separate table.

STEP II: *Distributing Background Sheets*

Each participant is given a copy of the background sheet and a copy of the appropriate department sheet. The participants are instructed to read these handouts, beginning with the background sheet.

STEP III: *Selecting Roles*

Within each department the instructor distributes the appropriate role sheets and gives each remaining member a copy of the observer sheet. All participants are asked to read their sheets, but are cautioned not to share the comments.

STEP IV: *Distribute Name Tags and Explain Activity*

Each participant is given a name tag that identifies his or her role. The instructor has the participants put on their tags.

The instructor emphasizes the importance of maintaining roles during the role play and then elicits and answers questions about the task. After telling the department managers that they have thirty minutes in which to conduct their meetings and their decisions, the groups are told to begin.

STEP V: *Announce Decisions*

A the end of the thirty-minute period, the instructor stops the group meetings and asks the managers to spend five minutes announcing their decisions to their subordinates and explaining their rationales.

STEP VI: *Conclude Roles*

The role plays are concluded. The observers are asked to provide their groups with feedback, and the remaining members within each group are asked to share their reactions to the feedback.

STEP VII: *Process Roles*

The four managers are instructed to form a circle in the center of the room, and the remaining participants are asked to form a circle around the managers. The instructor leads a discussion with the managers, requesting that the remaining participants listen but not participate. The following questions form the basis of the discussion:

1. How did the details of your role affect the way in which you directed the department meeting? How did these details affect your decision?
2. How might your decision have been different if you had not been required to play a role?
3. How did you deal with the conflicts that arose?
4. How effective were your methods for managing conflict?

DISCUSSION QUESTIONS

After the managers have completed their discussion, the instructor leads a total-group discussion by eliciting answers to the following questions:

1. What were the consequences of your role behavior during this activity?
2. How did you feel about the constraints that your role placed on you?
3. How did the roles in your group affect the interaction of the members?
4. How might you have behaved in the same situation if you had not been required to play a role?
5. In your back-home work group, what methods does your supervisor use to manage conflict? How effective are these methods?
6. What steps can you take in the future to help to manage conflict in your own work group?

EXHIBIT 36–1 DATATRAK BACKGROUND INFORMATION

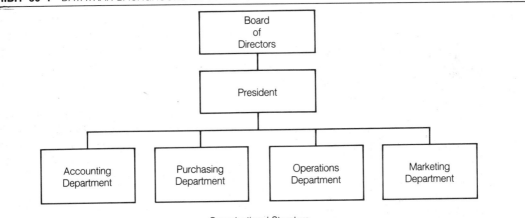

Organizational Structure

Products

Datatrak manufactures computer hardware and software designed to meet the specific needs of individual customers.

Organizational Objectives

The company's objectives are as follows:
- To manufacture computers designed to meet the specific needs of individual customers.
- To accomplish manufacturing in a manner that is cost effective to customers and that generates substantial revenue for the company and its stockholders.

Present Situation

The country is currently in the worst recession that it has ever experienced. Unemployment has reached 30 percent and is rising.

The stock market has closed each day for the past several months in a downward trend that, some economists fear, may lead to a stock-market crash.

Datatrak, your employer, is feeling the effects of the recession and is presently trying to cope with a reduction in sales and profits. An outside auditing firm has audited the company's books and determined that if the company is to survive the recession, it must reduce expenses. Consequently, the board of directors has just announced that, as a cost-reducing measure, each department must lay off one employee. Each department manager has been asked to meet with his or her subordinates in order to elicit input and opinions regarding which position should be terminated; then the manager is to make the ultimate decision. The department meetings are to take place in a few minutes.

EXHIBIT 36–2 DATATRAK ACCOUNTING
DEPARTMENT BACKGROUND
INFORMATION

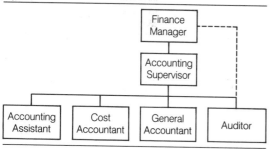

Job Descriptions

Finance Manager

Responsible for managing the Accounting Department and for presenting pertinent financial data to the president and the board of directors to facilitate timely and sound business decisions.

Accounting Supervisor

Responsible for directly supervising the accounting personnel and establishing and monitoring departmental budgets. Also responsible for other duties as assigned by management. Reports to the finance manager.

Accounting Assistant

Responsible for typing reports, providing assistance to the accountants and the auditor when necessary, and helping to put together the monthly operating report. Also performs a monthly bank reconciliation.

Cost Accountant

Responsible for accurately recording and classifying the cost of materials and properly accounting for work in progress, finished goods, and the cost of goods sold. Also responsible for providing the general accountant with this information for the preparation of the monthly operating report.

General Accountant

Responsible for preparing the balance sheet, the statement of income and retained earnings, the statement of changes in the financial position, and the monthly operating report.

Auditor

Responsible for ensuring that all departments comply with company financial policies and procedures. Also responsible for conducting periodic audits of inventories as necessary. Reports to the accounting supervisor for routine matters, but has the authority to consult the finance manager or to report directly to the president regarding significant matters.

Rumors About the Department

1. The accounting supervisor has no real work other than to report weekly to the finance manager and then to communicate the manager's wishes to others.
2. The accounting assistant habitually arrives late, frequently socializes in other departments, and often calls in sick.
3. The cost accountant is rumored to be interviewing for positions with several competing companies.

EXHIBIT 36–3 DATATRAK PURCHASING
DEPARTMENT BACKGROUND
INFORMATION

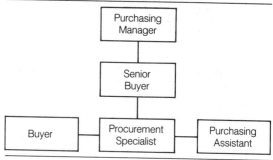

Job Descriptions

Purchasing Manager

Responsible for planning and supervising the effective procurement of materials and supplies requested by all departments within the company. Also responsible for ensuring that such items are bought after firm but fair negotiations and are delivered on a timely basis at the requested place and in excellent condition.

Senior Buyer

Responsible for planning and supervising the procurement of material and supplies requested by all departments within the company. Also responsible for ensuring that such items are bought after fair negotiations and are delivered promptly and without damage.

Buyer

Responsible for procuring materials, equipment, and services at the lowest possible cost consistent with the requirements of sound company operation. Also responsible for selecting vendors through an evaluation of price, availability, specifications, and other factors.

Procurement Specialist

Responsibilities are the same as those of the buyer.

Purchasing Assistant

Responsible for providing stenographical and other services necessary to maintain and support the functions of the Purchasing Department. Duties include transcribing material from handwritten or typed copy to final form through the use of word-processing equipment and operating terminal equipment to transmit and store textual and statistical information.

Rumors About the Department

1. The buyer is receiving kickbacks from vendors.
2. The senior buyer is eligible for early retirement, but wants to work for a few more years to build a larger retirement fund. This person frequently arrives late and leaves early, apparently without regard for the consequences.
3. Although the company has a policy against nepotism, the procurement specialist has a close relative in upper management.

EXHIBIT 36–4 DATATRAK OPERATIONS DEPARTMENT BACKGROUND INFORMATION

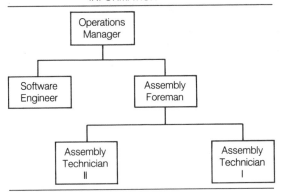

Job Descriptions

Operations Manager

Responsible for the final design, assembly, and packaging of all computer hardware and software. Also responsible for keeping assembly costs to a minimum while maintaining maximum quality and ensuring that all orders are completed on time. Supervises two people, a software engineer and an assembly foreman.

Software Engineer

Responsible for providing the software to meet each customer's needs. Also responsible for providing customers with manuals and training sessions on computer use and user language. Designs software diagnostic programs for troubleshooting the software packages. By virtue of experience and training, is the software expert in the company.

Assembly Foreman

Responsible for ensuring that computer parts are stored and assembled properly. Also responsible for checking each computer after assembly to ensure that it is operational, properly packaged, and sent to the warehouse. Makes sure that the proper tools and equipment are available to assemble each machine. Supervises assembly technicians I and II.

Assembly Technicians (I and II)

Responsible for assembling and packaging new computers and any spare parts required for existing computers, performing maintenance on tools and equipment necessary for assembling, and delivering packaged computers to the warehouse for shipping. Strong background in electronics required for both positions.

Rumors About the Department

1. The assembly foreman is given to back stabbing and to frequent verbal outbursts that upset people throughout the organization.
2. The assembly technician II is a free spirit who is often late to work and frequently calls in sick.
3. The operations manager, who was the software engineer before being promoted, spends a lot of time helping the present software engineer.

EXHIBIT 36–5 DATATRAK MARKETING DEPARTMENT BACKGROUND INFORMATION

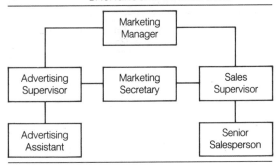

Job Descriptions

Marketing Manager

Responsible for effectively coordinating the delicate balance between the national coverage of advertising and sales. Exercises control over both the advertising supervisor and the sales supervisor in order to maintain this balance. Tasks include implementing budgets passed on by superiors, effectively reporting department sales to superiors, and informing superiors of advertising needed to maintain proper market coverage.

Advertising Supervisor

Responsible for managing all company advertising, maintaining a close relationship with the Operations Department in order to promote product lines, and advertising as effectively as possible within the limits of the budget. Works directly with the marketing manager.

Advertising Assistant

Responsible for preparing all advertising layouts and coordinating all advertising efforts with various media. Good art background required.

Marketing Secretary

Responsible for processing all paperwork for the department; answering all phone calls; and effectively managing all office equipment, such as copiers, typewriters, teletypewriter devices, and so forth.

Sales Supervisor

Responsible for setting all sales quotas, covering major accounts, and solving any and all major sales problems. Must be sensitive to market needs and must maintain a close working relationship with the Operations Department so that each sale can meet the customer's time requirements.

Senior Salesperson

Responsible for covering existing accounts in an assigned territory and acquiring enough new accounts to meet a quota.

Rumors About the Department

1. Although the company has a policy against nepotism, the sales supervisor is related to the president. Also, sales have been deteriorating since the sales supervisor has held this position.
2. The marketing manager spends many work days playing tennis.
3. The marketing manager shows favoritism toward the marketing secretary.

EXHIBIT 36–6   DATATRAK OBSERVER INSTRUCTIONS

During the department meeting, you are to listen and observe carefully and make notes regarding answers to the following questions. After the role play has been concluded, you will be asked to share these answers with the members of your department.

1. What types of conflicts arose?

2. What methods did the manager use to manage these conflicts?

3. How did the other department members respond to these methods?

4. How did the manager gather information from the subordinates?

5. How did he or she use that information to make the ultimate decision?

6. How would you describe the mood of the department at the beginning of the meeting?

7. How did this mood change as the meeting progressed?

IV

Organizational Dynamics

Change

Organizational Culture

Power and Politics

37

School of Education: Case of a Contracting Organization

"How negative do you feel today, Slocum?" inquired Johnson, who was the assistant dean for programs and chairman of the reorganization committee, half in jest and half seriously of the educational administration professor. The school reorganization committee was meeting to discuss problems arising from the recent reorganization of the school.

The school had begun as a Department of Education and Psychology within a small teachers college. In 1964, Psychology became a separate department, followed in 1967 by the Elementary and Secondary Education Departments. Special Education, Educational Administration, and Counselor Education were separated out in 1970. Finally in 1973, the Student Teaching Department was formed (see Exhibit 37–1).

Dr. Anderson had been dean since 1967. Prior to that he was Chairman of the Department of Education and Psychology. Having been at the university since 1948, he was now nearing retirement. A man of integrity, he was respected by most of his faculty.

The Dean had tried to persuade the School of Education faculty to reorganize in 1972 and 1975. He had proposed combining the departments of Elementary Education, Secondary Education, and Student Teaching to form a Teacher Education Department. The other departments were to remain intact. Both attempts at reorganization failed in the face of considerable faculty opposition.

By 1979, when the Dean made his third attempt at reorganizing the school, conditions had changed. Student credit hours (SCH) within the school had decreased by 14% since 1975. Full-time-equated (FTE) faculty positions had decreased 6%. The Department of Psychology was the only department that was growing. Their SCHs had increased 12% and their FTE 32% since 1975 (see Exhibit 37–2). If the Department of Psychology was excluded from the School of Education figures, the school decrease in SCH for 1975–80 was 27%, and the decrease in FTE was 20% (see Exhibit 37–3).

The Provost supported the reorganization. The university had originally been a

Written by Mahmoud A. Moursi and Susan K. Smith. Reprinted with permission of Mahmoud A. Moursi, Professor, Central Michigan University.

247

EXHIBIT 37–1 SCHOOL OF EDUCATION: CASE OF A CONTRACTING ORGANIZATION
ORGANIZATION CHART, AUGUST 1979

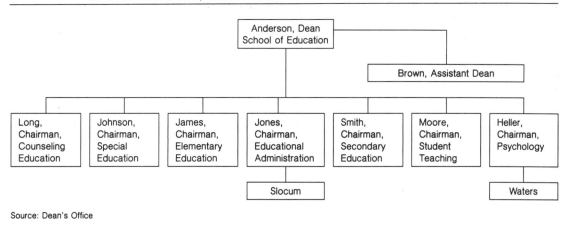

Source: Dean's Office

teachers college, but changes in the job market and accompanying changes in student career interests had resulted in the development of a new mission for the university. The education of teachers was no longer the basic purpose of the university. Rather, the professional education of business men and women was the university's new mission.

Since the university used a "student driven" model, declining enrollment in the School of Education had resulted in a decreased allotment of full-time-equated teaching positions to the school. Under these circumstances, contracting the organization from seven to three departments, was an appropriate response from the point of view of the Provost's office.

The decrease in FTE faculty positions was causing problems for the school since 85% of its faculty were tenured. Four departments, Counselor Education, Secondary Education, Elementary Education, and Educational Administration, were fully tenured. Most of the faculty had been with the school for many years (see Exhibit 37–4).

In August 1979, the Dean proposed a more sweeping reorganization than he had in 1972 and 1975. Not only were Special Education, Student Teaching, Secondary Education, and Elementary Education to be combined into Teacher Education, two of the remaining three departments, Counselor Education and Educational Administration, were to be combined into Educational Services (name changed later to Counseling, Educational Administration, Library Materials, and Community Leadership). The Psychology Department, as before, was to remain untouched.

The reorganization would require some people to move to different buildings so that members of the same department could be together (see Exhibit 37–5).

An implementation committee, chaired by the Dean and consisting of representatives from each of the departments, was charged with developing a proposal on which the faculty could vote on November 9.

The proposal was based on the Dean's recommendation, and presented only one reorganization plan. The committee had added a transitional structure, departmental units, to the Dean's proposal (see Exhibit 37–6).

The units, corresponding to the former departments, would be headed by unit

EXHIBIT 37–2 SCHOOL OF EDUCATION: CASE OF A CONTRACTING ORGANIZATION
ON CAMPUS SCH[1] PRODUCTION, FTE[2] TEACHING POSITIONS, 1975–1980

	1975-76	1976-77	1977-78	1978-79	1979-80	% Change 1975-80
SCHOOL Education						
SCH	89,600	87,184	86,229	84,620	77,339	−14%
FTE	141.71	137.71	138.32	134.53	133.28	−6%
DEPT Counselor Education						
SCH	4,758	4,345	3,505	3,432	3,173	−33%
FTE	10.79	8.96	8.47	7.17	7.13	−34%
DEPT Elementary Education						
SCH	12,679	12,401	12,284	11,835	10,707	−16%
FTE	22.20	19.80	20.04	19.47	19.80	−11%
DEPT Educational Administration and Library Science						
SCH	6,163	4,911	5,092	4,436	3,823	−38%
FTE	10.78	11.38	11.45	10.33	10.14	−6%
DEPT Psychology						
SCH	31,065	33,422	35,689	36,318	34,560	+12%
FTE	37.01	39.92	46.19	47.61	48.92	+32%
DEPT Secondary Education						
SCH	10,324	9,696	7,903	7,623	6,715	−35%
FTE	16.70	15.37	13.10	11.79	11.64	−30%
DEPT Special Education						
SCH	7,200	6,787	6,730	6,405	5,983	−17%
FTE	10.51	10.13	9.98	10.77	10.29	−2%
DEPT Student Teaching						
SCH	17,411	15,622	14,971	14,372	12,210	−30%
FTE	33.22	31.05	28.12	26.26	24.99	−25%

[1]SCH: student credit hours
[2]FTE: full-time-equated
Source: Office of University Planning and Research

coordinators. According to the proposal, the continuation of the units depended upon the departmental task forces created to develop departmental procedures. Each department would also be directed to form a program task force charged with reviewing programs and curriculum. The task forces would have time limits within which to complete their work. In addition, an ongoing School Organization Committee would be formed and charged with resolving problems that arose out of the reorganization.

The proposal was voted upon in November and passed 61 to 27. Most of the support for the proposal came from the two departments least affected by the change: psychology and student teaching.

Psychology was not really involved since that department was not changed and members did not interact very much with the rest of the school faculty.

Student teaching consisted primarily of off-campus faculty who supervised student teachers in various locations throughout the state. As a result, they were more aware of the need to update the school's curriculum and were supportive of the Dean's desire to make programmatic changes in the school. They had attempted to bring about changes in curriculum themselves but had been rebuffed by the on-campus faculty.

EXHIBIT 37–3 SCHOOL OF EDUCATION: CASE OF A CONTRACTING ORGANIZATION
SCH [1] AND FTE [2] OF SCHOOL OF EDUCATION, EXCLUDING PSYCHOLOGY DEPARTMENT

Year	1975-80					Differences:
	1975-76	*1976-77*	*1977-78*	*1978-79*	*1979-80*	*1975-80*
School SCH	89,600	87,184	86,229	84,620	77,339	−12,261
Psych SCH	31,065	33,422	35,689	36,318	34,560	+3,495
School-Psych SCH	58,535	53,762	50,540	48,302	42,779	−15,756
% Decrease, SCH	—	8%	6%	4%	11%	−27%
Psych. as % of Total School SCH	35%	38%	41%	43%	45%	
School FTE	142	138	138	135	133	−9
Psych FTE	37	40	46	48	49	+12
School-Psych FTE	105	98	92	87	84	−21
% Decrease, FTE	—	7%	6%	5%	3%	−20%
Psych as % of Total School FTE	26%	29%	33%	36%	37%	

[1]Student credit hour
[2]Full-time-equated
Source: University Office of Planning & Research

Johnson: All right, let's get going. Last week we looked over Wells and Moody Hall to see where we could put people and I think . . .

Slocum: Forget it. The people in my department are not going to move out of Wells into Moody Hall. They like the offices they have now; they've been there a long time and they don't want to move in with those guys in Moody Hall. Some of them are even afraid of the rats "psych" has over there. We didn't want to go in with Counselor Education in the first place. I've been a professor of Educational Administration throughout my career. Now I'm a professor of Counseling, Educational Administration, Library Media, and Community Leadership. The other people in my profession don't even know what that is! Another thing, we don't have anything in common with those counselors. They're all wrapped up in people and their emotions. We take a straightforward, objective view of problems. We're concerned with systems, not individuals.

Johnson: I know there are problems with putting those two departments together, but each one is too small to continue as a sepa-

rate entity. With decreasing resources the Dean had to get rid of the small departments. I'll admit I thought he should have put Coun-

EXHIBIT 37–4 FACULTY TENURE, FALL 1980

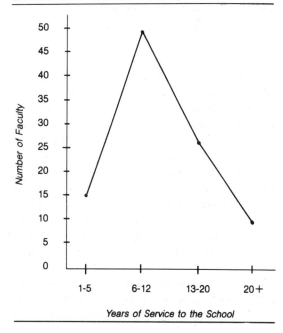

EXHIBIT 37–5 DEPARTMENTAL LOCATIONS

Pre-reorganization: Location of Departments

Fenwick	Wells	Moody
Psychology Special Education	Student Teaching Secondary Education Elementary Education Education Administration and Library-Media	Counseling Education

Post-reorganization: Location of Departments

Fenwick	Wells	Moody
Psychology	Teacher Education Student Teaching Secondary Education Elementary Education Special Education	C.E.A.L.M.C.L.[1] Counseling Education Educational Administration Library-Media

[1]Counseling, Educational Administration, Library Media, and Community Leadership.

selor Education in with the school psychologists in the Psychology Department. They at least have something in common.

Waters: No way. The school psychologists are in my department and they wouldn't stand for it. The credentials of school psychologists and counselors are completely different. School psychologists have much more extensive training requirements than counselors. Putting those two groups together wouldn't work at all. You know, someone should have paid more attention to how this whole thing was going to come out. There is a lot more involved in change than just drawing boxes on an organization chart. This reorganization has had a big impact on people: both faculty and staff.

Johnson: Let's get back to the space problems. The Dean wants Educational Administration to move into Moody and Special Education to move out of Fenwick into Wells. That way each of the departments will have all their people in the same building.

Smith: Well I hate to break this up, but I have a class at 11 and I have to get back to Wells Hall. It would sure help if we had release time to work on these committees. Some of my people are complaining about the way the departmental task forces are cutting into

their class preparation time.

Johnson: OK, we'll meet again next week. Wait a minute, Smith, and I'll walk to Wells with you. I need to stop at the Dean's office.

Later on their way across campus, Smith, who was chairman of the new Department of Teacher Education and former chairman of the Secondary Education Department, asked Johnson how the faculty in Special Education felt about the reorganization.

Johnson: They're very concerned. As you know, a lot of them are relatively young and new to the University. Going from a department of 7 to one of 56 is quite a change. They are especially concerned about getting tenure. The rest of the faculty in the teacher education department don't know them very well and they are not that familiar with special education. How are the special education faculty going to be evaluated? Also, it's well known that Secondary Education has four more tenured positions than it should have according to the Provost's office, and that when people leave those positions, they won't be replaced. It looks to me as though it's going to be hard for any of my people to get tenure and if anyone has to be laid off, they'll be the first to go.

Smith: Well, I hope it doesn't come to that.

EXHIBIT 37–6 SCHOOL OF EDUCATION: CASE OF A CONTRACTING
ORGANIZATION
ORGANIZATION CHART, AUGUST 1980

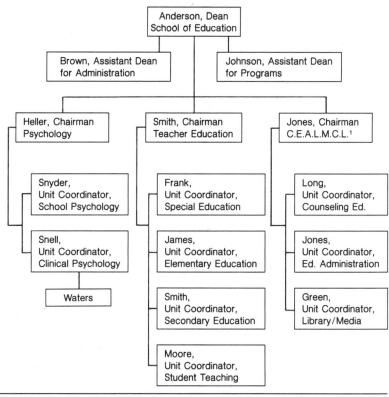

[1] Counseling, Educational Administration, Library Media, and Community Leadership.

Although do you realize that in 1971, 2,300 people were recommended for certification and this year we're only recommending 900? What concerns me are these confounded units. Here I am, chairman of the department, and the unit coordinators are acting like department chairmen. They're signing drop and add cards, approving budgets, and recruiting staff. The units are acting just like mini-departments.

Johnson: That's because this is a year of transition. The units are supposed to fade away after this year, according to the Dean. Not everyone agrees with that though.

Smith: That's for sure. Some of my faculty maintain these units can go on forever if the department decides to keep them. To hear them talk, there hasn't been any change at all.

Johnson: Then what's the point of the reorganization?

Smith: Beats me, but keeping these units is a neat way to finesse the reorganization.

Johnson: Why do you suppose psychology wasn't touched by any of this?

Smith: Rumor has it that the Dean didn't want to do anything that might encourage them to leave the school. After all, they're the only department that's growing and if they went to Liberal Arts, we would lose a lot of FTE.

Meanwhile, two of the Counseling Education faculty were discussing the reorganization over their morning coffee.

Miller: I'm supposed to go to one of those task force meetings again this afternoon. What a waste of time!

Terry: And all for nothing, too. The only money the reorganization saves is a couple of department chairperson's salaries, and that doesn't amount to anything.

Miller: Let's face it. The real reason the Dean wanted this reorganization is so that he can go out in a blaze of glory!

Terry: That's for sure. We don't have a thing in common with those guys from educational administration. I hope they never do move over here.

Later that day, Johnson, who had become the second assistant dean as a part of the reorganization, met with the Dean.

Dean: How did your meeting go this morning, Mike?

Johnson: About the same. Slocum is dragging his feet and we can't seem to resolve the space issue. Educational Administration probably isn't going to move unless you tell them they must.

Dean: It's frustrating to have all this resistance. They don't seem to realize how important this is to the school. We need to cut costs and the reorganization will allow us to reduce administrative expenses. More than that, it will permit us to be more flexible. We have to expand our mission beyond that of educating the classroom teacher. We could be educating people who are training personnel outside the classroom, such as in the private sector. Also, with the emphasis on "mainstreaming" we need to have special education faculty interacting with elementary education and secondary education.

Johnson: I agree with your reasons for reorganizing, Dean, but unless you take a stronger stand it's not going to happen. There are many people opposing the change, and unless you use stronger leadership, these committees are going to study it to death.

The next morning the Dean met with the other assistant dean, Dr. Brown, who was also a professor of psychology.

Dean: Good morning, Louise. I wanted to speak with you about the reorganization. You talk to a lot of people. How do you think it's going?

Brown: Well, in teacher education it's beginning to come along. The chairman has a nice informal way about him that will bring those people around eventually. Jones, on the other hand, is coming on rather strongly. Most of the people in his department are maintaining their old territorial boundaries and hoping the reorganization will go away.

Dean: What do you think about the relocation of educational administration to Moody at this point?

Brown: Financially, it has to be done. We must reduce some of these administrative expenses. I hope you are successful in persuading them to move. If you force them, however, I am afraid they may bring in the faculty union.

After Dr. Brown left, the Dean pondered his options. Should he continue to let the departmental task forces and School Organization Committee try to resolve the problems of the unit structure and the allocation of space, or should he play a stronger role in the process? He would be retiring in a year or two, and he wanted to accomplish the reorganization before leaving. The Dean thought about how he had devoted his entire professional life to the growth and development of the school. Now he had one more task, getting the organization into a stronger position to cope with its changing environment. He needed that reorganization! How could he get it?

38

Mail Route Improvement vs. the Manana Principle[1]

"Postal proposal rejected," said the headline, and the opening statement of the newspaper article left no doubt: "The U.S. Postal Service has rejected as 'garbage' a computerized route system for mail trucks that a Kansas State University professor says would save millions of dollars." Dr. Leonard W. Schruben, a research agricultural economist who had developed the LOCKSET method some eight years ago while at Stanford University, was stunned. During his years of experience with the method he had found no case in which the dispatching methods used by firms or government agencies had resulted in a routing with fewer miles than was discoverable by an appropriate version of LOCKSET.

About two years ago he had focused his attention on the U.S. Postal Service, which operates one of the nation's largest truck

fleets. A pilot study for the Topeka postal district showed that the routes designed by the computer outperformed the manually designed mail distribution system. He was certain that if the Postal Service implemented his method, substantial cost savings could be realized without any reduction in service.

Postal officials, who had participated in his work, had repeatedly expressed their confidence in the study's success, and Schruben simply did not understand the Postal Service's decision. What had gone wrong?

THE TRUCK DISPATCHING PROBLEM

Basically, the truck dispatching problem can be defined as the optimization of routes for a fleet of trucks used for delivery from a central depot to a large number of delivery points. It is designed to allocate loads to trucks in such a manner that all demands are supplied and that the total mileage covered is minimized.

There are several different operations research methods available to solve carrier

---

1 One of the most subtle forms of resistance to change is to ostensibly accept and encourage the innovator, to publicly proclaim support of innovative goals and while doing that to build in various safeguards devised to control, delay, and to ultimately nullify real change. We call this tactic, which leads innovative action to peter out while at the same time giving the organization the public semblance of progressiveness, the manana principle.

Reprinted with permission of Karl Dickel and James W. Gentry, Professor, Oklahoma State University.

routing problems, none of which has been found to be very successful by practitioners. The typical method in use is still one of trial and error. The dispatcher looks at a map, picks out routes consistent with available carrier capacities, and then by trial and error attempts to find shorter routes.

THE LOCKSET METHOD

Schruben's LOCKSET method is based upon an algorithm first developed by Clarke and Wright, and uses a sequential procedure to solve carrier routing problems. It starts from an initial solution in which each delivery is made on a one-stop route. Then, a successive aggregation of routes is carried out according to the highest distance-saved coefficient, which is the time saved by combining two routes as opposed to making two separate trips. The procedure is very flexible and many restrictions can successfully be built into the algorithm (travel time and truck capacity restrictions, special equipment trucks, bulk deliveries, road conditions, etc.).

LOCKSET tends to provide a "good" rather than an optimum solution. Since the procedure consecutively "locks" points into routes, it excludes them from further consideration; thus it is possible to preclude the best solution. On the other hand, LOCKSET reduces the number of possible alternatives considerably. An exact method would require the calculation of $\frac{1}{2}n!$ different combinations for a problem with n delivery points. Analyzed with LOCKSET, the same problem needs only $\frac{1}{2} \cdot n \cdot (n-1)$ calculations, or $1/(n-2)!$ of the explicit enumeration approach. Thus, the greater the magnitude of the problem, the greater the relative efficiency of LOCKSET. For instance, a problem with only 15 delivery points requires a mere 105 distance-saved coefficients compared with an astronomical 654 billion possible alternatives.

SUCCESSFUL INDUSTRIAL APPLICATIONS

The technique's performance has been tested against results of dispatching methods used by firms of different sizes, with various delivery configurations and different numbers and capacities of trucks. For example, LOCKSET was used to route trucks for a Massachusetts feed manufacturer, a Pennsylvania grocery chain, an Iowa meat packer, a Minnesota dairy, a Nebraska milk hauler, a Kansas soft drink bottler, as well as a California egg distributor. In none of the cases did the management procedure use a shorter set of routes than was discovered by LOCKSET.

Typically, the application of LOCKSET did not result in a drastic change in the routes, while distance savings ranged between 8% and 12% . In some cases, however, savings up to 20% were realized. Interestingly, small operations experienced the largest savings. Yet, distance savings are not the only outcome, as LOCKSET has provided a variety of other valuable results, such as:

1. reduction in fleet size,
2. better utilization of available truck capacities,
3. balancing of routes,
4. marginal delivery costs for existing as well as new customers,
5. optimal location of outside storage facilities, and
6. evaluation of driver performance.

EXPERIENCES WITH KANSAS SCHOOL DISTRICTS

The reorganization of school bus routes in several Kansas school districts has been one of the most extensive applications of LOCKSET so far, and it illustrates the method's first application by a governmental agency.

In the 1970–71 school year, the 308 Kansas school districts spent almost $15 million for busing pupils to and from schools. In many districts the transportation item is second only to teacher salaries, thus representing an important area for potential cost savings.

The service requirements for busing school children is very restrictive, compared with most commercial operations, and those differences necessitated modification in the procedures successfully used to solve commercial problems.

By 1973, LOCKSET had been adopted by 10 school districts and the computer routes met or exceeded all standards of the manual routes. The saving in total mileage usually amounted to about 10%, and the reduction in the number of buses was even more substantial (between 10% and 30%). In general, the average length of ride could be reduced. In some cases, the computer-designed routes increased the longest ride for students but in no case did a student have to ride longer than the maximum 60 minutes allowed by state regulations. In most situations, computerized routes tended to shorten long rides more than lengthen short rides. Waiting periods for pupils could be reduced and a better coordination of class and bus schedules could be obtained.

All parties agreed that the computer may neglect consideration of the human element, and that the final analysis had to be left to human judgment. If necessary, the computer had to be overruled. As an example, in Unified District 224 with two schools in Clifton and Clyde, the computer proposed that one of the families in each district should switch schools. The children involved asked to remain with their old school friends and teachers. After deliberation by the Board of Education, the computer was overruled. Due to this procedure, there was generally no dissatisfaction or rejection of the new routes by the pupils and their parents.

The cost to install the LOCKSET method in a district ran from $1,500 to $5,000, de-

pending on the size of the district and the number of routes. Annual maintenance of the system was estimated to run $1,000 to $3,000. All districts were able to save a multiple of these costs. For instance, the study for district 383, Manhattan, cost $3,000 and resulted in saving more than $9,000 in the first year of operation. Furthermore, three of the 22 buses in use could be eliminated. In the succeeding years, savings could be improved even further.

Following these successful applications, Schruben offered the Kansas school system an interesting alternative: for $400,000, a statewide reorganization of bus routes could be carried out that would save the state an estimated one million gallons of gasoline a year. However, this proposal did not produce any definite action. While many superintendents appeared before legislative committees to advocate a comprehensive statewide study, there was noticeable reluctance to employ the method independently. Some superintendents felt that it was either "inappropriate" or "too costly" for them, and some also feared that parents might regard a change in bus scheduling as unnecessary. Yet Schruben blamed the failure of his proposal on bureaucracy. He supposed that the reluctance of school districts to employ his study was primarily caused by the fact that the state funds most of the school district's transportation costs. Up to now, only a few more school districts have revised their transportation schedules on a voluntary basis.

THE POSTAL PROPOSAL

On January 21, 1976, Schruben made a report available to the general public in which he claimed that the U.S. Postal Service could save more than $40 million annually, without any reduction in service, if they reorganized their mail delivery routes by his method. Further savings, he said, could be realized with comparatively minor adjustments in schedules and by selected closings.

Coincidentally, Edward V. Dorsey, a senior assistant postmaster general for operations, happened to visit Kansas City on the same day to talk to area postal managers about the grave financial situation of the U.S. Postal Service and to ask for ideas from the managers on things they could do to cut costs. "We've got to use every measure we can to reduce costs," he said, and he added that costcutting programs could include abandoning Saturday delivery, limiting special delivery services, or not processing mail as fast as is now done.

Schruben's study had been initiated in June 1974 when the Postal Service granted him authority for access to Highway Contract Route records at the Topeka Sectional Center Facility (SCF). The Topeka SCF is one of 545 in the United States and it serves the 133 post offices with zip codes whose first three digits are 664, 665, 666, and 668. All sorting other than bulk mail for the individual post offices is done at the facility. At the time of the study the SCF used 32 trucks, of which 14 served "main" routes originating in Topeka. The other 18 trucks served "subroutes" originating from 9 outlying transshipment stations. The trucks run to the end of the line when dropping mail in the morning and return to their point of origin in the evening to complete the daily pickup leg. To meet service standards, all mail has to leave Topeka by 4:15 A.M., and the latest delivery time has to be 6:30 A.M. for first-class mail, 7:30 A.M. for second class, and 9:00 A.M. for third- and fourth-class mail.

Both Leonard Stadler, manager of logistics for the Topeka center, and Ralph Kingman, director of mail processing, aided Schruben in the procurement of necessary data and showed great interest in the study. On October 7, 1975, more than one year after the work had begun, Schruben submitted a first draft of the manuscript to them, soliciting their comments and requesting their review. A week later,

Schruben and his assistant held a conference with Kingman and Stadler, in which every route was individually reviewed. Stadler suggested a few changes that were made on the spot. After that, the postal representatives agreed that the computer routes would perform successfully, and authorization to publish the report was given some weeks later.

THE RESULTS OF THE STUDY

"Computer designed routes would provide better service than manually designed routes in most cases," Schruben said in his press release. "Computerized routes would result in earlier mail delivery to many communities in the Topeka mail distribution center. In no case would mail be delivered later than with manually designed routes."

As the report showed, only 20 of the 32 trucks were needed, resulting in the reduction of 150,000 miles and a savings of $80,000 a year. The average arrival time of first-class mail in the morning was reduced from 6:00 A.M. to 5:47 A.M., for second-class mail from 6:18 A.M. to 6:01 A.M., and for third- and fourth-class mail from 6:51 A.M. to 6:27 A.M.

"If the Topeka routes were typical of other mail distribution centers in the U.S.," Schruben concluded, "annual savings of approximately $500,000 and $40 million, respectively, for Kansas and the nation could be passed on to those who use the mail." Compared with his experience with other delivery routing systems, he found that the design of the Topeka manual routes was equal to or better than that of many private businesses and other government agencies. Even so, the computer-designed routes offered substantial savings of about 20%, and preliminary results of a second study indicated similar savings for the star routes at Springfield, Ill.

An estimated $7,500 annually would be needed to develop and maintain computer routes for mail distribution centers like that in Topeka, and "who can't afford to spend $7,500 to make an $80,000 saving in transportation costs?" In addition, further savings could be possible by discontinuing or consolidating smaller post offices, and the computer could help estimate both potential savings and changes in service associated with each such closing or consolidation.

Finally, the report suggests revising the method of awarding mail routes. "Route design and bidding procedures deprive the Postal Service of possible benefits by excluding contractor participation in route design. Contractors now bid on the routes and the lowest qualified bidder for each route is awarded the contract. Judgment as to the number and design of routes depends entirely on the skill and experience of the officer designing the routes. It is not tested by the bidding process, so it may result in inefficient route design and unnecessarily high costs." Schruben believes that computerized routing could encourage participation by contractors in route design if bidding were conducted in the same manner as real estate bidding often is, allowing an individual to bid on an entire tract rather than small, individual parcels.

THE RESPONSE

"I believe the study has merit," Stadler said to journalists, "and I think the computer would be faster and more accurate, but I don't believe the savings would be as great as he quotes."

"From the time the study was made, there have been several thousand miles reduced manually. Four of the trucks have been eliminated since that time."

"And some things would be more inconvenient. For instance, from what I have seen, it would require a big truck, like a semi, to pick up mail at St. George. That would be too inconvenient—it's just too large a truck to back in and everything there."

"Finally," Stadler said, "figuring the mileage of the trucks isn't feasible because they are let on bids. We don't care how many trucks someone says they're going to use, if they give us one bid. If we furnished our own trucks, that would be a different story."

The report as well as Stadler's statements received great publicity and, as Schruben says, "a number of people commenting to me were glad that the Postal Service showed promises of modernization and a willingness to explore new ideas that might result in savings."

On February 2, 1976, William R. Roberts, Wichita postal district manager, sent a letter to R. P. Koenigs, director of the central region logistics division, in which he criticized Schruben's study most severely. Some days later, the same letter was released to the press.

"Schruben's bulletin was immediately followed by many newspaper articles and TV coverage that was unfavorable to the U.S. Postal Service, but very favorable to Professor Schruben," Roberts said. "A partial review of the proposal by the Wichita postal district, however, does not substantiate Professor Schruben's highly publicized potential cost savings to the USPS. In fact, additional routes would be required to make his proposal usable."

"The problem was not the computer. It was the lack of essential data, incomplete understanding of our transportation schedules and frequencies by programmers (probably students), a lack of knowledge of our service requirements, and a few other minor problems. The result was 'garbage in and garbage out' of the computer."

His criticism was followed by an enumeration of problem areas that he found made the computer routes unworkable. Most important of all, he said, the proposal did not allow service standards to be met and it contained erroneous mileage figures for most truck routes. As an example, he pointed out that the study had neglected to mention that first-class post offices are required to receive mail from trucks leaving Topeka prior to 4:00 A.M., and that it showed mileage figures of 126.2 instead of 13.0 miles or 77.8 instead of 17.9 miles. However, the most aggravating error, he stated, was the attempt to send a mail truck from Grantville to Tecumseh, over the Kansas river where there is no bridge. "In view of the above problems and erroneous data," he concluded his letter, "further analysis of this highly publicized report is not deemed necessary."

SCHRUBEN BACKS HIS PROPOSAL

"I have checked every substantive statement critical of the study that you mentioned in your letter to R. P. Koenigs. Without exception, each one is false," Schruben countered in a letter to Roberts on February 12, 1976, and the subsequent enumeration of incorrect conclusions reads like a lecture to Roberts.

"Nowhere does the report state the early trucks (those leaving Topeka prior to 4:00 A.M.) are not needed. I do not understand how anyone could read the report and reach any other conclusion."

"You confuse route lengths with distance mail travels from Topeka. The mileage figures you labeled erroneous are distances mail travels from Topeka to the last stop, even though it may be carried by as many as three different trucks on three different routes before it arrives at its final destination. This is clearly spelled out in the report."

"There is no inference in the report that the computer would route a truck from Grantville to Tecumseh over a river where there is no bridge. The computer used actual routes in laying out routes and takes into account road conditions. If it is necessary to backtrack to find a bridge or a freeway exit five miles down the road, the computer schedules accordingly. That was the case in the Grantville to Tecumseh link. The extra

miles are because there is no direct bridge between these two locations."

"It is most unfortunate that you did not fully acquaint yourself with the plan. By your own admission, your comments are based on a 'partial analysis' and a 'quick summary' of the report. A complete analysis and summary could have prevented erroneous interpretations and shown two public institutions cooperating to save taxpayers and postal users money without diminishing services."

"Because of the implications for my reputation and that of the University in the publication of your letter, we deem it essential to make public a summary of the above. Also, any further public statements by you that are not factual will of course be closely examined for effect on my reputation and that of the University."

The public reaction to this dispute may be reflected in a statement on *The Salina Journal's* Page of Opinion: "There's considerable evidence that Postal Service officials wouldn't recognize a good postal service plan if it kicked them in the shins. And like most bureaucrats, they don't want 'outsiders' telling them how to run their Service, even if they don't know how themselves."

Subsequently, Schruben was not given any other opportunity to talk to area postal managers. "They frankly refused to talk to me," he said. "Obviously some people had gotten cold feet, and I would not be surprised if there has also been some pressure from superiors. Stadler's change, for instance, is a clear symptom for me."

THE FINAL REJECTION

On February 17, 1976, E. V. Dorsey sent a letter to Duane Acker, President of Kansas State University, in which he expressed the Postal Service's appreciation of Professor Schruben's work, and explained their objections to the plan. "There are some misunderstandings on his part (both qualitative and quantitative) which render his work less immediately applicable than might otherwise be the case," he said.

"First, I would like to emphasize that the transportation costs are generally irrelevant to the analysis of a recommendation to close or retain a small post office.

"Professor Schruben's work assumes that minimization of vehicle miles results in an optimum network. This is not always correct. There are many instances (including some in the Topeka area) where a higher mileage solution results in both a lower cost and lower energy utilization solely because it allows use of smaller vehicles on long mileage elements of the operation.

"Finally, the models are vastly more expensive to utilize than Professor Schruben estimates. I can only assume that Professor Schruben failed to include the labor costs of data collection in his estimate of $7,500 per location. Even so, his point that computer-assisted scheduling is financially attractive, albeit overstated, is still valid.

"The Postal Service is already highly committed to the concept of computer-assisted scheduling technology. Where the state of art has proven adequate, we have moved aggressively to implement its use.

The Postal Service is currently recovering in excess of $3 million annually from our efforts, and the trend is dramatically upward."

A later inquiry about the savings potential of Schruben's plan made by Senator Robert Dole (Kansas) rendered a similar reply from the U.S. General Accounting Office. The letter, postmarked April 30, 1976, said further that "it appears that the Topeka study has paralleled the work of the Service. Although the Topeka study and the Service's Star Route Simulator both propose using computer assistance for improving star routes, these efforts were pursued independent of each other. Service headquarters officials stated they were not aware of the Topeka study until January 1976."

On May 18, 1976, the Postal Service released a final statement to the press. It concludes: "The conclusion that the Postal Service rejected out of hand Dr. Schruben's proposal for a computerized routing system for mail trucks is simply not true. Dr. Schruben's plan was carefully weighed by postal officials, and was found not applicable to our needs."

39

Municipal Light

In 1902 the citizens of Hamilton passed a proposal to develop a source of hydroelectric power for street lights and other public purposes. Up until that time all power had been supplied by private companies. During the first half of the twentieth century, a number of dams and steam-generating plants were developed in order to supply a large portion of Hamilton's power needs. The existence of Municipal Light also served as a rate regulator for electric power purchased from private companies. Since its beginning in 1902, Municipal Light has developed into one of America's most efficient electric utilities, powered almost entirely by nonpolluting hydroelectric generating facilities. This self-supporting, tax-paying utility maintains rates that are among the nation's lowest (less than half the national average), with but two rate increases in 66 years. In addition to low rates, Municipal Light provides a spectrum of consumer services: electric range, electric water heater, and electric heating system repair service at no charge—except for parts; advice on heating and air conditioning; free estimates on electric heating costs; advice on use and care of electric appliances; recipes and other household hints; advice on adequate wiring; 24-hour emergency light trouble service; and water-heater rental as low as $1.25 monthly. As a consequence, Municipal Light has built up a good image in the minds of consumers for low rates and free services.

Municipal Light employs approximately 1,800 women and men for the Hamilton service area and the hydroelectric projects. Employees have considerable pride in their organization and enjoy the company's good image with customers. Many jobs have been passed from father to son, and in a number of instances three generations are represented on the Municipal Light payroll. In many cases, several members of the same family are currently working in the organization. Obviously, many traditions and norms have evolved over time with respect to employee relations—among peers as well as among superiors and subordinates. Approximately 700 of the 1,800 employees are represented by the International Brotherhood of Electrical Workers.

In 1972 Charles Newman was appointed superintendent of Municipal Light. He was a retired Air Force brigadier general with a distinguished military career and experience in managing large-scale weapon procurement programs. The appointment was controversial because many Municipal Light workers, as well as some members of the city council, contended that the superintendent should have had experience in an electrical utility. The mayor and a majority of the council, however, felt that managerial skills were transferable and that Mr. Newman was the right person for the job at that particular time. They were concerned that Municipal Light was entering a new era in which the emphasis would have to be placed on cost savings in order that rates could be held down to the current very attractive levels. In this context, the new superintendent accepted a mandate that emphasized public responsiveness, and he implemented programs designed to develop a greater sensitivity to the needs of Municipal Light's customers and owners and to provide them with more effective, efficient service.

An outside consulting firm—Donner, Blitzen, and Associates—was hired to conduct a comprehensive study of the organization—the first in its 70-year history. A year later, the study conclusions pointed the way toward an annual saving of over $2 million for the utility's rate payers, plus substantial increases in the speed and efficiency of customer service. An automated customer information system (CIS) was designed to provide near-instantaneous customer data from a control computer. By eliminating duplicate filing systems and reducing incidents of error, CIS would save an estimated $1 million annually. A proposed management reporting system involved a broad range of coordinated reports to assist Municipal Light managers in evaluating performance and analyzing work procedures on a regular, systema-

tized basis. Another recommendation involved a work management system to establish a project priority and scheduling procedure together with more precise work control and documentation in the engineering and operations area of the utility. A proposed organization and systems planning and coordination report would provide the necessary research capability and control to coordinate the new and ongoing utility programs. It was anticipated that implementation of all the recommendations should take approximately three years.

Municipal Light receives over 18,000 telephone calls a day for service and information, plus several hundred of an administrative nature. In April 1974, an automated centrex telephone system replaced equipment that had been installed in 1935. The new electronic switching means faster, more efficient service for Municipal Light customers.

Automation, plus implementation of the Donner, Blitzen, and Associates study, has resulted in certain personnel changes, reductions in some areas, and additional hiring in others. When the automation program was first started in 1970, the utility made a firm commitment to all personnel that there would be no layoffs or reductions in salary—a commitment that Municipal Light has stood by during the past years. To retain personnel for certain jobs in the utility, a skill redistribution program was created as an ongoing effort. To complement the skill redistribution program as well as to provide opportunities for all personnel to upgrade performance in various disciplines, Municipal Light established a training division in June 1973. The newly formed section was authorized to ascertain training needs in the utility and to develop appropriate courses to augment the already established tuition reimbursement and other education programs. Courses have been conducted in office and technical skills as well as in the management area.

Municipal Light has a firm commitment to Hamilton's Affirmative Action Program. The target for reaching minority parity within the service area is 1975, while 1978 is the goal set for equal representation of women. In 1974, women were admitted to training programs in the electrical trades, an area from which they had been historically excluded. This program was coordinated with the International Brotherhood of Electrical Workers, the Civil Service Commission, and the Hamilton personnel department.

In 1972, Superintendent Newman established a Citizens Policy Advisory Committee, consisting of 14 members who represented a wide spectrum of the community. Their recommendations have been included in policy deliberations on matters such as rates, generation and research, street lighting, underground policy, energy marketing, finances, and environmental impact.

On Wednesday, November 22, 1972, the following story appeared in the Hamilton *Harbinger*.

NEWMAN SUSPENDS 16 AT MUNICIPAL LIGHT

PRIVATE DETECTIVES TURN UP "ABUSES"

City Light Superintendent Charles Newman disclosed yesterday he has suspended 16 field employees and reprimanded two for abusing coffee break periods.

Newman said he hired a private detective firm to shadow Municipal Light crews for one week after getting complaints from citizens that some men were taking extended coffee breaks at their Hamilton cafés.

The investigation also turned up possible abuses of coffee break times by "15 to 18" employees of the Hamilton Engineering Department, according to George Everest, principal assistant city engineer for operations.

However, Everest said he cannot say if there are any actual violations in his department until he has had each reported case checked out. This is being done now.

The three cafés involved, Everest said, are near 2d Avenue and Barstow Street, 7th Avenue N.E. and Interlake Way, and N. 34th Street and Stevens Way N.

Newman said two Municipal Light employees were suspended for 10 days without pay, five were suspended for two days and nine for one day. Two others received letters of reprimand.

The superintendent said at least one of the disciplined employees was also disciplined in a similar investigation three years ago for the same thing.

Everest said his department also has to discipline employees from time to time for coffee break time abuses.

The private detective agency placed the three locations under surveillance during the work week of October 30 through November 3 and made its reports according to vehicle license numbers.

The private eyes timed the length of time crews spent in the cafés. Normal time allowed for coffee breaks is 15 minutes in the forenoon and afternoon, Everest said.

Newman said: "We talked to our people involved and they admitted the abuses. The severity and frequency of the violations varied."

Newman stressed that the infractions involved only a small minority of Municipal Light workers and "I continue to be amazed at the dedication of 99% of our employees."

He said those abusing lunch or coffee break periods not only are gypping the city, "they are also cheating on their fellow employees."

"I will not stand for this."

He said most of the violators "had been around for a while." He said that if any "extenuating circumstances" turn up later, the disciplinary actions will be rectified.

"We're not against coffee breaks—just the abuse of them" Newman declared.

The president of the security agency involved maintained that his agents did not spy upon employees of the utility. Their job was to check only on vehicles and that this task fell within their overall contract of protecting Municipal Light facilities and equipment. Citizen reaction was quick and varied. Some supported management in its efforts to "shape up" employees. Others felt that this goal, however meritorious, was overshadowed by the sneaky tactics used. They emphasized that control and discipline should be handled within the organization via normal managerial procedures.

This episode touched off a series of disputes within the organization, some of which were given publicity in the press. Two of the four city council members who voted against the superintendent at his confirmation hearing in 1972 said publicly that Newman hadn't done badly. One stated, "On balance, I would have to say he's done a good job." Another observed, "I like a number of things he's done, changes that I favored such as reducing personnel and opening up the utilities operations. I also hear about morale problems among the rank-and-file workers. There are pluses and minuses. . . ." The majority of the council who supported Newman in the beginning reaffirmed their position by stating, "Yes, we think he is doing a good job, making the kinds of changes we wanted to see." In December 1973, supervisory personnel—not Newman—suspended six more utility workers for coffee break abuses. This time, supervisory personnel did the surveillance rather than the security firm. Newman stated, "Those who were abusing their privileges were being unfair to their fellow workers. I felt that the previous management had failed to stop such abuses and that I must. Letters from the public supported the disciplinary actions 50 to 1."

During this period, a new discipline code was written, at the request of employees, to make penalties more equitable. According to Newman, union leadership failed to attend drafting sessions. The code was put into effect on March 21, 1974. In early April, two foremen were suspended for three days for alleged coffee break abuses. One of the foremen, Arnold Knutson, claimed that his crew had to move its truck out of a customer's driveway at 4 PM. Because it was too late to set up again and get anything accomplished by quitting time, he decided to take the crew back to a substation for a coffee break before quitting at 4:30. He maintained that they had not taken a normal 15-minute break during the afternoon. The new rules specified that crews would return to the main dispatching area rather than stop at substations en route. Jack Simmons, the other foreman, did not comment on the specifics of his case, but did say that he wasn't even aware of any new rules covering suspensions, discharges, and other disciplinary measures. Other workers suggested that the new rules were adopted unilaterally by Municipal Light Superintendent Charles Newman

without approval of the Civil Service Commission. Newman's comment was, "Municipal Light insists on being able to discipline employees when they fail to put in eight hours' work for eight hours' pay. There are standing work orders, dating back to 1970, explicitly requiring crews to return to headquarters at the close of their last job for the day. Loafing away from headquarters to round out the work day is not acceptable work procedure." He stated that citizens had complained that the two work crews involved were parking their trucks and loafing for 30 minutes or longer at the end of their work day.

The next day, about 700 workers of the electrical workers' union walked off the job, refusing to return until the suspensions were rescinded. By the second day, the strike had spread to over 1,000 of the 1,800 employees. An ad hoc committee representing the workers presented the following demands in the form of a memo to Superintendent Newman, the mayor of Hamilton, and the city council. The demands included:

1. Rescinding the suspensions of the two foremen
2. Resignation of Superintendent Newman
3. Suspension of the new work rules until they are approved by the employees, the union, and the Civil Service Commission
4. The development of an employees' bill of rights
5. The suspension of implementation of new programs that appeared to have exceeded the ability of the organization to absorb changes.

The superintendent responded by saying that he was willing to hold the suspensions in abeyance and meet with the ad hoc committee.

40

Changing a Corporate Culture: Can Johnson & Johnson Go from Band–Aids to High Tech?

On Albany Street in gritty New Brunswick, N.J., stands Johnson & Johnson's sleek new headquarters. The modernistic aluminum-and-glass structure designed by I. M. Pei stands in marked contrast to Kilmer House, the undistinguished brick building nearby that was its home from the late 1890s until last year. The new architectural face is richly symbolic, for it mirrors the more subtle changes under way within one of the most consistently successful companies in the world.

Best known to consumers for such brands as Band-Aids and Baby Shampoo, J & J has embarked on an accelerated move into far more sophisticated medical technologies. The shift poses big risks, since success depends on whether J & J can manage businesses very different from those it has dominated. And to achieve his goals, Chairman James E. Burke is tinkering in subtle but important ways with a management style and corporate culture that have long been central to the company's success.

MARKETING PROWESS

A good deal is at stake: In addition to its consumer brands, J & J holds powerful and profitable franchises in hospital supplies and prescription drugs. For years, these product lines have flourished under a marketing-dominated, decentralized management structure. While scores of companies are struggling to eliminate corporate bureaucracies and give power back to operations, J & J is already there.

The people running its 170 "companies" enjoy autonomy unheard of in most corporations. Most divisions have their own boards. Corporate headquarters staff is a scant 750 people. And only one management layer separates division presidents from the 14-member executive committee to whom they report.

It is obvious why J & J is held up as an example of decentralization's virtues. Its earnings growth in the last 10 years has averaged 13% annually. The company says 55% of 1983's $6 billion in sales and much of its $489 million in earnings came from products that are No. 1 in their markets. And the resuscitation of its Tylenol pain reliever after the 1982 deaths of seven people who had taken cyanide-laced capsules, its repositioning of Baby Shampoo for the adult market, and its come-from-nowhere move to No. 2 in infants' toys demonstrate its legendary marketing prowess.

But while J & J's core businesses remain solidly profitable, Burke believes that maturing markets limit long-term growth potential. Moreover, scientific and technological advances promise to revolutionize health care. Thus, the push into technology "is absolutely critical to the future and to the present," he states flatly. Without it "we would be heading toward being just another company."

So since 1980, J & J has acquired 25 companies, many in promising, high-tech markets. Burke, who became CEO in 1976, has positioned J & J in products ranging from intraocular lenses and surgical lasers to magnetic-resonance scanners for diagnostic imaging.

Now, however, the longtime dominance of marketing and sales executives and the insularity of J & J's units could seriously impede the company's ability to push successfully into these new businesses and to react swiftly to changing competitive conditions in health care. Burke himself recognizes that the company's success will require greater cooperation among corporate units. And he has found that such cooperation can be hard to obtain. Former J & J executives assert, for example, that at least two key managers of J & J's Ethicon Inc., the world's largest maker of sutures, left during a struggle to persuade the unit to go along with a centralized ordering-and-distribution effort deemed critical to maintaining J & J's leading position in hospital supplies.

Learning to manage new businesses is also a major task, as evidenced by the management problems that have plagued the push into medical equipment, where losses have been heavy. One big reason for the red ink is the investment made to position companies such as Technicare Corp.—a maker of diagnostic-imaging equipment, purchased in 1979—for the long haul. The money was spent mainly to develop new products, including magnetic-resonance (MR) machines that provide strikingly clear images of the body's tissue without using radiation.

Dollars alone, however, will not solve the problems at these businesses:

Extracorporeal Inc.

Product-development problems at Extracorporeal, bought in 1978, left its dialysis equipment business with outmoded offerings when the market changed. J & J took a $38 million write-off last year and put the dialysis business on the block.

Ortho Disgnostic Systems Inc.

Organizational turmoil has hurt this maker of blood-analysis equipment and reagents. From 1977 to 1981, the marginally profitable Ortho went through four presidents. Long a leader in the field, Ortho failed to latch on to hot new technologies in the 1970s. "It was a general management and research management failure," admits executive committee member Verne M. Willaman. As a result, Ortho has been forced into an expensive catch-up effort. And although J & J denies them, rumors persist that Ortho, too, will be sold.

Technicare Corp.

Customer relations problems stemming from reportedly overengineered products that were hard to use have hurt Technicare. It has lost $110 million since 1979, according to Larry N. Feinberg, an analyst at Dean Witter Reynolds Inc. In computer-assisted-tomography (CAT) scanners, these difficulties helped General Electric Co. to snatch the top spot away from Technicare.

Some outsiders predict the same thing could happen with MR machines, which GE just started selling.

Burke acknowledges that his company's record in medical equipment is undistinguished, grading the efforts anywhere "from E-minus to A-plus." But he says: "One of the things we insist on here is that everybody understands part of their job is to fail. You don't move forward unless you make mistakes." The willingness to admit problems and try to learn from them is a J & J strength. The key question, however, is whether the company can apply the lessons to its new businesses.

More than one successful CEO has found that changing his company's mix of businesses is a lot easier than changing managers' attitudes. William T. Ylvisaker succeeded in transforming Gould Inc. into an electronics company only by replacing dozens of key managers. At Emerson Electric Co., a corporate culture that made a religion of cost-cutting and the bottom line threatens Charles F. Knight's ambitions in high tech. And Ruben F. Mettler has experienced some problems getting TRW Inc.'s divisions to share their expertise so the company can make maximum use of its considerable technological strengths.

J & J is discovering that developing and marketing high-tech equipment requires markedly different management skills than selling the products that generated its rapid growth. J & J was founded in 1885 by three Johnson brothers. But the next generation—in the person of "the General," Robert Wood Johnson—is most responsible for shaping the company into its present form. Under the General's rule from 1938 to 1963, the decentralized structure that is J & J's hallmark took shape, and the company introduced many of its most dominant products.

PILLS VS. HARDWARE

The General also wrote the corporate cre-

do, which states that J & J's first responsibility is not to shareholders or employees but to "the doctors, nurses, patients, to mothers, and all others" who use its products. While many high-minded statements of corporate purpose are written and forgotten, J & J's is not.

That tradition may also explain why, despite Burke's ambitions in new technologies, virtually all of the 14 members of J & J's executive committee have consumer-marketing or pharmaceutical backgrounds. And all have been at the company at least 11 years.

After a stint at Procter & Gamble Co., Burke joined J & J in 1953 and rose through the marketing ranks to become chairman in 1976. Initially, Burke ran the Band-Aid, dental-floss, and first-aid-kit businesses. As chairman, he personally led the marketing campaign to revive Tylenol. And colleagues say Burke foresaw the shift of emphasis in health care to early detection and prevention of illness.

Because its strength is in making and marketing consumer products, some competitors and J & J alumni doubt the company can become a leader in medical equipment. "What pill people have done well in hardware, and what hardware people have done well in pills?" asks GE's chairman, John F. Welch Jr. "The road is strewn with people who have gone far afield [from the businesses they really know]."

The lack of experience in medical equipment probably helps explain why Burke has moved cautiously in the field. At $74 million, J & J's acquisition of Technicare is its largest. And even though research-and-development spending has doubled since 1979, and will continue to rise, there is a limit to J & J's daring.

In MR scanners, for instance, GE's Welch makes no bones about his willingness to spend whatever it takes to be the leader. Technicare President Joseph G. Teague, however, says: "We don't have it as a realistic strategy to be No. 1" in the U.S. in several years. Matching GE's expenditures dollar for dollar, he adds, could be "frivolous and very expensive."

The questions of J & J's ability to make it in medical equipment go far beyond its financial commitment. More important is whether it has the management talent. The company's only clear high-tech success is Iolab Corp., the $50 million maker of lenses that are implanted after the surgical removal of cataracts.

Although J & J installed its own man, John R. Gilbert, as president about a year after buying Iolab, he has demonstrated a willingness to use new management approaches. He spent considerable time learning the manufacturing process, talking to physicians, and questioning the company's founders, who had left—on amicable terms. Iolab's results have been impressive: Sales have jumped nearly fivefold since the acquisition. If J & J had tried to manage Iolab like one of its more established companies, "we would have failed," concedes Herbert G. Stolzer, Gilbert's boss on J & J's executive committee.

J & J's attempts to manage other medical equipment acquisitions have not been similarly successful. Like many big companies, it has had trouble keeping the entrepreneurs who build the acquired companies. "The thinking is, perhaps understandably, 'Follow us, we have the keys to the kingdom,' " says one alumnus. J & J's financial systems and controls so bothered some managers at Extracorporeal, for instance, that they left, former J & Jers say. "That drives a lot of entrepreneurs crazy," concedes Burke.

Nothing better illustrates that the J & J system does not always contain the keys to the kingdom than its experience with Extracorporeal's dialysis business. Soon after J & J bought the company in 1978, prices for dialyzers—the filters used to clean blood—plunged as the government limited medicare reimbursements. When cost-conscious customers began reusing dialyzers, J

& J found itself at a disadvantage, because competitors' products could be prepared for reuse more easily.

'SEA CHANGE'

J & J failed to adapt. As Burke explains it, J & J is so accustomed to selling products used once—often in sterile environments— "that it was appalling to us to think that those things would become reusable."

The kind of cooperation and communication that Burke deems essential for all J & J companies also has been alien to its culture. Burke believes that sharing R & D and marketing resources is a key to speeding product development. That, he says, will enable J & J to regain share in such traditional markets as hospital supplies and to exploit new opportunities created by the movement toward preventive health care. For example, he says, combining J & J's expertise in magnetic resonance and biotechnology could revolutionize diagnostics.

But even Burke acknowledges that persuading divisions to work together has required "a sea change in attitude" for J & J managers so used to independence. One J & J unit, notes J & J President David R. Clare, even refused to take managers from other J & J companies.

Burke and Clare have moved to break down the walls. They have increased the movement of managers between companies and placed more importance on corporate-level committees whose function is to facilitate the exchange of information between companies.

But mixed signals from the top have left some divisional managers confused about just how committed to togetherness their leaders are. A case in point: Johnson & Johnson Products, which sells bandages and splints; Surgikos, a maker of surgical gowns and disinfectants; and Ethicon, the suture division, recently proposed that the three package their products in a customized surgical kit. But to their frustration, the divisions' managers have yet to secure New Brunswick's approval.

So it is no surprise that as J & J top managers preach the gospel of cooperation, some in their congregation react with more skepticism than faith. Nowhere is this more evident than in New Brunswick's tribulations in inducing its hospital-supply companies to work together—an effort one former J & J executive dubs "the company's single biggest move away from decentralization."

In a belated attempt to respond to increasing hospital cost-consciousness and the inroads American Hospital Supply Corp. has made into its business, J & J created its Hospital Services Co., which is giving volume discounts to some 24 hospitals on products from seven J & J companies. Crucial to making the plan pay off will be the likely development of a central, computerized ordering system that should considerably reduce customer paperwork and, finally, match what its competition created in 1976.

LESS GRUMBLING

Some J & J managers have resisted the effort long past a sensible point. "People got fired for not supporting [Hospital Services]," says a former J & Jer who did stints in three of the companies involved. Although J & J denies this, it concedes that managers at Ethicon were resistant to change. Edward J. Hartnett, a company group chairman in New Brunswick, says, "The feeling was, 'I don't really need it.'"

Perhaps because centralization is such a sensitive issue at J & J, Burke and Clare sharply deny that Hospital Services is even a baby step in that direction. The companies involved in the effort will maintain separate sales forces—an indication that the two executives understand that instilling a cooperative spirit will take patience and time. Clare points to J & J's Absorbent Technology Group—a four-company effort to develop products for several markets—as an exam-

ple of how hostility fades once a payback is evident. Clare himself had to muscle the companies into participating. But now that the group has three products under development, grumbling has diminished.

Burke and Clare have plenty of time. While some consumer markets, such as Band-Aids, are maturing, they are still solidly profitable. Indeed, J & J's 1981 withdrawal from the U.S. disposable-diaper market is the exception rather than the rule. In the last year, J & J rolled out a record six consumer products, ranging from a shampoo for the more brittle hair of women over 40 to a disposable dust cloth that eliminates the need for sprays.

J & J's record in pharmaceuticals demonstrates that there are areas of high science and technology that it indisputably knows how to manage. The $1.2 billion combined sales of its four pharmaceutical divisions make J & J the fifth-largest drug company in the U.S. More than 40% of its R & D spending, which last year totaled $405 million, or 6.8% of sales, went to pharmaceuticals. Such investments already appear to be bearing fruit: J & J now has twice as many new drugs undergoing animal testing as it did five years ago.

Indeed, as significant as the internal challenges at J & J are, another important one comes from without—namely, government efforts to curtail hospital expenditures on sophisticated medical hardware. Burke argues that such hardware can identify health problems before they become catastrophic—and catastrophically expensive to treat.

But given uncertainties clouding the medical technology markets, GE's Welch cautions that the wisest strategy is simply to have "the best. There's no room for the third-best machine." In hardware, Welch scoffs that J & J is no match for GE. His advice to Burke: "People who go afar from what they know run into some ground holes." Burke's challenge is to prove J & J can climb out of them.

41

That's Easy for You to Say

It all began on labor day weekend in 1982. Allan A. Kennedy was sitting in a low beach chair on the shore in front of his cottage on Cape Cod. Next to him was his friend and fellow consultant Tony Merlo. As they relaxed there, watching the sailboats drift across Cape Cod Bay, drinking beer, and listening to a Red Sox game on the radio, Kennedy turned to Merlo and, with the majestic eloquence suited to great undertakings, said: "Gee, Tony, you know, we ought to start some kind of business together."

This identical thought has, of course, passed between countless friends ever since the discovery of profit margins. Coming from most people, it would have fallen into the general category of loose talk. But Kennedy was not most people. For one thing, he was a 13-year veteran of McKinsey & Co., the management consulting firm, and partner in charge of its Boston office. More to the point, he was the co-author of a recently published book that offered a startling new perspective on corporate life—one that challenged the whole way people thought about business.

The book was entitled *Corporate Cultures*, a term that was itself new to the language, and it dealt with an aspect of business that, up to then, had been largely ignored. Broadly speaking, that aspect involved the role played by a company's values, symbols, rites, and rituals in determining its overall performance. Citing examples from some of the country's most dynamic companies, Kennedy and co-author Terrence E. Deal showed that these "cultural" factors had a major effect on the attitudes and behavior of a company's employees, and were thus of critical importance to its long-term success.

By any measure, the book was a groundbreaking work, challenging, as it did, the rational, quantitative models of corporate success that were so popular in the 1960s and '70s. But its impact had as much to do with its timing as its content. Published in June 1982, during a period of economic stagnation—with unemployment at 9.5%, the prime over 16%, and trade deficits soaring to record levels—*Corporate Cultures* offered a welcome antidote to the doom and

Prepared by Lucien Rhodes. Reprinted with the permission of *INC.* Magazine, June 1986. Copyright © 1986 by INC. Publishing Company, 38 Commercial Wharf, Boston, MA 02110.

gloom that was abroad in the land. Like *In Search of Excellence*, which appeared a few months later, it suggested that Japan was not the only nation capable of producing strong, highly motivated companies that could compete effectively in the international arena. America could produce—in fact, was already producing—its own.

What the book did not detail, however, was how corporate cultures were actually constructed. The authors could describe a particular culture and demonstrate its effects, but they offered few clues as to how a company might develop a culture in the first place. So the news that Allan Kennedy was going into business was greeted with more than passing interest among the followers of corporate culture. Here was an opportunity to find out how a living, breathing culture could be created, and the creator would be none other than the man who wrote the book.

After an extensive survey of business opportunities, Kennedy and Merlo decided to develop microcomputer software for sales and marketing management. They felt this was their most promising option, given the anticipated growth of the microcomputer market and their own experience as consultants. Acting on that assessment, they resigned from McKinsey and, in February 1983, formally launched Selkirk Associates Inc. with four of their friends.

Kennedy had lofty ambitions for Selkirk. More than a business, he saw it as a kind of laboratory for his theories. He wanted it to function as a society of professional colleagues committed to building a culture and a company that would stress collaboration, openness, decentralization, democratic decisions, respect, and trust. In this society, each individual would be encouraged to devise his or her own entrepreneurial response to the challenges of the business.

For Kennedy, this was not a long-term goal, something that would evolve naturally in the fullness of time. On the contrary, it was a pressing, immediate concern. Ac-

cordingly, he focused all his attention on creating such a culture from the start. "I spent lots of time," he says, "trying to think about what kind of values the company ought to stand for and therefore what kind of behavior I expected from people." These thoughts eventually went into a detailed statement of "core beliefs," which he reviewed and amplified with each new employee. In the same vein, Kennedy and his colleagues chose a "guiding principle," namely, a commitment to "making people more productive." They would pursue this ambition, everyone agreed, "through the products and services we offer" and "in the way we conduct our own affairs."

And, in the beginning at least, Selkirk seemed to be everything Kennedy had hoped for. The company set up shop in Boston, in an office that consisted of a large, rectangular room, with three smaller attachments. Each morning, staff members would pile into the main room and sort themselves out by function—programmers and systems engineers by the windows; administrators in the middle; sales and marketing folk at the other end. In keeping with Kennedy's cultural precepts, there were no private offices or, indeed, any physical demarcations between functions.

It was a familial enterprise, informed with the very qualities Kennedy had laid out in his statement of core beliefs. The work was absorbing, the comradeship inspiring. Most mornings, the staff feasted on doughnuts, which they took to calling "corporate carbos," as a wordplay on "corporate cultures." They began a scrapbook as an impromptu cultural archive. Included among the memorabilia was "The Ravin'," an Edgar Allan Poe takeoff that commemorated Selkirk's first stirrings in earlier temporary headquarters:

Once upon an April morning,
   disregarding every warning,
In a Back Bay storefront,
   Selkirk software was begun:

True, it was without a toilet,

    but that didn't seem to spoil it.

To strengthen their bonds even further, the staff began to experiment with so-called rites, rituals, and ceremonies—all important elements of a corporate culture, according to Kennedy's book. Selkirk's office manager, Linda Sharkey, recalls a day, for example, when the whole company went out to Kennedy's place on Cape Cod to celebrate their common purpose with barbecues on the beach. "The sun was shining, and we were all there together," she says. "It was a beautiful day. That's the way it was. We didn't use the terms among ourselves that Allan uses in the book. With us, corporate culture was more by seeing and doing." Sharkey remembers, too, Friday afternoon luncheons of pizza or Chinese food, at which everyone in the company had a chance to talk about his or her accomplishments or problems, or simply hang out.

Kennedy was pleased with all this, as well he might be. "We were," he says, "beginning to develop a real culture."

Then the walls went up.

The problem stemmed from the situation in the big room, where the technical people were laboring feverishly to develop Selkirk's first product, while the salespeople were busy preselling it. The former desperately needed peace and quiet to concentrate on their work; the latter were a boisterous lot, fond of crowing whenever a prospect looked encouraging. In fact, the salespeople crowed so often and so loudly that the technicians complained that they were being driven to distraction. Finally, they confronted Kennedy with the problem. Their solution, which Kennedy agreed to, was to erect five-foot-high movable partitions, separating each functional grouping from the others.

In the memory of Selkirk veterans, "the day the walls went up" lives on as a day of infamy. "It was terrible," says Sharkey. "I was embarrassed."

"It was clearly a symbol of divisiveness," says Kennedy.

"I don't know what would have been the right solution," says Reilly Hayes, Selkirk's 23-year-old technical wizard, "but the wall certainly wasn't. It blocked out the windows for the other end of the room. Someone [in marketing] drew a picture of a window and taped it to the wall. The whole thing created a lot of dissension."

Indeed, the erection of the walls touched off a feud between engineering and marketing that eventually grew into "open organizational warfare," according to Kennedy. "I let the wall stand, and a competitive attitude developed where engineering started sniping at marketing. We had two armed camps that didn't trust each other."

As if that weren't bad enough, other problems were beginning to surface. For one thing, the company was obviously overstaffed, having grown from 12 people in June 1983 to 25 in January 1984, without any product—or sales—to show for it. "That was a big mistake," says Kennedy. "We clearly ramped up the organization too fast, particularly given the fact that we were financing ourselves. I mean, for a while, we had a burn rate of around $100,000 per month."

Even more serious, however, was the problem that emerged following the release of the company's initial product, Correspondent, in February 1984. Not that there was anything wrong with the product. It was, in fact, a fine piece of software, and it premiered to glowing reviews. Designed as a selling tool, it combined database management, calendar management, word processing, and mail merge—functions that could help customers organize their accounts, track and schedule sales calls and follow-ups, and generate correspondence. And it did all that splendidly.

The problem had to do with the price tag, a whopping $12,000 per unit. The Selkirk team members had come up with this rarefied figure, not out of greed, but out of a commitment to customer service—a goal to which they had pledged themselves as part of their cultural mission. In order to provide such service, they figured, a Selkirk representative might have to spend two or three weeks with each customer, helping to install and customize the product. Trouble was, customers weren't willing to *pay* for that service, not at $12,000 per unit anyway. After a brief flurry of interest, sales dropped off.

"We just blew it," says Kennedy. "We were arrogant about the market. We were trying to tell the market something it wasn't interested in hearing. We took an arbitrary cultural goal and tried to make it into a strategy rather than saying we're a market-driven company and we've got to find out what the market wants and supply it." Unfortunately, six months went by before Kennedy and his colleagues figured all this out and began to reduce Correspondent's price accordingly.

By then, however, Selkirk's entire sales effort was in shambles, a victim of its commitment to employee autonomy. Sales targets were seldom realized. Indeed, they were scarcely even set. At weekly meetings, salespeople would do little more than review account activity. "If a salesman said each week for three weeks in a row that he expected to close a certain account, and it never happened," says Merlo, "well, we didn't do anything about it. In any other company, he would probably have been put on probation." As it was, each of the participants entered the results of the meeting in a red-and-black ledger book and struck out once again to wander haphazardly through uncharted territory. "The mistake we made," reflects Merlo, "was using real money in a real company to test hypotheses about what sales goals should be."

Finally, in June 1984, Kennedy took action, laying off 6 people. In July, Correspondent's price was dropped to $4,000 per unit, but sales remained sluggish. In Sep-

tember, Kennedy laid off 5 more people, bringing the size of the staff back to 12.

One of those laid off was the chief engineer, a close friend of Kennedy's, but a man whose departure brought an immediate ceasefire between the warring factions. That night, the remaining staff members took down the walls and stacked them neatly in the kitchenette, where they repose to this day. "We felt," says Sharkey, "like we had our little family back together again."

With morale finally rebounding, Selkirk again cut Correspondent's price in the early fall, to $1,500. This time, sales responded, and, in November, the company enjoyed its first month in the black.

But Selkirk was not yet out of the woods. What remained was for Kennedy to figure out the significance of what had happened, and to draw the appropriate conclusions. Clearly, his experiment had not turned out as he had planned. His insistence on a company without walls had led to organizational warfare. His goal of providing extraordinary service had led to a crucial pricing error. His ideal of employee autonomy had led to confusion in the sales force. In the end, he was forced to fire more than half of his staff, slash prices by 87%, and start over again. What did it all mean?

Merlo had one answer. "We're talking about an experiment in corporate culture failing because the business environment did not support it," he says. "The notion of corporate culture got in the way of tough-minded business decisions." He also faults the emphasis on autonomy. "I don't think we had the right to be organized the way we were. I think we should have had more discipline."

Kennedy himself soon came around to a similar view. "Look in [the statement of core beliefs] and tell me what you find about the importance of performance, about measuring performance or about the idea that people must be held accountable for their performance," he says. "That stuff should have been there. I'm not discounting the importance of corporate culture, but you have to worry about the business at the same time, or you simply won't have one. Then you obviously won't *need* a culture. Where the two come together, I think, is in the cultural norms for performance, what kind of performance is expected of people. And that's a linkage that wasn't explicit in my mind three years ago. But it is now." He adds that, if the manuscript of *Corporate Cultures* were before him today, he would include a section on performance standards, measurement systems, and accountability sanctions.

On that point, he might get an argument from his co-author, Terrence Deal, a professor at Vanderbilt University and a member of Selkirk's board of directors since its inception. Deal does not disagree about the importance of discipline and performance standards, but he questions the wisdom of trying to impose them from above. The most effective performance standards, he notes, are the ones that employees recognize and accept as the product of their own commitment, and these can emerge only from the employees' experience. "One of the things that we know pretty handsomely," says Deal, "is that it's the informal performance standards that really drive a company."

In fact, Kennedy may have gotten into trouble not by doing too little, but by doing too much. Rather than letting Selkirk's culture evolve organically, he tried to impose a set of predetermined cultural values on the company, thereby retarding the growth of its own informal value system. He pursued culture as an end in itself, ignoring his own caveat, set down in his book, that "the business environment is the single greatest influence in shaping a corporate culture." Instead, he tried to shape the culture in a vacuum, without synchronizing it with the company's business goals.

In so doing, Kennedy reduced corporate culture to a formula, a collection of generic "principles." It was a cardinal error, if not an uncommon one. "There are a lot of people," says Deal, "who take our book literally and try to design a culture much as if they're trying to design an organization chart. My experience across the board has been that, as soon as people make it into a formula, they start making mistakes." By following the "formula," Kennedy wound up imposing his own set of rules on Selkirk—although not enough of them, and not the right kind, he now says. The irony is that a real corporate culture allows a company to manage itself *without* formal rules, and to manage itself better than a company that has them.

Deal makes another point. Kennedy, he observes, might be less concerned with performance today if he had not hired so many friends at the beginning. Friends are nice to have around, but it's often hard to discipline them, or subject them to a company's normal sanctions. Over the long run, Deal says, their presence at Selkirk probably undermined the development of informal performance standards.

Kennedy himself may have played a role in that, too. He estimates that, over the past year, he has spent only one day a week at Selkirk. The rest of the time he has been on the road as a consultant, using his fees to help finance the company. In all, he has sunk some $1 million of his own money into Selkirk, without which the company might not have survived. But it has come at a price. "Nobody had to pay attention to things like expenses, because there was a perception of an infinite sink of money," Kennedy says.

The danger of that perception finally came home to him last summer, when three of Selkirk's four salespeople elected to take vacations during the same month. The result was that sales for the month all but vanished. Kennedy had had enough. "I told the people here that either you sustain the company as a self-financing entity, or I will let it go under. I'm unwilling to put more money on the table."

And yet, in the end, it was hard to avoid the conclusion that a large part of Selkirk's continuing problem was Allan Kennedy himself—a thought that did not escape him. "I've got a lot to learn about running a business successfully," he says, "about doing it myself, I mean. I think I know everything about management except how to manage. I can give world-class advice on managing, but—when it comes right down to it—I take too long and fall into all the traps that I see with the managers I advise."

Whatever his shortcomings as a manager, there is one thing Kennedy can't be faulted for, and that is lack of courage. Having drawn the inevitable conclusion, he went out looking for someone who could help him do a better job of managing the company. For several months, he negotiated with the former president of a Boston-based high-tech firm, but the two of them were unable to come to terms. Instead, Kennedy has made changes at Selkirk that he hopes will achieve the same effect. In the new structure, Merlo is taking charge of the microcomputer end of the business, while Betsy Meade—a former West Coast sales representative—has responsibility for a new minicomputer version of Correspondent, to be marketed in conjunction with Prime Computer Corp. As for Kennedy, he will concern himself with external company relations, product-development strategies, and, of course, corporate culture.

Kennedy is full of optimism these days.

He points out that, despite its checkered history, Selkirk has emerged with a durable product and an installed base of about 1,000 units. In addition, the company will soon be bolstered with the proceeds from a $250,000 private placement. Meanwhile, he says, some of the company's previous problems have been dealt with, thanks to the introduction of a reliable order-fulfillment process, the decision to put sales reps on a straight commission payment schedule, and the establishment of specific sales targets for at least the next two quarters. "I think we have much more focused responsibility," he says, "and much more tangible measures of success for people in their jobs."

Overall, Kennedy looks on the past three years as a learning experience. "There are times when I think I should charge up most of the zigs and the zags to sheer rank incompetence," he admits. "But then there are other times when I look back and say, 'Nobody's that smart, and you can't do everything right.' In life, you have to be willing to try things. And if something doesn't work, you have to be willing to say, 'Well, that was a dumb idea,' and then try something else." Now, he believes, he has a chance to do just that.

In the meantime, he is in the process of writing another book. He already has a proposal circulating among publishers. In his idle moments, he occasionally amuses himself by inventing titles. One of those titles speaks volumes about where he has been: *Kicking Ass and Taking Names.*

42

Culture Shock

"Tell us the bicycle story," a voice called out to the man in the pin-striped suit standing at the front of the room.

"No-o, not the bicycle story," another voice moaned.

It was early on the first Friday evening of September 1984, and 90-some employees of Sequent Computer Systems Inc. and their spouses and friends, in ties and jackets and silk dresses, were sitting on the carpet like kindergartners.

"You really want to hear it?" the man in the suit asked incredulously. He had sandy hair, a beard, thick glasses, and two buttons on his lapel; one said "Sequent=Easy to Do Business With," the other, "Casey Powell." He was Sequent's president. That afternoon, the Portland, Ore., company had introduced its first product, a new type of supermicrocomputer, and Powell had just shown an abbreviated version of the slide show he had been taking around to editors and industry gurus all week. The box itself, about the size of a dorm-room refrigerator, blinked red lights from a table behind him. There was wine to drink, stuffed mush-

rooms to eat, and five kinds of cheesecake in the next room, yet the people in front of him were asking for what sounded like a bedtime story.

"No," yelled a chorus of voices.

Powell cleared his throat, and several people reached for their wine.

"I'll tell the short version," he said, hooking his thumbs behind his lapels.

"Boy," said Powell. "Bicycle. One hundred dollars." People laughed.

The long version began "Once upon a time," and most people at Sequent knew it by heart. It was a hokey story Powell had made up about a little boy who wanted a bicycle more than anything else in the world—and not just any old two-wheeler, but a "very flashy bike" that cost $100. Being "a real process person," this boy set himself "measurable goals" to make sure that at the end of the year he would have enough money to buy his bicycle. He figured that, giving himself two weeks off for vacation, he needed to save $2 a week, or 40¢ a day, or 5¢ an hour to earn the money in a year. The moral, of course, was the

Prepared by Susan Benner. Reprinted with the permission of *INC.* Magazine, August 1985. Copyright © 1985 by INC. Publishing Company, 38 Commercial Wharf, Boston MA 02110.

importance of setting goals and working hard for what you want.

Powell never told the end of the story— even the beginning had become a joke— but it was still a company ritual. Whenever Sequent reached a goal, a nickel would be dropped ceremoniously into a special jar.

For this particular occasion, Sequent's engineers had planned to buy a bicycle, which they would pass on to the marketing group to symbolize the transfer of responsibility for the company's progress. But money was tight, so Roger Swanson, the director of software, had borrowed a Schwinn Pixie from his daughter Kris. Swanson had attached plastic bugs to the handlebars, representing the problems the software people still had to work out. When Powell was finished with the story, Swanson wheeled out the bicycle and handed it over to Barbara Slaughter, the director of marketing.

People clapped, then stood up and wandered back to the wine and the stuffed mushrooms. "No, I'm *not* going to ride it," Slaughter said. "I'm wearing a skirt."

For an anthropologist trying to define the "corporate culture" at Sequent Computer Systems, the bicycle story would be a good place to start. Like much of the rest of Sequent's culture, Powell's fable was manipulative, self-conscious, even silly—and carefully thought out to focus the attention of every person in the room where management wanted it, on the achievement of yet another milestone on the company's planned path to success.

An industrial Margaret Mead wouldn't have to stop with nickels and bicycles, however. There would be all kinds of strange artifacts and rituals to examine.

Take the red light on the manufacturing floor, which gets turned on whenever anyone finds a quality problem on a production line. The entire line then shuts down, with the red light burning day and night until the problem is solved.

Or take the objects displayed in the glass case next to the computer room: the Dom Perignon bottle that was emptied after the company was named for the second time; the photo of all the dogs, kids, spouses, and employees at the company's first annual camping trip; the silver baseball bat used by Gary Fielland, Sequent's computer architect, to tap the people he needed for the second product.

Sequent even held "culture classes." Three days before the company was to ship its first product, 22 employees spent an entire working day in a local motel talking about shaping their company's culture. "No" was not an acceptable R.S.V.P., even if the software wasn't debugged yet.

But most of all, a visiting anthropologist with his or her eyes even slightly open would soon see that at Sequent—beyond any single artifact or ritual—the culture *is* the company. As Barbara Slaughter puts it, "We really believe it's how we work together, not our technology, that's going to make or break us."

Casey Powell has never read any of the popular Business Books he classifies as "how to books." But he and the rest of the people at Sequent are refining the management of corporate culture into a high art. They believe that the environment a company provides for its employees is the key factor in how well they work together to achieve company goals. From the beginning of Sequent's two-plus years of existence, Powell and his three vice-presidents, Scott Gibson, Dave Rodgers, and Larry Wade—along with Barbara Gaffney, the company's human resources director— made culture a deliberate priority, and they have nurtured Sequent's values, heroes, and rituals as carefully as a parent nurtures a child.

It makes you wonder where the dedication came from.

On a Tuesday morning in the fall of 1982, Casey Powell flew down from Oregon to the Santa Clara, Calif., headquarters of Intel Corp., one of the world's leading semiconductor companies, where he was then employed. A boyish-looking 37-year-old general manager who had joined Intel seven years earlier as a salesman, Powell was four months into what was perhaps the biggest challenge of his career—the turnaround of a $100-million microprocessor operation.

The turnaround was crucial to Intel. The microprocessor operation represented 10% of the company's total revenues, and that summer, IBM had announced it was dropping Intel's latest microprocessor product, the 8086, to use a competitive chip in its Displaywriter. Intel management was nervous. The semiconductor industry was in a slump, and for the second year in a row, profit margins were a fraction of what the company liked to consider the norm. Powell had 30 minutes at an executive staff meeting to explain how he intended to proceed.

Powell knew that several of the executives present thought he could do his job better if he moved to California. Although the operational part of the job was based in Oregon, the marketing program, known as Operation Checkmate, was corporate, and the executives had wanted him to lead it from headquarters. Powell had told them that he would not move. He had moved for Intel twice in the past three years; he had been in Oregon only 16 months, and his daughters were just beginning to learn their friends' last names. Although he thought Intel was one of the best-managed companies in the world, and wanted to continue his rise within it, he and his wife liked the more traditional values of the Pacific Northwest and did not want to raise their children in the Bay Area.

Powell is a natural performer, with a salesman's love of telling stories and a stage actor's feel for an audience, and he generally enjoys presentations, even the tough, confrontational kind for which Intel had earned some notoriety. He appreciated Intel's emphasis on achievement and the formal management-by-objective system that allowed ambitious managers like himself to set high goals for themselves, then earn the rewards of reaching them. Although his turnaround was taking longer than expected, Powell was sure that Operation Checkmate would work. His task that day was to convince the rest of management that he was right.

At Intel, such grilling of managers is officially called "constructive confrontation"; privately, it is called "destructive confrontations," "guerrilla warfare," and "table pounding." Although the intensity of the inquisitions is sometimes hard on newcomers and the thin-skinned, most Intelites are proud of their willingness to point out weaknesses in one another's thinking, and they enjoy working for an organization that demands high performance. So it didn't surprise Powell when one of the executives interrupted his presentation to ask questions. What was surprising was the direction the questioning soon took.

As the Intel inner circle cringed, a second, very senior executive started asking a series of questions that were, according to one of the men present, "depersonalizing." The tone was that of an officer berating a cadet who hadn't done his homework, and the message was tied in their minds to Powell's unwillingness to move to the Bay Area. They say they will never forget the faces.

Here was Powell—a loyal, hardworking employee who had done well on the Intel grading system ever since he joined the company—standing in front of them saying "Yes, sir" and "No, sir" as if he were back in military school. And here was a senior executive lighting into him in a way that the most battle-hardened Intel veterans found too painful to watch. Finally, two of them told the executive that if he wished to continue this line of questioning, he should do it somewhere else. The executive called a break, and everyone left the room. In the hall he apologized, but Powell, according to friends, was so upset that he turned around without saying anything and walked off.

It was one of the few times Intel veterans can recall a "constructive confrontation" turning into a personal attack. The outburst would serve as a reminder of what could happen when the pressure got so intense that people forgot a basic tenet of a management-by-objective system, which is the faith that talented people, given an objective and the freedom to do things the way they think best, will produce results. It changed Casey Powell's life—and, as it turned out, the lives of a lot of other people as well.

Powell refuses to comment on this incident for publication, but shortly afterward, he told a friend that he was going to execute the marketing plan in the manner outlined in the meeting, and then quit. The senior executive later apologized again, and praised the marketing effort as one of the best ever executed at Intel. But Powell never looked back.

He realized that he was tired of solving problems that were the result of someone else not doing something right. So when a venture capitalist asked if he would like to try turning around a troubled company, Powell said he would rather deal with his own mistakes. He decided to start a company that would: a) provide him with a job in Oregon; b) enable him to work quickly and efficiently, which was one of the things he liked about Intel; c) give him the opportunity to satisfy professional goals without sacrificing his family; and d) create a working environment that would motivate people as well as Intel did without beating them up.

It was an ambitious agenda, but Powell set about making it happen in a very systematic way. Over the next several months, while still working at Intel, he approached a number of the people he wanted to help him. He was looking not only for outstanding track records and talents, but for people who shared his values.

The first person he talked to was Scott Gibson, a 30-year-old boy wonder from the Midwest who years earlier had become Intel's youngest general manager. Gibson was extremely bright and possessed of an enormous capacity for detail that complemented Powell's intuitive management style; he was also interested in building a company that valued both people and achievement. Systems architect Gary Fielland had a streak of pragmatism that let him focus his inventiveness on the kind of product an embryonic company needed. Larry Wade, another general manager who had spent much of his professional life at DEC, was looking for a way to make money and have fun—with fun defined as working with people he enjoyed and producing something beneficial to society.

After agreeing to work together, Powell, Gibson, Fielland, and Wade quickly and discreetly chose 13 other Intel employees and one engineer who was working as a consultant in England.

On January 17, 1983, all 17 Intel-ites resigned.

That night, they celebrated at the Upper Level Pub, a bar at a nearby shopping mall. They sat at a long table in the back drinking beer and talking about the shock waves at the company, the attempts to get them to stay, and the local TV coverage describing them as "the cream of the crop" at Intel. One of the first toasts of the evening was about allowing the simultaneous accomplishment of company goals and personal objectives. The last toast was made as the sun came up.

There were 15 men and three women, ranging in age from 23 to 39, wearing everything from pinstripes and shined loafers to T-shirts and running shoes. Some were close friends, some knew each other only by reputation. All had agreed to buy stock, to work for as long as six months without salary while the company lined up financing, and to do whatever was necessary to make the company succeed. For months, this included taking home the company garbage in large plastic bags; there was no dumpster on the premises.

Within days, they had arranged a lease on a "deathlike space" in Portland recently vacated by a company on the road to bankruptcy. They negotiated what they came to call "very special terms"—six months use for free—persuading the owners that they would benefit later when Sequent got its financing.

That first Saturday they held a "Name the Company" party to which they invited family, friends, business associates, and *The New York Times*. More than 100 people ate, drank, and wrote suggestions on large paper banners hung on the walls. They vetoed such names as Trillium, Topaz, and Osprey, settling on Sequel, the name of a local rock band.

After the party, they gathered to write down their corporate objectives. Powell was the Thomas Jefferson, holding the pen longer than anyone else. Ten drafts later, they came up with six objectives, involving profitability, customer satisfaction, market domination, "a culture that rewards our employees for their contributions," "an organization that provides individuals with the means to accept the maximum responsibility for the overall success of their company," and acceptance of community responsibility.

During the next two months, they worked on their business plan and negotiated for various necessities of life—furniture, telephones, a copy machine, legal and accounting advice, and a VAX computer—all on "very special terms."

In April a group of well-known venture capitalists, led by Reid Dennis of Institutional Venture Partners, agreed to pay an unprecedented $5.2 million for 35% of a company that consisted of 19 people and a business plan the size of a small-town telephone book.

At the end of the month, the founders received their first paychecks, for $1, suitably framed for hanging in cubicles.

By then, they had begun work in earnest on their first product. It was to be a multiprocessor parallel computer, meaning that a number of microprocessors were to be put into one box and linked together with software and hardware. Although other companies had put more than one microprocessor in a box before, each microprocessor had been dedicated to a particular function. Sequent's machine was to be the first in which the microprocessors could work either on the same task at the same time or on different tasks at the same time. The low-end configuration (2 processors) was to be competitive with workstations. The high-end (later determined to be 12 processors) was to be competitive with superminicomputers, and even, it turned out, with the low-end of Cray Research—type mainframes.

Powell and his crew believed that they could carve out a significant market for their computer, but to do so, they had to get there first, with a quality machine. The pressure to produce was intense enough to strain any culture. Yet unlike so many other start-ups, Sequent never lost sight of the kind of company it had set out to build.

People took great care with recruiting, for example, and refused to change their style just because their need increased. "We saw a few people who fit our technical needs, but didn't really fit in," says Roger Swanson, the software director. "There was one case I remember very well. I was in need of a particular kind of engineer. Our schedules were beginning to slip because we didn't have the people. Larry Wade and I had a long talk about one fellow. I really needed this person. And Larry said, you know, it just doesn't feel right. This fellow was just too laid back. And I said, Larry, I have to agree with you when I think about it. But it was really hard to make those trade-offs."

The concern didn't stop once a person

signed on. Periodically, Barbara Gaffney, Sequent's unofficial minister of culture, led workshops in which about 20 employees would spend the day talking about whether the company was living up to its values.

One of those values dictated that there would be no walls between departments. Everyone, not just the managers, was expected to walk around the building to find out what was going on. Marketing people were expected to show their faces in engineering, engineers in manufacturing. People were expected to serve on cross-functional task forces, and got graded on cross-functional interactions during their performance reviews.

Scott Gibson—vice-president of operations and finance, and inventor of the red-light process—put his desk on the manufacturing floor.

At a cost of $2,500, Sequent installed a terminal in every employee's house so family members could talk to one another all day—and so employees could go home for dinner or to tuck in their children even when they had to work until midnight. There were family parties, camping trips, ski trips, and picnics. On weekends it was not unusual to find children crawling around on the carpets.

The company started a yearbook, written mostly by employees' spouses, with sections on people, kids, culture, and the year's significant events. The 1983 edition includes the bicycle story, complete with photo of Sequent's jar of nickels.

In order to foster a sense of shared responsibility, employee involvement in even the smallest decisions was encouraged. Barbara Gaffney once came back from a conference to find her office stacked with ice chests and cans of pop. It had been converted into a soda-tasting stall. It seems that as the company had grown, the percentage of vending-machine slots dedicated to natural drinks had declined, and one day a software engineer had rebelled. To find the best natural sodas to occupy the availa-

ble slots, Dave Rodgers, the vice-president of engineering, had organized a blind tasting. (The winner was Ol' Bob Miller's Natcherly sodas.)

Powell, meanwhile, played the symbolism of small events instinctively. Even at Intel, he had been the kind of manager who delegated operational and strategic responsibilities to top managers he trusted, leaving himself free to wander around the cubicle maze or the manufacturing floor or to make his own coffee. Now that he had his own company, he was as apt to talk about not leaving coffee rings on the furniture as to comment on the schedule. People could walk into his office any time—like everyone else, he had a cubicle with no door—and offer him a cookie, or sell him a mug to raise money for the yearbook or tell him they might not finish a particular task on the appointed day. Powell could bear down on a problem, but he would always offer to help, and then he would do what he said he would do, whether it was bringing in a pizza for the people who were working through dinner or buying an expensive engineering tool. Then he would let the people know that the life or death of the company depended on them getting their piece of the machine done on time.

It all added up to a carefully cultivated message that this company really cared.

What no one knew was, would it make any difference when the going *really* got tough?

By the fall of 1983, the walls had been painted, the floors carpeted, and the loaner furniture replaced with desks and chairs in the company colors—gray and cranberry. The head count had doubled, and the company name had been changed from Sequel to Sequent because of a trademark conflict. As people settled into a routine of working 60 to 80 hours a week, start-up life seemed to be living up to its promise—except that the hardware group was missing some of its deadlines. Not by much—a day here, a week there, two weeks somewhere else—

the kind of slippages that were said to go with the engineering territory at larger, more established companies.

But Sequent was neither large nor established.

Roger Shelton first heard that the hardware schedule was in serious trouble in early November. Like most of the other hardware engineers, Shelton had spent the previous few months buried in the design of his own piece of the machine, and although he was vaguely aware that "things were not happening as quickly as we had thought," he had not stopped to worry about the bigger picture.

Shelton, like everyone else at Sequent, had a computer terminal on his desk. Important messages were announced by the terminal with a little beep, then green letters would run across the screen in a ribbon like a news flash on television. Although most of the messages had something to do with food—the morning cookies have just come in, or there is popcorn in the kitchen—the message that Friday afternoon announced an ad hoc, all-employee meeting in the cafeteria.

There were not enough chairs, so most people stood. Powell was direct: They were behind. They were approaching a big, externally visible milestone—their first anniversary, a key board of directors meeting, and the deadline for providing the first physical proof that the company could do what it said it would do. If they kept moving at their current rate, the hardware would not be up and running until February 15, which was not good enough. They were starting to go out for their second round of financing, and beginning to talk to customers. They had to have working hardware by January 17.

Powell had talked to Gibson, Wade, and Rodgers, and they all thought it could be done. But it was going to take the help of every person in the company. This was not some big corporation where, if they were a month late, they were a month late. If this

hardware wasn't finished on time, their desks and chairs might go away. The bank might come for their terminals and their CAD machines.

To keep attention focused on the problem, Powell had had buttons made up. He and Gibson and Wade and most of the rest of the company would wear green "How Can I Help?" buttons. Rodgers and the engineers on the critical path would get red "Priority" buttons. People with green buttons were to do anything to remove obstacles for the people on the critical path, whether it was getting them coffee, registering their cars, or talking to the vendors that were supposed to be supplying them with parts and services. These were all obstacles, he said, all the same. All obstacles had to be removed.

Powell passed out the buttons, and everyone went back to work. The whole thing took less than 15 minutes. The buttons cost $73.50. And every person in the company now knew what had to be done.

Shelton went back to his desk with a red "Priority" button pinned to his shirt. Although Powell had presented the buttons as a device to make the rest of the company aware of the gravity of the situation, Shelton and the other hardware engineers got another not-so-subtle message. "I think it was a way to make sure we understood how important what we were doing was," explains one engineer.

"We were already working hard," says Shelton, "but now there was this sense of 'Gee, we really need to get done.'"

It was symbolic management in action. Powell hadn't solved the problem; in fact he hadn't even defined it. (Rodgers had done that in his regular meetings with the director of hardware and his wanderings around the engineering cubicles.) He had merely clarified the company's priorities and driven a stake into the ground.

Powell didn't even go to the second meeting, scheduled for the next day, a Saturday. Neither did Gibson or Wade. This meeting, which lasted three hours, was for the hardware engineers; their director, Walt Mayberry; their vice-president, Dave Rodgers; and two guests, Barbara Gaffney and Roger Swanson. Gaffney was there because she knew the people in the company well enough to suggest who might help. Swanson was offering the services of the software group.

Mayberry, a quiet man with glasses and carefully trimmed hair, started by presenting the historical data—how they had fallen behind—and the new schedule, which he described as "reasonably aggressive, but possible." But Shelton and most of the other hardware engineers thought the situation was out of their control. A hardware engineer designing a circuit board first develops a set of schematics that describe the logic of the board, then designs the placement of the components on the board. Then, at a small company like Sequent, he sends this design out to a layout vendor, which lays out the design to scale and makes a "physical interconnect" for the photographic mask from which the physical boards are fabricated. Shelton had sent out a board to a California vendor in September, and although the standard layout time was four to six weeks, the board had still not come back. Another vendor had laid out another engineer's design incorrectly and sent Sequent a chip that didn't work. The company would fix the chip, it said, but it would probably take another eight weeks. The engineers didn't see anything they could do.

What Powell, Gibson, Rodgers, and Wade were telling them, said Mayberry, was that the whole company was going to pitch in. It was OK to take risks, OK to spend money to get things done, OK to insist that the vendors deliver what was promised. Rodgers was working on the design. Gibson had volunteered to talk to vendors. But they needed the engineers to tell them where they could help.

One engineer said that if someone else could design a piece of test software, he could concentrate on a more critical task. Another engineer had once seen boards laid out in a week, but he was pretty sure it had cost a lot of money. They spent an awful lot of time in meetings, another engineer pointed out. As the engineers offered suggestions, Mayberry wrote them down. After the meeting was over, everyone went back to work.

They came in on Sunday, too. People had been working 12 hours a day, six days a week; now they came in seven days, and instead of going home at midnight, they stayed until two in the morning. Gone were the days when they could grab a sandwich and a couple of video games at the Inner Space Deli down the street. They had to look at their watches to figure out what day of the week it was. "Sometimes you'd be in a meeting and you'd find out the guy next to you hadn't been home for 24 hours," Mayberry says. People actually wore their buttons, and if a person with a "Priority" button had a question for a person with a "How Can I Help?" button, the "How Can I Help?" person dropped whatever he was doing.

Gibson flew down to talk to the layout vendor, and decided to start another company working on the same design. He visited other vendors, telling them Sequent's life depended on them. He offered cash bonuses to get them to complete the work in record time—2 weeks instead of 4 or 6 weeks, and once even 2 weeks instead of 12 weeks. When a vendor came through on a particularly tough schedule, Gibson sent the company a singing telegram.

Rodgers took off his tie, sat down in front of a terminal, and only got up to go to the bathroom and to find out what was going on. Every afternoon around four o'clock, he and Mayberry would stroll by the cubicle of each person with a red button and ask what that person had done that day. Was it what he had said he would do? Was it the most important thing? Did he have any problems? Could anyone help? It made an engineer think twice about talking for more than 30 seconds over a cup of coffee, or taking off more than 24 hours for Christmas.

The visits helped draw attention to the task that needed to be done—but they worked because the help offered was not just symbolic. When he had problems, Shelton says, "I told them what they were, and they fixed them. I'd say, 'We really need another logic analyzer, and it costs $18,000.' Or, 'We're standing around waiting to get onto the engineering work-stations, and they cost $60,000 or $90,000.' In 18 hours they'd get us a rental, and then if we really needed another one, they'd buy it. The people who control the money at most companies don't even know what the problems are."

Soon it was apparent that the group was catching up.

It was dark inside the cake, and Casey Powell was shivering.

The date was January 17, 1984, Sequent's first anniversary, and Powell had lost a bet.

By the end of December, when the hardware engineers were clearly making up lost time, Barbara Gaffney had decided the time was ripe for a small wager, which became known as "The Challenge." As keeper of the culture, Gaffney was partially responsible for seeing that company milestones were celebrated with all the ceremony the occasions warranted. She talked to Dave Rodgers, who was all in favor of the idea, provided the stakes were more humiliating than the usual dinner or lunch.

If the hardware group met its deadline. Rodgers suggested, they should make their president jump out of a cake with "due pomp, circumstance, and little else." Gaffney had the proposal drawn up with scrolls and flourishes. The document was signed by the hardware engineers and presented to Powell at a company meeting.

The deadline had been met. Now the hardware engineers—with a crowd of oth-

er Sequent employees, about 50 in all—were waiting in the manufacturing area to see him jump naked out of this cake.

"Wheel me out," Powell yelled. "I am not going to do this."

"I have a small piece of attire for you to use," said Dave Rodgers. The top of the cake was cracked open, and in floated a paper towel. Powell could hear the hardware engineers laughing.

"Will it cover?" Rodgers asked.

"Wheel me out," Powell yelled.

"No," Rodgers said. "This is it."

Flashbulbs popped, a videotape rolled, and one of the women looked away as Rodgers lifted the top of the cake, then opened the sides. The president of Sequent Computer Systems stood up wearing the red yarn wig, the bulbous red nose, and the puffy suit of Bozo the Clown.

"The real Casey Powell!" someone called out through the applause.

Lights reflected off Powell's glasses. He pushed up the mask, shook the hands of the hardware group, and said he had never had more pleasure losing a bet in his life. A champagne cork popped.

The hardware challenge was just the first of many. Sequent went on to complete its second round of financing for $7.5 million. There was a software challenge, and it was Roger Swanson's turn to buy the pizzas. In September, the company unveiled its first product, the Balance 8000, and began shipping units out for independent testing. In December, it shipped its first boxes for revenue. One potential investor called the testing companies and told Sequent that the evaluations he got were the best he had ever heard. Last March, Sequent completed its third round of financing for $10 million.

By this time, members of the sales force were working on yet another challenge, which would turn them into "bound serfs" at the next anniversary party if they didn't meet their sales goals. And Powell's Bozo wig had long since taken its place in the artifacts case, next to the Dom Perignon bottle.

"Was it really a motivator?" Mayberry reflects. "No. We did wheel in a cake. Casey did jump out. It was something to talk about. Some people thought it was a bit hokey. But it was a focus.

"In retrospect, it was an event in the corporate culture."

43

Measuring Excellence: Applying the Lessons of Peters and Waterman

Goals

I. To help participants identify an organization's degree of excellence.*

II. To heighten the participants' awareness of the effect of management attitudes and practices within organizations.

Group Size

Six to eight individuals preferably with different degrees of work experience.

Time Required

Approximately three and one-half hours (with optional activities).

Materials

I. A copy of the Measuring Excellence Theory Sheet for each participant.

II. A copy of the Measuring Excellence Work Sheet for each participant.

_____
* As defined by T. J. Peters and R. H. Waterman, Jr., in *In Search of Excellence: Lessons from America's Best-Run Companies*, Harper & Row, 1982.

III. A newsprint flip chart and a felt-tipped marker for each group.

IV. A newsprint flip chart and a felt-tipped marker for the instructor's use.

Physical Setting

A room large enough so that each group can work without disturbing the other group(s). Movable chairs should be provided.

Process

STEP 1: *Introduction (10 min.)*

The instructor announces the goals of the activity, distributes copies of the Measuring Excellence Theory Sheet, and asks the participants to read this handout.

STEP 2: *Overview (15 min.)*

The instructor presents an overview of the eight characteristics of organizational excellence identified by Peters and Waterman, provides examples of these characteristics, and then elicits and answers questions.

Reprinted from Leonard D. Goodstein and J. William Pfeiffer, (Eds.), *The 1986 Annual: Developing Human Resources*, San Diego, CA: University Associates, Inc., 1986. Used with permission.

STEP 3: *Analysis (30 min.)*

Each participant is asked to think of an organization with which they are familiar and to evaluate that organization in terms of the 8 basic characteristics. The participants are then told to read the instructions to the work sheet and then to complete the sheet independently. The instructor mentions that the participants' work sheets will be collected and that their responses will be discussed by the entire group, but that the participants need not put their names on their work sheets unless they wish to do so.

STEP 4: *Totals (15 min.)*

The Instructor collects the work sheets and tallies on newsprint all participant responses to Item I.

STEP 5: *Discussion (40 min.)*

The instructor leads the entire group through a discussion of the responses to Item I. As the participants identify areas of agreement and disagreement as well as the overall levels of their responses, the instructor summarizes their findings on newsprint.

STEP 6: *Excellence Examples (20 min.) (optional)*

The instructor reads aloud each participant's paragraph describing an example of one of the eight basics of excellence (Item II on the work sheet). After each is read, the participants are asked:

1. Which of the eight basics of excellence the incident exemplifies;
2. How frequently such incidents occur in the organization;
3. How many of the participants knew about the incident before this announcement of it; and
4. What conclusions can be drawn from this discussion of the incident.

STEP 7: *Excellence Omissions (20 min.) (optional)*

Step VI is repeated using each participant's example of an omission of one of the basics of excellence (Item III on the work sheet).

STEP 8: *Group Discussion (15 min.)*

The instructor leads a discussion during which the participants determine which of the eight basics of excellence should be emphasized more strongly in organizations. As these basics are identified, the instructor lists them on newsprint.

STEP 9: *Action Plans (30 min.)*

The instructor asks the participants to assemble into their individual groups. Each group is asked to choose one of the eight basics that requires a stronger emphasis and to devise an action plan of specific steps that an organization could take to help promote this basic. The instructor emphasizes that each plan should incorporate goals, strategies to be used, action steps to be taken to accomplish strategies, specific personnel to be responsible for the various steps, and target dates for completing the steps. Each group is given a newsprint flip chart and a felt-tipped marker and is asked to select a member to record the group's plan as it is devised.

STEP 10: *Closure (25 min.)*

The instructor reconvenes the total group and asks the participants to share their reactions to the planning phase and about the actions that they plan to take.

MEASURING EXCELLENCE THEORY

In their popular book entitled *In Search of Excellence: Lessons from America's Best-Run Companies*, Peters and Waterman outline the *eight basics of excellence* that they found to be characteristic of thirty-seven of the most successful companies in the United States. These eight basics are as follows: [1]

1. **A bias for action**—a preference for doing something—anything—rather than sending a question through cycles and cycles of analyses and committee reports.
   not
   Paralysis by analysis—a preference for waiting to act until all issues and possible ramifications have been studied exhaustively.

2. **Staying close to the customer**—learning his preferences and catering to them.
   not
   Close to the organization—characterizing the customer as an intrusion into organizational functioning.

3. **Autonomy and entrepreneurship**—breaking the corporation into small companies and encouraging them to think independently and competitively.
   not
   Top-down control—concentrating control exclusively within the ranks of management and discouraging independent thinking.

4. **Productivity through people**—creating in *all* employees the awareness that their best efforts are essential and that they will share in the rewards of the company's success.

not
Productivity through forced labor—assuming that employees must be forced to work, cannot or will not make meaningful contributions, and should not share in the organization's success.

5. **Hands-on, value driven**—insisting that executives keep in touch with the firm's essential business.
   not
   Remote control, driven by policy manuals—allowing executives to remain in the background, removed from the firm's essential business.

6. **Stick to the knitting**—remaining with the business the company knows best.
   not
   Diversify widely—emphasizing wide diversification to achieve a synergistic effect.

7. **Simple form, lean staff**—few administrative layers, few people at the upper levels.
   not
   Complex form, top-heavy staff—a complex structure and systems, many people at the upper levels.

8. **Simultaneous loose-tight properties**—fostering a climate where there is dedication to the central values of the company combined with tolerance for all employees who accept those values.
   not
   Totalitarianism or anarchy—fostering a climate that depends on the enforcement of unbending controls or one that allows employees to pursue unbridled self-actualization.

---

[1] "Learn how the best-run American companies use these EIGHT BASIC PRINCIPLES to stay on top of the heap!" from IN SEARCH OF EXCELLENCE: *Lessons from America's Best-Run Companies* (Warner paperback edition) by Thomas J. Peters and Robert H. Waterman, Jr. Copyright © 1982 by Thomas J. Peters and Robert H. Waterman, Jr. Reprinted by permission of Harper & Row, Publishers, Inc.

MEASURING EXCELLENCE WORK SHEET

I. Indicate the degree to which each of the following eight basics of excellence is emphasized in your organization. Write "H" in each blank that corresponds to a basic that receives *heavy* emphasis, "M" in each blank that corresponds to one that receives *medium* emphasis, and "L" in each blank that corresponds to one that receives *light* emphasis.

_____ 1. A bias for action
_____ 2. Staying close to the customer
_____ 3. Autonomy and entrepreneurship
_____ 4. Productivity through people
_____ 5. Hands-on, value driven
_____ 6. Stick to the knitting
_____ 7. Simple form, lean staff
_____ 8. Simultaneous loose-tight properties

II. In the space provided below, write a paragraph describing an incident that occurred in your organization that you consider to be an *example* of one of the eight basics of excellence.

III. In the space provided below, write a paragraph describing an incident that occurred in your organization that you consider to be an *omission* of one of the eight basics of excellence.

44

Meadville State Prison

INTRODUCTION

Meadville State Prison is one of four major correctional facilities in the state. Until recently, it operated strictly in a custodial role, making very little effort to rehabilitate the inmates.

The organization of the prison consists of three departments reporting to the warden. An administrative staff, consisting of the purchasing, maintenance, health care, and recordkeeping departments, is considered as being apart from the mainstream of prison activities. A rehabilitation director heads a staff responsible for the training and counseling of inmates in preparation for their re-entry into civilian life. The deputy warden is in charge of the guards and is responsible for the security of the prison.

The situation at Meadville has experienced a change and is presently in a state of conflict. Before describing this conflict, it is essential that the personalities involved and the prior state of affairs be explored.

BACKGROUND

Warden Aaron Hunsacre has been an administrator at Meadville for 15 years, the first five of which were spent as a deputy warden and the last ten as warden.

On completing his high school education, Hunsacre immediately enlisted in the Marines, where he hoped someday to become a high ranking officer. Although he completed Officer Candidate School, he became bitter when he did not rise above the rank of major. Finally, in 1963, after 13 years in the service, he decided to accept the deputy warden position at Meadville. Several motives prompted his acceptance of this job, but foremost the implicit understanding that the warden's job would be his when the present holder retired in five years. The thought of being head honcho at a large prison was very appealing; he felt that the several years he had spent as an MP (military policeman) in the Marines had adequately prepared him for the position.

From this point on, events seemed to fall neatly into place for Aaron: he moved into the vacated warden's position at the end of five years and influenced the hiring of an old ex-Marine buddy, Eugene Halter, to fill

This case was prepared by Becky Fox, Steve Hardy, Jim Kreiner, and Kitty Putzier under the supervision of Theodore T. Herbert. The case is not intended to reflect either effective or ineffective administrative or technical practices; it was prepared for class discussion. Reprinted by permission of Theodore T. Herbert.

the deputy warden spot. Aaron was very content with his job, feeling that he had achieved a secure position of power and prestige in society as well as in the organization—after all, he was responsible directly to the *governor* of the state!

Aaron interpreted his job as warden as one of maintaining firm control in managing inmates. He had to punish and keep those people who threatened society out of sight. With this orientation, he hired employees who advocated strict enforcement of the rules and tolerated little misbehavior on the part of the inmates. He was very suspicious of younger, college-trained persons and held most of their theories in contempt. Whenever it could be avoided, he refused to hire college graduates.

DEPUTY WARDEN

Eugene Halter, the deputy warden, was supposed to take care of the daily operations of the prison, having the responsibility of supervising the guards who controlled the prisoners. He was to report any problems to the warden, as well as keep him informed of daily occurrences.

After Eugene had completed his stay in the Marines, he returned to school and received a two-year technical degree in criminology. It was at this point that he went to work at Meadville, a decision based on the encouragement of his friend, Aaron. He felt that this institution offered him the opportunity to rise someday to the top. Consequently, he took his job very seriously and was careful not to rock the boat in matters affecting Aaron's perceptions of the way he executed his job. After seven years with Meadville, Eugene had become Aaron's "yes man"; Eugene always avoided telling Aaron things that might upset him.

The deputy warden took his lead from Aaron and became an almost tyrannical enforcer of order. (In response to his commands, it became a standing joke for the prisoners, as well as some guards, to salute behind his back and garble his last name to sound like Heil Hitler!) The prisoners held Eugene in contempt; most of the guards regarded him with awe. It was felt that his actions to carry out his responsibilities bordered on being sadistic and that overall he was extremely power hungry.

THE CAPTAIN OF THE YARD

Jeb Slatka was responsible for the guards and inmates in one of four sections of Meadville. He had been captain of the yard for five years, working his way up through the ranks by advancing from guard through sergeant, to watch officer, and finally to captain. He was now fifty-two with 21 years of service at the prison. Most of Jeb's earlier work experience had been in the military as an army noncom. After his combat tour of duty in Korea, the peacetime army no longer had an appeal for him. He had decided not to "re-up" and was looking for a job when an opening for a guard at Meadville came to his attention. The job seemed to suit his temperament, and he took it.

Jeb's office acted as the center for all yard communications. As a result of the custodial goals of the institution, primary interest was placed in the hour-by-hour reports on the location and movements of the prisoners. In addition, all orders, assignments of men, requests, and reports had to pass through his office and communications center. The line work supervisors, under these conditions, although equal in rank to the guards, had lower status and were obliged to take orders from the guards. This situation had evolved because the custodial goals of order and control were of prime importance. Meaningful work and rehabilitation were insignificant in the eyes of the warden and, therefore, to his guard staff. Other activities that might interfere even slightly with security just were not allowed.

THE GUARDS

Although all other functions in the prison had operated under authoritarian and narrowly defined limits, much discretionary authority had been given to the guards insofar as their relationship to the prisoners was concerned. The guards had almost always been backed by their supervisors. This condition, in fact, had given the guards, as a group, more power than the line work supervisors and other rehabilitative personnel. The inmates recognized this power and considered it in all of their actions. The guards' position of power over the prisoners was enhanced by the psychological domination arising from the regimentation, frequent head counts, assemblies, and imposed silence during all supervised activities. Hence, the use of punishment was infrequent and usually unnecessary.

When imposed, punishment for control had few rules and was based on the individual guard's determination of insubordination. This created a situation wherein the accused had no rules, no forewarning, and no recourse for appeal. The uncertainty of the infliction of punishment as a means of control, not justice, produced an underlying and everpresent terror in the prisoners, especially at the lower hierarchical levels. Any of the very infrequent rewards were made only for prisoner conformity.

THE INMATE SOCIETY

The authoritarian, custodial nature of the Meadville prison operation had created a no-frills environment, with few privileges available to the inmates. Under these conditions, one might have expected the men to become coequals and ready to rebel against the system at any chance. This was not the case. A highly structured inmate society, aimed at adjustment rather than rebellion, had developed. This society was led, rather surprisingly, by the least violent and aggressive men.

Although the inmate society, like the prison authorities, demanded that all prisoners be treated alike, interpersonal relations founded on dominance and subordination were the rule. The ability to exercise coercion was highly valued, not for the power, but because it was a means to achieve the goals common to all inmates: integrity and safety from official sanctions. As it currently existed, the inmate society had a static, sharply defined structure and power hierarchy aimed at attaining these goals. The society enforced member conformity through punishments usually more severe than those used by the prison officials.

When a new inmate or "fish" (just caught) arrived, he wasn't given a book of regulations defining his position. The shock of entering the prison, the capricious nature of discipline, the secrecy, and the regimentation all made the new man very dependent on any veteran inmate to whom he could attach himself. He needed an experienced man to teach him about the undefined and uncertain tolerances of the guards and to give him any insights vital for making life even the slightest bit more pleasant.

The new man was, in time, introduced to the prison grapevine. The grapevine was usually inaccurate, but it created and circulated the myths that helped to explain satisfactorily otherwise inexplicable (to the inmates) events. It helped the new men to adjust to prison life. The grapevine also helped, through the myths that held the prison officials in contempt, to create and maintain a degree of dignity and group unity.

The new, not yet accepted fish found himself lumped together at the bottom of the inmate society with those inmates whose prison jobs, behavior, or outside ties created suspicions that they might act as informers to the officials. The least a new

Clan control (handwritten)

man had to do to gain, or a current member to retain, membership in the society was to conform to the group norms. These included rejection of the outside world and to take any punishment without talking. A man who had gained seniority and the confidence of the membership and was able to explain, predict, or control in part the circumstances that others could not, would probably emerge as a leader. These leaders, because they had power, were mediators between their inmate followers and the officials. They were allowed to talk to the guards, which was not permitted for men in lower positions.

Referent power (handwritten)

When conditions were stable, as things had been for the many years of the warden's custodial stewardship, the inmate society actually acted as a support for the authoritarian, custodial system. The inmate leaders had responsible contacts with the guards and had a voice in the assignment and distribution of privileges. This interaction between the officials and inmate leaders helped both sides achieve common, mutual goals of peace, order, and adjustment. In this way, each hierarchy was able to maintain its position of power and advantage.

reciprocal (handwritten)

THE REHABILITATION STAFF

dont fit in (handwritten)

The rehabilitation services department at Meadville is directed by Polly Hoover. Polly has her master's degree in social work. Before beginning graduate school, she worked for several years as a counselor in the State Detention Center for juvenile delinquents. Polly was an outstanding student during her graduate work, and at thirty-one she is quite a bit younger than any of the previous directors. Polly has been at Meadville for almost two years now, and her staff is still making adjustments to her rehabilitation plans.

Polly is quite an idealist and believes strongly in the modern goals of therapy, treatment, education, and rehabilitation. She espouses the belief that if discipline is absolutely necessary, it must be administered in such a way as to preserve the dignity of the inmate.

The rehabilitation staff is made up of one full-time psychologist, a librarian, a part-time art instructor, two full-time vocational instructors, and another social worker (besides Polly).

Sam Fall, the prison psychologist, is fifty-three years old and quite comfortable with his position at Meadville. He is much more comfortable than he was 15 years ago when he was still struggling to make a go of his private practice. When this position opened up 12 years ago, Sam jumped at the chance to, for once in his life, have a steady income he could count on, without the worries and responsibilities he faced when he was self-employed. Sam looked forward to spending the next 12 years waiting out his retirement.

Sam's formal responsibilities included scheduling private counseling sessions with inmates, which took up most of his time. He was also to conduct group therapy sessions, keep certain office hours for visitation by inmates, and maintain each inmate's file, updating it as to treatment and progress. He also served in an advisory capacity to the rest of the rehabilitation staff as well as the custodial staff.

The librarian, art instructor, and shop teachers were responsible for their own areas only and planned and coordinated their curricula with the advice and approval of the director. If Polly thought it necessary, Sam was called in for consultation.

The resident social worker was responsible for placing inmates in jobs within the prison in such areas as the kitchen, the laundry, and the library. He also directed prison recreational and social activities and assisted the director, Polly, in maintaining supportive relationships between prisoners and their families and friends and between prisoners and supportive volunteer organizations.

Polly was quite enthusiastic about getting outside groups more involved in the prison and trying out some of the rehabilitation techniques that she had researched during her graduate work. However, most of her staff had a less optimistic view of rehabilitation than she. Most of their efforts were directed toward keeping peace among the inmate society, rather than toward rehabilitation.

It was no secret that most of the inmates regarded the whole idea of rehabilitation as a joke. They played the game because they knew that, if they didn't, parole was a virtual impossibility. Sam Fall was not one of the most perceptive people when it came to human behavior, but even he had begun to realize that during personal counseling sessions, the inmates' responses had begun to follow predictable patterns.

Polly had become frustrated with the lack of support her rehabilitation efforts were receiving at Meadville. In fact, she was considering looking for a job elsewhere, where the attitudes of the administration were more enlightened. However, a riot at neighboring Roland State Prison brought the need for prison reform to light, and Polly felt that maybe now her ideas would be considered seriously.

THE CHANGE

The news was full of the explosive situation at Roland State. No one knew exactly how the riot started; accidently caught in the middle was a group of college freshmen from the local university who happened to be touring the facility as a field trip in psychology. Six of the group, four males and two females, had been held hostage along with four guards and a clerk from the prison's administrative staff.

The confrontation lasted for four long days with the prisoners demanding improved treatment in exchange for the hostages. The state police were prepared to attack the prisoner-controlled area and

regain control by force. The fact that innocent bystanders, not a part of the prison system, were involved generated national public interest. People realized that the activities within a prison system can affect the general public and became very interested in the situation that led to the riot.

Jay Cole supplied the desired information and is considered the man most responsible for settling the riot and obtaining the release of the hostages unharmed. Cole is a local TV personality with a late-night talk show. Several months before, Cole and his station filmed a documentary on prison conditions at Roland State and conducted interviews with inmates. The show went relatively unnoticed when first aired, but during the riot the program was repeated nationwide during prime time. Cole's program and his genuine concern about prison conditions convinced a large segment of the public that reform was overdue, and that the prisoners had legitimate complaints. Governor Wendell, well tuned to political pressures, saw a way to end the riot and take the initiative for reform. He selected Jay Cole to negotiate with the prisoners and offered to establish a state commission for prison reform in exchange for the hostages. The prisoners trusted Cole and agreed to the governor's terms. Cole promised the prisoners that he would keep the activities of the commission in the public eye to assure that real action would be taken.

The newly formed state commission visited Meadville and informed the warden that rehabilitation must be emphasized. A portion of the Commission's findings states that:

consequently, it has been determined by our investigations that the 70 percent recidivism rate and the increase in severity of crimes committed by those released from prison indicate that prisons should take a more active part in attempting to rehabilitate inmates. Prisons must be made into something other than breeding places of hate-filled and vengeful individuals if we expect these individuals to one day re-enter our society.

The governor has also visited Warden Hunsacre and made it clear that prison reform is one of his major goals. He wants specific actions that the voter can relate to, for use in his re-election campaign next year. He reminded the warden that Jay Cole will keep this issue alive and will insist on real action, not just paper plans and programs.

The State Commission for Prison Reform presented all prison staff with a copy of the newly developed guidelines for achieving the desired changes in the state's prison system. Most of the guidelines are aimed at assuring more humane treatment of inmates and providing more opportunities for rehabilitation. The prison staff is to be responsible for maintaining a separate file on each inmate. These reports are to be filled out by both custodial and rehabilitative staff and are to be updated weekly. Each report is to include descriptions of all rehabilitation programs and efforts in which the inmate is involved, the results of the program and progress of the inmate's attitudes and behaviors, and an evaluation of custodial cooperation.

These reports are sent to the rehabilitation director who evaluates them and summarizes the progress of the inmate population in reaching the goals set forth by the commission. These summaries will be sent to the State Commission for Prison Reform, and all inmates' files will be made available for the commission's examination.

Also the rehabilitation staff was increased by the addition of two full-time counselors to assist in implementing the new guidelines.

Aaron realized that he had no choice other than to accommodate the wishes of the Commission for Prison Reform. Although he felt that these new goals of the governor's had their basis in political vote rallying and were not expected really to ac-

complish anything, he knew he would have to make a pretext of implementing them or else lose his job. He confided the following to Eugene:

Listen, I'm not about to let that Wendell and his commission come in here and tell me what to do. As far as I'm concerned, these new rehabilitation goals are nothing but a lot of hogwash! I'm only putting up with this rehabilitation director and her division because there's no way around it— but I'll tell you—they're really out in left field when it comes to understanding what a prison system is all about. They must think we're running a _____ day care center here instead of a prison. Thieves, murderers, and nogood bums!—that's what we've got here, and there's no way anyone's going to make upstanding citizens out of that lot. Give these guys an inch and they'll take a mile. I'm sure I've made my point and you know what I mean—don't give them that first inch!

Eugene transmitted Hunsacre's sentiments to the guards and let it be known that under no circumstances were security and control over the prisoners to be lessened. In turn, the guards were expected to remind the prisoners of exactly who was in charge and that nothing had changed.

On the other hand, Polly could not have been happier. She felt that with the governor and the commission behind her, she was finally going to have some clout in implementing her rehabilitation strategies. She expressed these beliefs in a discussion with her newly enlarged staff:

I've been waiting a long time for this kind of backing and finally we've got it. Now maybe we can make the warden see the kind of progress we can make with the prisoners if they're just treated like respectable human beings. Warden Hunsacre has told me I'm free to do whatever I want with this program and I'm sure we've got his full cooperation.

Various programs were created for the prisoners in the hopes that their self-improvement would be forthcoming. Participation in vocational education classes was encouraged, as well as participation in the formal therapy and rap sessions.

After several months of organizing and establishing these programs, Polly felt that she wasn't making as much progress as she had hoped. She felt that her social workers were facing a subverted resistance from the guards. Although the guards always seemed to listen to the rehabilitation staff, often their actions were inconsistent with the advice. Behind the staff's backs, guards apparently continued to belittle the inmates and exercise control in the way they felt necessary. The rehabilitation staff learned this through the complaints of some of the prisoners. At first, Polly could not understand why the guards were being so uncooperative, but then attributed it to laziness and unwillingness to exert the effort to interact decently with the prisoners.

The guards viewed their situation differently, as is evidenced by this conversation between two of them:

This rehabilitation stuff is for the birds. I don't know about you, but I'm getting a little tired of listening to their preaching about how we should respect these hooligans. "Try to get to know them better," they say—ha!—I know all I care to know and that's too much. I know who signs my paycheck, and if he wants the cons to toe the mark, that's what he's going to get.

Yeah. Things ran a lot better around here before rehab got so high-and-mighty. These social workers are always siding with the inmates and believing their accounts over ours. You should hear some of the stories I've heard prisoners tell—sheesh! Those rehabs are a gullible bunch, they fall for any sob story.

During the ensuing months, problems between the rehabilitation staff and the warden's group increased drastically. Minor occasions for interaction between the two groups seemed to assume more importance, and tensions increased. Guards complained that the rehabilitation staff was too lax in their dealings with the inmates, which endangered security. One guard confronted a rehabilitation teacher with the following:

Three times last week I had to confiscate weapons from inmates that they got from your class. You may think they're only harmless tools, but in the hands of most of these fellows they're as lethal as any gun or knife. You just don't understand that these guys can't be trusted, do you?!

Oftentimes, a guard would, as a form of punishment, not permit a certain inmate to attend a class or self-help session. Conflicts then arose because teachers and social workers felt that the classes were too important for inmates to be arbitrarily denied.

The inmates were caught in the middle of the situation. Those in the top level of the prisoner hierarchy knew that their best course of action was to stay on the guard's best side and avoid any siding with the rehabilitation staff. Taking their cue from the façade used by the guards, those prisoners would go through the motions of "being rehabilitated," when in fact they thought it was a joke. However, in the lower echelons of the ranks of prisoners were those inmates who were trying to get the best deal for themselves by playing the staff against the guards. They could covertly "squeal" to the rehabilitation workers and gain sympathy without much fear of reprisals or sanctions from fellow inmates. It was these individuals, because they didn't conform to the main prisoner group, which wanted compliance and safety from prison sanctions, that increased conflict between the warden and guards and the rehabilitation staff.

It became evident to Polly that the warden was not really being very cooperative in helping her to meet her rehabilitation goals. One day the two confronted each other in the explosive argument which follows:

Polly: Listen here, Hunsacre! I get the impression you don't care at all about what I'm attempting to do with these prisoners. You tell me one thing and the next time I turn around you're doing the opposite. I can't get anywhere with your guards either, and I *need* their cooperation. It looks like I may have to go to the state commission if you don't make a few changes.

Aaron: What have I been trying to tell you all along!? Get your head out of the clouds and return to earth, will you? Don't try and put the blame on me because your program is a flop. Sometimes I think I'm the only one around here who's living in the real world. You're so blind you can't see what a mess you're making of everything. The only way to handle prisoners is with firm control and the sooner you realize that, the better off we'll all be. I wouldn't be so anxious to broadcast this mess to the commission if I were you; you just might be cutting your own throat!

45

Missouri Campus Bitterly Divided over How to 'Reallocate' Funds

On the campus of the University of Missouri here, the signs of spring came late and were decidedly makeshift: a white sheet bearing the spray-painted legend "SOCIAL WORK IS HERE TO STAY" draped from windows in Clark Hall; a crudely lettered placard taped to a glass door in Memorial Union defiantly announcing, "HELL NO, HOME EC WON'T GO!"

Hasty construction accounted for the homemade quality of the signs, for as the academic year drew quickly to a close, many students and faculty members were surprised to find themselves fighting for their academic lives—the survival of their programs.

In a year in which this campus has had to contend with a host of financial problems—some fabricated, critics allege—April was the cruelest month. It was on April 2 that proposals to "reallocate" nearly $12 million in operating funds over the next three years were announced. Among them were recommendations to eliminate two of the university's 14 colleges and to reduce substantially the offerings in five others.

The ensuing controversy divided the campus. "It has set department against department and colleague against colleague," says one dean. "It's civil war, with everyone trying to gore everyone else's bull."

In mid-April, the faculty voted to call for the resignation of Chancellor Barbara S. Uehling if she did not withdraw the proposals.

By the time graduating students were preparing for last week's commencement exercises, the subject of their conversations—whether or not they had jobs—also seemed to be a prime topic of talk among many members of the faculty and staff.

What led to this course of events was a decision last summer by President James C. Olson to take action "to preserve and even enhance the quality of the university in a time of severely limited resources."

"The university has coped with 10 years of inadequate funding by making cuts across the board," he says. "It became clear that a continuation of that policy was a prescription for mediocrity."

Mr. Olson announced last July that the university would attempt to save approxi-

Written by Paul Desruisseaux. Reprinted with permission of *The Chronicle of Higher Education*, copyright © 1982.

mately $16 million over the next three years to finance pay raises as well as library, laboratory, and other improvements. He told the chancellors of the four Missouri campuses that their first priority was to be the development of an adequate compensation plan for the university staff. His plan was supported by the university's Board of Curators.

President Olson's goal is to bring salaries at the university up to the average of those at member institutions of the Big 8 and Big 10 athletic conferences—institutions that, he says, "are comparable to Missouri in mission." At the start of the 1981–82 academic year, Missouri had the lowest salary average in that comparison group, 8.9% below the midpoint.

Mr. Olson instructed the chancellors to find money for salary adjustments "by reducing the quantity of what you do rather than the quality."

That met with approval on the Columbia campus, where Chancellor Uehling has said "the concept of shared poverty is not viable for a competitive university," and where the faculty has been on the record for five years in opposition to across-the-board budget cuts.

The 24,000-student campus, biggest in the system, is scheduled for the largest reductions: as much as $12 million, or about 5% of its operating budget.

The curators adopted procedures for the "discontinuance" of program, and the university established four criteria for reviewing them: overall quality, contribution to the university's mission, need for the program, and financial considerations. Application of the criteria was left up to the individual campuses.

"On two occasions I identified to the deans the ways in which we might go about this task," says Provost Ronald F. Bunn, who is faced with reducing the budget for academic programs by $7 million.

'A QUALITY MATRIX'

According to Mr. Bunn, most of the deans suggested that he take on the task. The Faculty Council recommended the same. "This was an administrative job," says David West, the council chairman and a professor of finance. "We wanted the administration to make its proposals, and then we'd take shots at it."

Mr. Bunn reviewed all of the campus's academic programs himself, rating them according to the four criteria established by the president. He compiled what he calls "a quality matrix," which resembles the box score of a baseball game. The programs that ranked lowest he proposed reducing.

Specifically, the provost recommended the elimination of the School of Library and Informational Science and the College of Public and Community Services (with the possible retention of its masters-in-social-work program). He also recommended major reductions in the College of Education, the College of Engineering, the School of Nursing, the College of Home Economics, and the School of Health Related Professions. In some cases the reductions would mean the elimination of one or more departments within those colleges.

All told, campus officials estimated that the cuts in academic programs would affect 2,500 students and as many as 200 faculty and staff members. Since tenure regulations require the university to give tenured faculty members 13 months' notice of plans to eliminate their jobs, the reduction proposals would have little effect on the 1982–83 budget.

When university administrators announced their plans on April 2, those in the academic programs predictably provoked the greatest response.

'IT INFURIATES ME'

An ad hoc committee of faculty members and students was charged with reviewing the provost's recommendations and conducting hearings.

Individuals in the targeted programs have been outspokenly critical of Provost Bunn's judgment.

"We are the only accredited library-science program in Missouri, and it infuriates me—as a citizen as much as anything—that this campus, unilaterally, has made the decision to eliminate programs that exist nowhere else in the state," says Edward P. Miller, dean of the library school. "I don't think the provost could have done a worse job of abrogating the criteria for review if he tried."

Bob G. Woods, dean of the College of Education, who supported the idea of programmatic cuts, says he was prepared to reduce his budget by as much as $500,000, but when he learned that reductions of $1.2 million were required, he changed his mind. "I want the process to be refuted as unnecessary at this time," he says.

Officials in the College of Home Economics charge that the recommendations to eliminate two departments there were based on outdated information. "The decision regarding my program was based on a three-year-old internal-review document," says Kitty G. Dickerson, chairman of the department of clothing and textiles, who is in her first year at Missouri. "I was brought here to strengthen this department. There were 35 recommendations in that internal review, and we have already addressed all but three. But there was never an opportunity to let it be known that we have made this enormous progress."

Martha Jo Martin, assistant dean of home economics, says that eliminating the two departments would cost the college its accreditation and half of its enrollment.

Opposition was not limited to those in programs proposed for reduction. Says Andrew Twaddle, a professor of sociology, "My main concern is not with the actual targeting of programs but the fact that the administration made these decisions with little input from the faculty, except for a select group of its supporters.

"I honestly don't know what the university's real fiscal situation is—there are so many conflicting figures flying around, and no one is backing them up very well," he adds. "But according to the bylaws of this campus, the faculty is supposed to make academic policy, and when you're talking about what is or is not to be taught at the university, you're talking about policy."

Others are concerned about the impact of the proposals on women and minorities.

"We are assuming that the university is aware of its commitment to affirmative action," says W. L. Moore, an assistant professor of education and chairman of the Black Faculty and Staff Organization. "But we have not been kept informed, and we are very skeptical of all that is being done in this area."

Mr. Moore says his organization has determined that the proposed cuts would affect 63% of the black faculty members. The university's Office of Equal Opportunity says the figure is 33%. The discrepancy is due to the administration's inclusion of nonteaching blacks in its figures, says Mr. Moore. "But the precise number doesn't matter, because even 33% is too high a price to pay," he adds.

Of the campus's 620 black undergraduates, 255 are enrolled in targeted programs, says H. Richard Dozier, coordinator of minority-student services. "Blacks weren't admitted to this institution until 1950, and they make up only 3.7% of the student body," he says. "These cuts would be regressive."

Blacks on the campus have asked the administration for assurances that the university's five-year affirmative-action goals will be met.

There is also some feeling on the campus that faculty salary raises are being used as, in the words of one dean, "a smokescreen" for an attempt to change the institution from a multipurpose university to a research university. One reduction target, home economics, is, according to officials of that college, one of only two areas of study identified in federal farm-bill legislation as being part of the educational responsibility of a land-grant institution.

While some opponents of the proposals were testifying before the review committee, others were mustering support for them. Students, faculty members, and alumni mounted massive letter-writing and phone calling campaigns aimed at state legislators and the university's curators. Rallies were held, petitions circulated, press conferences staged. The Missouri State Teachers Association expressed outrage. The State Senate's Education Committee held a hearing.

On April 7, the Columbia campus's student senate passed a resolution denouncing the academic review.

On April 19, the faculty voted 237 to 70 to call for the resignations of the chancellor and the provost if the reduction proposals were not withdrawn. The vote, however, has been criticized—by, among others, Chancellor Uehling herself—for not being a true representation of the sentiments of the campus's 2,038-member faculty. Last November, when the faculty voted against midyear salary increases if they were to come at the expense of campus jobs, more than 800 members cast ballots.

THE 'POINT MAN'

The author of the resignation resolution, George V. Boyle, says he believes the vote was representative.

"We should not be cannibalizing ourselves in order to give people raises," says Mr. Boyle, director of labor education, a program not affected by the provost's proposal. "When you encounter heavy seas and the best plan the captain offers is to lighten the load by throwing crew mem-

bers overboard, I think the crew has to try and come up with something better."

"Our approach to these reductions," says Provost Bunn, "required that I become the 'point man,' and the discussion stage has subsequently become an adversarial one: The source of the recommendations—me—has become as much a subject of debate as the recommendations themselves. It has also become a highly political one, and I think it's unfortunate that the debate has been brought to the legislature and the curators before we have completed the review process on campus."

Chancellor Uehling also came in for some personal criticism when the campus learned that she was among the final candidates for the chancellorship of the 19-campus California State University system. She took herself out of the running for that job last week and announced that she was committed to working for policies that would enable the Columbia campus "not simply to survive but to carry into the future even greater strength than before."

The chancellor says she is not surprised by the demonstrations of hostility. "It's a very frightening and painful process," she says. "I can understand the anger on the part of some, but I still think our greater obligation is to the institution as a whole."

Ms. Uehling says that while she will not review or comment on the recommended proposals until they come to her in their final form, she supports the process and is convinced of its necessity.

"For the past five years, the State of Missouri has provided the university with budget increases that have amounted to only one-half the rate of inflation," she says. "When I came, the faculty was already on the record in opposition to across-the-board cuts to provide salary raises, and we must bring salaries up to attract and retain quality people. We *have* lost some good people.

"We have no hidden agenda. Our only agenda is our determination to take charge of our own fate. We are trying to anticipate the future so that we won't have to engage in crisis kind of planning. There are enough signs of an impending erosion of our quality to make us want to get ahead and start doing what we do smaller and better."

There have also been signs that the state can't afford to support the university to any greater extent. Missouri voters in 1980 passed an amendment prohibiting the legislature from increasing appropriations unless there were corresponding growth in the state economy. In 1981, Missouri ranked forty-sixth in state-tax-revenue growth, one of the reasons the governor, on two occasions, withheld portions of the university's budget totaling 13%.

Nevertheless, some critics charge that salary increases—if they are essential now—could be provided for next year without eliminating programs, since there has been a slight increase in the state appropriation from what was originally expected, and a 17% hike in student fees.

"If you take a short-term view, it's possible to conclude that we could have an acceptable level of salary adjustment for the coming year," says Mr. Bunn. "That isn't the case if you're looking ahead. Some on campus feel that it isn't important for us to strengthen our salary structure, but in my judgment that is a very narrow view of the aspirations this campus should have for itself."

To be sure, there is faculty support for the administration. "I think the faculty who approved of this strategy previously ought to be heard from again," says John Kuhlman, a professor of economics. "I don't think we can afford to sit back and watch a few departments create this big fight with the provost."

Adds Sam Brown, chairman of the psychology department, "It would be difficult to find anyone to say they'd favor the cannibalization of their colleagues' jobs for the sake of a salary raise. But ignoring the

source of funds, I can say as a department chairman that one of the major problems I face is insufficient salary increments for faculty."

OTHER IMPROVEMENTS SOUGHT

According to Provost Bunn, when salary raises are given out, they will not be distributed uniformly but will be based on individual merit and the salary market in the particular field.

While salaries will have the highest claim on the "reallocated" funds, the provost also hopes there will be enough money to strengthen equipment and expense budgets—"to bring them back to at least the real-dollar level of three years ago."

The provost said he would consider seriously the advice offered by the committee reviewing his proposals. What is not an option, in his view, is to back away from the $7 million in savings that his proposals would provide.

When it reported to the provost May 6, however, the review committee announced that it had voted to weaken the effect of all but one of the proposed reductions. Mr. Bunn is expected to submit his final recommendations to the chancellor by the end of this week.

The Board of Curators, at meetings on May 6 and 7, conducted lengthy discussions of the reallocation process underway at the Columbia campus. The result, William T. Doak, president of the board, told the press, was that the curators were so divided on the question that had a vote been taken on the proposals they would have been rejected.

"We are trying to plan for a very uncertain future," says President Olson, "and I'm not sure we've yet found the mechanism for doing that. We are seeking it."

Chancellor Uehling is expected to submit her reallocation proposals to President Olson sometime in June. The curators are scheduled to vote on the proposals in July.

"The board's resistance to any program eliminations has certainly given those who favor such a course of action cause for pause," says the Faculty Council's David West, who has supported the process from the outset. "There has been much more visible and vocal opposition to the process in the past four weeks than there had been support for it up to that time."

On the Columbia campus, faculty mem-bers were circulating petitions calling for votes of confidence and of no confidence in the administration. Mr. West says he is advising those faculty members not to call for campuswide votes at this time.

"There has already been too much confrontation, and faculty votes would just prolong it," he says. "I think everyone should try to gather additional information and rethink his position. And try to find some means by which all of this division can be mitigated."

46

Political Processes in Organizations

The purpose of this exercise is to analyze and predict when political behavior is used in organizational decision-making and to compare participants' ratings of politically-based decisions with ratings of practicing managers.

Politics is the use of influence to make decisions and obtain preferred outcomes in organizations. Surveys of managers show that political behavior is a fact of life in virtually all organizations. Every organization will confront situations characterized by uncertainty and disagreement, hence standard rules and rational decision models can't necessarily be used. Political behavior and rational decision processes act as substitutes for one another, depending upon the degree of uncertainty and disagreement that exists among managers about specific issues. Political behavior is used and is revealed in informal discussions and unscheduled meetings among managers, arguments, attempts at persuasion, and eventual agreement and acceptance of the organizational choice.

In the following exercise, you are asked to evaluate the extent to which politics will play a part in 11 types of decisions that are made in organizations. The complete exercise takes about one hour.

STEP 1: *Individual Ranking (5 minutes)*

Rank the 11 organizational decisions listed on the scoring sheet below according to the extent you think politics plays a part. The most political decision would be ranked 1, the least political decision would be ranked 11. Enter your ranking on the first column of the scoring sheet.

STEP 2: *Team Ranking (20 minutes)*

Divide into teams of from three to seven people. As a group, rank the 11 items according to your group's consensus on the amount of politics used in each decision. Use good group decision-making techniques to arrive at a consensus. Listen to each person's ideas and rationale fully before reaching a decision. Do not vote. Discuss items until agreement is reached. Base your deci-

Thanks to Don Hellriegel for suggesting the idea for this exercise. The scoring sheet is based on Jeffrey Gandz and Victor V. Murray, "The Experience of Workplace Politics," *Academy of Management Journal* 1980, 23, 237–251.

sions on the underlying logic provided by group members rather than on personal preference. After your team has reached a consensus, record the team rankings in the second column on the scoring sheet.

STEP 3: *Correct Ranking (5 minutes)*

After all teams have finished ranking the 11 decisions, your instructor will read the correct ranking based on a survey of managers. This survey indicates the frequency with which politics played a part in each type of decision. As the instructor reads each item's ranking, enter it in the "correct ranking" column on the scoring sheet.

STEP 4: *Individual Score (5 minutes)*

Your individual score is computed by taking the difference between your individual ranking and the correct ranking for each item. Be sure to use the *absolute* difference between your ranking and the correct ranking for each item (ignore pluses and minuses). Enter the difference in column 4 labeled "Individual Score." Add the numbers in column 4 and insert the total at the bottom of the column. This score indicates how accurate you were in assessing the extent to which politics plays a part in organizational decisions.

STEP 5: *Team Score (5 minutes)*

Compute the difference between your group's ranking and the correct ranking. Again, use the *absolute* difference for each item. Enter the difference in the column 5 labeled "Team Score." Add the numbers in column 5 and insert the total at the bottom of the column. The total is your team score.

STEP 6: *Compare Teams (5 minutes)*

When all individual and team scores have been calculated, the instructor will record the data from each group for class discussion. One member of your group should be prepared to provide both the team score and the lowest individual score on your team. The instructor may wish to display these data so that team and individual scores can be easily compared as illustrated on the bottom of the scoring sheet. All participants may wish to record these data for further reference.

STEP 7: *Discussion (15 minutes)*

Discuss this exercise as a total group with the instructor. Use your experience and the data to try to arrive at some conclusions about the role of politics in real-world organizational decision-making. The following questions may facilitate the total group discussion.

1. Why did some individuals and groups solve the ranking more accurately than others? Did they have more experience with organizational decision-making? Did they interpret the amount of uncertainty and disagreement associated with decisions more accurately?
2. If the 11 decisions were ranked according to the importance of rational decision processes, how would that ranking compare to the one you've completed above? To what extent does this mean both rational and political models of decision-making should be used in organizations?
3. What would happen if managers apply political processes to logical, well understood issues? What would happen if they applied rational or quantitative techniques to uncertain issues about which considerable disagreement existed?
4. Many managers believe that political behavior is greater at higher levels in the organization hierarchy. Is there any evidence from this exercise that would explain why more politics would appear at higher rather than lower levels in organizations?
5. What advice would you give to managers who feel politics is bad for the organization and should be avoided at all costs?

SCORING SHEET

Decisions	1. Individual Ranking	2. Team Ranking	3. Correct Ranking	4. Individual Score	5. Team Score
1. Management promotions and transfers					
2. Entry level hiring					
3. Amount of pay					
4. Annual budgets					
5. Allocation of facilities, equipment, offices					
6. Delegation of authority among managers					
7. Interdepartmental coordination					
8. Specification of personnel policies					
9. Penalties for disciplinary infractions					
10. Performance appraisals					
11. Grievances and complaints					

	Team Number						
	1	2	3	4	5	6	7
Team Scores:							
Lowest individual score on each team:							

47

Utopia Inc.

One day last summer, a very young Israeli boy named Zohar rode his tricycle out onto the floor of a factory near his home. He was looking for his grandmother, one of the packers. But she wasn't there at her usual station; gone to the bathroom, apparently. So someone found a little chair for Zohar where he could wait and help his grandmother when she returned.

This factory, oddly enough, is a suitable place for small boys to visit their grandmothers. The big shed is filled with sunlight from a glass wall that looks out over some sand dunes to the Mediterranean. The machines, mostly injection molding devices, are clean and safe. And many of the workers are the age of grandparents, and seem to know one another very well. Many of them seem to know Zohar, too.

An interesting sort of factory, clearly. But also the engine room of a very profitable business, Plasson, which last year had sales of $15 million for its owners, the 550 members of a kibbutz called Ma'agan Michael on the coast of Israel. "Plass" stands for plastic, "on" for the Hebrew word for power; a kib-

butznik won a contest by coming up with that name about 21 years ago when Ma'agan Michael decided to go into business. It proved prophetic. Plasson now generates about 70% of Ma'agan Michael's revenues (the rest comes from the much more traditional kibbutz activity of farming), and has lifted its collective owner to a position among the richest kibbutzim in Israel. Plasson has production facilities—partly owned and partly subcontracted—in Italy, Venezuela, and Mexico, and its products are sold all over the world. In the United States alone, the company has conquered as much as 90% of certain segments of its market. Its crowning success came when Taiwanese imitators shamelessly started to brand their knock-offs "Plasson-type." In a keenly competitive, worldwide field, Plasson is the undisputed standard of excellence.

But the company is extraordinary in other respects as well. Allowing children on the factory floor is the least of it: The factory was designed with just that sort of thing in mind, certainly with grandparents in mind.

Prepared by Robert Rosenberg. Reprinted with permission, *INC.* Magazine, February 1985. Copyright © 1985 by INC. Publishing Company, 38 Commercial Wharf, Boston, MA 02110.

Yosef "Yossi" Cohen remembers how it happened. The decision to found a factory didn't come easily to Ma'agan Michael, Cohen explains. Factories seemed to go against every kibbutz tradition and ideal. From the beginning, the kibbutz movement was uncompromisingly socialist and egalitarian. On a kibbutz, all wealth (except personal possessions) is supposed to be held in common; all work is shared according to each person's ability; all goods are distributed according to each person's need; all decision making is arrived at democratically by all members of the kibbutz.

Factories threatened those ideals, Cohen goes on. Factories meant—what else?—going into business, and going into business implied, in a socialist scheme of things, a whole host of evils: money-envy, bosses and workers, class hostility, alienation, and all the other dreadful consequences of capitalism. For years, then, the kibbutz movement remained basically agrarian. Only in farming—"with the wind in our hair and the soil beneath our feet," as kibbutzniks put it—only in this most basic of human enterprises could the kibbutz hold fast to its ideals of equality.

And Ma'agan Michael prospered as an agricultural community. Its dairies, fisheries, banana and cotton plantations, and poultry farm were among the most productive in Israel, perhaps in the world. But the kibbutz wanted to grow, both in membership and in influence in Israeli society; and there was no way it could do this without establishing a growing economy for itself. Once they had cultivated all the land, built all the chicken coops, and stocked all the ponds, agriculture could never provide such a growing economy. So they had to find some engine of economic development—a factory.

Even so, Cohen recalls, they might never have done it, certainly not in the way they did it, if it hadn't been for the kibbutz's elderly. The founders' parents, then the founders themselves, would be getting old; and kibbutz ideology knows nothing of retirement and the "sunset years." On a kibbutz, self-worth is measured in work, in a person's contribution of labor to the community. Old people could not work indefinitely in the fields and fisheries. A factory, therefore, if it were designed to be clean and safe, would extend their productivity, and hence perhaps their very lives.

So Ma'agan Michael got itself a factory, and entered the capitalist world. Has it watered down the kibbutzniks commitment to absolute equality? Certainly not, says Yossi Cohen. The company belongs to the community as much as the land does. The community founded it, put up the money for it, provided all its personnel. Naturally, therefore, it is the community that decides what to do with its profits—plow them back into the business or invest them in such community improvements as schooling or color television. "The entire system of the kibbutz," says Cohen, "makes anything but completely horizontal decision making impossible."

In effect, the kibbutzniks of Ma'agan Michael practice a form of socialism in one company—and it is a highly entrepreneurial, innovative, and profitable company at that. All of which leaves the capitalists with whom they do business a little bewildered. Jack Dubrovsky, a partner in Diversified Imports, D.I.V. Co., of Lakewood, N.J., Plasson's exclusive import agents for the United States and Canada, says, "It's a large democracy they've got there. But you'd have to call it a social democracy. It's more like a big family. You have the feeling you're doing business with a family. There's a lot of concern, a lot of pride, all the good things you've got in a family."

Much of the family environment is maintained through job rotation. Job rotation has been part of kibbutz ideology for generations. Four years ago, for example, Eli Zamir, a kibbutznik, left his post as general manager of Plasson, which he had held for five years, to become general secretary of the Israeli kibbutz movement. His place was taken by Ilan Tassler. Job rotation serves the ideal of social equality by under-·mining occupational specializations. The assumption is that by diversifying each individual's work throughout the enterprise, indeed throughout the kibbutz, cliques will be broken up, incipient hierarchies will be flattened, and everyone will gain a good deal of common experience with everyone else. But at Plasson, job rotation has another point as well, a business point as tough-minded as any American could wish for. Movement from this job to that, ensures a constant circulation of fresh ideas and enriched experience through every workstation in production and sales.

Seeing Itzik Kantor at Ma'agan Michael, it is difficult to imagine him as a globe-trotting businessman Kantor is in charge of all of Plasson's export markets and he is the closest thing to a founder that the company has. Easy-going, clad in typical kibbutz attire (blue shorts, blue shirt, sandals), as accessible to a younger man with domestic troubles as he is to an engineer with a new design on his CAD/CAM system, Kantor looks as though he would be uncomfortable anywhere else. Especially, perhaps, cutting tough deals in the capitalist world.

Of course, in 1961, when the kibbutz sent him on his first venture into the capitalist world, Kantor didn't have any products to sell. He was 35 years old, working as a sort of master mechanic, assigned to keep the farm's machinery in good repair. His other qualifications to lead the kibbutz into business were no more impressive—or wouldn't have been, say, to a typical venture capitalist. "What can I say?" one of Kantor's friends offered. "He was a garagenik."

On the other hand, Itzik Kantor didn't need venture capital. He had that already. It was in Ma'agan Michael's treasury, the collective savings of his fellow kibbutzniks, and, if necessary, additional funds that would be supplied by kibbutzim of the same ideological bent. He also had a fairly clear mandate as to the sort of factory he should be looking for. The machinery had to be safe, clean, and physically easy to use; this for the elderly, of course. It also had to conform to the principle that the means of production, the machinery, should be as much as possible like hand tools, which can be picked up or laid down at the will of the worker, not at the dictates of an assembly line.

With these guidelines, Kantor went off to find a factory for Ma'agan Michael. The research took him and a few fellow members about a year and a half. Almost from the start, he realized that whatever they made, it would have to be for export. Israel's internal markets were too small to sustain the kind of growth that Ma'agan Michael expected. Export meant the possibility of government loans, but it also meant mass production, and as Kantor searched around Israel he discovered that the Israelis' mass production of sophisticated industrial goods was at least 10 years behind the times. In Europe, however, he found what he was looking for—injection molding machinery for plastics.

So Itzik Kantor, former mechanic, came home to propose that Ma'agan Michael set up a plastics factory. With this proposal, the "horizontal decision making" process went into action. In fact, several recognized institutional bodies were already involved: the kibbutz Secretariat, for example, whose two officers are elected on alternate years, and an Economic Resources Committee, composed of the elected managers of the money-making kibbutz enterprises, at that time fishing and agriculture. The final decision, however, rested with the General Assembly, which is composed of all members of the kibbutz, 550 of them today, 350 when Kantor proposed his factory, who meet every Saturday evening to debate, often with classic Israeli vehemence, everything from kibbutz morals and direction to the triumphs and travails of individual members.

It was an extraordinary decision that Kantor put before them. Used to thinking of themselves as sitting in a political assembly, or even as a court of law, here they were being approached as investors: to put up some portion of their community's wealth to establish a company and compete for profits in the capitalist world. And they were being asked to commit more than money. The investors in this business would also be its board of directors, its labor union, its stockholders, and its sole source of manpower. After hearing the recommendations of the kibbutz committees, the General Assembly told Kantor to go ahead: They would take the risk.

The degree of risk may be imagined from the fact that Kantor was for some time unclear about what products they would make with their injection molding machines once they got them. "I knew we'd have to make something of higher quality than was being made in Israel at that time," he recalls, "and most importantly it would have to be something new." The machinery would take care of the "higher quality"; it would be state-of-the-art. But what about the "something new"?

To answer that, Kantor looked to his own and his comrades' experience. "We could draw on the expertise available on the kibbutz," he says. "Something that we, as farmers, would be able to come up with that other farmers worldwide would be able to use, would find necessary, or at least better than anything else on the market." The practical as well as the philosophical underpinnings of the new enterprise would remain in the soil.

A new design for chicken cages was what they came up with first. The kibbutz's experience with chicken cages was the same as that of poultrymen all over the world. They were either made of wood, in which case they didn't last long, or they were made of metal, which made them heavy. Plasson's first product was plastic poultry cages, which were durable and

light. A bit later they went into toilet reservoirs, the first sophisticated ("and aesthetic," Kantor insists) ones on the Israeli market. Neither product was what one would call an instant success; nobody remembers what the revenues for Plasson's first year of business amounted to. The breakthrough chicken cages moved slower than the toilet reservoirs. One shipment of cages sat on the Amsterdam docks for three years before anyone bought them. In Israel, distributors stubbornly clung to iron cages—until they were forced over to the plastic by porters, the men who actually carry the birds to market. Plasson had little difficulty persuading the porters of the merits of the plastic cages.

The chicken cages were Plasson's first international success. Then, in the late 1960s, the company began coming out with a line of products that has made Plasson a byword for excellence throughout the multibillion-dollar poultry industry, especially in America.

The line was designed around a new invention for an old necessity—watering chickens. Plasson's drinker is a bell-shaped plastic device, colored a distinctive bright red, that is hooked up to a water source by valved tubing. The valves keep the water level constant, while the bell keeps it free of mash and other impurities. Nothing so effective had ever before been made for the purpose. But because it was novel, and because it cost more than rival products, Plasson's bell encountered heavy going.

By the mid-'70s, however, the kibbutz's American distributor, Diversified Imports, was reporting that Plasson had 35% of the American market for broilers and 90% of the breeder market. (Poulterers have a much bigger investment in breeders and so can more easily justify the greater cost of the Plasson bell.) Then in January 1978, at an Atlanta trade fair, Diversified Imports introduced Plasson's turkey drinker. "It was wild," says Dubrovsky. "Plasson's factory couldn't even begin to keep up with orders that came in. In one year, we had 80% of the turkey market."

Last fall, Plasson entered the 15-million-to-25-million-units-per-year American commercial egg market, another subset of the industry, with a new patented product that the kibbutz has been researching and testing for the past three or four years. In addition, Plasson's engineers and machinists have prepared a patented entry into the broiler market, for introduction late this year. They want to lift their share from their current one-third to the 80% they enjoy in the turkey coops. After that, they plan to develop something for the baby chicks, the last drinker market still eluding Plasson's products. Each product must be designed specifically for the size of the different types of poultry.

Kantor had understood from the chicken-cages days that the kibbutz was in markets in which the business cycle was short and merciless. Plasson was thus committed to innovation, whether it liked it or not. "Before the sales start to slump," Kantor explained to his fellow workers, who are also, remember, his investors and neighbors, "we have to find something new to produce." The market's whip hand in this instance belongs to the kibbutz's Taiwanese competitors. From the moment a new Plasson product makes a market for itself, the Taiwanese crank out a cheaper version. The quality, of course, is not always comparable. Dubrovsky tells the story of a farmer who complained to one of Diversified Import's distributors about the priciness of a Plasson item. The farmer had in his hand a familiar bright red bell which, he said, had cost him a whole lot less than what the distributor was charging for *his* bright red bell. The distributor thereupon endeavored to instruct the farmer in differentials of quality and price.

"Take a hammer to it," he said, pointing to the farmer's bell. The farmer did, and put a big dent in the plastic. "Then," says Dubrovsky, "he told the guy to take a ham-

mer to the Plasson bell. Well, that hammer bounced right back and damn near clawed the farmer's eyes out. Since then we tell people who can't tell the difference between our products and the Taiwanese, 'Take a hammer test—and watch out for your eyes!' "

But there is another reason that Plasson is so relentlessly driven to innovate—namely, Ma'agan Michael's refusal, so far, to employ outside labor. By hiring workers from nearby towns, the kibbutz could relieve a number of problems. It could buy more machines, expand production capacity, and thereby hang on much longer to the market demand for any given product. With this lengthening of the business curve, in turn, the pressure to innovate would relax slightly.

A number of kibbutzim in Israel have, in fact, recruited labor, both Arab and Jewish, from outside the collective. Ma'agan Michael will not; voters in the General Assembly have repeatedly turned the proposal down. Everyone has his own reasons for refusing this "opportunity." For Yossi Cohen, it reminds him of a visit he made in 1963 to a plastics factory in the Bronx, just to see what they were like, these machines that Itzik Kantor proposed to bring to Ma'agan Michael. "Frankly," he recalls, "I wasn't very impressed. The manager told me that of five machines, only three were working. I asked about the others, and he told me something I couldn't believe, I couldn't understand. He said that one of the workers threw—deliberately threw—something into the machine to make it stop and slow down production." The tough old man pauses for effect. "That, my friend, could never happen here."

Kantor makes the same point in ideological terms. "We are now all workers and owners," he says, "union members and stockholders. This is right. With outsiders here, there would be two classes of workers, and I wouldn't want that. It would immediately result in different motivating elements for different workers." For Boaz Tamir, Kantor's son-in-law and a PhD candidate in political science and management at Massachusetts Institute of Technology, it is a matter, almost, of domestic continuity: "Besides the problems of salaries, pensions, and all the rest of it—problems which don't exist among ourselves—with hired labor you wouldn't be able to count on the workers the way you can count on the person who lives next door to you, who eats dinner with you on the holidays, who takes picnics with you, and whose children go to school with your children."

"Of course it's not all idyllic around here," says Yossi Cohen. "Kibbutzniks aren't angels. We're flesh and blood like anybody else. But our system makes it possible for social tensions, the ordinary tensions of daily life, to be dealt with in ways the city doesn't allow. And that gets reflected in the way people work here. They are committed to the kibbutz and, therefore, to the job."

The primacy of work shows up in any number of ways. Nobody ever gets fired at Ma'agan Michael, and codes of behavior permit personal eccentricities that many Western enterprises would frown upon. (One grandmother at the factory, for example, comes to work at two o'clock in the morning, puts in her six hours, returns home for a nap, then spends the rest of the day with her grandchildren.) On the other hand, with respect to work, to pulling one's own weight, the social and moral pressure can be as firm and uncompromising as any "capitalist boss." Idlers don't belong.

From the business point of view, however, perhaps the most extraordinary aspect of this "workers' capitalism" is something else. Jack Dubrovsky describes it as confidence. "They've got this incredible confidence in the value of their products," he says. He attributes the confidence to experience. The factory, in a way, is just a service for the kibbutz farm, where its products are tested and retested by the people—

friends, fellow workers, fellow investors, farmers—whom it was set up to serve. If the products prove good for the farmers of Ma'agan Michael, then, and only then, will they be marketed to the other farmers of the world.

And there is another aspect of this confidence—the trust that the workers/stockholders/neighbors give to Itzik Kantor or whoever else happens to be circulating around the globe as international sales coordinator. It is a job that brings with it a terrible responsibility. Decisions must be made that risk the wealth of his neighbors and friends, his entire community—often under circumstances that don't permit calling a meeting of the General Assembly. Trust is the key factor in this arrangement. "Itzik can travel and make decisions," says Boaz Tamir, the young management student, "decisions that involve many millions of dollars. He can do that because he knows that the kibbutz is behind him, is ready to accept his decisions." And Itzik, for his part, is conscious of this trust every moment that he is abroad. "Of course, I'm aware of the fact that this isn't my own money," he says. "It's the whole kubbutz's money that we're dealing with here. That's a huge responsibility, and it sometimes frightens me. But that's why I work so hard."

But, naturally, there is trust on his side as well. Many times, having just clinched a big, unexpected order, Kantor will call back to Plasson to order what is known at Ma'agan Michael as a "mobilization." With that one word, posted on the bulletin board, he can summon volunteers from all over the kibbutz to work the machines of the factory. They will work on Saturdays, their only day off, giving up drives into the Galilee or picnics on the beach; everybody will—teenagers and grandparents, agricultural workers and engineers at the research and development facilities, everybody. And the only "overtime" they will be paid is in gallons of free ice cream. Much of what

American businesspeople would call Plasson's corporate culture can be explained by the state of Israel's society and political problems. When a Ma'agan Michael worker sees himself or herself as laboring "under the gun" to meet a production demand, or as being "on the front line" of Israel's struggle to earn foreign currency, these clichés come close to describing an actual state of affairs. Last December, the entire kibbutz of 1,200, including all of the children, mobilized to put in a day's work—and profits—to aid the famine-stricken people of Ethiopia.

Yet societies and individuals may respond in all sorts of ways to emergencies—selfishly as well as altruistically, by hunkering down and by opening up. Military metaphors can't explain all of Plasson's high morale. There is also the kibbutz ideals—and maybe, too, little details like having a factory where small boys can go visit their grandparents.

V

View From the Top

48

Palace Products Company

You are J. C. Kramer, Executive Vice-President of Palace Products Company. John Maguire, President of Palace Products, hired you from another company and you began work only one week ago. You were to train under Walter Hopkins, who was Executive Vice-President for one year until his retirement. You have 22 years of experience working in manufacturing companies, with 10 years at middle and upper management levels. You have a Bachelor of Science Degree in Engineering.

Walter Hopkins is critically ill, and will not be returning to work. You have not been with the company long enough to learn very much about the management system. You have just had time to learn the names of other managers. John Maguire wants you to assume full responsibility as Executive Vice-President because you are an experienced manufacturing executive. He told you that you are in complete control of internal operations. He does not want to interfere in your decisions because his role is to work with people in the environment and with International Controls Company, the company that purchased Palace Products two years ago.

HISTORY

Palace Products was started in 1948 by John Maguire and two other World War II veterans. They invented a flow control device and pooled their resources to develop and manufacture it. Palace Products grew rapidly, and now produces control valves to regulate almost anything that flows through pipe. Palace originally established a niche as an innovative new product leader in the field of control valves and flow control instruments. Over the last 10 years, however, innovation has been less frequent. The products are rather standard. Other companies are gaining a new-product edge, and Palace has gradually exper-

Prepared by Richard L. Daft. This case is adapted from several sources, including James B. Lau, "Crofts Products Company," *Behavior in Organization: An Experiential Approach* (Homewood, IL: Richard D. Irwin, 1975), 269–277; Harry R. Knudson, Robert T. Woodworth, and Cecil H. Bell, "Electronics, Incorporated," *Management: An Experiential Approach* (New York: McGraw-Hill, 1979), 128–138; E. Paul Smith, "You Are Bob Waters, Assistant Administrator at Unity Hospital," distributed by the Intercollegiate Case Clearing House, Soldiers Field, Boston, MA 02163; and the authors' own management experiences.

ienced a decreasing market share. Palace Products was taken over two years ago by International Controls Co. in a friendly merger. To date, Palace has kept substantial autonomy from International.

THE SITUATION

Palace Products is located in central Ohio. It has a capital investment in excess of $30,000,000, and produces seven major products for civilian (82%) and government markets (18%). Four products represent distinct types of control valves, and three products are instruments for flow control regulation. A control valve and instrument are typically combined to fit a specific flow control application. Palace also produces many valves on a custom order basis to meet unusual applications.

A fifth major product, called the 830 Butterfly Valve, is under development.

Flow control products have a variety of applications in refineries, pipelines, and utilities. Industrial applications represent 70% of Palace's business. Small control valves are used in virtually every home and building, and account for about 30% of total sales.

Palace's employees now include 64 engineers and 38 technicians. There are approximately 1,200 production employees who work two shifts. The manager in charge of production is Keith Malone. He has been in his current job for less than a year, but has been with the company about 21 years. His previous job included manager of quality control and manager of the machine shop. The marketing manager is Ray Thomas, who has been in his job four years. He was promoted from field sales manager into his present position. He is now responsible for the field sales manager (Mike McKay) and for the advertising and research manager (Bruce Parker). Marketing functions include promotion, merchandising, market research, market development, and di-

rect sales to customers. Sixty-five employees work in the marketing department.

Pete Tucker is the manager in charge of research and development. Tucker has a Masters Degree in Electrical Engineering. Prior to his promotion 30 months ago, he was the manager in charge of electrical engineering. The Research and Development Department includes 19 engineers and several technicians. Pete Tucker refuses to appoint anyone to supervisor roles because he believes his people should work as a team. Because of John Maguire's strong interest in research and development, nearly 8% of Palace's profits are allocated to this function.

The Engineering Department is managed by Bill Urban. Engineering typically implements the products created in Research and Development. Several engineering specialties are represented within the department, including electrical, mechanical, product, and systems engineering. The contracting specialist handles technical details involved in contracts with clients.

Al Wagner is in charge of employment and administrative services. His responsibility also includes community relations. This department has a staff of 19 people. Wagner transferred from the corporate personnel department over 18 months ago.

The finance manager is Ed Brock. He has been in his job about two years. Brock has an M.B.A. and is a specialist in management information systems. He is responsible for general and cost accounting, payroll, the computer unit, and accounts receivable and payable. Finance has a staff of about 20 people.

The demand for control valves has traditionally fluctuated with general business activity, especially construction. When construction and business activity is high, the control valve business booms. For the last two years, industry output has been stable, and the number of units shipped by Palace

EXHIBIT 48–1 ORGANIZATION CHART FOR PALACE PRODUCTS CO.

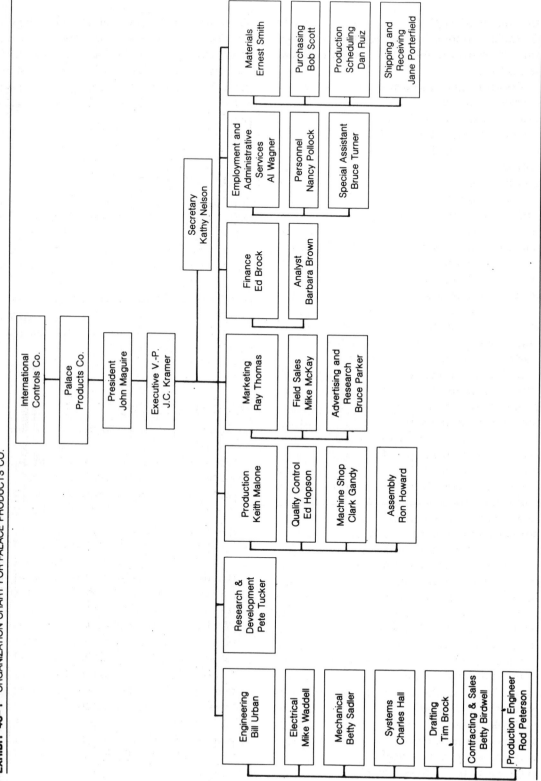

has declined slightly. Palace is not yet in financial trouble, but money is tight. High interest rates on short-term loans is drawing off cash.

Control valve innovation follows developments in electronics, metallurgy, and flow control theory. Developments in these fields are used by manufacturers to increase the sensitivity and efficiency of valves and instruments. Recent developments in electronics have led to new control valve applications based upon miniaturization and automatic controls. Palace has been working for three years on a new control valve design called the Butterfly. This design has the potential to regulate the flow of liquids at 75% of the cost of traditional designs.

Palace has a reputation for product quality and reliability. Engineering, research, and production have traditionally been important departments in the company.

In the single conversation you had with Walter Hopkins before he became ill, he confided to you that Palace should retrench for the next two years or so until economic conditions improved. He insisted that Palace's reputation for product quality would hold the customer base if the marketing department concentrated on servicing established customers rather than on finding new customers. Hopkins said that Maguire always wanted more money budgeted to R & D for new developments, but he disagreed. New products have been an enormous hassle, and Hopkins could not see their contribution to profit. He believed new products were more trouble than they were worth. Hopkins planned to concentrate on improving internal efficiencies. "Cutbacks now will leave us lean and strong for the economic upturn ahead." He also said, "One dollar saved in production is worth $3 in sales."

Hopkins also confided to you that a staff member from International Controls Company headquarters suggested to President Maguire that a project or matrix form of structure be adopted at Palace. Maguire isn't sure whether that is a good idea, but most managers, including Hopkins, don't see any need to change organization structure. They are more concerned with human resources—finding and keeping good people.

SATURDAY, MARCH 7

You were appointed Executive Vice-President on Thursday, March 5. On Friday morning you got word to all those reporting to you (see Exhibit 48–1) asking them to write you a memorandum if they had any issues to be discussed with you. By Friday night, your in-basket contained the memoranda below. You take these memoranda home for evaluation so you can plan your next week's activities.

YOUR ASSIGNMENT

Study the memoranda and answer the following questions:

1. What are the four most important problems facing you? Specify and rank the problems in priority order of importance. What are the two least important problems facing you?

2. What techniques will you use to work on the problems during the coming week? Be specific. State exactly how you plan to approach and solve the problems listed in response to question 1.

3. What overall strategy should Palace Products adopt? Should the company cut back, retrench, and stress efficiency? Should it invest heavily in research and development in order to be innovative and reestablish itself as a product leader?

4. Based upon the information available to you, is a change in organization structure warranted? What would you recommend to Maguire?

PALACE PRODUCTS COMPANY

OFFICE MEMORANDUM   DATE: March 6, 1983

TO: J. C. Kramer
FROM: Kathy
SUBJECT: Your Meetings and Correspondence

Here are the memos that came in today. Mr. Maguire's memo is on top. Your luncheon appointments for the week are as follows:

Tuesday, March 10	11:30 AM–1:30 PM	Award lunch
Wednesday, March 11	12:00 AM–1:30 PM	Peter O'Reilly of O'Reilly Construction Co.
Thursday, March 12	10:00 AM–1:00 PM	Corporation meeting
Friday, March 13	12:30 PM–2:00 PM	Mrs. Rogers of the United Way

The following meetings were already scheduled by Mr. Hopkins.

Tuesday, March 10	8:00 AM–9:00 AM	Weekly staff meeting. This will include a discussion of new policies and procedures by Al Wagner and expanding opportunities for women by Nancy Pollock. A program for using less energy will be proposed by Bruce Turner.
Wednesday, March 11	9:00 AM–10:00 AM	Meet Chamber of Commerce representative.

See you on Monday.

PALACE PRODUCTS COMPANY

OFFICE MEMORANDUM   DATE: March 6, 1983

TO: J. C. Kramer
FROM: John Maguire, President
SUBJECT: New Products and Corporate Meetings

J.C., let me welcome you aboard once again. I'm looking forward to working with you. I will be out of town for the next two weeks but will get together with you immediately upon my return.

I am quite concerned that Palace continues developing new control valve products and adding to our line. New developments have not been progressing very well, and decisions will have to be made in the near future for allocating funds and people to this endeavor. Could you get together right away with Pete Tucker and find out what new developments they would like to work on? We need to have these ideas consolidated and to select promising projects in the near future.

By the way, would you also check into the progress of our new model 830 butterfly valve? I've heard grumblings from two customers, but told them I didn't believe there was any problem. Where is the monthly report? It should have been on my desk by March 1st. Would you please have that completed and bring it to my office?

One other thing. I'm scheduled to attend the International Controls Company meeting on Thursday at 10:00 AM Since I will be out of town, could you attend for me? We do not have to make a presentation and the corporation will send me a copy of the minutes. The executives from the other companies within International Controls will be there, and you can meet them.

I look forward to seeing you when I return.

PALACE PRODUCTS COMPANY

OFFICE MEMORANDUM   DATE: March 6, 1983

TO: J. C. Kramer, Executive Vice-President
FROM: Ray Thomas, Marketing Department
SUBJECT: Model 830 Butterfly Valve

I understand that the new model 830 butterfly valve will not begin production for another two months. We have had repeated delays introducing this new system. It was originally scheduled to begin production last August, then January 1 of this year. Now the earliest date appears to be May 1. This is creating a serious problem for us, because we've been telling our customers about it and they want to have an opportunity to experiment with it. I anticipate a 30–60 day lag from the beginning of production before we will have products ready for delivery to customers. One of the salesmen heard from a customer that a small control valve company in Texas was about to introduce a new butterfly valve.

Another urgent matter is the model 820 retrofit. This should go on the market immediately. It also needs to be priced low or it could affect sales. Our retrofit is a small item, but it is badly needed because it will provide the precision control our competitor's products already have. Mr. Hopkins agreed with me that every effort should be made to have this product in the field immediately. We have promised our customers that the retrofit would be ready for delivery on April 1.

The sales forecasts for this year were based on the expectation that new products would go into production and sales as planned. Further delays in the introduction of the model 820 retrofit and the model 830 butterfly valve could seriously reduce sales forecasts for the year.

PALACE PRODUCTS COMPANY

OFFICE MEMORANDUM   DATE: March 6, 1983

TO: J. C. Kramer, Executive V.-P.
FROM: Ernest Smith, Materials Manager
SUBJECT: Material Costs and Inventory Needs

I have been concerned for a long time about our steadily increasing materials costs. Due to the nature of our business almost 30% of our direct costs are materials-related. Walter Hopkins agreed with me that we should do everything possible to increase efficiency at Palace Products. Reducing materials costs was a top priority for him. My people work hard to reduce costs and establish decent manufacturing schedules, but we can't do it alone. We always have to revise production schedules because of manufacturing problems, especially with the new models. My purchasing people don't get word on what to buy until the last minute, and then their materials need to be rush ordered and expedited. This increases costs at least 10%. By the time we get the materials, another design change may be underway, so the parts we rush-ordered may not be appropriate. Because of the way Engineering, Research, and Production work, our material costs are almost out of control.

Another important matter is the inventory problem. During the spring and summer we receive many small orders for one or two items. Setting up and manufacturing a special order is expensive. Sometimes after we complete the order the customer will decide they want one or two more of the same item. This means two setups for the same product and customer. For approximately $275,000 we could keep these small orders in inventory and fill orders much more efficiently. Ed Brock in Finance tells me he doesn't have $275,000 for inventory. Walter Hopkins agreed with me that this was another priority in our efforts to increase efficiency. An investment in inventory would be the best thing for this company right now.

The final problem are the designs for the model 830 butterfly valve. We need to get these designs finalized so we can establish decent manufacturing and purchasing schedules. The model 830 is supposed to go into manufacturing shortly, but as yet we have not been able to get a parts list that we can rely on. How can we go into production without acquiring parts? I wish the people in Engineering and Research would be more cooperative on this.

PALACE PRODUCTS COMPANY

OFFICE MEMORANDUM   DATE: March 6, 1983

TO: J. C. Kramer
FROM: Barbara Brown
SUBJECT: Request for Appointment

Since you have an open door policy, I must see you. I am about to resign from the company and want to discuss it with you before I make the final decision. I have been here for six months. The assignments I am receiving from Mr. Brock simply are not challenging. I am not having any impact upon Palace Products Company. The projects I have been assigned are small and do not utilize the theoretical and analytical abilities I acquired during my M.B.A. training.

My mid-year progress report was excellent, which frustrates me even more. I would rather be rewarded for making a major contribution to this company than for doing small projects. I have tried to explain the problem to Mr. Brock, but he hardly has time to discuss it. He says he understands, but still hasn't assigned me to do anything really important. It is becoming clear to me that the Finance department does not control anything here at Palace Products Company.

PALACE PRODUCTS COMPANY

OFFICE MEMORANDUM   DATE: March 6, 1983

TO: J. C. Kramer, Executive Vice-President
FROM: Al Wagner, E. & A.S.
SUBJECT: Employment of the Disadvantaged

I received important information at a personnel meeting last night. The word is out that federal equal opportunity agencies will be looking at industrial plants in this area during the next six months. Currently, we have a very low ratio of disadvantaged employees. We may be in serious trouble.

I believe we should begin a crash program to employ 50 non-whites in all areas of the company. In order to save time, we should not use our normal testing procedures for these employees. Besides, our regular aptitude and intelligence tests may open us to charges of discrimination. Of course we can continue to use these tests for our normal employment of whites.

A crash program may involve some increased training and labor costs. Increased costs are better than losing government contracts. Besides, employing the disadvantaged is the right thing for Palace Products to do.

PALACE PRODUCTS COMPANY

OFFICE MEMORANDUM   DATE: March 6, 1983

TO: J. C. Kramer, Executive V.-P.
FROM: Bill Urban, Manager, Engineering
SUBJECT: Engineering Activities

There is really not too much to report from here. Things are in good shape. I would like to give you a complete briefing on our activities and plans whenever your schedule will allow it. For now, I would like to call four things to your attention.

1. I heard a rumor that International Controls was planning to centralize many of the contracting and engineering activities to the corporate level. This would mean a transfer of people to corporate headquarters, and many of our activities would be done away from this plant. I think this is a terrible idea because centralized engineers wouldn't know the details of what we're doing here. The International people seem to think it would save money by consolidating engineers into a central facility and allow them to use up-to-date equipment. That would be a poor tradeoff in my opinion.

2. We continue to be short-handed by two engineers. Betty Sadler and Charles Hall both told me that some of their people have job offers from other companies. We may have to make counter-offers in the next few weeks.

3. A related item is the need to send five people to the American Engineering Society meeting in Las Vegas. Some of the engineering and research people want to report in a scientific paper some of the theoretical work behind the 830 butterfly valve. They will conduct a full-day session. This would be a great reward for them, but it will

cost $7,500. We will need your approval because this will be well in excess of the travel budget.

4. The model 820 and model 830 developments seem to be coming along quite well. There is no urgency, but we do not have the most recent data and the final report from R & D. R & D claims we already have the data, but I think they are too busy to write the final report. We can't make the final decisions about production designs until we know the exact figures. I discussed this with Walter Hopkins last week, and he was going to see Pete Tucker about it.

PALACE PRODUCTS COMPANY

OFFICE MEMORANDUM DATE: March 6, 1983

TO: J. C. Kramer, Executive Vice-President
FROM: Nancy Pollock, Personnel
SUBJECT: Award Lunch

Don Jameson, a machinist, has been with the company 35 years and is being given an award as the most senior employee. He has been with the company since its founding, and a luncheon has been scheduled for him on Tuesday, March 10, from 11:30 to 1:30. It will be held in the luncheon room at the Townshire Hotel.

Walter Hopkins was going to present a company pin and give a brief talk. He always believed it was good human relations to emphasize the company's interest in those working here. Several of the senior production employees will attend the luncheon. Keith Malone agreed to substitute for Walter, but I'm sure you will also want to attend Don's luncheon.

PALACE PRODUCTS COMPANY

OFFICE MEMORANDUM DATE: March 6, 1983

TO: J. C. Kramer, Executive V.-P.
FROM: Al Wagner, E. & A.S.
SUBJECT: Reporting on the Model 820 and Model 830

I have attached a note from Bruce Turner, a bright young employee with the company. It reflects the problems he is having and I have not been able to do much about it. The memo illustrates the lack of cooperation when we try to coordinate new product developments.

Dear Mr. Wagner:

One of my most important jobs is coordinating the monthly report for the Model 830 butterfly valve. In the initial meeting with you and Ed Brock from Finance, we worked out a monthly reporting plan for the 830 project. The plan was designed to record budget expenditures, and to keep upper management informed on the progress of each aspect of the development. We have tried to use a similar procedure for the Model 820 retrofit.

I'm getting no cooperation whatsoever. As it turns out, I am nothing but a pencil-pusher. I am having no influence at all on running and coordinating the 830 program. The departments are not taking this project seriously, no matter how many memos I write. R & D

wants to do its own thing. Pete Tucker tells me that I give too much emphasis to reporting procedures and that I can expect the final report in a month or so. He says he is busy with important new developments, and the 830 is now old stuff. Keith Malone in Production says that they are having problems, and have not yet started production, but I don't know why. Marketing is pressing me to get the report moving, but they don't provide any useful information either. None of the departments bother to meet my deadline for a monthly report. As an administrative coordinator, I can't enforce compliance. What should I do?

Bruce Turner

PALACE PRODUCTS COMPANY

OFFICE MEMORANDUM DATE: March 6, 1983

TO: J. C. Kramer, Executive Vice-President
FROM: Edward Brock, Finance
SUBJECT: Integrated Management Information System

After a long struggle, we finally completed our computer-based integrated management information system last month. It cost $110,000, but will be well worth it. The new system will provide daily, weekly, or monthly information about sales, production scheduling, the status of customer orders, vendor deliveries, and the like. The system will also provide me with more detailed cost accounting data.

Unfortunately, although we debugged the computer software, the system is not working very well. One problem is that the managers are not providing the correct information and they are not using it. They are maintaining their own reports. They don't seem to want me to have the detailed figures I need for the cost-accounting reports. This system is important to the efficient operation of this company. Another problem is that we aren't using the most recent technical developments for data processing. I've set aside $60,000 for acquiring updated equipment. We will have the best MIS in the industry.

Walter Hopkins gave me his full backing to install the MIS. Would you talk to the other managers about adhering to the rules and procedures necessary to make the system work? Any assistance you can give me will be greatly appreciated. My staff and I have spent almost full time on this project for several weeks.

PALACE PRODUCTS COMPANY

OFFICE MEMORANDUM DATE: March 6, 1983

TO: J. C. Kramer
FROM: Keith Malone
SUBJECT: Model 820 Retrofit

I can't possibly make the production schedule for the Model 820 retrofit if I also have to be concerned about beginning production of the new Model 830 butterfly valve. The research, engineering, and marketing people are driving us crazy. Engineering keeps making design changes, and marketing people keep coming out to the shop to see when they can get their hands on the finished products. My people are working overtime to make production changes to meet design changes so the 820 won't be delayed any further. I strongly recommend that we stop all production activities on both the 820 and the 830 until all design issues are resolved once and for all.

I see that I made a mistake in accepting the 820 for production. The engineering people convinced me that there would be no more changes but they did not have the final figures ready for me. It turns out they weren't clear about the final design. I won't make that mistake again.

By the way, can you get the finance people off my back? They have installed a computer system and want to have us run everything into that computer. It creates a lot of extra work for us at a time when we don't need extra work. The computer has not been debugged, so my people still have to keep their own reports.

PALACE PRODUCTS COMPANY

OFFICE MEMORANDUM   DATE: March 6, 1983

TO: J. C. Kramer, Executive V.-P.
FROM: Pete Tucker, Manager, Research and Development
SUBJECT: New Products

Our most pressing need is to get budgets approved for new developments. John Maguire has always supported new-product development in this company. Our people in R & D have a number of original ideas, and they are ready to start working on them. We will need a budget allocation of about $325,000 beginning April 1. We will have the people to allocate full time to the projects then. Would you contact Ed Brock about assigning the needed budget to us? He hasn't even responded to my memos. And please don't ask for a lot of formal plans and approvals. My people are very creative, which is their strength, and paperwork inhibits them. Palace Products has been a success because of new-product developments, and we need to maintain our momentum.

I also want to call your attention to problems in Production and in Engineering. The Model 820 retrofit has turned into a joke. We gave those people a perfect retrofit design, and somehow things have been screwed up so that it is not yet in production. It may be the people in production engineering or a lack of cooperation in the machine shop. Somebody was not able to follow through on an excellent design.

I have also heard that Engineering and Production are having problems with the new Model 830 butterfly valve. I want to assure you that everything is under control. We have completed the design work and the final report will be written as soon as we have some free time. Engineering has all the figures they need. I admit there were some slippages in the development of the 830. One hangup was due to the failure of the system to pass the high pressure flow control tests, but we anticipate no further difficulty. I don't see any reason why Engineering and Production should not be able to meet their schedules. By far the most important thing for us is to get the $325,000 so we can commit ourselves full time to new developments.

49

Panalba

The purpose of this exercise is to analyze the decision-making actions of an organization faced with conflicting responsibilities to its constituents and to society. This exercise may be conducted as a role-play, with members representing various constituents, or as an "unaffiliated" group decision process.

Strategic actions/planning in an organization may take into consideration constituents internal and external to its operations. Stockholders, employees, the board of directors, competitors, and government are a few of those to be considered. In the following exercise you will be challenged to determine the course of action to be taken by a major pharmaceutical manufacturer in the face of various demands.

STEP 1: *Group Assignment (5 min.)*

The class will be divided into groups of seven people. Each group will read the problem description below; the instructor will assign either the "Financial Accounting" or the "Social or Interest Group Accounting" to each group.

STEP 2: *Group Decision (20 min.)*

After reading the problem description each group will discuss and propose a course of action to be followed for the U.S. market. Select from the possible solutions A, B, C, D, or E.

STEP 3: *Group Decision (5–10 min.)*

Repeat step 2 for the foreign markets, again selecting from solutions A, B, C, D, and E.

STEP 4: *Class Discussion (20 min.)*

Each group will briefly present its proposal and justification. The class will then discuss the relevant issues in relation to the theories and models that may have been presented earlier in classroom lectures and discussions. The following questions are provided to stimulate the discussion.

DISCUSSION QUESTIONS

1. Which constituents and environmental factors must the company consider? Which are most important?
2. What role should the constituents play in the decision-making process? Should the

Abstracted from "Social Irresponsibility in Management," J. Scott Armstrong, *Journal of Business Research*, 5 (Sept. 1977), 185–213.

company involve each in making a decision?

3. How would you describe the strategy of the Upjohn Corporation before the Panalba incident? What strategic shift, if any, would your course of action require?

4. What do you think are the internal cultural values of the Upjohn Corporation? How would these support the strategic goals of the company?

5. Can you cite other instances when an organization's cultural values conflicted with society's? How was this resolved?

6. Can organization theory teach managers to act ethically?

BACKGROUND INFORMATION FOR PANALBA

Assume that it is August, 1969, and that Upjohn Corporation has called a Special Board Meeting to discuss what should be done with the product known as "Panalba."

Panalba is a fixed-ratio antibiotic sold by prescription, that is, it contains a combination of drugs. It has been on the market for over 13 years and has been highly successful. It now accounts for about $18 million per year, which is 12% of Upjohn Company's gross income in the U.S. (and a greater percentage of net profits). Profits from foreign markets, where Panalba is marketed under a different name, are roughly comparable to those in the U.S.

Over the past 20 years there have been numerous medical scientists (e.g., the AMA's Council on Drugs) objecting to the sale of most fixed-ratio drugs. The argument has been that (1) there is no evidence that these fixed-ratio drugs have improved benefits over single drugs and (2) the possibility of detrimental side effects, including death, is *at least* doubled. For example, these scientists have estimated that Panalba is causing about 14 to 22 unnecessary deaths per year, i.e., deaths that could be prevented if the patients had used a substitute made by a competitor of Upjohn. De-

spite these recommendations to remove fixed-ratio drugs from the market, doctors have continued to use them. They offer a shotgun approach for the doctor who is unsure of his diagnosis.

Recently a National Academy of Science—National Research Council panel, a group of impartial scientists, carried out extensive research studies and recommended unanimously that the Food and Drug Administration (FDA) ban the sale of Panalba. One of the members of the panel, Dr. Eichewald of the University of Texas, was quoted by the press as saying, "There are few instances in medicine when so many experts have agreed unanimously and without reservation" (about banning Panalba). This view was typical of comments made by other members of the panel. In fact, it was typical of comments that had been made about fixed-ratio drugs over the past 20 years. These impartial experts believed that while all drugs have some possibility of side effects, the costs associated with Panalba far exceed the possible benefits.

The Special Board Meeting has arisen out of an emergency situation. The FDA has told Upjohn that it plans to ban Panalba in the U.S. and wants to give Upjohn time for a final appeal to them. Should the ban become effective, Upjohn would have to stop all sales of Panalba and attempt to remove inventories from the market. Upjohn has no close substitute for Panalba, so consumers will be switched to close substitutes that are easily available from other firms. Some of these substitutes offer benefits that are equivalent to those from Panalba, yet they have no serious side effects. The selling price of the substitutes is approximately the same as the price for Panalba.

It is extremely unlikely that bad publicity from this case would have any significant effect upon the long-term profits of other products made by Upjohn.

The following possible solutions were considered by the Board:

    A. Recall Panalba immediately and destroy.

B. Stop production of Panalba immediately but allow what's been made to be sold.

C. Stop all advertising and promotion of Panalba but provide it for those doctors who request it.

D. Continue efforts to most effectively market Panalba until sale is actually banned.

E. Continue efforts to most effectively market Panalba and take legal, political, and other necessary actions to prevent the authorities from banning Panalba.

You, as a member of the Board, must help reach a decision at today's meeting. The Chairman of the Board, Ed Upjohn, has provided this background information to each of the board members. He is especially concerned about selecting the most appropriate alternative for the U.S. market. (You must decide which of the possible alternatives is *closest* to your preferred solution.)

A similar decision must also be made for the foreign market *under the assumption that the sale of Panalba was banned in the U.S.* This decision will be used as a contingency plan.

FINANCIAL ACCOUNTING

To assist with this decision, the Chairman had asked the Controller's Office to make some quick estimates of what would happen as a result of each course of action. These estimates are summarized in the memo from the Controller.

MEMO: To E. G. Upjohn, Chairman of the Board
FROM: Samuel Hardy, Controller (copies to Board of Directors)

The following estimates were prepared on very short notice by the Controller at Upjohn. As a result, these figures should be regarded as crude estimates as to what will happen. After-tax profits at Upjohn *prior* to this crisis have been predicted to be $39 million for 1969. The figures below are estimated losses from this prediction under each alternative. The figures represent only the financial losses to Upjohn stockholders.

Alternative	Estimated LOSSES* (In millions of dollars)
A. "Recall Immediately"	20.0
B. "Stop Production"	13.0
C. "Stop Promotion"	12.0
D. "Continue Until Banned"	11.0
E. "Take Actions to Prevent Ban"	4.0

* This estimate represents present value loss to Upjohn and covers all items (e.g., lawsuits, legal fees, expenses involved with recall). The losses would be spread out over a number of years.

SOCIAL OR INTEREST GROUP ACCOUNTING

To assist with this decision, the Chairman had asked the Controller's Office to make some quick estimates of what would happen as a result of each course of action. These estimates are summarized in the memo from the Controller.

MEMO: To E. G. Upjohn, Chairman of the Board
FROM: Samuel Hardy, Controller (copies to Board of Directors)

The following estimates were prepared on short notice by the Controller of Upjohn. As a result, these figures should be regarded as crude estimates as to what will happen. After-tax profit at Upjohn *prior* to this crisis had been predicted to be $39 million for 1969. The figures below are estimated losses from this prediction under each alternative for each group. All other important effects from this decision have also been estimated.

Alternative	Estimated LOSSES* (in millions of dollars)			
	(1) Stockholders	(2) Customers	(3) Employees	(1)+ (2)+(3) Total Losses
A. "Recall Immediately"	20.0	0.0	2.0	22.0
B. "Stop Production"	13.0	13.6	1.8	28.4
C. "Stop Promotion"	12.0	16.8	1.2	30.0
D. "Continue Until Banned"	11.0	19.6	1.0	31.6
E. "Take Actions to Prevent Ban"	4.0	33.8	0.2	38.0

* These estimates represent present value losses to each group that is affected by this decision. The losses to customers represent deaths and illnesses caused by Panalba for which no compensation is received; losses to employees represent lost wages and moving expenses beyond those covered by severance pay and unemployment benefits.

50

Recreation Products, Inc.

By early 1969 Leroy Harden and James Nicklus were indeed satisfied with the rapid growth in Recreation Products, Inc. They were aware, however, that this very growth could produce organizational strains; they were concerned that any such tendencies not be overlooked but be dealt with. They realized that the rapid growth in RPI had moved them further from operational control and might lead to problems in coordination among the functional units. They were also determined that one key current organizational relationship, selling several product groups through a single force, continue to operate as they continued to pursue their strategies of acquisition and rapid growth.

HISTORY

In 1964 Nicklus and Harden left McKinsey to look for a company to purchase and manage. After a five-month search, they purchased Gorman Manufacturing Company, an established but unimaginative maker of lawn sprinklers. Gorman had what Nicklus and Harden were looking for: a consumer product with an established reputation for quality but a feeble marketing effort. The two men felt that their M.B.A. education and consulting experience plus an infusion of younger, more aggressive management talent could markedly improve Gorman's profitability and growth.

Recreation Products, Inc. (RPI) developed as the founders expanded their original ambitions into the larger concept of a leisure-time recreation company. In early 1969 the firm was an agglomeration of eight youth, recreation, lawn, and sports equipment companies, all acquired in a carefully developed strategy that would eventually take RPI into most areas normally defined as "leisure time" or "recreation." Between 1965 and 1967, RPI grew at about 15%. RPI acquired four firms and grew from sales of $1,291,000 to $9,631,000, and its net income after taxes rose from $81,000 to $536,000. Exhibit 50–1 presents key financial data for the period 1965–68.

EXHIBIT 50-1 KEY FINANCIAL DATA FOR PERIOD OF 1965-68

	1968		1967		1966		1965	
Sales	$17,662,000		$ 9,631,000		$ 7,324,000		$ 1,291,000	
Gross margin	5,839,000	33%	3,584,000	41%	2,296,000	31%	506,000	39%
Income before taxes	1,922,000	11%	1,004,000	10.4%	432,000	6%	138,000	10.4%
Net income	962,000		536,000		235,000		81,000	
Earnings per share	$ 1.08		$ 0.76		$ 0.40		$ 0.23	
Working capital	5,673,000		2,547,000		2,176,000		141,000	
Net plant and equipment	7,095,000		2,686,000		2,360,000		671,000	
Shareholders' equity	8,177,000		1,380,000		676,000		121,000	
Number of plants	7		4		3		2	
Number of employees	1,700		700		530		120	

Stock Price Movement
(bid-asked prices)

Insured 4/68	5/1/68	6/1/68	7/1/68	8/1/68	9/1/68	10/1/68
13	33-35	41-44	43-45	45-48	48-51	58-62
Insured 11/1/68	12/1/68	1/1/69	2/1/69	3/1/69	4/1/69	
61-65	68-72	63-67	68-72	55-59	59-63	

Capitalization, 1,039,000 shares 20 percent held by top officers

Source: Annual reports.

The first acquisition was Rich Spray Gun Company, picked up in 1965 and merged into Gorman. Since the two product lines were similar, this marriage was relatively easy to effect organizationally. Next came Tom Carver, Inc., the world's largest manufacturer of archery equipment. Nicklus and Harden were attracted to this company because of potential for savings in operating costs and the possibility of increasing sales by streamlining the organization and providing increased marketing punch.

They felt certain they could accomplish this by substituting RPI management procedures for those of the founder, Tom Carver, a professional archer. Leroy Harden described the situation as it developed:

Tom Carver is still on the payroll. Only now he is doing what he likes to do best. This includes promoting Carver products by traveling the United States staging archery tournaments and attracting attention to his entourage, a stuffed animal caravan. Tom Carver is to Carver's product line what Colonel Sanders is to Kentucky Fried Chicken.

In 1967 RPI acquired Nile Sled Company, makers of Snowbird sleds since 1889. Once

again the pattern was consistent with the general strategy: a branded consumer product with accepted quality but moribund marketing ideas. James Nicklus commented on the marketing inputs RPI had to inject to rebuild Snowbird sales:

This Snowbird situation really took an effort. This company virtually dominated the sled market during the 1920s. By 1967, they were lucky to have 15%, and I'll bet part of that was a gift. This company probably survived because nostalgic fathers insisted their children have the same sled they once used. The products were generally overpriced and unwanted by dealers. We had to redesign the sleds to make them competitive, cut prices to chain stores, and really promote them at retail. We also had to win back dealers with special promotional offers as well as the lowered prices.

In 1968, RPI accelerated acquisition growth by absorbing four more companies. First came Brockman Sprinkler. This purchase was designed to widen the product line in lawn and garden equipment. In March 1968, RPI picked up Green Thumb Company, manufacturers and marketers of indoor plant care products. In June the group moved into still another new field by acquiring Quality Arms Company. Quality Arms manufactured quality lines of firearms, both handguns and shoulder guns. This "top of the line" product group included Tournament Caliber firearms for competition accuracy as well as a complete array of hunting rifles and shotguns. Finally, in October 1968, RPI added to its line of winter products by acquiring Alpine Industries, a Canadian maker of toboggans and other winter sporting equipment. Alpine was also intended to provide an entrée into Canadian markets. Thus, by February 1969, Recreation Products, Inc. consisted of the broad product groups shown in Exhibit 50–2.

STRATEGY

The key elements of RPI strategy were formulated explicitly by Harden and Nicklus during 1966 as a reaction to factors in the environment. They saw two significant trends that strongly affected the growth possibilities of the companies managed at that time. One trend was the rapid *growth* in demand for leisure-time products and services. The factors contributing to this demand are generally known: (1) gradual shortening of workweeks, from today's 38–39 hours to estimates of 20 hours by the year 2000; (2) changing population mix, such that the number of young families, ages 25–34, will increase by 46% in the next decade alone; (3) rising disposable income per capita, projected to increase by 45% by 1975; and (4) increased education and better

communication, which serve to "socialize" Americans to use their free time actively.

The second trend, equally important in RPI's competitive environment, was the changing nature of distribution methods for leisure products: *the emergence of the high-volume mass merchandiser.* This evolution brings significant changes in the way goods are moved: self-service, point-of-sale displays, increased importance of packaging, and more sophisticated promotion techniques. It also brings centralized buying of chains and cooperative groups of independents.

The result of these two trends is the cornerstone of RPI strategy: to market various leisure-time products through a single sales force. Mr. Nicklus commented to the case writer:

This choice is more significant than might seem to be the case at first glance. The most obvious result is, of course, the economies of the selling effort spread over several products. Because the products are not highly technical, one salesman can handle the various lines. Equally significant, however, is an ability to provide the buyers at larger distributors with facts and data quickly and concisely. What we are working toward is a two-tiered salesforce: (1) a small number of expert salesmen who can provide these buyers the benefits of our centralized information on several product groups and (2) a larger number of "retail detail" men who stock shelves, handle promotional material, etc., at the various retail outlets. The result is that we are able to overpower most of our competitors in dealing with buyers; these competitors are still organized

EXHIBIT 50–2 PRODUCT GROUPS AND PRODUCTS

Archery	Firearms	Lawn and Garden Equipment	Winter Products	Commercial and Industrial Products
Tom Carver	Quality arms	Gorman Manufacturing Company	Snowbird	Farm equipment
		Rich Spray Gun Company	Alpine Industries	Private brands
		Green Thumb Company		Government sales

as though they were selling to a network of small retailers. In fact, over 50% of the sales of products such as ours are sold through mass merchandisers.

Mr. Harden, commenting on questions of strategy, added:

In terms of where we hope to take RPI, we are really still in Phase I. Our present lines can easily be handled by one salesforce. The questions I grapple with are what happens when sales of our present groups (and acquisitions to be made in these existing lines) reach $100 million or more and we move into fields such as travel, education, or entertainment. We might have to leave Recreation Products, Inc. at that time as a separate organization and start almost from scratch with the added services. You know, we can go a long way under the umbrella "leisure time" and "recreation."

To provide even more direction to these strategic goals, RPI has translated them into specific financial objectives. The first page of the 1968 RPI annual report sets forth these objectives and invites stockholders to evaluate the efforts of the management team in its pursuit of their accomplishment:

Since formation of the company in November 1964, our objective has been to build a major business enterprise engaged in the manufacture and marketing of leisure-time products. At that time we established financial and operating goals as follows: (1) 15% annual sales increase through internal growth; (2) 50% annual sales increase through acquisition; (3) net income equal to 6% of sales and a minimum annual increase in earnings per share of 25%.

ORGANIZATIONAL STRUCTURE

In 1969, Recreation Products, Inc. was organized functionally into three major units: marketing, operations (production), and product development. A fourth unit, the controller, provided centralized accounting, finance, and customer relation activities for the group at the corporate level. While no formal organization chart existed,

Exhibit 50–3 portrays the case writer's impressions of how it might have looked. Approximate ages are presented in this exhibit, and those men with M.B.A. degrees are noted.

MARKETING

The marketing unit performed essentially two types of functions: sales management and product management. Since marketing was critical at RPI, product managers occupied key roles in the operations of the firm. Mr. Nicklus indicated the scope of their responsibilities:

I'm sure the concept of the product manager is a familiar one. Most of the large consumer products companies, General Foods, Procter & Gamble, Kellogg, etc., are built on product managers. Around here, though, the term connotes a much broader span of responsibilities than I think exists in most firms. Our PMs are responsible for product strategies, market evaluation, merchandising and advertising tools, just as are their counterparts at General Foods. However, a more appropriate term at Recreation Products, Inc. would be product general manager. We hold these guys responsible for the product planning and for monitoring the ongoing situation to see that plans are fulfilled [in reference to the rough organization charts constructed by the case writer]. We don't really believe in these lines and boxes. If problems at a plant are holding back a product's sales, we expect the product manager to be on the phone immediately talking to the plant manager to iron out the problems. You know if I see a forecast not being met, I'll expect that PM to know why this exists, and what he plans to do about it. Similarly, if a PM expects to be under or over forecast in any particular quarter, it is his job to work with the plant manager to adjust production to avoid stocking out or excessive inventories. This information doesn't move up to Ralph Spiegel [director of marketing] and then down. It moves by the shortest route.

Product managers were each responsible for a particular product line: archery, winter products, lawn and garden equipment, firearms. In some instances, a line included

EXHIBIT 50-3 ORGANIZATION CHART

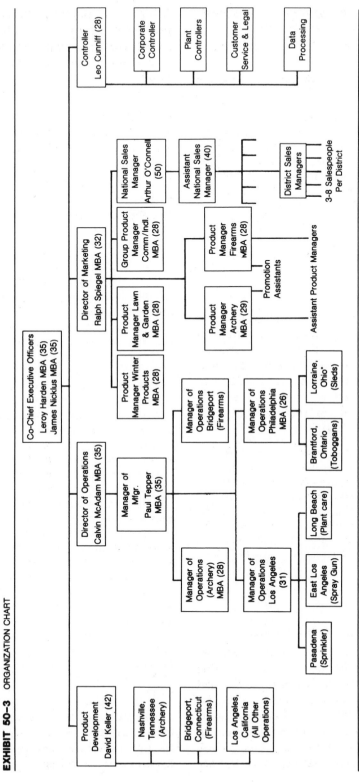

*Under construction.

more than one type of product; for instance, the PM for lawn and garden equipment handled sprinklers (acquired with Gorman Manufacturing Company), spray guns (once made by Rich), and the indoor plant care products of Green Thumb. The various products in a line might be manufactured at different plants, as is in fact the case in the above example. Thus, the product manager had to maintain contact with various plant people—the manager of operations and workers at each specific plant—as well as the salesforce and the director of marketing, to do his job.

Bob Vroom, product manager for lawn and garden equipment, described the facets of his job to the case writer:

I'll tell you the one thing I could use most around here, a 30-hour day! But we really relish the work and the responsibility that goes with being a product manager. I spend a good portion of my time at daily "firefighting" chores like attending to a problem raised by a customer or something popping up at the plant. And over the course of a month I am usually engaged in a few specific projects, such as planning a new product or altering packaging on an existing one. Of course, I spend quite a bit of time preparing the budgets and forecasts for next fiscal year. And I guess the remainder of my time is spent monitoring the current performance of my product line and keeping everyone aware of its status.

Jacob Sanford, product manager for archery, added:

I have to do most of my planning around and between "firefighting" on daily operations. You'll usually find the lights on around here until 9:00, often much later. But I think most PMs do it because of their stake in RPI and their large measure of responsibility for their product line. This stake in the company motivates me to go across functional areas when necessary.

The salesforce was divided geographically, with each person responsible for sales of all product lines within a geographic area. In 1969 the national sales area was divided into seven districts, each headed by a district manager. The district managers reported to Arthur O'Connell, the national sales manager. As of 1969 these district managers (DSMs) were dividing their time between selling and administrative duties. The DSM usually handled the larger accounts: centralized buying offices of chain stores and the larger independents. He would sometimes be accompanied by various product managers in calls to these large chains, usually at the beginning of the selling season for a particular product. The purpose of this joint effort would be to provide the intensive information and data mentioned earlier as a critical element of the marketing strategy.

The field salespeople usually called on smaller accounts and handled shelving, promotional material, and similar needs at individual outlets of the chain retailer. Mr. O'Connell commented on the current situation in the sales force.

RPI is really in a state of transition, a state of rapid growth. We began in 1968 with 15 salesmen; by December we had 50. What we are doing is moving toward our eventual target of a two-tiered sales organization. But if you're looking for an established formal organization, I doubt if you'll find it. As the force expands we must be constantly thinking of the future personnel demands. We have men in the field selling who will some day be district or area managers. Some of the men are obviously more talented than others; some possess far greater potential to grow with us. So at the present, our fieldmen have varying assignments. Some perform primarily the "detailing" functions at specific retail outlets. Others do the selling to larger buyers, or at least participate in this effort.

This marketing unit was headed by Ralph Spiegel, a 32-year-old M.B.A. Mr. Spiegel, a former product manager, had been made director of marketing in early 1969. Since the previous director had left RPI in June 1968, the position had remained unfilled while Messrs. Harden and Nicklus waited for a replacement to develop. In the interim Mr. Nicklus became more deeply involved with coordinating the efforts of the marketing organization.

OPERATIONS

Calvin McAdam, 35-year-old M.B.A., headed the operations organization. Reporting to Mr. McAdam were four managers of operations, each responsible for plants producing a particular product line. In early 1969, Paul Tepper, also an M.B.A., joined the group as the manager of manufacturing under Mr. McAdam and assumed responsibility for monitoring the day-to-day operations of the various plants. This new position was intended to reduce the extraordinary work load carried by Mr. McAdam.

I'm really glad to have Paul around here. Shifting part of my responsibility to him should permit me to spend some time on areas that I just haven't been able to get around to yet. We really haven't yet fully defined his job, as he has been here only a month. Right now I expect him to be on top of all current operations, that is, assuring the plants are meeting their production plans, meeting their cost reduction goals, and watching inventories.

As you know, I'm usually involved in our acquisitions in the early stages, because we usually have to make a number of significant changes in the production system of these firms. We are committed to our stockholders and the financial markets for making our profit estimates, and that often means getting these acquisitions turned around pronto! I also hope to devote more time now to specific projects, for instance, developing proposals for new plants or additions and developing a uniform labor policy for all plants.

The managers of operations were given full responsibility for the plant or plants under their supervision. They were responsible for translating marketing forecasts into production quotas and for monitoring ongoing operations to assure it met these goals. Allan Temple commented to the case writer on what this responsibility meant:

You know, we're shrewd enough to realize that

even though we spend a great effort planning around here, we have to retain the flexibility to react to the inevitable changes. That obviously makes the smooth operation of a product line highly dependent on the personal relationship between guys like me and their product manager. I'm on the phone to Bob Vroom (product manager for lawn and garden products) several times a week. When he sees a likely deviation from the marketing plan, he'll alert me to watch the inventory. If this confirms his thoughts, we will discuss the changes necessary in my production plan. Of course, he'll have to justify these changes to Ralph Spiegel [director of marketing], but it will be his decision. I don't see how we'd effectively handle the situation without this continuous personal contact.

PRODUCT DEVELOPMENT

Most product-development activities were centralized in Los Angeles, with only the groups at Nashville, Tennessee (archery), and Bridgeport, Connecticut (firearms), remaining at those particular plants.

David Keller, director of product development, commented to the case writer:

Like the rest of RPI, the product-development unit is constantly in a state of transition. We are working toward centralizing everything here at Los Angeles. At the present, the plants at Nashville and Bridgeport are still in need of work on production processes, so there are engineers at these plants.

The typical sequence of a particular project usually began with a suggestion from a product manager for a new or modified product, from a manager of operations for a process change, or from a designer or engineer in the product development group. A preliminary feasibility analysis was done, with time and dollar commitments estimated. Mr. Keller discussed the more frequent contacts he maintained during a project.

During the early phases of a project, I'm in pretty close contact with the particular PM or manager of operations who suggested the project. We gradually develop a cost-benefit analysis to see if the project warrants further work. Gradually, the director of marketing will be brought in, and sometimes the director of operations. And, of course, a "go/no-go" decision on all but very small projects will usually involve the top guys, James Nicklus and Leroy Harden.

CONTROLLER

In early 1969 the controller's office had recently been expanded as more and more functions were centralized under the responsibility of Mr. Leo Cunniff, the controller. Typical corporate accounting functions were directed to L.A. even before the group had data-processing facilities. Because the A/R and A/P data were there, it was a logical step to establish a central office for handling customer service: orders, complaints, and reports requested by customers. The data-processing unit provided data for use by both marketing and operations managers. Mr. Cunniff talked about the current problem areas with the case writer:

At present we have two chief areas of concern. Our present crisis stems from the fact that we are now doing our own data processing in-house, ratther than having it done by a service bureau. We're still in the "debugging" stage, so our output isn't getting to product managers or operations people as fast as it should. But this is temporary I'm sure, and we'll get it working.

Secondly, we're now thrashing around the idea of having plant controllers report to their respective plant managers, rather than to me. The intent would be to provide these MOs with more responsive information on their respective operations. The change is now being considered both by myself and by people in operations, particularly Paul Tepper [manager of manufacturing].

THE ANNUAL PLANNING PROCESS

Board Chairman Leroy Harden explained why there was an emphasis on planning at Recreation Products, Inc.:

Given our backgrounds, it's not hard to understand why we are so thorough in our

planning efforts around here. James and I were consultants, exposed to a broad range of situations where we could observe a number of different planning systems. Most of our marketing organization comes from companies like General Foods, Procter & Gamble, and Xerox—so we have the benefit of knowing how these rather sophisticated firms went about it. And most of us are MBAs, so I'm sure we're all still recovering from the pounding of "planning is a way of life."

He continued:

Detailed emphasis on planning fits integrally with the style of James and myself here at RPI. We both believe it is possible to make certain types of decisions once, and then disseminate procedures for how these recurring problems should be handled. We have seen so many examples of rather simple decisions being made over and over, each time with a new analysis. In this vein, we are convinced that a strong emphasis on planning forces our people to think in strategic terms. With well-thought plans, the everyday events can be interpreted in the context of the larger plan. Planning also contributes to setting goals and specific action routes to accomplishing these goals.

Because RPI was essentially a marketing organization, planning began with the individual product managers. In late spring product managers began their planning effort for the following fiscal year (beginning November 1). These men were responsible for the preparation of five formal documents, covering in general the industry and market and potential new products, and specifically sales forecasts and budgets for various marketing expenses. The "bottom line" figure for product managers was one that measured sales dollars minus all marketing expenses controllable by PMs, such as advertising and promotion. As mentioned earlier, PMs were held entirely responsible for the performance of their product line. Thus, their completed product plans also specified the efforts they expected to make to increase market share or sales dollars: efforts such as special promotions, new product introductions, intensive advertising campaigns, etc.

As these product plans were the basis for forecasting efforts by other units, substantial pressure existed for these men to produce accurate plans. Ralph Spiegel, director of marketing, explained this to the case writer:

I'm sure it is obvious we use our planning system as a mechanism to coordinate efforts of the various units of the company. As such, it is imperative that we get accurate plans from our product managers. While it is sometimes difficult to do, I try to be just as upset when a PM has underforecast as when he falls short of his goals. Of course, each PM has to project at least a 15% annual gain in sales; as a matter of corporate strategy, these are our overall goals. But I want these guys to formulate a marketing strategy they think will be effective, and then give me forecasts based on what they really expect to happen, not just tack 15% onto last year's sales figures. We're a long way from being perfect at it, but we are getting closer. And since these PMs have total responsibility for a product line, I believe there is strong motivation to give me good data, rather than leave themselves a "cushion" in their forecasts.

Based on the individual plans of the product managers, the sales organization made its annual forecasts and established targets. The sum of all PM forecasts was reviewed by the national sales manager (NSM) and the director of marketing to determine whether the total load could be handled by the salesforce. The figures were broken down by the NSM to specific sales quotas for each district by product line and by quarter. District managers then further divided the district among the various salesmen, again by product line by quarter. Once these quotas had been established, the sales managers have them as a basis for evaluation, unless they receive a formal correction by a PM of his forecast.

On the operations side, the planning effort once again began at the bottom and moved upward. A PM's forecast for his line

was given to the manager of operations (MO) responsible for plants producing those products. As the sales forecasts were estimated by quarter, the MOs would then translate this data into volumes by quarter. From this information, production rates, standard cost data, and inventory levels were established; these then became the standards against which these MOs were evaluated.

These MOs were also responsible for initiating requests for capital expenditures. As a part of the annual budgets, managers of operations were expected to submit capital expenditure proposals that met RPI's corporate criteria for ROI and payback period. The director of operations, Mr. McAdam, would review these requests and consult Messrs. Harden and Nicklus if it were necessary to place priorities because of limited available funds.

Once the MOs had established operating forecasts and submitted them to Mr. McAdam, these figures became the basis for measuring performance. Weekly and monthly reports showing key ratios, operating costs, and inventory were reviewed by Mr. McAdam. MOs were also responsible for initiating a cost-reduction program as a part of each annual forecast. They were then measured on meeting these cost-reduction targets.

FUNCTIONAL INTERFACES

Many of the managers were concerned, in some way or other, with the interfaces between functional areas. While often not stated in precise terms, these men were aware of the potential for problems at these boundaries. The case writer posed this possibility to various managers; the comments below reflect their concern. The problems of multiple products/single salesforce will be discussed later and are not specifically mentioned below. Chairman Leroy Harden commented:

I can think of a few ways in which we have tried

to "manage these interfaces" as you put it. Clearly the most general fact is our informal communication and the access everyone has to everyone else. Being M.B.A.s James and I expect these men to have an orientation broad enough to fit their job into the more general picture. We also expect them to be problem oriented: to go where they have to and speak to whomever they need, to solve their particular problem.

Secondly, our detailed emphasis on planning and review allows each unit to operate without being totally dependent on other functional units. Once our annual plans are established, the PMs and MOs practically live with each other, going across the functional boundaries. And since PMs have responsibility for meeting sales forecasts, they have what I believe to be a very strong incentive to keep in touch with everyone necessary to do so, everyone being other managers in RPI, the salesforce, customers, suppliers.

Last, James and I have mentioned our belief that a lot of decisions in any firm can be procedurized. We hope to have made the process easier for our people by disseminating procedures and criteria. This provides a framework within which our managers can work.

Mr. Temple, manager of operations for lawn and garden equipment, added:

The procedures around here are what I call "methodology procedures," that is, general guidelines. I used to be with a large, rather prosaic metals organization, and there I considered the procedures stifling. Here, they are really the formalized thoughts of Leroy and James. These men really serve as the ultimate resource around here. Whenever there are arguments that can't be resolved they enter the discussion. Leroy usually handles operations and control, while James oversees the marketing side. And believe me, when it gets kicked upstairs, it gets solved.

Calvin McAdam, director of operations, added his thoughts on the topic:

I believe the most critical mechanism for operating across the functions is keeping communications channels open. We have a couple of ways of keeping these channels forced open. First, the mass of written data that flows at

RPI serves to provide communication. We get weekly reports and monthly reports on plants; equally precise data is provided on how products are being moved by salesmen. Second, I believe there is a pressure downward to keep information flowing upward. For example, there are plenty of instances where one of my MOs will have indications that some costs are rising, etc., but this would not appear in a report for two or three weeks. I have made it clear that I want such information as soon as they get these first indications. Obviously, this cuts down our reaction time to such contingencies. When I get information on inventories or quality control, for example, the product manager and I can go over it and discuss a possible course of action immediately.

There are, however, a couple of things I'm concerned about as we grow as an organization. I see first signs that we're nearing the size where informal mechanisms become more rigid. I know this has happened personally in at least one instance. In the past, I would react to a PM's first thought that he was over or under forecast by reworking the production plans for the plant involved. Recently, though, I find myself less willing to accept his first indications. There have been times when my quick reaction meant changing a production flow, only to have to reestablish the old volume as the product line got back on forecast. As a result, I generally won't have MOs rework their operating forecasts until the product manager is certain enough of the change to formally commit himself by changing his forecasts in writing.

More significantly, the interface I am most concerned about is that between operations and product development. As I see it no one in PD is responsible for coordinating the efforts of product-development people and the operations people on a particular project. I don't believe David Keller [director of production development] can do this; he has to manage so many different projects. As a result, my MOs are really assuming this responsibility by default. This is tough on them, since they already have plenty to do. The solution that comes to my mind is to have one of the product development engineers assume formal leadership of the project group. Then when the project is ready for production it would be handled by the MO.

Walter Grace, manager of operations for winter products, also commented on handling the interdependencies:

I really believe we have just overwhelmed the potential problems by the type of people we have at RPI. We have MBAs with experience in well-run companies or consulting organizations—a collection of good, honest, greedy, capable people. Everyone has that problem-solving orientation imbedded at the business school. When [Ralph] Spiegel was the product manager for archery, they couldn't keep him out of the Nashville plant; he was always snooping around, figuring a way to do something better. I am not convinced, however, that this alone will permit us to function effectively as we grow. There are a few things I believe we have to try to do. The relationship between PMs and MOs during the planning cycle has to be maintained. I have sensed the tendency for PMs to make their forecasts assuming the best of all possible worlds. Once I even saw a PM complete his unit forecast unaware that his plant could not possibly crank out the predicted volume. I think we have to try and keep a slight bit of manufacturing orientation a part of the PM's perspective.

It also seems likely to me we might end up decentralizing the product development units. Two of them operate out of particular plants already, in Bridgeport and Nashville. And the operations people are already integrally involved in the process. I think the centralized PD group may lose its flexibility across product lines. Perhaps the solution would be "decentralized" product (and process) development at the plants with a headquarters staff providing specific expertise in packaging, materials, design, etc.

MULTIPLE PRODUCT—SINGLE SALESFORCE

Another topic of general concern was that of the single salesforce. Mr. Nicklus commented:

We are always thinking about the implications of selling a group of products through a single salesforce. While this concept seems to work well for some very large marketing firms, we want to make certain that as we grow in size, we make any modifications necessary to keep this system working here at RPI.

Mr. Nicklus continued his comments in this regard:

What we have really done is encourage a "tunnel vision" perspective on the part of the product managers by giving them full responsibility and rewarding them for performance of their time. To compensate for this, I look to the director of marketing and national sales manager to resolve any frictions which arise. And, of course, I am usually pretty involved in things, especially if a conflict can't be settled.

The national sales manager and director of marketing did have several mechanisms to translate the product managers' forecasts into salesmen's quotas and to monitor their efforts in meeting these quotas. The primary tools have been mentioned previously: the planning process itself and the review to assure that the salesforce could handle the total job as determined by the various PMs. In addition, most of the product lines were seasonal in nature, so it was possible to schedule intensive sales efforts for the various products so that they did not occur simultaneously. Thus, the salesmen's yearly routine normally included a sequence of peak efforts plus a continuing selling job of much less intensive nature.

Arthur O'Connell, national sales manager, commented further:

I feel we have good data with which to insure that the salesmen concentrate where it will be most effective. District managers get weekly reports showing sales calls, orders booked, and dollar volume for each man, for each product line. There is also a "super" bonus for the salesman who achieves this target sales goal in each product group.

District Sales Manager Jim Grabowski also spoke on this topic:

Our salesman routes himself through his territory, subject to the review of myself and Mr. O'Connell. The frequency with which each customer is called upon is also determined by the individual men, based on our expectation of the importance of the account. Again, his choices are subject to review. By watching the reports for call frequencies and sales by product line, I can usually spot a situation where quotas might not be met. This might be symptomatic of a man feeling low, since he is so distant from us and his home, or it could be just a poor salesman. The super bonus at RPI also depends on every man in the district meeting his overall dollar quotas. Obviously, I'm very interested in finding out about potential trouble spots quickly, for the sake of my bonus as well as those of my men.

There are a couple of other areas I think we have to work harder on. First, we aren't getting good communication between the salesmen and product managers. These men in the field can supply valuable information on the market and competitors; we haven't yet brought the two groups together. I think it would also be valuable for the salesmen to provide estimates on potential sales of various lines by customer. This might help the PMs in their forecasts. Secondly, we are still establishing individual quotas from the top down. I've read many places that since we are paying these guys based on their accomplishing these quotas they ought to bear some responsibility for establishing them.

INCORPORATING ACQUISITIONS

Leroy Harden described the acquisition process:

We've had enough experience at making acquisitions to have distilled a few generalizations. The process can be visualized in four stages.

First, James and I evaluate the opportunity in the context of our established strategy. Does this situation fit? Can it take us where we want to go? Next we enter a period of negotiating with the present owners as to the value of the firm. Being human, these owners generally want more than a firm is worth; sometimes they seem to expect us to pay them for value we intend to introduce by making changes.

The third stage is probably the most critical: to arrange for integrating an acquisition into Recreation Products, Inc. We take a task force into the new firm, usually someone from marketing, operations, and control. Each of these

men analyzes the situation he finds and is responsible for developing an "action plan." This plan should tell us, in specific language, what has to be done to turn this company into a contributor to the company. We spend quite a bit of time as a task unit, preparing changes we believe necessary.

The action plans indicated what types of inputs RPI expected to inject into an acquisition, both in the immediate future and over the longer term. In most cases to date the immediate emphasis was on reducing general overhead expenses and instituting cost control measures in the plants. More significant were the sophisticated marketing ideas and techniques that RPI brought to bear: products were added and others discontinued to strengthen the line, some products were altered and improved to be more attuned to changes in the markets, and more emphasis was placed on providing retail outlets with data helpful in making their decisions as to product mix and space allocations.

Potential acquisitions could reach Messrs. Harden and Nicklus through a variety of sources. Product managers might suggest a firm for its addition of products to the existing line. Salesmen could pass back information on possible candidates. Outside sources, such as business brokers, etc., might supply leads. And Mr. Harden and Mr. Nicklus spent much of their time keeping up on possible acquisition sources.

Walter Grace contributed some thoughts on possible dysfunctions in the acquisition process:

I think we might be failing to gear up for longer term development of an acquisition. There is tremendous pressure to turn a problem situation around as quickly as possible because we can't afford the losses that could be incurred. We are committed to earnings growth, and we can't have our existing operations support a losing situation for long. As a result, we tend to cut it apart if necessary to accomplish our transition quickly.

While a change in ownership and operating procedures was bound to have an impact on existing personnel, the severity of the changes varied and could be considerably less disruptive than is implied above. In a typical company before acquisitions, much of the administrative work was usually handled by the owner and one or two assistants. On several occasions these people, who were often involved in negotiating the role, had elected not to remain with the company. Plant personnel were usually retained, although the force might have been reduced by some amount. Engineers and most plant supervisors remained with the firm. In most cases, the original companies relied on manufacturers' representatives for their sales effort. Therefore, no large salesforce had to be disbanded.

RPI had not yet faced the difficulties of acquiring a larger company with a highly technical product line. They had not yet faced the situation of having to rely on existing managers for detailed market information, or on engineers for highly technical product and process characteristics. Mr. Grace commented on this subject:

As we grow and take larger firms, we will probably face the possibility of having to keep existing management. As we get further from where we are, we might in fact need them for their expertise to compensate for our not knowing the specifics of the business.

IMPLICATIONS OF GROWTH

Many of the managers realized that a continuation of the rapid growth at RPI could mean changes in its structure or procedures. Thus, many had comments relevant to a discussion of the implications of this potential growth. Mr. Harden commented:

I devote quite a bit of time thinking about this. "Growth" for RPI means something distinct from what it has for most other firms, and even conglomerates. In addition to extrapolation of trends in existing products or markets, growth often means to us completely new markets. This usually means subsuming an existing firm, with

its own ways of doing things, into our present, organization. Whereas conglomerates normally operate new acquisitions as semiautonomous units, we incorporate them into our present structure. As we move further from our existing lines into leisure services, for instance, we will have to learn new tasks, develop new expertise. I think you'll agree, it's exciting and certainly very challenging.

I see growth forcing us to gradually replace our informal access to one another with more formal mechanisms. Not that we want to but I think size and distance will force us to. James and I will always want as much personal involvement as possible, but I believe size, and in time diversity, will force us to spend more of our time working with acquisitions and less working with the existing lines. In fact, hiring Paul Tepper is a step in the direction of providing for someone to monitor our established operations. Calvin McAdam will now spend more time working on acquisitions and special projects.

Our growth potential poses a unique pressure on James and myself, that is, providing the opportunities for our existing management team to develop and grow. We have been able to attract such talent by giving them responsibility and challenging tasks today, but also by promising them opportunities for more of both tomorrow. I personally feel a greater pressure to provide these opportunities than I do to perform for the "auction judges" of the financial markets.

The potential growth of the salesforce at RPI was well planned, and in rather specific detail. The broad intention was for the size of territory covered by each man to gradually contract as he (1) penetrated more of the potential customers in his area, (2) carried more products and possible new product lines, and (3) convinced each customer to take more products from the lines offered. Indices had been developed to anticipate when new men were needed and where each new man would go. This planning for the force's expansion extended five years into the future and was closely watched for accuracy and relevance to the next time interval. Plans were also developed to add to the administrative capabilities of the salesforce by adding additional levels of zones, regions, etc. Ralph Spiegel, director of marketing, made additional comments on the subject:

The potential always exists here for competition among the product managers for the resources of RPI, in several aspects. Already, I can see the competition for the efforts of the salesforce. Arthur and I try to control this by translating the individual forecasts into a total forecast and insuring it can be met. The plans for expansion of the salesforce are also designed to reduce this potential bottleneck.

A second potential bottleneck could develop, I feel, in competition among PMs for product development or capital expenditure dollars. Right now product development effort is allocated on a "first-come-first-served" basis. If a PM wants a new product, process change, etc., he will request a product from David Keller. David will accept projects that meet our established ROI criteria until his budget is exhausted. Thus, the only way we can determine priorities among products is to bring in James Nicklus. And yet we might want a disproportionate share of product development going into a product with greater growth potential, for example.

A final possibility is that the nature of our selling task will change as we grow, and as our salesforce matures. Right now the effort is primarily on building the sales of a narrow line to a customer who bought it from the firm that we took over. A secondary emphasis is on developing new customers. As we mature, I think greater emphasis will be placed on getting a particular customer to carry all our lines. We will also find a way to get better information back from the field. And I think we might gradually increase our efforts in providing customer service. While we are prepared to provide such service now, many of our customers don't know yet how much help we can provide.

Another existing mechanism for provid-

ing for growth in the sales force was the unit bonus system for rewarding districts. Jim Grabowski, a district sales manager, discussed this:

We know that one thing that can seriously damage a salesman's morale is to have part of his territory taken away after he has cultivated it. We have tried to cope with this by placing a heavy reliance on the total effort of a district as the basis for determining bonuses. Then, as we contract these territories, we hope the transition will be smoother. This team effort feeling also helps keep my men from feeling they are alone in the field. I think it brings them one step closer to RPI.

Walter Grace, manager of operations for winter products, also commented on the ramifications of growth at RPI:

I don't think we are really geared up to provide for product introduction in the long run. I think this is because of our strategy of acquiring new lines by acquisition. However, we must continue to innovate with new products to remain competitive. Many of these innovations must come from within the present organization rather than by acquisition.

Calvin McAdam, director of operations, added his thoughts on the implications of growth:

I think we have to do two things with our people as we expand. First, James and Leroy will of necessity be less involved in ongoing operations. We have to compensate for their not being the final arbiter around here. More important, we still must attract capable people to the organization. This, I think will be more difficult than it has been in the past. We'll have less to offer in terms of growing with the firm, as most of us are the benefactors of getting in on the ground floor. Someday we'll have to attract people on the same criteria as does General Foods.